RUSSIA AND THE MIDDLE EAST:
VIEWPOINTS, POLICIES, STRATEGIES

RUSSIA AND THE MIDDLE EAST:
VIEWPOINTS, POLICIES, STRATEGIES

Edited by FYODOR LUKYANOV

East View Press
Minneapolis, MN

RUSSIA AND THE MIDDLE EAST: VIEWPOINTS, POLICIES, STRATEGIES
Edited by Fyodor Lukyanov

Published by East View Press, an imprint of East View Information Services, Inc.
10601 Wayzata Blvd | Minneapolis, MN 55305 USA | www.eastviewpress.com

Library of Congress Cataloging-in-Publication Data

Names: Lukyanov, Fyodor, 1967- editor.
Title: Russia and the Middle East : viewpoints, policies, strategies / edited
   by Fyodor Lukyanov.
Description: First edition. | Minneapolis, MN : East View Press, 2019. |
   Includes index.
Identifiers: LCCN 2019020204 | ISBN 9781879944756 (pbk.)
Subjects: LCSH: Islam and politics. | Terrorism--Middle East--Prevention. |
   Russia (Federation)--Foreign relations--Middle East. | Middle
   East--Foreign relations--Russia (Federation) | Middle East--Politics and
   government--21st century.
Classification: LCC DK68.5 .R88 2019 | DDC 327.47056--dc23
LC record available at https://lccn.loc.gov/2019020204

Cover design by Carol A. Dungan
Layout design and composition by Ana K. Niedermaier

Printed in the United States of America
ISBN: 978-1-879944-75-6

First Edition, 2019
3 5 7 9 10 8 6 4 2

CONTENTS

PART TWO

Tactics and Interactions: Falling Into the Same Traps

2.1. Countering Terrorism

2.2. À la Guerre Comme à la Guerre (Military Analysis)

PART THREE

The Middle East as a Factor of World Order (and Disorder)

3.1. The Arab Spring: Democracy and Revolution

FOREWORD

Russia's military intervention in the Syrian conflict in September 2015 not only heralded a new phase in that war but also signaled Russia's full-scale return to the Middle East and international diplomacy. Moscow's deployment of a limited but decisive contingent of armed troops, above all from the Aerospace Forces, tilted the tide of battle against Islamic State (ISIS), and probably saved Damascus from occupation, with all of the horrors that would have ensued. Russia reasserted itself as a great power not only on the field of battle but also in the complex diplomatic maneuvering as multiple actors sought to achieve contradictory outcomes in the region. Only a year earlier, Moscow had intervened in Ukraine, drawing upon itself a sanctions regime, which has since intensified.

However, rather than constraining Russian policy, the Russian leadership headed by President Vladimir Putin were further convinced that the country's strategic interests no longer coincided with those of the West, other than in practical matters of conflict avoidance and the struggle against common concerns, notably international terrorism and non-proliferation. The growing alienation of Russia from its earlier Atlanticist inclinations was confirmed. Since the much-talked about but increasingly insubstantial partnership with the West was running into the sands, Russia now felt that it should act in the way that it considered appropriate. Russia was emboldened in international affairs, and its military activism and diplomatic initiatives in the Middle East have been the result. Contrary to stereotypical views in the West, Russian policies in the region are not simply intended to displace the West or to buttress authoritarianism, but reflect the view that Western policies in the region have mostly been disastrous. If multipolarity means anything, it entails a broader multilateralism in the management of regional issues; and out of this, perhaps better policies will emerge.

These are the issues analyzed in this book. The essays go back to 2005, when Russia was still stinging from the Anglo-American invasion of Iraq two years earlier. Bringing together some of the leading Russian policymakers, academics and analysts, this collection of articles from the journal *Russia in Global Affairs* provides a unique insight into Russian thinking. The journal itself has become a forum where some of the most important Russian and global debates about international affairs take place. The openness of the debate may surprise some readers, but the public sphere in Russia remains lively and diverse. This is especially the case when dealing with a region as complex as the Middle East, with its heavy legacy of external interventions and multiple conflicts.

Several aspects stand out in the accounts presented in this book. First, without exception all of the contributors express commitment in one form or another to international society and the institutions of global governance, above all the United Nations. This is accompanied by repeated calls for the observance of international law. It goes without saying that the behavior of great powers does not always accord with their normative commitments, yet this does not diminish the importance of the latter. The expressed convictions in these articles help map the mental and political universe of Russia today. Although there are assertive strains, the overall sentiment is far from anything like revisionism. Instead, the emphasis is on making the existing international system work better, rather than overturning the present order to create something new. In other words, Russia emerges as an overwhelmingly status quo conservative power. Its insertion into the Syrian conflict was not designed to shake the world order, but to preserve it.

Second, the Middle East is a region in which power and ideology interact in unique ways. Russia has long been involved there, but in the early post-cold war years it became a marginal player, although not without some influence in specific policy areas, notably energy and interventionism. However, after the military intervention in Syria, Russia has emerged as a classic "great power" in the region. It is debatable whether this accords with the country's national interests, at a time when it is facing so many domestic developmental and economic challenges. The tightening sanctions regime has now broadened to cover Russia's alleged meddling in the 2016 US presidential election and other issues. In the short term, Russia's intervention has been extraordinarily successful, judged in terms of its stated goals. It prevented Damascus from falling to ISIS; it stabilized the regime of President Bashar Assad; it pinned down militants from the Caucasus who otherwise may have returned to cause mayhem in Russia; it provided Russia with a military foothold in the region; but above all, it forced the other powers to reckon with Russia as a major diplomatic actor. This is not so much an end in itself as a reflection of Moscow's view that the traditional dominant actors in the region have been irresponsible when they have not been incompetent, and usually a combination of the two, which has only exacerbated existing conflicts and prevented their resolution. Through adroit diplomacy, Putin managed to remain on good terms with all the other actors in the region, including Israel, Saudi Arabia and Iran, however incompatible they may be with each other. Even relations with the US in this regional context have been pragmatic and businesslike, establishing a model of relations that could apply elsewhere.

Third, several articles deal with the "inside-out" question – the danger of Middle Eastern conflicts spilling out and provoking larger confrontations. This was the case in 1956, 1967 and 1973, and remains the case today. This question also covers the problem of international terrorism, a complex issue whose roots today lie largely, although not entirely, in the region. This is a matter of particular concern to Russian policymakers. For these reasons, analysis of contemporary Islamic movements is so important.

The fourth issue is the "outside-in" problem – the degree to which outside interests stimulate and exacerbate regional divisions. This has long applied to energy politics, and in particular to Western concerns over oil supplies and pricing, and access to oil fields. Policy towards Iran was long shaped by these concerns, and resulted in several interventions. Oil was undoubtedly a factor, although probably not the primary one, in the invasion of Iraq in 2003. Security of energy supplies is obviously also a factor in relations with Saudi Arabia and the other Gulf states. A related issue is arms supplies, with the Middle East one of the primary destinations for the arms industry in the US and the UK. For Russia, energy politics and arms sales are important, but are not as determinative as for the Western powers.

The fifth point is reflected throughout the volume, although not always directly. It has to do with world order issues, and in particular challenges to the pattern of Western hegemony established after 1945 and reinforced after 1989. The Middle East is a region particularly sensitive to shifts in great power relations, and it is also typically the first to feel the effects. The emergence of new actors and processes immediately affects the region. The reemergence of Russia as a great power, along with the arrival of China as a serious new actor, is accompanied by the establishment of an anti-hegemonic alignment by the two powers. This alignment is reinforced by the creation of international groupings, notably the Shanghai Cooperation Organization, intended to counterbalance Western alliances.

Sixth, non-proliferation issues have taken on a new urgency with the US's withdrawal in 2018 from the Joint Comprehensive Plan of Action (JCPOA), signed in July 2015. This move has placed the Iran nuclear program once again back on the agenda. The enduring hostility between the US and Iran is one of the greatest threats to peace in the region. Israel is a nondeclared nuclear power, and if other states feel threatened, they too may be tempted to take that route.

This book provides a rewarding field of analysis of these questions and many more. It is a rich mix of issue analysis and policy prescription. There are plenty of differences among the authors, yet all provide material of interest to anyone trying to understand Russian thinking about the Middle East.

Richard Sakwa, University of Kent

PREFACE

In autumn 2015, just over two weeks after the start of the Russian military operation in Syria, Russian President Vladimir Putin spoke at the annual Valdai International Discussion Club forum. A Russian participant asked the head of state whether it made sense to get involved. After all, the risks were high, losses inevitable and combat actions unpredictable. In addition, there was no exit strategy, which could entail long-term negative consequences. "Fifty years ago, the streets of Leningrad taught me one rule: If a fight is inevitable, you have to strike first," Putin responded without missing a beat.

This quip was later often cited as a typical example of how the Russian leader understands political actions and the essence of international politics. However, it is equally important to note that it was said specifically about the Middle East.

After the collapse of the Soviet Union, that region remained on the periphery of Russian diplomacy for a time. Foreign policy was so focused on trying to make Russia a part of the "expanded West" and integrate it into the "community of civilized nations" that it simply retreated from many parts of the world (both intentionally and due to a lack of resources). This was especially true of regions that had been an area of stiff competition between the USSR and the West. The Middle East was not only one such region, but was perhaps the most important arena of ideological and geopolitical confrontation, second only to Europe. And it is fairly symbolic that the Syrian conflict became a pretext for Russia's military-political return to the international arena as a full-fledged superpower and top player. This has been a Russian foreign policy goal – at times tacit, then openly declared – since the early 1990s.

The Great Game of the second half of the 20th century played out to a considerable degree in the Middle East. It was not a periphery, since it was close to Europe, the main arena of a systemic confrontation between the East and West. Meanwhile, decolonization had created almost limitless possibilities for competition between the new "masters of the world" – the USSR and the US. The sociopolitical systems that the leaders of the regional states embraced (capitalism or socialism) did not play a principal role – both were given a markedly local flavor. However, competition for geopolitical loyalty oriented toward either Moscow or Washington took on very harsh forms. The region was rocked by political cataclysms – coups, wars, religious and ethnic persecutions. However, despite it all, this bipolar confrontation paradoxically ensured a kind of stability. To be more exact, the dividing lines were clear, and were enforced not so much by the [local] governments as by the "big brothers."

The Middle East was supposed to be the beginning of a "new world order" as envisioned by optimists at the end of the cold war. The first proving ground was Saddam Hussein's invasion of Kuwait in August 1990, which was met with unprecedented rejection by the entire global community. For the first time (which turned out to be the last), Moscow and Washington acted together in favor of an international military operation to liberate Kuwait and punish Iraq for its aggression. Operation Desert Storm in early 1991 seemed to mark a new era of postconfrontation, ushering in a joint approach to solving global problems, including through force. Even a few years earlier, such a thing was impossible in principle: The region, and in fact the entire world, was divided into spheres of influence in which the global patrons guaranteed military and political protection to their protégés against their opponents and the opposing superpower.

Routing Iraq from Kuwait did not usher in an era of new global politics, for the simple reason that the system of two superpowers ceased to exist when one of them disappeared. The balance of forces that had determined the situation in the world for more than four decades was suddenly replaced by the dominance of the US, the only "hyperpower" (to use the terminology of French politician Hubert Védrine). Russia, the legal successor of the Soviet Union, withdrew from the competition. Meanwhile, the Middle East was left hanging: The powerful wave of democratization that shook the world in the late 1980s and early 1990s (Eastern Europe, Central Eurasia, the Far East, Africa, Latin America) essentially passed this region by.

However, stability [in the Middle East] turned out to be illusory. The disappearance of the cold war hastened what Zbigniew Brzezinski called a global awakening. The rise of international terrorism, whose most obvious roots can be traced to the Middle East, combined with the hobbling of the entire system of regime-states born of decolonization in the early and mid-20th century to turn the region into a ticking time bomb and then an inferno of global significance. After Sept. 11, 2001, events began to develop incredibly quickly. In the 15 years between 2001 and 2016, the Middle East experienced just about all forms of turmoil – outside interference, civil wars, an explosion of religious extremism, the collapse of political systems and the disintegration of entire states. As has always been the case historically, these changes were largely driven by the great powers. Their interventions – especially those undertaken by the US – destroyed the existing order and provoked a chaotic and practically uncontrollable transformation.

Why was the Middle East the specific place where Russia returned to the stage as a global player? There are several reasons. The first is Russia's vulnerability to the threat of the Middle East's radicalization – something that Russia, given its large Muslim population, has faced since the 1990s. In this sense, Putin's aforementioned remark easily fits the logic of countering distant threats before they inevitably reach Russia.

Moreover, the Middle East is the region that best fits Russia's foreign policy "toolkit," so to speak: i.e., sufficiently effective modern Armed Forces and the ability to use them (especially after the reforms of the late 2000s and early 2010s); a solid knowledge of the region gathered during the Soviet Union's activity there; a strong and professional diplomatic tradition; the Middle East's weariness of unopposed US dominance, which had become increasingly dysfunctional since the start of the 21st century; post-Soviet Russia's lack of ideological dogmas that would limit room for maneuvering; and an adherence to realpolitik, which suits the Middle Eastern states much better than any other approach.

All these factors came together in the mid-2010s, when all the concepts that various players had been trying to implement in this part of the world simply fell through. Meanwhile, the region itself had descended into the chaos of deconstruction, with the possibility of a complete loss of control. Russia unexpectedly became a game-changer that altered the dynamics of the situation.

Of course, only time will tell whether it changed or simply stalled that momentum. Six to eight years ago, it seemed that the Middle East was a festering wound in an otherwise steadily developing world. The feeling is different today – the Middle East is both a reflection and the quintessence of the highly complex changes affecting the entire world order.

This collection of articles, carefully selected by the editors of Russia in Global Affairs and East View Press, presents views and findings from the best Russian experts, standing diplomats and statesmen, prominent politicians and public figures. Contributors include the late Yevgeny Primakov, dean of the Russian diplomatic and intelligence corps; current Minister of Foreign Affairs Sergei Lavrov; current Minister of Energy Alexander Novak; Ambassadors Extraordinary and Plenipotentiary; Members of the Russian Academy of Sciences; and others.

While each article in our collection deals with a specific issue or element related to the Middle East in general and Russia's foreign policy in the region, in their entirety they provide a window into the dynamic evolution of attitudes and views espoused by the Russian expert community and policymakers. They fit together within a comprehensive system of analysis, forecasts and scenarios of foreign relations in the region and beyond.

Fyodor Lukyanov

Editor in chief, *Russia in Global Affairs*
Chairman, Presidium of the Council on Foreign and Defense Policy
Research Director, Valdai International Discussion Club

ACKNOWLEDGMENTS

All articles in this collection were originally published in the online journal *Russia in Global Affairs* (*RGA*) and have been selected exclusively for East View Press. The contents have been freshly edited, and in some cases condensed for brevity. Text omitted by East View editorial staff is designated with an ellipsis (. . .). In other cases, the original authors chose to abbreviate certain text (for example, quoted material from a report or public speech); such omissions are indicated by asterisks (***). Some additional information that may be helpful to the general English-speaking audience is provided by in-text annotations enclosed in brackets. More detailed and extensive clarifications, as well as other background facts and quotations, are provided in endnotes following each article.

The first group of people we wish to acknowledge are the translators who worked with the original Russian copy to produce the English-language versions published in *RGA*. In addition, the following members of the *RGA* editorial staff deserve credit for bringing the present collection to light. Fyodor Lukyanov, editor in chief, curated and selected compelling and valuable material by prominent statesmen, analysts and scholars. Alexander "Alex" Solovyov, associate editor, worked tirelessly with many of the original authors to add corroborative material, including source citations, and in general served as an essential conduit of communication between the Russian and American sides. His work was supported by Evgeniya Prokopchuk, assistant to the editor in chief, who kept up perfect communication between the authors and editors and did an incalculable amount of paperwork, while always remaining cheerful and helpful. Lead designer Natalia Zablotskite expertly made new versions of most images, significantly improving their quality. We express gratitude to all of them for their diligent efforts.

On the American side, we wish to thank: Matthew Larson, for editing the English-language copy, supplying annotations and indicating points that needed additional citations; Carol Dungan, for her patience and creativity in designing the book cover; Ana K. Niedermaier, for her resourcefulness and eagle eye for detail in the design and composition of the book as a whole; and Sarah Buchlaw, for her perspicacious proofreading of the final copy.

Finally, we would like to thank Richard Sakwa at Kent University (UK) for writing the Foreword, as well as Ron Suny (University of Michigan) and Stephen Blank (American Foreign Policy Council) for their encouraging comments on the advance copy.

We hope that the perspectives offered in *Russia and the Middle East* will serve scholars, analysts, students and the general public for years to come in reaching a more nuanced understanding of a crucial region of our world.

Laurence Bogoslaw

Chief Editor and Publishing Director, East View Press

PART ONE
Strategy: Regional Problems in Global Perspective

PART ONE

1.1. Decades of International Insecurity

THE UNITED NATIONS: CHALLENGES OF OUR TIME

Yevgeny Primakov

The UN Charter provides for all possible ways to collectively counteract threats to security and stability. So the question is not how to amend the Charter, but how to best use the great potential of this document, as well as the potential of the UN Security Council and the UN as a whole.

The events of recent years – especially the 9/11 terrorist attack on the US – have moved peace and security to the forefront of global issues. The 9/11 tragedy made everyone realize the seriousness of the danger posed by international terrorism. This form of terrorism manifested itself in the worst possible form: a self-sufficient organization that is not connected to any state and that seeks to become an independent international player. The terrorist organization Al Qaeda, which is not supported officially by any state, stands to acquire this menacing position in the world.

The hostile goal of this organization has been explicitly expressed by its leader, Osama bin Laden: the creation of a single Islamic caliphate. The method for achieving the declared goal is to destroy the secular regimes in the Muslim-populated countries (such as Turkey, for

This article originally appeared in *Russia in Global Affairs* Vol. 3, No. 1, 2005.

example), as well as moderately secular states (Saudi Arabia). At the same time, bin Laden has declared a "merciless war" on the US, which he argues supports such regimes, as well as on those countries that oppose extremist Islamic groups advocating the ideas of separatism.

What distinguishes Al Qaeda from traditional international players is not civilization or religion. The opposing sides comprise, on the one hand, dangerous extremist movements that preach a medieval "zoological" attitude toward peoples and nations; and, on the other, the rest of the world that is guided by the values of modern society.

International terrorism has acquired a fundamentally new form and is now becoming dangerously intertwined with many traditional threats:

- the threat of the proliferation of weapons of mass destruction, which has been aggravated by a real possibility of its coalescence with international terrorism;
- unsettled regional conflicts, especially in the Middle East, which create a fertile ground for the spread of international terrorism;
- the ominous existence of "failed states" where the authorities are unable to prevent humanitarian catastrophes, genocide, mass exodus of refugees, etc.;
- narcotics trafficking as a source of financing international terrorism;
- religious extremism (not fundamentalism, but extremism), which in some countries is joining forces with international terrorism, thereby inflaming separatism (this factor has already had a destabilizing effect in some states, and may lead to even more disastrous consequences);
- the threat of the world being divided along the religious axis, which has manifested itself in sweeping attacks against Islam as a "dangerous" religion; these attacks are splitting the international community, spurring terrorist acts and undermining efforts to counter international terrorism.

There is a real threat that international terrorism may use globalization, as well as scientific and technological progress, to carry out its attacks.

'Hierarchy of Threats' Counterproductive

The newly emerging challenges to humankind are creating a fundamentally different international environment that requires new approaches to the security problems of individual states and the international community as a whole. It is necessary to determine what these approaches should be.

Some politicians and pundits divide the threats into "hard" and "soft." On the one hand, there are threats to security that emerge either because of aggressive actions by another state or as a consequence of an unstable situation. On the other hand, there are the so-called "soft" threats: poverty, disease, unemployment, etc. It is argued that the UN should combat the soft threats, since its mechanism is not tailored to a rapid and efficient reaction to security threats.

However, such conclusions are groundless.

First, the UN Charter provides for all possible ways to collectively counteract threats to security and stability. True, the UN Security Council has sometimes failed to optimally use its authority, and its efficiency should be improved on the basis of coordinated agreements. However, in practical terms, the Security Council has proven that it is able to assume a fundamentally new approach to applying provisions of the UN Charter. For example, following 9/11, the Security Council provided an essentially new interpretation of Art. 51 of the UN Charter, which provides for the use of force in self-defense in case of an attack by a nonstate entity. Furthermore, the UN Security Council endorsed sanctions against the Taliban movement and created the Counter-Terrorism Committee (CTC). It has made decisions on the use of force in support of democracy and human rights (for example, in its Resolution No. 940 of July 31, 1994, the Security Council authorized all member countries "to form a multi-national force***and use all necessary means" to restore democracy in Haiti).

The Security Council has demonstrated its ability to adapt to new challenges and threats, and this international body bears a major responsibility for maintaining international peace and security. So, there is no need to bypass the Security Council when taking decisive steps or using force.

Second, the ongoing events in Iraq graphically demonstrate the shortcomings of those tactics that ignore the UN and rely instead on unilateral action. It is noteworthy that since the failure of the US operation in Iraq, those who only recently were obsessed with the idea of unilateralism – that is, the independent and preventive use of force that ignores the UN and are regarded as "legitimate" – are now returning to this international organization. It has become obvious that the US has no chance of extricating itself from the Iraqi dead-lock without UN assistance.

Third, it is counterproductive to build a hierarchy of threats or pit them against each other; threats are interrelated. Although inter-national terrorism is not directly rooted in poverty, which is the fate of most people on the planet, it results to a large extent from past or present discriminatory policies against those who live outside the "golden billion" countries. Discrimination – be it political, economic or cultural – nurtures terrorism.

Fourth, the significance of the various threats is viewed differ-ently in various parts of the world. In Africa, for example, the main threat is considered AIDS, which is responsible for approximately 30 million deaths. In actuality, many countries outside the golden billion are threatened not by terrorism, but by disease, poverty and hunger.

Effectiveness of the Multilateral Mechanism

Under the UN Charter (Chapter VII), the Security Council is respon-sible for determining the presence of a threat, an act of aggression or a violation of the peace. It also considers measures that should be taken to maintain and restore international peace and security. And finally, it organizes and implements these measures, including urgent military action.

The UN Charter directly mentions the possibility of taking compulsory measures as preventive means (Art. 50). At the same time, the Charter does not contain criteria for resorting to the use of compulsory measures, including preventive ones. Therefore, it is necessary to define such criteria. The following is a list of those circumstances that should require coercive actions from the UN Security Council:

- An acute humanitarian crisis, such as the mass murder of civilians, gross violations of international humanitarian law, rights to life and property, and the mass exodus of refugees. More often than not, such circumstances occur in tandem with the collapse of a country's central government or a severe internal conflict.

- The inability of the central government to take control over nonstate entities that operate on the country's territory and pose a threat to international security.
- The violation of the Nuclear Non-Proliferation Treaty, especially if there is a possibility of nuclear arms being transferred to a terrorist organization.
- Any state harboring international terrorist organizations that are found to be launching large-scale terrorist acts against other states (in this case, the state under attack also has the right to self-defense under Art. 51 of the UN Charter).

Under Chapter VII of the Charter, the "criteria of interference" can be approved by a UN Security Council resolution. At the same time, there is no need to make amendments to the Charter itself. The aforementioned circumstances are not related to shortcomings of the UN Charter, but to flagrant violations of its provisions and those documents that have been adopted to improve it.

Naturally, specific circumstances will require detailed consideration before there can be any legitimate interference in a state's internal affairs. The possibility of such interference should not be ruled out in situations where there is a regional or international threat to peace and security. This premise does not mean a rejection of the principle of states' sovereignty per se, rather, it emphasizes that the ban on interference in a state's internal affairs is firm unless internal developments there present a real threat to either part or all of the international community. What's more, preventive interference cannot be undertaken if it is based on a party's subjective decision concerning the threat level of a particular regime, or on the decision to use force unilaterally. Both the determination of the threat level and the resolution on the use of force should be based only on a joint decision.

Preventive use of force should be preceded by a UN demand that the government of the state in question must take urgent measures to stop activities that threaten the international community.

Refusal or inability to meet this demand should be taken by the Security Council as the basis for sanctioning coercive – use-of-force or nonuse-of-force – measures. Accepting the possibility of using force in principle, the international community should specify that any forceful intervention is permissible in strictly limited situations as a last resort, and only following a decision by the UN Security Council. Any subsequent actions must be under the oversight of the Security Council and with full observance of international law.

Security Council decisions must be based on apparent and uncontestable facts, as well as proven information. The unfortunate experience of military action against the Federal Republic of Yugoslavia and Iraq, unauthorized by the UN Security Council, proves that establishing facts for justifying the use of force was the weakest point. It is in our common interest to give this factor the most serious consideration.

Adapting Multilateral Bodies to New Threats

Raising the efficiency of the UN Security Council is paramount. The combination of two principles – justice and UN capability – may be used as a conceptual approach to this problem. Of course, the composition and structure of the Security Council, which emerged as a result of the disposition of forces after World War II, cannot remain intact forever. The time has long passed since Germany and Japan were set apart from the rest of the world by their defeat in the war. Since the UN came into existence 60 years ago, other crucial changes have taken place in the world as well. A significant number of former colonies and semi-colonies have become sovereign states. Today, they play an active and independent role in international politics, while enhancing their status in the global economy (India serves as a good example).

It is imperative that the composition of the UN Security Council be brought into line with present-day realities. Therefore, the primary goal is to increase the number of its permanent and nonpermanent members. Furthermore, there should be stricter observance of the principle of geographic representation in the Security Council, particularly as it concerns Africa and Latin America. At the same time, too great an increase in the number of Security Council members would contradict the idea of maintaining and consolidating the capability of the UN. As for the right to veto, it should be made clear that, as a multilateral mechanism efficiently acting in the name of peace and security, the UN cannot exist without the power of the veto. The history of the League of Nations is quite instructive in this respect. Yet it would be no less destructive for the UN to grant the veto right to many countries. I believe that only the five permanent UN Security Council members should enjoy this right.

Opponents of the UN argue that the permanent members of the Security Council are often unable to reach a consensus on questions concerning the use of force in response to the most acute security threats. Such arguments are unfair regarding situations that undeniably threaten international security. To increase the potential for coordinating steps on fundamental security issues within the Security Council, it is expedient to amend its working procedure to a certain extent. The existing procedural innovations should be used on a wider scale, particularly with respect to expanding cooperation between UN Security Council members and the leading states providing peacekeeping contingents for UN operations.

The permanent members of the UN Security Council should consider possibly adopting a joint declaration stating that they will act with maximum responsibility and restraint from invoking their veto right (this proposal has already been discussed and the probability of working out a coordinated document is rather high at the moment). Furthermore, members of the Security Council could forward a politically binding statement that they will spare no effort to reach a consensus in the Security Council on key questions relating to security and stability.

Other, more significant solutions (not involving amendments to the UN Charter) are also possible, but it would make sense to discuss them in detail after determining the format of expanding the UN Security Council.

The Security Council should focus on specific conflict situations as stipulated by the UN Charter. To this end, the Security Council would better free itself of the so-called "generic" debates that deal with questions that fall under the jurisdiction of the General Assembly (problems involving women, children, AIDS, protection of UN personnel, etc.). Efforts should be directed toward effectively using other multilateral structures of crisis management, as well as to adapt these structures, if need be, to new threats. This concerns, above all, the CTC and the UN Security Council Committee on sanctions against Al Qaeda, the Taliban and their associated individuals and entities (Committee 1267).

The planned reorganization of the CTC and the decision already in effect to strengthen the potential of Committee 1267 (Security Council Resolution No. 1526) expand opportunities for cooperation between these two bodies in matters where their counterterrorism tasks intersect. It is important that the sanction list of Committee 1267 – the only tool of its kind to counteract terrorism – be actively used and constantly revised.

The rich experience that is being gained through the interaction of the CTC and Committee 1267 can also be applied to working out a Counterterrorism Charter. This charter should contain a set of specific obligations to eliminate terrorist organizations and their branches; block financial flows; prevent the transit of arms, explosives and terrorists; and extradite those accused of terrorism (as listed by the Anti-Taliban Committee). Refusal to obey the regime to be established by this charter should be regarded as unacceptable. Such refusal (and not just opinions of some countries) could provide a basis for condemning a particular country (or countries), thus prompting subsequent sanctions against them.

It makes sense to more actively involve other sanction committees of the UN Security Council, particularly African ones (considering the growing threats from this continent), as well as expert groups established by the Security Council to monitor the observance of the sanctions. Operating under their mandates, these structures could contribute to determining those threats that may be linked to regional conflicts.

Military Dimension

To make the UN a working mechanism – i.e., an alternative to a unilateral decision on the use of force – it should acquire a military dimension. Thus, it is necessary to continue the practice of conducting operations approved by the Security Council within the format of coalitions of interested states (operations in Albania, East Timor, Afghanistan provide positive examples). It is equally important to work out a system of measures to strengthen the UN's potential for carrying out multifunctional operations to maintain and, if required, restore peace (using force). In this connection, it makes sense to form permanent UN rapid deployment forces stationed with regard to "hot spots." Moreover, the UN could sign special agreements with certain regional organizations and individual states stipulating that in case the Security Council makes a relevant decision, they will employ their rapid deployment units to conduct operations either under the UN flag or jointly with the UN.

Another promising direction is to form within the UN a sort of expert pool comprising representatives of interested states possessing a solid intelligence potential. Intelligence services of various countries already exchange information to uncover potential crises as early as possible and choose optimal ways to neutralize them. However, as was the case with the US prior to the 9/11 attacks, even the availability of certain information failed to help them uncover the terrorists' plans. The US experience proves the need for joint analysis of information and constant monitoring of crisis situations.

The UN should establish a structure capable of performing practical management functions in postconflict conditions, such as the coordination of reconstruction and other UN rehabilitation projects.

The international community succeeded in overcoming the cold war, which was an extremely dangerous period in its history. There is no doubt that it has enough power to cope with the new challenges, and to find ways to guarantee stability on the planet and the wellbeing of peoples.

THE FUNDAMENTAL CONFLICT

Yevgeny Primakov

*If Israel annexes the Arab territories it occupied in 1967, it will
soon cease to be a Jewish state, as the ratio between the Jewish
and Arab populations there will inevitably change in favor of
the latter due to birth rates.*

Research in the field of international relations and world economics
would be untenable without an analysis of regional conflicts, among
which the Middle East conflict takes a special place. This is perhaps
the longest-running regional conflict in the world. It has already
surpassed other conflicts in the number of states involved and the
frequency with which it enters the critical stage of large-scale armed
clashes. Yet these are not the only factors determining the impact
that the Middle East conflict has on the dynamics of the international situation.

Threat of Globalization of the Middle East Conflict

The Middle East conflict is unparalleled in terms of its potential for
spreading globally. During the cold war, amid which the Arab-Israeli

This article originally appeared in *Russia in Global Affairs* Vol. 7, No. 3, 2009.

conflict evolved, the two opposing superpowers directly supported the conflicting parties: The Soviet Union supported the Arab countries, while the US supported Israel. On the one hand, the bipolar world order that existed at that time objectively contributed to the escalation of the Middle East conflict into a global confrontation. On the other hand, the Soviet Union and the US were not interested in such developments, and they managed to keep the situation under control.

The behavior of both superpowers during all the wars in the Middle East stands as proof. In 1956, during the Anglo-French-Israeli military invasion of Egypt (which followed Cairo's decision to nationalize the Suez Canal Company) the US – contrary to the widespread belief in various countries, including Russia – not only refrained from supporting its allies but insistently pressed – along with the Soviet Union – for the cessation of hostilities. Washington feared that the tripartite aggression would undermine the position of the West in the Arab world and result in a direct clash with the Soviet Union.

Fears that hostilities in the Middle East might acquire a global dimension could also have materialized during the Six-Day War of 1967. Prior to its outbreak, Moscow and Washington urged each other to cool down their "clients." When the war began, both superpowers assured each other that they did not intend to get involved in the crisis militarily and that that they would seek to negotiate terms for a ceasefire at the UN. On July 5, chairman of the Soviet government Aleksei Kosygin, who was authorized by the Politburo to negotiate on behalf of the Soviet leadership, used a hotline for this purpose for the first time. After the USS Liberty was attacked by Israeli forces, which later claimed the attack was a case of mistaken identity, US president Lyndon Johnson immediately notified Kosygin that the movement of the US Navy in the Mediterranean Sea was only intended to help the crew of the attacked ship and to investigate the incident.

The situation repeated itself during the hostilities of October 1973. Russian publications of those years argued that it was the Soviet Union that prevented US military involvement in those events. In contrast, many US authors claimed that the US reaction thwarted Soviet plans to send troops to the Middle East. Neither statement is true.

The atmosphere was truly quite tense. Sentiments in both Washington and Moscow favored interference, yet both capitals were far from taking real action. When US troops were put on high alert, Henry Kissinger assured Soviet ambassador Anatoly Dobrynin that this move was largely for domestic reasons and should not be seen by Moscow as a hostile act. In a private conversation with Dobrynin, president Richard Nixon said the same, adding that he might have overreacted, but this had been done amid a hostile campaign against him over Watergate.

Meanwhile, Kosygin and foreign minister Andrei Gromyko at a Politburo meeting in Moscow strongly rejected a proposal by the defense minister, Marshal Andrei Grechko, to "demonstrate" the Soviet military presence in Egypt in response to Israel's refusal to comply with a UN Security Council resolution. Soviet leader Leonid Brezhnev took the side of Kosygin and Gromyko, saying that he was against any Soviet involvement in the conflict.

This suggests the unequivocal conclusion that control by the superpowers in the bipolar world did not allow the Middle East conflict to escalate into a global confrontation.

After the cold war, some scholars and political observers concluded that the real threat of the Arab-Israeli conflict going beyond regional frameworks ceased to exist. However, in the 21st century, this conclusion no longer matches reality. The US military operation in Iraq changed the balance of forces in the Middle East. The disappearance of the Iraqi counterbalance has brought Iran to the fore as a regional power claiming a direct role in various Middle East processes. I am among those who believe that the Iranian leadership has already made a political decision to create nuclear weapons of its own. Yet Tehran seems to have set a goal of achieving a technological level that would allow it to make such a decision under unfavorable circumstances (the "Japanese model"). Israel already possesses nuclear weapons and delivery vehicles. Under such circumstances, the absence of a Middle East settlement opens the dangerous prospect of a nuclear collision in the region, which would have catastrophic consequences for the whole world.

The transition to a multipolar world has objectively strengthened the role of states and organizations that are directly involved in regional conflicts, which increases the latter's danger and reduces the possibility of controlling them. This refers, above all, to the Middle

East conflict. The coming of Barack Obama to the presidency allayed fears that the US could deliver a preventive strike against Iran (under George W. Bush, it was one of the most discussed topics in the US). However, fears have increased that such a strike could be launched by Israel, which would have unpredictable consequences for the region and beyond. It seems that President Obama's position does not completely rule out such a possibility.

Terrorism: Danger of a Clash of Civilizations

Another aspect of the highly negative impact of the Middle East conflict on the international situation is the 21st-century challenge: terrorism. The Middle East, or rather the Arab-Israeli conflict, has become an incubator of international terrorism. Many extremist and terrorist organizations and groups, including Al Qaeda, have emerged and developed under the influence of this conflict. The military actions Israel takes to oppose terrorists, which often are disproportionate and cause suffering to the civilian population, not only fail to narrow the scope of terrorist activities but, on the contrary, broaden it.

The danger of this "vicious terrorist circle" can be seen in the theory of the "clash of civilizations," which has become popular in the West. Humankind has hardly recovered from the ideological confrontation between capitalism and communism when a new division of the world is now predicted – this time along religious and civilizational lines. This theory is particularly elaborated in works by American political scientist Samuel Huntington. He views the clash of civilizations as the basic conflict of the present and argues that such clashes are inevitable. The popularity of this theory is seen in the frequency with which Huntington's works are cited in various publications, including works on geopolitics.

Unfortunately, works by Russian scholars lack proof of the invalidity of Huntington's theory. Meanwhile, there is a dire need to study the impact of globalization on various civilizations and analyze the effects of the convergence of not only their material parts but also cultures and dialectics that do not negate the individuality of the civilizational development of nations when such convergence takes place.

Tensions between Western and Islamic civilizations do exist, and it is no use turning a blind eye to them. But these tensions stem not from the essence of these so-called "irreconcilable antagonists" but from the crisis of dialogue between them, which has been replaced with confrontation and even armed struggle. The Middle East conflict plays a special role in this context, which certainly increases the cost of its settlement.

The Arab-Israeli conflict has one more important dimension, as it has a destabilizing effect on the entire Middle East region, which has 68% of the world's oil reserves (not including Arab North Africa, which has also been affected by the Middle East conflict). A recurrence of the events of 1973, when Arab states stopped oil supplies to the West, is unlikely. Yet the US military operation against Iraq, which accounts for almost 10% of the world's oil resources, has already removed this country from the list of major oil exporters for years to come.

Despite the development of alternative energy sources, oil and gas will continue to be primary energy resources for the next few decades. Therefore, stability in the Middle East is and will be of paramount importance, especially once the main consumers of Middle East oil start overcoming the present recession. The jocular saying "The energy crisis has made the light at the end of the tunnel go off" is in fact not so jocular.

I would also like to emphasize that the Middle East region, which has been least hit by the global economic crisis, will be of special value in the postcrisis period as an object of foreign investment. Huge financial resources accumulated in the Gulf area bode well for that possibility.

Comprehensive Settlement or Separate Solutions?

What capabilities does the international community now have to settle the conflict in the Middle East? What does history teach us in this respect?

First, it must be said that the Middle East conflict cannot be settled militarily. This was confirmed once again by Israel's latest major military operation in the Gaza Strip against the Palestinian Hamas movement. Interference from the UN Security Council made Israel cease combat actions and withdraw its troops from Gaza. This time, the US departed from its usual practice of vetoing Security Council resolutions critical of Israel. There is reason to believe that the US will continue to abide by this position with regard to Israel's military offensives because of a possible reaction from the Islamic world. In any case, the US, along with the other permanent members of the Security Council, will oppose a military solution to the Arab-Israeli conflict.

The use of force is unproductive in terms of the objective interests of Israel itself. It has military advantages over Arab countries, but it has very limited capabilities to use these advantages to annex occupied Arab territories – and not just because of the absence of international support. If Israel annexes the Arab territories it occupied in 1967, it will soon cease to be a Jewish state, as the ratio between the Jewish and Arab populations in it will inevitably change in favor of the latter due to its birth rates. There are grounds to believe that not only the leaders of Israel, but the bulk of its political class are aware of this.

The impossibility of a military solution to the Middle East conflict emphasizes the need for a comprehensive settlement. Back in Soviet times, there were two contrasting approaches: The Soviet Union advocated a comprehensive settlement, while the US favored separate agreements between Israel and individual Arab countries. As a result, Israel signed peace treaties with Egypt and Jordan. Was the Soviet Union right in its approach? In retrospect, some authors support the American policy line. I do not. Obviously, the ability to reach a comprehensive settlement was simply ignored when preparing agreements with individual Arab countries. Moreover, it was not even stipulated that these would be interim agreements paving the way to an overall solution.

Aware of the complexity of the process and the impossibility of achieving settlement overnight, the Soviet Union never opposed intermediary measures leading to a clearly defined and mutually agreed goal – a comprehensive settlement. At the same time, the Soviet logic was dictated by the fact that the conclusion of separate agreements removed one Arab country after another from the settlement process and thus complicated the solution of another issue – the settlement of Israeli-Palestinian and Israeli-Syrian relations. Both these "tracks" involve basic territorial problems. And it is not accidental that, despite the Egyptian-Israeli and Jordanian-Israeli peace settlements, endless armed clashes have been taking place in the region for more than 30 years now, including two Israeli interventions in Lebanon – in 1982 and 2007. Both interventions were comparable in scale and number of casualties to the wars of 1967 and 1973, which took place before the conclusion of the Egyptian-Israeli peace treaty.

Without a comprehensive settlement, it is impossible to end the state of hostility between Israel and the Arab world in general, or to guarantee stability of what has already been achieved in Israel's relations with Egypt and Jordan. Without a comprehensive settlement, radical Islamist forces have good chances of destabilizing the situation in the region, especially in key Arab countries like Egypt and Saudi Arabia.

The foundation for a comprehensive settlement of the Middle East conflict was found in the following formula: the territories occupied by Israel during the 1967 war in exchange for peace in Arab countries' relations with Israel. This implies not only the recognition of the Israeli state but also the establishment of full-scale diplomatic and other relations with it. This formula, established at the Madrid Peace Conference (1991), meant universal recognition of the undeniable truth that Israel's withdrawal from Arab territories and security guarantees for Israel were the only way to achieve settlement in the Middle East. I would like to emphasize: The assent of all Arab states and the Palestine Liberation Organization to the "Madrid formula" means their absolute waiver of the demand that Israel withdraw to the borders originally defined for it by the UN General Assembly. (As a result of the first Arab-Israeli War of 1948-1949, Israel's territory expanded significantly.)

Creation of a Palestinian State as Cornerstone of Settlement

The settlement of the Palestinian issue entails resolving several problems, the main one being the creation of a Palestinian state, as provided for back in 1947 by the UN General Assembly's decision on the partition of Palestine into separate Jewish and Arab states. There is now a global consensus on this issue, which includes the US and the European Union. The previous Israeli government, led by Ehud Olmert, also recognized the need to create a Palestinian state. I do not think that incumbent Israeli prime minister Benjamin Netanyahu's negative position on this issue is final, although he is likely to make his consent to the establishment of a Palestinian state conditional on some concessions from the latter. The process of creating a Palestinian state involves difficult negotiations on other issues such as the borders of this state, the rights of refugees and the future of Jerusalem, which must become the capital of the two states.

I do not share the view of those who think that all these problems are insoluble; they can be solved if Israel renounces its practice of establishing settlements in the occupied West Bank. Israel is expanding existing settlements and establishing new ones despite UN Security Council resolutions and the negative attitude toward this practice from a majority of states, including not only Russia, China and European countries but now also the US.

Borders. They could be defined by making minor changes to armistice lines and even exchanging some territories.

Refugees. Their right to return does not mean that all refugees will want to return. Most of them may choose financial compensation, which will allow them to give up living in Palestinian camps and settle in the future Palestinian state or in some other Arab country. Separating the issue of refugees' right to return from the issue of a mechanism for implementing the return, including compensation, was discussed at informal talks between former Israeli minister Yossi Beilin and member of the PLO leadership Yassir Abd Rabbo. The two parties reached an understanding.

Jerusalem. It was none other than US president Bill Clinton who proposed dividing Jerusalem into Israeli and Palestinian sections in his settlement plan.

As for the Israeli-Syrian track, success in this field depends entirely on Israel's consent to Syria's sovereignty over the Golan Heights, occupied by Israel since the war of 1967. Damascus has expressed its desire to negotiate with Israel. Factors that make such negotiations possible include the position of those in the US who are not interested in further rapprochement between Syria and Iran, which would inevitably happen if a Syrian-Israeli settlement is not reached. The new Israeli government is divided over this issue. Foreign minister Avigdor Lieberman has publicly rejected the possibility of returning the Golan Heights to Syria. Defense minister Ehud Barak, who represents the Labor Party (Avoda) in the government, holds a different opinion.

Success in the Syrian-Israeli peace process would also help solve Israeli-Lebanese problems.

Why No Continuity in the Settlement Process?

Attempts to achieve a Middle East settlement have been made in three forms: direct Arab-Israeli negotiations, an intermediary mission by the US, and an international intermediary mission by the US, Russia, the EU and the UN – the present Quartet on the Middle East. Past experience has demonstrated the futility of two of these three forms: attempts by the conflicting parties to come to an agreement on their own, without the involvement of outside forces, and the monopolization of the intermediary mission by the US.

Recent examples of that include the termination of the Israeli-Palestinian negotiating process after the Netanyahu government came to power in Israel and the failure of the promise given by former US President George W. Bush to achieve a peace settlement in the Middle East before his presidency expired. The White House did not confine itself to words. US Secretary of State Condoleezza Rice has actually bypassed the Quartet aside, spending more time in the Middle East in 2008 than in any other region of the world. It was not fortuitous that the White House named the US city of Annapolis as the venue for a Middle East summit, intended to mark the start of the final stage of a settlement.

I would like to mention just one factor contributing to the failure of the process started in Annapolis. To ensure the broadest possible Arab participation in that meeting (including Syria, of course), Rice said that the Annapolis summit would be followed by an international conference on Middle East settlement in Moscow. This implied the continuity of the process, with the active participation of Russia and other members of the Quartet. Given all that, Moscow decided to support the American initiative to convene an international meeting in Annapolis. President Vladimir Putin, Foreign Minister Sergei Lavrov, his deputy Aleksandr Saltanov, and other Foreign Ministry officials played the main role in this decision.

I, too, took part in the settlement efforts. Shortly before the Annapolis summit, on behalf of President Putin, I met with the president of the Palestinian Authority, Mahmoud Abbas, as well as Israeli prime minister Ehud Olmert, Israeli defense minister Ehud Barak, Syrian president Hafez al-Assad, Egyptian president Hosni Mubarak, and Arab League secretary general Amr Moussa. In Damascus, I also met with the head of Hamas's political bureau, Khaled Mashaal.

The keynote of all those meetings was the idea of continuity in the Middle East settlement process, which the planned Moscow peace conference was to ensure several months after the Annapolis meeting. For example, Syrian president Assad linked his consent to send a Syrian delegation to Annapolis with the idea of holding a follow-up conference in Moscow. His position was shared by the other officials with whom I talked.

However, the Moscow peace conference never took place. It was repeatedly postponed throughout 2008. Then it was announced that the conference would be held in the spring of 2009. The main reason why the Moscow conference was not held as scheduled was the unwillingness of the US, which cited the opinion of Israel, while Israeli leaders, in turn, cited Washington's unreadiness.

In view of the changes in the political leadership of Israel and the differences among Palestinians that have divided them into supporters of the Fatah and Hamas movements, I think holding a peace conference in Moscow in the present circumstances and without thorough preparation would be counterproductive.

But this conclusion does not mean that headway in the Middle East settlement process is now impossible. Despite the enormous difficulties and obstacles that have accumulated on this path, chances for success do exist.

First, there is reason to believe that US president Barack Obama, concerned by the situation in Afghanistan, Iraq, Iran and Pakistan, will take the Middle East settlement problem much more seriously than his predecessor. Washington can exert a decisive influence on Israel to press the Netanyahu government to solve problems with Palestinians and Syrians. Naturally, the strong pro-Israel lobby in the US will stand in the way of the White House's resolute measures to influence the Israeli leadership, but today this lobby has somewhat lost its strength as many former supporters of Israel's radical measures now feel the need for a peaceful settlement. Another encouraging factor in this regard is that President Obama has not let neoconservatives, famous for their anti-Arab lobbying, onto his team.

Second, Arab countries – primarily Egypt and Saudi Arabia – have taken a constructive position and have a positive impact on Palestinians.

Third, before Israel attacked the Gaza Strip, Tel Aviv and Fatah had drawn closer to each other on some sensitive issues. At least they had moved from refusing to discuss them to exchanging views.

Finally, Moscow's role and policy can be a very important re-source in settlement efforts. Unlike the other Quartet members, Russia has good relations not only with Israel, Iran and Syria, but also with Fatah, Hamas and Hezbollah.

Using the experience gained, the Quartet could work out a compromise plan on all major settlement issues. This plan should be handed over to the conflicting parties as a collective decision of the US, Russia, the EU and the UN. Let us remember how Israel was created. Was it not the international community that dictated the decision to partition Palestine and create Israel and an Arab state in Palestinian territory?

The proposed plan should include the establishment of a nuclear-free zone in the Middle East. This problem is exacerbated still further today. Israel's nuclear armaments and concerns about Iran's possession of nuclear weapons encourage nuclear ambitions among other countries in the region. Israel opposes the establishment of a nuclear-free zone. But its position may change if an Arab-Israeli settlement is linked to Iran's verifiable renunciation of nuclear weapons.

Of course, the path to a Middle East settlement is difficult. This task cannot be solved overnight. But active efforts must be made.

THE MODERN ERA AND THE CRISIS OF THE 1970s

Aleksandr Dynkin and Vladimir Pantin

The second decade of the 21st century, like the 1970s, is unlikely to be calm: We can expect a series of crises and imbalances. We cannot rule out geopolitical upheavals and changes, especially in the Middle East and the post-Soviet space. The crises will alternate with upturns; and despite pessimistic forecasts, the global trend of world development will not be disrupted.

The global financial and economic crisis of 2008-2009 has revitalized discussions about a change of the world order. Compared with the opinions voiced in the past two decades, including prophecies about "the end of history" and a "clash of civilizations," the crisis has brought the financial-economic paradigm to the forefront of the current debate. The recent (precrisis) mainstream forecasts of the future world order (such as "The Age of Nonpolarity"[1] by Richard Haass, president of the Council on Foreign Relations, or the report by the US National Intelligence Council "Global Trends-2025. A Transformed World"[2]) do not fully take into account the new realities and

This article appeared in *Russia in Global Affairs* Vol. 8, No. 3, 2010; it was first published in Russian in *Mirovaya Ekonomika i Mezhdunarodniye Otnosheniya*, No. 6, 2010. Content has been edited for the present publication. – *Ed.*

challenges emerging under the pressure of the current global crisis.

Admittedly, the crisis was caused by a global imbalance and will result in a new equilibrium due to changes in the alignment of forces in the world economy and international relations, as was the case after the 1929-1932 recession and the ensuing Great Depression, or after the 1969-1970, 1974-1975 and 1980-1982 crises. In the first case, World War II broke out, which resulted in the establishment of a bipolar world. In the second case, the crises contributed to the political mobilization of American society and its economic renewal, thus enabling the US to emerge as the sole superpower.

Will the ongoing crisis be an exception? Or have we entered another protracted age in which the world order will change? Will the new world order after the current crisis be more stable? What kind of world order will it be? How will the US's leading role in the world change, and what will happen to other major powers? . . .

In certain respects, the current situation in the Middle East resembles that of the late 1960s and the early 1970s. In September 1969, in response to Israel's actions (the Six Day War), the leaders of the Islamic countries decided to establish the Organization of the Islamic Conference (OIC); in 1973-1974, oil prices skyrocketed due to the policy of the Organization of Petroleum Exporting Countries (OPEC). Today, these organizations are again vigorously pursuing their policies, playing an ever-increasing role in the world economy and politics. The impasse in the Palestinian-Israeli conflict and worsening relations between Israel and Iran may provoke new conflicts in the Middle East, while US participation in military operations not only in Afghanistan but also in Pakistan (to prevent the Taliban from getting nuclear weapons) may make the Islamic world even more resentful of the West. A similar situation occurred in the early 1970s, after the Arab-Israeli wars of 1967 and 1973. There were acts of terror and hostage-takings at the 1972 Olympic Games in Munich and elsewhere.

However, the current situation is more acute than in the 1970s. Terrorism has grown to global proportions, and the "arc of instability" now stretches from North Africa and Palestine to North Korea, Indonesia and the Philippines. Of special concern is the "Asian end of the arc" – i.e., terrorist activity in Afghanistan and Pakistan, as well as potential conflicts in the Central Asian states. According to the head of the Anti Terrorist Center of the Commonwealth of

Independent States, Andrei Novikov,[3] the economic and social crisis in Central Asian states may force many young unemployed people to join international terrorist organizations. All these circumstances require closer cooperation between the US, the European Union and Russia to rebuff the terrorists and stabilize the world.

However, paradoxical though it may seem, the alignment of key political forces in the 2000s – despite the political changes that have occurred – somewhat resembles their alignment in the 1970s. True, the world has become more complex, interrelated and globalized since then, but the main political roles are still the same, although some factors and players have been replaced. International revolutionary communism has given way to Islamic fundamentalism, which is active in many countries, and China is playing the role of the second superpower now, albeit less powerful than the Soviet Union. The EU has taken the place of Germany and France, while South Korea, India and Brazil play the role of Japan, which developed rapidly in the 1970s. This shows certain conservatism (or succession) in the development of the architecture of international relations and world politics. The table below shows the basic similarities between the 1970s and the modern period.

The surprising similarity of the aforementioned processes and problems that, respectively, deteriorated in the 1970s and at present, indicate the presence of another round in global development where a new crisis replaces rapid growth, rather than the recurrence of situations in the world economy and politics. Compared with the 1970s, the world has changed dramatically, and many problems that were not resolved at the time, have reemerged in new forms and on a larger scale.

Conflicts and Upheavals in the Offing

If comparison of the current situation with the 1970s is at least partially justified, several important conclusions follow:

First, a certain weakening of the world leader, the US, is most likely temporary. The US has encountered unprecedented challenges in financial, economic, social and international relations. But as in the 1970s, as long as there are no serious challengers to world leadership, America's domination will persist, although this does not mean that it will continue forever or that the US's leadership is guaranteed.

TABLE 1. Basic Similarities Between Crises of 1970s and 2008-2010

Events	1970s	2008-2010
Military operations	• US war in Vietnam (1965-1972)	• US in Afghanistan: since 2001 • US in Iraq: since 2003
Financial crises, changes in financial policy	• US crisis (1969-1970) • Renunciation of Bretton Woods gold standard • Dollar devaluations (1971, 1973)	• Global economic crisis: 2008-2009 • Discussion of changes in the world financial system: new world reserve currency, possible dollar devaluation
Changes in world politics	• US renunciation of active foreign policy (1970s) Increasingly vigorous foreign policy of USSR and China	• Changes in US foreign policy under Barack Obama (as shown in speech in Cairo, June 4, 2009) • Increasing political activity of Islamic countries, China and Russia (since 2007)
Internal political changes in US	• Growing antiwar movement (late 1960s to early 1970s) • Social and economic reforms (1970s)	• Changes in US public sentiment Barack Obama's victory in 2008 Beginning of social and economic reforms
Imbalances in world order	• OPEC oil embargo (1974-1975) Revolution in Iran (1978-1979) Conflicts between Israel and Arab countries (1970s)	• North Korea challenge (2009) Iranian nuclear problem, internal conflicts in Iran (2007-2009) Problems in Israeli-Palestinian relations
Arms reduction talks (Washington/ Moscow)	• Richard Nixon's visit to Moscow (1972) • Missile defense treaties (1972) • SALT I (1972) • SALT II (1979)	• Obama's visit to Moscow (2009) • Draft of New START treaty
Mounting problems in world energy sector	• Oil price hikes, energy crisis (1974-1975) • Transition of US and Western Europe to new energy conservation technologies (1970s)	• Oil price fluctuations (2005-2009) Conflicts over oil and gas transit (2007-2009) • Discussions about establishing "gas OPEC" • Intensive launching of environmentally friendly energy sources in US and Europe

In the future, the world may see a real aspirant to world leadership, or this leadership may be shared among several power centers. This would cultivate the so-called multipolar world and, consequently, an increasing potential for the collision of interests and conflicts.

Second, if the analogy in question is justified, the world is likely to expect many economic upheavals and political conflicts within the next few years. The weakening of the US after the defeat in Vietnam prompted some leaders in the Arab countries and the Soviet Union to make rash decisions. Several years after the financial crisis of 1969-1971, the energy crisis of 1974-1975 broke out. The latter was caused by a dramatic increase in world oil prices due to the policies of the Arab states and other oil-producing countries after another war in the Middle East in 1973.

The analogy would suggest a new economic crisis that might break out in 2012-2013 after a period of growth. The general instability of the world financial and political system indicates a high probability of new upheavals.[4]

New conflicts in the Middle East or serious upheavals in the post-Soviet space may directly cause a new crisis. This primarily concerns Central Asia (one of the states of the region, namely Kazakhstan, has considerable oil reserves, while Turkmenistan boasts tremendous natural gas reserves), where the US, Russia and China are competing for influence. No less dangerous are the simmering conflicts in the Caucasus that accommodate oil-rich Azerbaijan and Georgia, where an oil pipeline to Europe runs. A political conflict in Ukraine threatening its integrity would be of even greater danger. It may provoke outside interference in its affairs. In this event, a dramatic worsening of relations between Russia and the West is quite likely.[5]

However, a possible new crisis and even a minute political retreat by the US would not imply the defeat of the West. In 1975, US troops had to pull out of South Vietnam, which temporarily weakened the US's foreign policy position and offered the Soviet Union an opportunity to strengthen its influence in the Third World. But while the Soviet Union was busy supporting revolutions in Asia, Africa and Central America, and funding the "socialist camp," the US, having learned a lesson from the Vietnam War, used the chance to reform its Army, making it truly strong, mobile and professional.

In addition, the US implemented other important reforms in the 1970s, paving the way to a dramatic increase in its international economic and political influence in the 1980s and the 1990s. The planned withdrawal of US troops from Iraq may serve as an analogy to the US withdrawal from Vietnam. Yet, as in the 1970s, it is unlikely to weaken the US; instead, it will enable it to focus on key economic, social and foreign policy issues.

The late 1970s were quite dramatic. In 1978-1979, a revolution broke out in Iran, which seriously compromised the US's positions in the Middle East and the Persian Gulf (the Greater Middle East, as they say now). The revolution brought an anti-US regime to power, led by charismatic religious leader Ayatollah Khomeini. But this regime was not pro-Soviet, so the weakening of the US's position in the Gulf did not imply an automatic strengthening of the Soviet position. In late 1979, the Soviet Union deployed troops in Afghanistan, starting a long war. Afghanistan turned into a theater of the "world war" of the bipolar era as diverse forces came together against the Soviet Union like Islamic (including pro-Iranian) fundamentalists, the US, West European countries and even China, which supplied weapons to the Afghan *mujahedeen*.

Therefore, even though the US's foreign policy position had noticeably weakened by the late 1970s, and its rival had attained maximum influence in the world, the Soviet Union, in effect, entered a deep economic crisis and became bogged down in Afghanistan. The US, having rid itself of the burden of the Vietnam War, emerged from a chain of crises and upheavals as a more consolidated and powerful state, whereas the Soviet Union's defeat in Afghanistan was the final bell toll before its breakup. A mere eight months after Soviet troops pulled out of Kabul, the Berlin Wall fell.

The global military and political consequences of both these wars were largely caused by economic processes. The economic crisis of 1980-1982 profoundly affected the US and Western states. But, unlike the crises of 1969-1971 and 1974-1975, the US position in the world improved in the long run, whereas that of the Soviet Union worsened.

Throughout the 1970s, the Soviet Union squandered considerable resources aiding its satellites and supporting revolutions and national movements, which took a heavy toll on its economic and political position. Economically, the Soviet Union was stagnating, and this period was later – under Mikhail Gorbachev – called "the age of stagnation." In the meantime, the US accumulated intellectual, technological, financial and political resources for a new growth spurt. It began in 1983-1984, together with an economic revival that gave impetus to a new technological revolution, the advent of modern information technologies, personal computers, the Internet, etc.

If we were to extend the above analogies into the late 1970s and early 1980s, that would lead us to expect political and economic upheavals in 2012-2020. They are likely to be caused by the development of new technologies (the integration of nano-, bio-, cognitive and information technologies, environmentally friendly energy sources and faster information transfer methods), changes in the geopolitical situation in the world, an imbalance of demographic processes in various regions of the world and ensuing mass migration, climate change, environmental problems, shortages of freshwater, and the spread of new epidemics. As a result, social and political conflicts may escalate in various regions.

Most countries will have to coordinate their efforts to address numerous problems. In these conditions, one might expect increased demand for global governance and effective leadership that would bring together countries with different traditions, religions and cultures. Only the US can be such a leader in the near future. It is important that the leading country be ready for this global challenging task and avoid the temptation to be guided by its own momentary interests.

New Trends

Globalization is among the new trends that set the beginning of the 21st century apart from the 1970s. It was globalization that caused such different and seemingly unrelated processes as the emergence of the global information market; the instantaneous overflow of financial assets from one country to another; the rapid economic growth of China and other Asian countries; the rapid spread of new technologies, institutions, democratic and semi-democratic regimes; intensive communication among millions of citizens of various countries; global migration; and global international terrorism. New global markets are emerging, providing financial, legal, educational and medical services and highly skilled specialists. The "experience economy" is gaining greater significance, as are international sports, cultural and high fashion events. The current crisis, too, largely relates to globalization processes.

Globalization has its pros and cons, obverse and reverse, advantages and shortcomings. It is necessary to learn to govern globalization, but no country can do it on its own, not even such a powerful one as the US. Therefore, the leading countries will have to learn to effectively interact within Group of 20 and other international formats. Of course, finding compromises and consensus within the G-20 is a more laborious task compared with doing the same within Group of Eight.

Among other new trends (and political risks), one should note the threat of the proliferation of nuclear weapons, climate change, freshwater shortages and the spread of new epidemics. The danger of Iran or North Korea attaining nuclear weapons is considerable, but it can never compare with the horrendous prospect of the Taliban getting Pakistani nuclear weapons to blackmail the world. There was no such threat in the 1970s, but now the international community will have to counteract it. The growth of the influence of aggressive Islamism poses a danger to all the leading countries, including the US, the EU, Russia, India and China.

As for challenges posed by climate change and freshwater shortages, they, too, have a clear political dimension. Many analysts predict that the upcoming conflicts and wars will be caused not so much by oil supply problems as the fight for freshwater resources.[6] On top of that, the world is facing global epidemics such as AIDS, atypical pneumonia and swine flu, fraught with grave economic and political consequences.

The ongoing rapid technological changes are both advantageous and risky. For example, the relatively cheap ($1,500) human genome mapping might cause a wealth of ethical and other problems in four to five years. Any insurance company or bank may demand the mapping of its client's genome, which implies an invasion of privacy and vulnerability to outside interference. Cloning, cyber-terrorism, and trade in internal organs may become side effects of the rapid and uncontrollable development of new technologies.

Thus, compared with the 1970s, the present-day world is more dynamic, globalized and risk-prone. The new trends considerably influence the picture of the modern world, political processes and international relations, yet some historical situations look similar.

The 1970s are already two generations in the past; much has changed since then, but the logic and sequence of events in crises and transitional periods are changing much more slowly.

***

The above parallels between the modern day and the 1970s allow us to identify some prospects with a certain degree of probability.

First, the next decade, like the 1970s, is unlikely to be calm: We may expect a series of crises and imbalances. We cannot rule out geopolitical upheavals and changes, especially in the Middle East and the post-Soviet space (Ukraine, Moldova and some Central Asian states in which the interests of Russia, the US and China intersect). These crises will alternate with upturns; and despite pessimistic forecasts, the global trend of world development will not be disrupted. At the same time, we will certainly see pronounced turbulence in the world economy and politics, intensive restructuring, and political and economic reforms both in individual countries and at the supranational level.

Second, the US will retain its world leadership position in the next few decades. At the same time, the role of China and other BRIC states (Brazil, Russia, India, China), and possibly the EU, will increase dramatically. Therefore, the unipolar world will gradually be replaced by a multipolar one. In these new conditions, the US will have to closely interact with the key political power centers (above all the EU, Russia, China and India) and search for acceptable compromises. The US, together with other countries, will have to strive to prevent the world from plunging into chaos, and preserve the governability of global processes. There are no serious aspirants to world leadership at present, but a weakening of the US may facilitate their emergence. At the same time, attempts to show strength at any cost, disregarding possible consequences, will weaken the US rather than strengthen it. A reckless demonstration of strength would certainly boost anti-American sentiment across the world.

Third, we should expect, as in the 1970s, serious changes in international politics and the global financial system, as well as reforms of international political, financial and economic institutions. Reforming the International Monetary Fund, the G-8 and the G-20 seems to be most urgent, but the UN should carry out reforms of its own as well. NATO, too, is looking for a new strategy. Russian President Dmitry Medvedev's initiative to build a new European security architecture will require creative efforts. We can no longer postpone its modernization. The task of world leaders, including the US and Russia, is to help implement these reforms. Meanwhile, both countries will have to decide in 2012 on the constitutional change of their leaderships or their reelection to a second term. China, too, is planning changes in its leadership in 2012. This implies a rather busy schedule of political and diplomatic work within the next three years, and by no means guarantees stability in the world.

Fourth, the uniqueness of the present moment is that no major global issue can be solved without cooperation with Russia – be it the stable development of countries in the post-Soviet space; the Israeli-Palestinian, Armenian-Azerbaijani or South Caucasus conflicts; an aggravation of the situation in Afghanistan and Pakistan; the nonproliferation of nuclear weapons; the nuclear threat from Iran and North Korea; missile defense problems; international terrorism; the new financial architecture; energy and water security; climate change; control over new technologies; or the danger of epidemics.

Finally, the awareness of the interdependence of various countries in the face of a possible financial-economic disaster, the priority of common strategic values and the de-ideologization of politics in the Euro-Atlantic space have given an unprecedented impulse to the appearance of good will in world politics. This impulse, if used correctly and in a timely manner, may prevail over national or transnational interests. If not, the "end of history" scenario may very likely come true.

Notes

1. Haass, Richard A. "The Age of Nonpolarity," *Foreign Affairs*, 2008: 87(3).
2. National Intelligence Council. "Global Trends-2025. A Transformed World," November 2008, https://www.files.ethz.ch/isn/94769/2008_11_global_trends_2025.pdf.
3. See: *Nezavisimoye voyennoye obozreniye*, July 3, 2009.
4. See, for example: Paul Krugman, *The Return of Depression Economics and the Crisis of 2008*. New York: W.W. Norton & Company, 2009.
5. See: V.V. Lapkin, ed., "Osnovniye tendentsii i perspektivy politicheskikh transformatsii v Rossii i v Ukraine v period 2004-2008 gg." [Main trends and prospects of political transformations in Russia and Ukraine, 2004-2008], Moscow, IMEMO.
6. See: V. Danilov-Danilyan, "Voda dorozhe nefti?" [Is water more expensive than oil?] *Argumenty i fakty*, 2008, Vol. 4, p. 45.

THE GLASS MENAGERIE OF NON-PROLIFERATION

Vladimir Orlov

There is no doubt that the international nuclear nonprolif-
eration regime entered a new phase in May 2015. The situa-
tion has worsened, and it will be more and more difficult and
expensive to correct it. The cooling of international relations
will make the NPT situation extremely fragile.

Once upon a time all the animals in the Zoo decided that they would
disarm, and they arranged to have a conference to arrange the matter. So the Rhinoceros said when he opened the proceedings that
the use of teeth was barbarous and horrible and ought to be strictly
prohibited by general consent. Horns, which were mainly defensive
weapons, would, of course, have to be allowed. The Buffalo, the Stag,
the Porcupine, and even the little Hedgehog all said they would vote
with the Rhino, but the Lion and the Tiger took a different view.
They defended teeth and even claws, which they described as honor-
able weapons of immemorial antiquity.
– Winston Churchill, "A Disarmament Fable" (1928)

This article originally appeared in *Russia in Global Affairs* Vol. 13, No. 3, 2015.

Hardly anyone placed high hopes on a successful outcome to the Review Conference of the Parties to the Treaty on the Non-Proliferation of Nuclear Weapons (NPT), which was held in April and May 2015 in New York. The atmosphere among its members was far from supportive. But the failure of the conference is a much more significant event than the simple inability of the participating states to reach agreement on the text of a final document that would summarize the five-year review cycle.

Background

The vast majority of countries in the world view the NPT as the cornerstone of the global security architecture. It has been joined by 191 states – more than any other international security treaty – and the number of NPT signatories continues to grow: At the latest conference, the treaty was joined by Palestine. Only four countries have never joined the NPT: Israel, India, Pakistan and South Sudan. North Korea has partially withdrawn, and is now a de facto nuclear weapon state and a nonparty to the treaty.

There are many doubts about how effectively some NPT provisions are being implemented. Yet no party to the treaty questions its necessity. In 1995, the NPT was extended indefinitely by consensus, without a vote. Thus, the very question of whether the Treaty is needed or not has been redundant in legal terms for two decades already. The same year, the NPT member countries adopted a package of decisions that served as the basis for the legally binding verdict on the treaty's extension. They included a resolution on the Middle East that called on all states in the region to accede to the NPT and establish a "zone free of nuclear weapons as well as other weapons of mass destruction."[1] This resolution has never been fulfilled.

All subsequent conferences have only reviewed the operation of the Treaty and sought – sometimes successfully, sometimes not – to formulate moves to ensure the most effective implementation of all NPT provisions, while keeping balance among its three pillars: non-proliferation (Arts. 1 and 2), disarmament (Art. 6) and the right to peacefully use nuclear technology (Art. 4). The four-week marathon review conferences ended with the adoption of the final documents by consensus, which was to serve as recognition of their success.

On the eve of the Review Conference in 2000, the situation did not look promising. The aggression against Serbia had exacerbated relations between Russia and the US. Tensions were growing between the US and China. In addition, the smell of war against Baghdad was already in the air, and the US was actively exploiting the theme of "weapons of mass destruction" to provide propaganda support for an invasion of Iraq. The conference's success was hanging by a thread until the last day – primarily because of difficulties with the wording of a statement on Iraq. However, the will of the majority of states helped them reach a compromise on the final document, which included "13 steps" toward nuclear disarmament. (However, not all of them have been implemented. Suffice it to mention the point that described the Russian-US Antiballistic Missile Treaty as "a cornerstone of strategic stability." [2])

The atmosphere at the 2005 conference in New York was quite different – sluggish and lacking the will to find solutions. Three countries – the US, Iran and Egypt – wanted the conference to fail (each for its own purely selfish reasons). And they succeeded.

Five years later, in 2010, the atmosphere changed again, and significantly. The recent conclusion of the New START Treaty by Russia and the US had heightened expectations among nonnuclear states that progress on nuclear disarmament could be accelerated. Hopes appeared that a solution to the Middle East problem could be found at a conference on the establishment of a WMD-free zone in the region. This generally favorable background helped adopt an ambitious final document that included a 64-point action plan,[3] the bulk of which was devoted to nuclear disarmament. It was not easy for nuclear-weapon states, including Russia, to adopt this document. However, they did not block it; the reason was that adopting the action plan would be a sign of constructive compromise, which would ultimately strengthen the NPT.

It is clear from today's perspective that the success in 2010 was illusory. The conference participants simply jumped the gun, for they did not have any solid basis for implementing the provisions set out in the action plan. Some of them could have been a travesty if implemented. Others were simply a failure. A conference on a Middle East WMD-free zone was never convened, although the final document had said this should be done no later than 2012. Preparations for establishing one began unjustifiably late. Israel avoided discussing its participation in such a zone; the US, apparently believing that it should not annoy its main ally in the Middle East over such an issue, allowed plans for the conference to be torpedoed.

The 2015 Context

The international background against which we gathered in New York in April 2015 was the worst since the cold war. Moreover, many signs in the current international situation suggest that the world has already entered a new cold war:

1. Two of the five nuclear states – Russia and the US – are in a tough, relentless confrontation.
2. The security situation in Europe has dramatically deteriorated.
3. Countries in the Middle East, especially Egypt, are profoundly disappointed over the lack of any progress in implementing the 1995 resolution on Israel's joining the Treaty – or, at least, in launching a dialogue on a Middle East WMD-free zone.
4. Multilateral disarmament is in a deep crisis, reflected in the long-term stagnation of the Conference on Disarmament in Geneva, as well as the inability to enact the Comprehensive Nuclear Test Ban Treaty. The latter was signed in 1996, but several countries, including the US and China, have not ratified it.
5. There are growing tensions in East Asia, including North Korea's plans to build up its nuclear missile program.

These five factors produced profound skepticism among many participants about the possibility of achieving any progress in nonproliferation and disarmament this year – and this despite significant progress in negotiations with Iran!

Many parties to the NPT did pay tribute to the success of multilateral diplomacy with regard to the Iranian nuclear program. Even though no comprehensive solution to this program had been found by the beginning of the conference and the very possibility of achieving a final solution has raised doubts, the attitude toward the Iranian delegation at the conference was very positive, and their contribution to the discussions was viewed as constructive. However, this positive dynamic proved unable to change the overall negative background.

The Beginning: Major Players

The beginning of the Review Conference – its first week, when the parties to the treaty set out their official positions at a plenary meeting – showed both the conference's potential and its limits. It also brought to light the main players.

Let's start with the five nuclear states. The US and Russia got right down to exchanging accusations in the first few days, and their accusations were not trivial. Usually, the US and Russia do not do this in public at NPT conferences. But this time, [US Secretary of State] John Kerry on the very first day accused Russia of violating the Intermediate-Range Nuclear Forces (INF) Treaty and the Budapest Memorandum (Canada, Poland, Estonia and, not surprisingly, Ukraine later joined in the criticism). In response, Russia accused the US and NATO of undermining the NPT by pursuing the "nuclear sharing" policy. As part of this policy, military personnel of allied countries without nuclear weapons of their own are taught to use nuclear weapons and participate in nuclear planning. Russia issued an unprecedentedly tough statement, urging "the US and NATO member countries concerned to ensure due compliance with the NPT obligations. If they cease to violate the Treaty, they will make their best contribution to strengthen the nuclear non-proliferation regime."[1] Another source of Russia's concern was the deployment by the US of a global missile defense system.

On the other hand, even amid these mutual accusations, the five nuclear-weapon states did not lose at least a semblance of unity. They adopted a joint statement[5] – insipid and commonplace, as usual, yet it sent a signal to the staunchest "disarmament radicals" [i.e., countries that strongly support disarmament – Ed.] that the five states were at least still coordinating their approaches. Russia and the US held a joint briefing on the implementation of the START treaty. However, the audience was small. Did the decreased interest in bilateral Russian-US arms control show that the world took the implementation of START for granted and was not worried about risks? Or did it show that most NPT parties viewed START as a correct yet insufficient step?

As regards the Budapest Memorandum, this issue was not given much attention at the conference. It was not even mentioned in the draft final document, nor was NATO's "nuclear sharing" policy.[6] This suggests that the parties performed a ritual "sword dance," threatening each other in public and then getting down to their joint work: After all, both the US and Russia are vitally interested in the NPT's viability.

There was disharmony among other nuclear states as well. The UK mainly sided with the US, but on some issues it took positions that were closer to those of the "disarmament radicals."[7] France, on the contrary, was firmly opposed[8] to the so-called humanitarian initiative, which calls for international attention to catastrophic consequences of nuclear weapons; it did not try to court the radicals, which objectively brought its position closer to that of Russia. Finally, China kept silent, avoiding bringing matters to a head – with only one exception, made to hurt Japan. Beijing did this distinctly and with maximum pain to Tokyo (on the issue of Hiroshima), after which it again went into pleasant hibernation.

Therefore, the unity of the five nuclear states was nothing more than a façade hiding deep differences – and not only between Russia and the US. At the same time, each of the nuclear states was happy to sit back and keep silent when it came to giving straight and clear answers to the "disarmament radicals." For some reason, they all wanted to pass the buck to Russia. Could this have been in order to accuse it of undermining the conference later?

Another collective player at the Review Conference – the Non-Aligned Movement (NAM) – was too large (over 110 members) to avoid being amorphous. Indonesia had been expected to play a significant role at the conference, but that did not happen. The leading role was taken by Iran, which played it elegantly.

Still another collective player is the Non-Proliferation and Disarmament Initiative (NPDI). This coalition largely includes countries that are under the US nuclear umbrella and act as a buffer between the "disarmament radicals" and the nuclear states (especially the US and UK), all while pursuing their own interests.

Now is the time to introduce those who have already appeared on the political scene under the collective name of "disarmament radicals." This is a significant and growing group of countries dissatisfied with the slow progress in disarmament and the lack of progress in implementing the disarmament resolutions adopted in 2000 and 2010. These countries are led by Austria, Switzerland, Mexico, Cuba and South Africa. Last year, Austria enlisted 159 states under its banners for the Vienna Conference on the Humanitarian Impact of Nuclear Weapons. (Mexico had convened a similar conference earlier, and South Africa may host the next one.) Austria issued the Austrian Pledge,[9] later renamed the Humanitarian Pledge, which proposed legally prohibiting nuclear weapons and won support from 93 countries.

This group is a serious force that should be neither ignored nor ridiculed. Austria-led efforts have seriously reconfigured the balance of power in the NPT review process. As nuclear states, Russia and France in particular have remained highly skeptical of the humanitarian initiative. Indeed, Austria, Mexico and some other countries that have initiated discussions of ethical and humanitarian issues (which are important per se) will seek a legal prohibition on the possession of nuclear weapons – like the prohibitions on two other forms of WMD, chemical and biological, that are codified in international conventions. It remains unclear whether this initiative will be undertaken within or outside the format of the NPT review process.

Now we come to the last informal group of countries: the Middle Eastern group. Like the Middle East itself, this group is marked by mutual suspicion – but this feeling is concealed when it comes to the subjects of Israel or a conference on a WMD-free zone. Arabs are of one mind when these issues are discussed. As a rule, their position is made public by Egypt, then Algeria, Tunisia and Syria chime in. The Gulf States, annoyed by Iran's diplomatic brilliance, say the same but under their breath, as it were. At this conference, Cairo took a very tough position, reminiscent of a preparatory committee meeting in 2013, when the Egyptian delegation slammed the door. The same year, US influence on Egypt markedly decreased.

Behind the Scenes

After the plenary week came work by the three main committees – on disarmament, nonproliferation and nuclear energy. Nuclear energy is probably the only NPT area where differences do not escalate into antagonism, and this committee adopted a consensus text. There are no prizes for guessing that the work of the other two committees proceeded with difficulties; hardly anyone expected consensus there.

Other important work went on behind the scenes. It revealed two opposite trends. The first was *unwillingness to compromise*; the second was the desire to *settle differences and seek compromise*.

The first trend was obvious among some of the five nuclear states, the "disarmament radicals," and some Middle Eastern countries, especially Egypt. Each country was guided by its own motives and avoided seeking compromise. For example, what France viewed as unacceptable concessions on disarmament issues looked to Austria and Mexico like insufficient measures.

The second trend seemed to fit the mood of the majority of delegates in New York: They had no illusions or excessively high expectations. They did not attempt to overextend themselves and exceed the 2010 Action Plan. Realizing that the general situation was not conducive to major moves and big achievements, the advocates of compromise were disposed to move forward in small yet tangible steps in order to return to their capitals with a final consensus document. For example, Spain, Brazil, Iran, Australia, Sweden and eventually Switzerland favored such a flexible approach.

Russia was also set to achieve results, not failure. It was with this intention that it presented a draft text on the Middle East for inclusion in the final document, which proposed that the UN secretary-general convene a conference on a WMD-free zone no later than March 1, 2016.[10]

But this group of countries, even though they were in the majority, did not have a leader or a mediator.

Climax and Denouement

The president of the conference, experienced diplomat Taous Feroukhi from Algeria, had to assume a leadership role. In the closing days of the session, she urged the participants to seek a compromise. With a close-knit group she began to prepare the final document, knowing that the French and Americans would not like some of its proposals, while the Austrians would find them weak. Yet she was set to achieve a balanced outcome.

We saw the draft text at midnight May 21. After I had read all 24 pages, I had to admit that Feroukhi and her small team had almost achieved the impossible. Of course, there was nothing revolutionary in the text – it was only a final document of another review conference. But the draft text made great progress on at least two key fronts.

First, the 19 points of the section that set out further steps for nuclear disarmament seemed to be acceptable to nonnuclear states,

which demanded "further progress." The section began by expressing "deep concerns pertaining to the catastrophic humanitarian
consequences of any use of nuclear weapons." Then it urged Russia
and the US "to commence negotiations at an early date to achieve
greater reductions in their stockpiles of nuclear weapons." The draft
document called on all nuclear states to "continue their engagement
on a standard reporting form," but "without prejudice to national
security."

The draft called on the eight states that had not yet ratified the
CTBT (and were thus holding the treaty hostage) to "ratify that
Treaty without further delay and without waiting for any other State
to do so." The last, 19th point recommended that the UN General
Assembly "establish*** an open-ended working group to identify
and elaborate effective measures for the full implementation of Article VI."

My first reaction was that this was a victory for the "disarmament
radicals" and surrender by the five nuclear states, which were torn
by differences. On second thought, however, I saw a reasonable and
mostly balanced compromise, and it became clear why the acting
head of the Russian delegation described the draft as "a very useful
effort on the part of Ms. Feroukhi that could have been adopted –
and should have been adopted."

The Middle East section was based on Russia's proposals, which
had been drafted after long consultations with Middle Eastern
delegates, above all Egypt. Israel, which attended the conference
as an observer country, was also present – in both body and spirit
(sometimes it seemed that the Americans or Canadians were voic-
ing not their own positions, but Israel's). The Israeli flag could be
seen at various sideline meetings. Continuing the tradition of recent
years, Russian officials repeatedly met with their Israeli counterparts
to discuss possible solutions and their degree of acceptability. Of
course, Russia also maintained dialogue with the US and the UK,
which until the last days of the conference seemed to be constructive. Sometimes it could even be heard on the margins of the conference that Russians and Americans "are again singing the same tune
on Middle East issues."

But it turned out that the tune was not the same. The US (as
well as the UK and Canada) strongly objected to the idea that
a conference on a nuclear-free Mideast should not be blocked by

Israel's disagreement. [The draft conference document] proposed that an agenda be drafted with the active participation of the UN Secretary-General, the US, the UK and Russia, so that 45 days later the Secretary-General could convene a conference, inviting all the countries of the region, including Israel, of course. And if Israel ignored the conference, that would not prevent it from taking place. In addition, the cofounders of the conference would not have the right to block it, either. This provision would solve the problem of endless waiting and would increase pressure on Israel.

Intensive consultations on the draft final document continued until 5 p.m. of the last day of the conference. As it soon became clear, disarmament matters proved to be mutually acceptable to all.

Failure came during the discussion of the Middle East issue – quite a déjà vu for NPT conferences. In those hours, all the delegates seem to have been held hostage by diplomatic consultations: Washington must have received calls from its New York delegation (the State Department, as far as I could understand, had no authority in such matters) and from Jerusalem.

The latter tipped the scales. The US told an overcrowded UN General Assembly Hall that the draft document's Middle East section was "incompatible with our [U.S.'s] long-standing policies"[11] (meaning that it gave Washington no right to block a nuclear-free Middle East conference) and that [the US delegation] could not adopt it. Simultaneously, the US accused Egypt of being intractable. The audience let out a collective sound of disappointment. It became clear then that those who wanted to find solutions were not just in the majority, but in the overwhelming majority. Yet they lost on that day.

South Africa lamented the failure to find a solution on the Middle East, which it said raised the question of how one NPT nonparty could influence the outcome of the conference's work in such a way. But it was too late. Iran made the only attempt to save the situation: it proposed that the review conference be suspended for further consultations, although it was already late at night.[12] The conference was suspended, but no miracle happened.

The 2015 Conference could have followed the 2000 scenario, when the unfavorable international background proved to be no obstacle to the common desire to adopt a joint document. Or it could have followed the 2005 scenario, when the conference showed no will to achieve a result. I thought (some of my Western colleagues disagreed with me, saying I was unreasonably optimistic) that in 2015, there were enough conducive factors to repeat the 2000 scenario. But the 2005 scenario prevailed, and the NPT lost.

What This Means

Let me make one thing clear. The future of the treaty was not at stake at this Review Conference. It remains in force indefinitely, whereas the review process has been uneven ever since the treaty entered into force in 1970. Some five-year periods are successful, and others are not. In addition, the adoption of a final document (or lack thereof) is not the main criterion for a conference's success; it's only a tangible part of it. Professor William Potter, a leading nonproliferation expert, said that a more important factor is what spirit prevailed at the conference: the spirit of cooperation or the spirit of confrontation. (By the way, the most successful NPT conference took place in 1995, when the Treaty was extended indefinitely; however, that conference failed to adopt a final review document.)

Let me make it even clearer: The lesson of the failed 2005 Conference shows that such failures stimulate in-depth work to correct mistakes and help mobilize efforts to make the next conference better.

Yet, despite these two caveats, I have to say that on May 22, 2015, the nonproliferation regime suffered a very serious defeat. At best, it has been thrown back a decade. With tensions growing on the European continent; with politicians talking again about the nuclear factor and the deployment of new nuclear weapons; and with the Intermediate-Range Nuclear Forces Treaty at risk of being lost, the NPT must stand firm, without any reservations.

Speaking of European security, it is time to think of how to strengthen the nonproliferation regime on the continent. One way to do this is by establishing nuclear-free zones and taking other measures aimed at nondeployment of nuclear weapons outside the national territories of nuclear states. Item number one on the agenda is the reduction of the risk of accidents involving nuclear weapons – those incidental risks whose consequences may be irreversible.

Another vital and unresolved issue is the relationship between offensive and defensive strategic armaments; a related one is the balance between nuclear weapons and new types of conventional strategic armaments. Unfortunately, despite their importance, these issues are of little interest to most Europeans. They seem to have adopted the Russian proverb: "We remember God only when we are in trouble."

At the same time, the Humanitarian Initiative and the Austrian Pledge will continue to gain momentum. In my opinion, these discussions are distracting us from key disarmament issues. Some even plan to turn this [nuclear abolition] movement into a platform that would be an alternative to the NPT, where they would work toward a Convention on the Prohibition of Nuclear Weapons. Would that help the NPT? Not at all.

But should nuclear states (Russia included) be afraid of disarmament radicals? Of course not. The nuclear "haves" should enter into dialogue with the "have-nots." All member countries of the Commonwealth of Independent States and the Collective Security Treaty Organization (except Russia and Tajikistan) and all BRICS members (again, except Russia) attended the Vienna conference. Perhaps France and Russia should learn from China, which does not shy away from [such] discussions but sends low-level delegations to them.

During the upcoming five-year review cycle, lines of tension whose contours are now only faintly visible may appear in Northeast Asia. How will nonnuclear Japan, which is modernizing its Armed Forces, react to a growing North Korean nuclear arsenal? Will a line of nuclear tension emerge between Japan, which is under the US nuclear umbrella, and nuclear China, which is ready to multiply its number of warheads at any moment?

Yet the most dramatic scenario may take place in the Middle East. Israel may be celebrating now; in tactical terms, the US has defended its interests. But how will Egypt respond? Where is the breaking point at which the Middle Eastern states will conclude that the 1995 decision has not been implemented and that no one wants to implement it? This may mean they will have to take the initiative into their own hands.

Since the failure of the [2015] conference, more and more people have blamed Egypt for it. Even if we agree that the Egyptian delegation took an inflexible position, one cannot help thinking that the Egyptians have been too patient. They have been waiting since 1995 – and nothing is happening. Sometimes it seems that no one really cares about a Middle East solution.

There is no doubt that the international nuclear nonproliferation regime entered a new phase in May 2015. The situation has worsened, and it will be more and more difficult and expensive to correct it. The cooling of international relations will make the NPT extremely fragile: All it takes is for one thing to break accidentally, and many others will also fall and break to pieces.

Notes

1. Resolution on the Middle East. 1995 Review and Extension Conference of the Parties to the Treaty on the Non-Proliferation of Nuclear Weapons. Final Document. Part I (NPT/CONF.1995/32 (Part I)). Annex. Decisions and resolution adopted by the Conference. New York, 1995, p. 13, https://undocs.org/NPT/CONF.1995/32(PartI).

2. 2000 Review Conference of the Parties to the Treaty on the Non-Proliferation of Nuclear Weapons. Final Document. Volume I. Part I. Part II. New York, 2000, p. 14, https://undocs.org/NPT/CONF.2000/28(PartsIandII).

3. Conclusions and recommendations for follow-on actions. 2010 Review Conference of the Parties to the Treaty on the Non-Proliferation of Nuclear Weapons. Final Document. Volume I. Part I. Part II. New York, 2010, pp. 19-29, https://undocs.org/NPT/CONF.2010/50%20(VOL.I).

4. Statement by Mikhail I. Ulyanov, Acting Head of the Delegation of the Russian Federation at the 2015 Review Conference of the Parties to the Treaty on the Non-Proliferation of Nuclear Weapons (General debate). New York, April 27, 2015, p. 11, http://www.un.org/en/conf/npt/2015/statements/pdf/RU_en.pdf.

5. Statement by the People's Republic of China, France, the Russian Federation, the United Kingdom of Great Britain and Northern Ireland, and the United States of America to the 2015 Treaty of the Non-Proliferation of Nuclear Weapons Review Conference. Statements. April 30, 2015, http://www.un.org/en/conf/npt/2015/statements/pdf/P5_en.pdf.

6. According to the "Conclusions of the Conference" section of the Final Document of the Conference: "Despite intensive consultations, the Conference was not able to reach agreement on the substantive part of the draft Final Document" (see https://undocs.org/NPT/CONF.2015/50(PartI)).

7. See, for example, "National report on the implementation of actions 5, 20, and 21 of the action plan of the 2010 Review Conference of the Parties to the Treaty on the Non-Proliferation of Nuclear Weapons," https://undocs.org/NPT/CONF.2015/29. For other proceedings involving Great Britain at the Conference, see https://undocs.org/NPT/CONF.2015/50(PartII).

8. See "Report submitted by France under actions 5, 20 and 21 of the Final Document of the 2010 Review Conference of the Parties to the Treaty on the Non-Proliferation of Nuclear Weapons," https://undocs.org/NPT/CONF.2015/10. For other proceedings involving France at the conference, see https://undocs.org/NPT/CONF.2015/50(PartII).

9. In December 2014. See https://www.bmeia.gv.at/fileadmin/user_upload/ Zentrale/Aussenpolitik/Abruestung/HIN.W14/HINW14_Austrian_Pledge.pdf. Another version available at http://www.icanw.org/wp-content/uploads/2015/04/ AustrianPledge-ICAN.pdf.

10. Conference on the establishment of a Middle East zone free of nuclear weapons and all other weapons of mass destruction: Working paper submitted by the Russian Federation, http://undocs.org/NPT/CONF.2015/WP.57.

11. Speech of the US Representative available at: http://webtv.un.org/www. unwomen.org/en/executive-board/watch/15th-meeting-2015-review-conference-of-the-parties-to-the-treaty-on-the-non-proliferation-of-nuclear-weapons/425244 2911001/?term=&sort=popular.

12. *Ibid.*

PART ONE

1.2. Islam and Islamist Movements

LANDMARKS ON THE ROAD TO JIHAD

Aleksei Malashenko

The 'Islamic threat' to the ruling regimes in Central Asia is currently nonexistent: The Islamists are not prepared to take certain risks at a time when any measures taken against them would not draw much criticism from the rest of the world. However, grounds for radical Islamic protests in the region still exist. The possibility also remains that existing Islamic organizations will survive, and new ones could emerge.

It has become rather fashionable today to give particular attention, as well as multiple definitions, to the various religious groupings now dotting the globe. Fundamentalism, neofundamentalism, Wahhabism, neo-Wahhabism, Islamism, integrism – these are just a few examples.

Occasionally, discussions over such terms take on a theological tone, and secular scholars must quote *ayats* from the Holy Qur'an and the Hadith to support their statements. Of course, people do need to exercise their intellects, but they sometimes overdo it and invent different definitions for one and the same phenomenon.

This article originally appeared in *Russia in Global Affairs* Vol. 1, No. 1, 2003.

Russians of the older generation may still remember a speaker at the 26th Congress of the Soviet Communist Party telling his amazed audience: "The struggle for liberation may be launched under the banner of Islam, as shown by early and recent history. But that same history also teaches us that Islamic slogans can be used by reactionary forces stirring up counterrevolutionary revolts."[1] What a universal guide to action for Vladimir Putin, Aslan Maskhadov, Islam Karimov and Juma Namangani!

Much water has flowed under the bridge since then, but the deep inner link between religion and politics has remained unchanged. Secularism is now interpreted in a much more "diplomatic" way, while religion is now perceived as a normal factor in the secular political world and public life in general.

These changes are particularly manifest in the Muslim world, where all political forces appeal to Islam. It is common these days for a proreform president and a fierce opponent from orthodox Islamist circles to begin their speeches with *"Bismillah"* ("In the name of Allah"). Central Asia is no exception; in a sense, it represents the rule.

Riddles of the Islamic "Threat"

The actual power of Islamists and the degree of their influence upon a particular society are difficult to judge, despite an avalanche of articles on this issue. An overwhelming majority of these articles stem from "information" regularly leaked to the press by various sources. These allegedly "official" statements, which originate from secret services, ambitious "spiritual leaders," and opportunistic politicians and analysts, serve to cloud the facts. The existence of radical Islam has long become a tool actively used by secular leaders to achieve their goals. Similarly, it is used by security and defense agencies that exploit the "Islamic threat" to pump funds out of the national budget.

In the past, experts sometimes portrayed Islamists (or whatever other titles they may have gone by) as the only effective oppositional force. And in some countries – e.g., Uzbekistan and Tajikistan – they really were. In other places, they enjoyed varying degrees of success. In Kyrgyzstan, they played a minor role in political processes, whereas in Kazakhstan, the Islamic forces found themselves cast by the wayside of political life. And in Turkmenistan. they simply do not exist as an organized movement. One must not rule out, however, that Muslim opposition may emerge in the land of the new "Gospel" (Rukhnama) written by Saparmurat Niyazov (1940-2006), Turkmenistan's "president for life" (otherwise known as *Turkmenbashi* – "father of the Turkmen people").

At various national and regional levels, double standards are widely used with regard to Islamist movements. The 'Islamic threat' never stops making the headlines of government-controlled publications and is a dominant theme of political statements. But if you ask a well-informed official in a private conversation how real this 'threat' is, he may merely shrug his shoulders. Some highly placed politicians in Central Asia know nothing at all about the existence of Islamist organizations in their countries, not to mention their leaders' names.

At the same time, it is generally believed that if chaos begins to run rampant throughout the economy, and the gap between the rich and the poor continues to increase along with blatant corruption, "they" will make [ordinary people] suffer the consequences. "They" are perceived as some sort of surrealistic force that is everywhere, yet nowhere. "They" are mighty, of course, but their actual rise to power seems as unrealistic as the end of the world.

It may be helpful at this point to outline specific periods of Islamist activity in Central Asia that are common to all the countries of the former Soviet Union. Our chronology of events, like any broad analysis, may lack full synchronicity. Furthermore, one may find many exceptions to the stages outlined below; nevertheless, they will help us identify distinct landmarks in history.

The first stage lasted from the late 1980s to the early 1990s. The landmark date in this stage was 1990, when the All-Union Islamic Party of Revival (IPR) was established in Astrakhan, Russia.[2] Naturally, independent Islamic organizations had existed in Central Asia before, but they were small and amorphous, with no ambitious goals. The IPR had numerous branches, which promoted the establishment of other parties and groups, large and small.

The year 1991 saw the establishment of the famous Adolat party in Uzbekistan, a kind of synthesis of the Soviet Union's voluntary people's patrols and moral police.[3] This party had been preceded by the long-forgotten Islamic Party of Turkestan, aka Hezbullah.[4] In the same years, the Alash National Freedom Party was founded in Kazakhstan,[5] and four Islamist groups emerged in Azerbaijan.[6]

In November 1991, the Islamic Revival Party (IRP) was officially registered in Tajikistan. The Muslim revival movement was in full swing.

But the "Islamic Renaissance" proved to be short-lived. In December 1991, following the first election in newly independent Tajikistan, the IRP entered into confrontation with the People's Front. In 1992, the Uzbek government began to suppress the Adolat party. Finally, Kazakh President Nursultan Nazarbayev refused to conduct negotiations with Alashists, whom he had labeled "fascists" in a fit of emotion.

Grapes of Wrath

The years 1992-1993 marked the beginning of the second stage, in which the suppression of political Islam intensified. At first, a few dozen opposition mosques were shut down, and soon the doors of hundreds of opposition mosques were closed; rebellious Muslim politicians and clergymen were sent off to prison.

Islamists who appeal to the Muslim religion in pursuing their objectives went into deep opposition, and more often resorted to military activities to achieve their political goals. In Central Asia and the North Caucasus there emerged special training camps for Islamic fighters. Tajikistan was torn by a civil war. Nationalistic Islamic movements – "the grapes of wrath" – ripened in Russia's Tatarstan region. The first president of the breakaway Republic of Chechnya, Air Force Major-General Dzhokhar Dudayev, declared a *jihad* (religious war) against Russia.

By the mid-1990s, Islamic radicalism became an ordinary political force in the former states of the Soviet Union. The main success of the Islamist movement was a peace agreement signed in 1997 by the United Tajik Opposition (UTO) and the government of Tajikistan.[7] This milestone led to the subsequent establishment of a real government coalition (however, UTO members reportedly do not feel at home in Dushanbe's corridors of power to this day).

The developments in Tajikistan demonstrated that the use of force alone against radical Islamists may have tragic and unexpected consequences. It is possible to reach an accord with them, thus turning enemies into partners, however difficult the working relationship may be.

At the same time, the civil war in Tajikistan, which took a heavy toll on human lives (tens of thousands of people were killed), came as an important trump card for all the Central Asian presidents. They blamed the outbreak of civil war on their bloodstained neighbor, whose weak political power had prevented it from preserving stability, thus forcing it into concessions with the "children of Shaitan" – fundamentalists.

Some analysts argue that another big achievement of the radical Islamists was the 1996 Khasavyurt agreement, signed in Moscow. However, this agreement did not increase the chances for a peace settlement in Chechnya and was eventually repudiated. Although some circles described it as a victory for the militant Islamists, one should not forget that Aslan Maskhadov, who signed the agreement on Chechnya's behalf, always opposed Chechnya's "Islamization" and the foundation of an Islamic state there. The Khasavyurt agreement heralded the victory of the Chechen separatist movement, not Islamism.

The Taliban as an Ideal

The beginning of the third stage can be dated to 1996. At this juncture, the Taliban rose to political power in Afghanistan. In Turkey, the leader of the Refah (Welfare) Party, Necmettin Erbakan, became prime minister. This was the first victory for the Turkish Islamists, with Refah winning the general elections for the first time in history. The second came in 2002, when Recep Tayyip Erdogan's Justice and Development Party won the general elections by a landslide. If such outcomes are possible in Turkey (a would-be member of the EU), one should not be surprised if and when they happen in Central Asia.

By that time, Islamists had become more consolidated and organized, as well as more experienced, in opposing a government that totally rejected all compromises. The radical Islamists now had a territory under their control, which made them less vulnerable in their struggle against secular authorities. Afghanistan became an international transfer point for arms traffickers, and an area where Islamic extremists and their allies from various countries could freely meet and share their experience. (In those years, Russian newspapers and television considered it good policy to regularly frighten their audiences by suggesting "a Taliban invasion of Kazan" or "an Islamic parade through Red Square.") Contacts between Islamists in Central Asia and Chechen fighters became more and more obvious. Russian troops identified Uzbeks among the Chechen fighters taken prisoner, and many Chechens were apprehended in Uzbekistan's Fergana Valley.

The establishment of a Taliban regime in Afghanistan had an immense demonstrative effect on Central Asians: "Look, those people have been able to establish a truly Islamic regime! Why not build such a state right here?" Needless to say, an overwhelming majority of Central Asians, even in the Islamist-dominated Fergana Valley, would not have been able to live even 10 minutes under a real government of the Taliban, who threw television sets out of windows and closed down public baths.

Yet, the myth of the Taliban regime's justness kept spreading. People, especially the poor, tend to always believe in a better future. This belief was strengthened by accounts of those who had visited Afghanistan during the reign of the Taliban. Many of them reported a decrease in corruption in that country, an evil that remains widespread among its northern neighbors.

In 1996, the strengthened Islamic Movement of Uzbekistan began to make regular raids in the Fergana Valley, fighting against Uzbek and Kyrgyz regular troops. The Kyrgyz town of Batken became a local "Battle of Stalingrad" in the war against Islamic fighters. Finally, in 1999, in a climax to the tensions, the "legendary" assassination attempt on Uzbek leader Islam Karimov was made. Even if we agree with those who are confident that the explosions in Tashkent had no relation to the Islamic opposition and were organized by other forces, we cannot fail to notice that the terrorist act coincided in time with the intensification of the opposition's activity.

Another important political force in Central Asia is the Hizb-ut-Tahrir al-Islami (Party of Islamic Liberation), which has become a favorite subject for reporters. Indeed, Hizb-ut-Tahrir members differ substantially from the more traditional "Islamic fighters." They have declared their devotion to nonviolent activities and launched a propaganda campaign among the population by spreading leaflets and enculturating people about the ideas and rules of Islam.

Eventually, the Uzbek authorities launched a crackdown on Hizb-ut-Tahrir members. Kyrgyzstan displayed more tolerance for them: They were arrested but then released. If they were put on trial, the sentences were not very severe. In Kyrgyzstan, Hizb-ut-Tahrir members resembled the *maquisards* (members of the French underground resistance movement during World War II), who fought Nazis out in the open and were not particularly keen on secrecy rules.

September 11: Intermission

The slow, grueling struggle for a caliphate and Islamic justice, marked by seasonal upsurges of military activities, continued until September 11, 2001. That day marked the beginning of a new, fourth stage in the history of the Islamic movement in Central Asia, as well as the whole world. It can be described as an intermission in the noisy religious and political performance.

The fall of the Taliban regime in Afghanistan, together with the large-scale offensive against al-Qaeda, placed the Central Asian radicals in a difficult position. Their flow of financial support began to dry up, together with the support they had once enjoyed from their Afghan allies. Finally, they lost many valuable fighters in Afghanistan as well: Uzbek Islamists were known to be among the fiercest fighters in the Taliban forces. Finally, no one knows the fate of the leader of the Islamic Movement of Uzbekistan, Juma Namangani, who has gone missing.[8]

A year after September 11, the "Islamic threat" to the ruling regimes in Central Asia was nonexistent. At this critical juncture, the Islamists are not ready to take risks; and an intermission has settled in the region. However, the grounds for radical Islamic protests still exist. There also remains the possibility that existing Islamic organizations will survive and new ones could emerge.

In the North Caucasus, the post-September intermission is long over. In a sense, the continuation of the Chechen conflict proves its special autonomy from [Osama] bin Laden and his people. The Middle East has seen no intermission at all. The war there continues, despite the strikes against international terrorism.

Attitudes toward people considering social changes in the context of Islam may differ, yet these people have a right to views of their own, even though their views may be utopian. The significance of an Islamic alternative for Central Asia should be neither underestimated nor exaggerated. The authors and followers of such ideas are unable to stir up society on their own, but they have good chances to promote their ideas quickly (and without any bin Ladens) if the general situation in their countries is aggravated. One must be constantly ready for such a turn of events everywhere, be it democratic Kyrgyzstan or authoritarian Uzbekistan – i.e., any country where the government is unable to markedly raise the standard of living and bring the population above the poverty line. Islamists may well establish cooperation with other political forces that are not "pure Islam."

Like the Chechen separatists, some members of the Islamic Movement of Uzbekistan like to compare themselves to wolves. Most likely, they (and we too) do not realize how true this comparison is: Both forces attack "sick" (i.e., socially vulnerable) state systems, truly resembling wolves who promote the health of the ecosystem in the wild by killing weak and sick animals. One gets the impression that Central Asia is awaiting the fifth stage of Islamic political activity. And no one can say when or how that fifth stage will begin.

Notes

1. Brezhnev, Leonid. "Report of the General Secretary of the Communist Party of the Soviet Union on Feb. 23, 1981 [at the XXVI Communist Party Congress]." *Krasnoye znamya*, Feb. 24, 1981, p. 3, http://sun.tsu.ru/mminfo/2012/000024359/1981/1981_046.pdf.

2. Guboglo, M.N. and Gryzlov, V.F., eds. *Dagestan: Ethnopolitical Portrait. Essays, Documents, Chronicle.* Vol. II: *Ethnopolitical Situation in the Essays and Documents of the Congress of Peoples of Dagestan, Multinational Parties, Movements and Religious Organizations.* Moscow: CIMO, 1994.

3. Officially the Adolat party was inaugurated in 1995 as a socialist-democratic party (see http://www.elections.uz/en/events/political_parties/74/); however, it was present in Uzbekistan's political landscape much earlier. See, for example: John Glenn, *The Soviet Legacy in Central Asia.* London: Palgrave Macmillan, 1999, p. 110.

4. As with many other radical Islamist organizations, this group was known by many names, including Islamic Movement of Turkestan, Islamic Movement of Uzbekistan, etc. Soon it was included in official lists of terrorist groups drawn up by Russia, the US and other countries. See, for example: Mikhail Falkov, "The Islamic Movement of Uzbekistan (IMU)," *Nezavisimaya gazeta*, Aug. 24, 2000, http://www.ng.ru/net/2000-08-24/0_idu.html/.

5. Uteshev, Dauren and Makashev, Erbol. "From the Soviet Political System Toward a Presidential Government." In M.S. Ashimbaev et al., ed. *Sovereign Kazakhstan on the Verge of the Millenium.* Astana: Elroda, 2001, pp. 64-65, https://docplayer.ru/60671538-Suverennyy-kazahstan-na-rubezhe-tysyacheletiy-sbornik-nauchnyh-sta-te-y-a-s-ta-n-a-elorda-s.html.

6. See, for example: Andrei Polonsky, "Islam in the Social Context of Modern Azerbaijan," *Istoria*, Vol. 28, 1999, http://his.1september.ru/article. php?ID=199902802.

7. UN Peacekeeping Missions list, http://www.un.org/ru/peacekeeping/ missions/past/unmotref.htm.

8. Since the original publication of this article, most media outlets throughout the world have concluded that Namangani was killed in Afghanistan in November 2001. See, for example: Richard Weitz, "Outside View: The Bombs of Tashkent," *UPI*, April 14, 2004, https://www.upi.com/Outside-View-The-bombs-of-Tashkent/24991082053894/.

THE MODERNIZATION OF ISLAM: HOW PLAUSIBLE IS IT?

Rafael Khakimov

Medieval Europe admired the erudition and wisdom of Muslim scholars. But as time passed, the concepts of creativity, rationalism and renewal vanished from the Muslim vocabulary. Critical analytical thinking was forbidden. The taboo on new interpretations of the Qur'an ossified thought and society.

Taklid and Ijtihad

There is a widespread perception shared by Muslims and non-Muslims alike that Islam is a uniform denomination; it has no multiple ethnic, geographic or any other differing forms. Ironically, this perception may intertwine with the exactly opposite view that nations develop their own Islamic traditions.

The world consists of many different nations that fail to merge even when they have the same faith. The Qur'an says: "And among His Signs is the creation of the heavens and the earth, and the variations in your languages and your colors" [30:22].[1] If it was Allah's will, He could make us one nation speaking in one tongue.

This article originally appeared in *Russia in Global Affairs* Vol. 1, No. 3, 2003.

Shiites and Sunnis (including their four schools of theology and law: the Hanbalites, Hanifites, Malakites and Shafiis), Ismailites, Sufis, etc. are groups representing particular trends within Islam that emerged in various historical epochs in order to suit the needs of rulers and certain social groups. The Hanbalites rejected rationalism and provided a traditional narrative about the Prophet Mohammad, or the Sunnah, which acquired the status of Islamic jurisprudence, thus ranking it with the Qur'an. At a later point, their teaching, so hostile to change, was taken up by the Wahhabites.

The Hanifites adopted a more flexible doctrine that permitted common law to be used in addition to the Shariah law. This doctrine, tolerant toward other ethnic traditions, made the day-to-day dealings with other nations much easier.

Each of the four Sunni schools of theology and law (*mazhabs*) developed its own distinctive features while appealing to certain nations or ethnic groups. Interestingly, the Tatars opted for Hanifism, which came to them from Asia, its major trading partner. In 922, the Baghdad caliphate sent the envoy Ibn-Fadlan to Bulgar on the Volga to persuade the Tatars to accept its version of Islam. The trip proved to be in vain, and pragmatic considerations gained the upper hand. The great interest that the Tatar rulers had in bolstering trade with Bukhara and Khorezm dictated their religious preference.

The *mazhabs* appeared in the ninth to 11th centuries as part of Islam's natural evolution and were subsequently canonized. Since then, Islam's main emphasis has been on maintaining unquestioning loyalty to the authority of the schools (this approach is known as *taklid*) and prohibiting new interpretations of the Qur'an. This worked to ossify thought and society; progress became a foreign concept to Islam. Medieval Europe admired the erudition and wisdom of the Muslim scholars. But as time passed, the concepts of creativity, rationalism and renewal vanished from the Muslim vocabulary. Digression and innovation were punishable by death even though the Prophet Mohammad preached: "Verily, Allah will send the *umma* [the human race] a man early each century to renew the religion."[2] How is it possible to reconcile these words with an uncritical interpretation of the tradition – i.e., *taklid*? These concepts contradict each other. Renewal goes hand-in-hand with independent thinking and critical analysis – i.e., *ijtihad*.

In Islam's formative years, criticism was employed even in relation to the Sunnah. However, critical analytical thinking was finally forbidden in the 10th century. As Muslim theologians put it, "the gates of *ijtihad* were closed," implying that there was no longer a need for new interpretations since the *mazhabs* had already interpreted everything. Even the renowned contemporary Turkish theologian, Haydar Bas, believes that the *mazhabs* have concluded the analysis of all religious issues based on the most trustworthy principles.[3] This statement is predicated on the assumption that human development has come to a standstill and there is nothing new in the whole world to discover. The Qur'an permits slavery, while Shariah law treats slaves as camels, or any other property. To conform to the interpretations of the *mazhabs*, we should have reinstated slavery, otherwise this norm, along with many others, needs to be revised.

Actually, it is not human development that has come to a standstill but Islamic thought. Muslim countries have fallen behind in basic research, high technology and engineering, which are now traditionally regarded as the West's domain.

Islamic reformers who have occasionally appeared on the scene in various Muslim countries were unable to turn the tide. They put their lives on the line but remained isolated anomalies that few people cared to talk about. Nonetheless, the Tatar nation witnessed Islamic reform in both theory and practice.

In 1804, Tatar theologian Kursavi wrote in his treatise calling for Islam's modernization: "You are not true and faithful Muslims. You have given up the Qur'an of Allah and the tradition of the Prophet." He repudiated the schools' teachings and suggested that Muslims turn to the Holy Book itself and critically assess the existing trends. At the same time, Kursavi rejected public opinion as a criterion of truth. He argued that a scholar, certain of the correctness of his position and its full conformity with the "direct path," could speak on behalf of Muslim society. He could use his own discretion even if the majority disapproved of his behavior. This idea was revolutionary, since it promoted the notion that the position of an individual with that of the community is one and the same. Kursavi was the founder of the religious trend of Jadidism (from the Arabic *al-jadid*, which means renewal or reform).

The whole thrust of Jadidism was based on encouraging critical thinking as opposed to insisting on unquestioning loyalty. It also supported increasing education for Muslims and promoting equality among the sexes; it advocated a tolerance for other faiths and openness to Europe's cultural legacy. The whole modern Tatar culture has its roots in Jadidism. Following the 1917 revolution, Jadidism's influence was felt in Mirsaid Sultan-Galeyev's theory of "Islamic socialism." The Bolsheviks, however, found this theory unpalatable, and its author fell victim to Stalin purges. However, his ideas were widely recognized throughout the Arab world. The last Tatar reformist theologian, Musa Bigiyev, was forced to leave the country in 1930.

Tatar reformers contending with stubborn medieval traditions presented yet another episode in the ongoing battle between progressive and reactionary forces. Today, at the beginning of the 21st century, and in the face of new challenges, Islam needs to tackle the very same problem of modernization.

Pluralism in Islam

Contrary to popular opinion, Islam is quite far from being monolithic. The Qur'an verses, which originated in the Meccan period, address humanity as a whole, "O mankind! We created you from a single (pair) male and female, and made you into nations and tribes, that ye may know each other" [49:13]. The Meccan verses do not differentiate between men's and women's rights. Furthermore, it forbids using force to gain converts to Islam and is explicitly tolerant of other creeds.

The Qur'an *ayats* (verses) that date back to the Medina period were written primarily for 7th-century Arabs. They declare war on pagans, commanding them to "slay them wherever ye catch them, and turn them out from where they have turned you out" [2:191]. Women are considered subordinate to men: "Men are the protectors and maintainers of women, because God has given the one more (strength) than the other, and because they support them from their means" [4:34].

The inconsistencies between the verses of the Mecca and Medina periods are self-evident. Therefore, Muslim legal experts declare that the Medina verses supersede the earlier Meccan ones. But the Prophet Mohammad presented the Meccan verses as the Qur'an's integral part. As we know, the original high-ranking teachers of the Qur'an received their instruction under the direct supervision of the prophet, and Mohammad saw to it with the greatest efficacy that the Qur'an's *surahs* (chapters) be learnt without omissions.

Interpretations of the Meccan and Medina verses should not center on their effectiveness or ineffectiveness, but rather on the dissimilarities in their targeted audiences and historical epochs. Putting things into historical perspective is paramount in today's interpretation of the *ayats*.

Wahhabism, for example, espouses violence in its relations with other religions and separate trends within Islam. This zeal for "pure" Islam is a variation of Hanbalism driven to its irrational extreme: It asserts that rational thinking is useless, since the Qur'an is something that cannot be understood; it can only be believed. This is an apology for traditionalism with its fear of the new. But the old interpretation has aged, thus necessitating new commentaries that are comprehensible to a modern person.

For example, during the Middle Ages, war against the unfaithful was an accepted norm, since the use of force in politics was also commonplace. Mohammad made the distinction between "minor" *jihad*, which presupposes the use of force, and "supreme" *jihad*, which permits the spread of Islam solely by nonviolent means, primarily through preaching the Qur'an: "Therefore listen not to the Unbelievers, but strive against them with the utmost strenuousness, with the [Qur'an]" [25:52]. The minor *jihad* was justified when Muslims were at risk of invasion by non-Muslims, or when Muslims decided to invade new territories. Such behavior was considered normal in the Middle Ages. But today we approach the issues of war and peace differently. That is why we should take *jihad* for what it literally means, "zeal," – i.e., the battle of the spirit against the material world, against the lack of faith within ourselves. The Lord read this meaning into the word *jihad*, therefore it is immutable. Minor *jihad* is just if it is pursued in self-defense or to curb violence and tyranny. Such an interpretation fits well not only with the Qur'an, but international law.

The era of the Prophet Mohammad knew no weapons of mass destruction. In his day, the call for war against the infidels carried a completely different meaning using entirely different means. Today, Muslims should adhere to the everlasting idea of universal solidarity, revealed to humanity in the Meccan period. For humanity pursuing good is one of the manifestations of Allah.

The Tatar Subcivilization

The Tatars were historically part of the Russian Empire and placed considerable strain on the nation's intellectual and physical resources. The Orthodox Christian state tolerated these Muslims only because it had no other choice, and it curtailed their rights as much as it could. In particular, the Tatars were not allowed to set up their own secular educational establishments, while the Tatar language could be used only for religious education. This helped make the leading *madrasahs* (Muslim schools) a breeding ground for progressive thought.

Economically and legally, Tatars were at a disadvantage when it came to competing with Russians. The Russian government did not feel obligated to provide funding for the Tatar educational system; this burden fell entirely upon the shoulders of Tatar entrepreneurs. To their credit, the literacy rate among Tatars reached 100% at the turn of the 20th century.

Finally, Islam's influence on Tatars was reinforced by the Russian policy of religious tolerance. The Russian government, concerned with the Orthodox Church, placed no constraints on the development of Tatar theology. This situation was unique because in Muslim countries, councils of *ulema* (theology scholars) had to comply with government policies and cater to the powers that be. Thus, Islam's modernization was something that came rather naturally to Tatar Muslims.

For the millions of Tatar Muslims who grew up in Russia, living in a secular state and being part of its centuries-old culture was just a matter of course. Today's Tatarstan, together with Russia, manufactures many high-technology products, which requires the development of intensive research capabilities, as well as a system of higher education. Since our main competitors derive from Western countries, we must keep up with their standards. In this respect, Tatarstan cannot look to Muslim countries such as Sudan, Pakistan, Iran, etc. These nations do not produce heavy trucks, planes, helicopters and so on, but consume them and, therefore, cannot directly assist us in becoming more competitive in the global marketplace.

The Muslim *umma* is a civilization uniting believers of the same faith. It coexists with separate nations, respecting their sovereignty. Each nation develops individually within a certain context that is governed by their climate, environment and other factors. Fate has made Tatarstan Islam's northern outpost, while, at the same time, placing it geographically and culturally between the West and the East. This fact accounts in large measure for the singular Muslim subcivilization in Tatarstan and in Russia.[4]

Euro-Islam: Key Concepts

According to a survey conducted to study trends among young Tatars, over 80% identify themselves as Muslims, but only 2% attend mosque at least once a week; 4% attend once a month. Avowed atheists make up less than 1% of the population in Tatarstan, yet the number of those who obey all religious instructions is also dismal. One to three percent of respondents attend lessons involving the basics of Islam or Orthodox Christianity.[5]

Young Tatars are enthusiastic about receiving a university education, and many favor studying abroad in Europe. They indicate a preference for the English language as a means of communication in business, politics and science. Thirteen percent of Tatar urban residents and 25% of villagers would like their children to have a solid command of the Arabic language. With regard to the Turkish language, this ratio is 10% and 19%; for the West European languages, the numbers are 74% and 33% respectively. The preponderance in the demand for West European languages is even more overwhelming among the younger generations. The use of the Arabic language tends to be reserved explicitly for religious functions or some specific professional activity.

Tatar citizens may have a poor command of their mother tongue, not practice their faith and know little about Shariah law and yet still identify with Muslims, as well as feel a cultural kinship with Islam. By the same token, Tatars have an equal appreciation for the cultures of Europe and Asia; this applies equally to secular as well as religious elements. The Tatar civilization, inherently open to other cultures, erects no barriers between the West and the East.

The term "Euro-Islam" denotes a modern form of Jadidism. It applies rather to Islam's cultural aspect, as opposed to its ritual, leaving this practice to the discretion of the individual. *Ijtihad* plays a pivotal role in Euro-Islam. As a method of Qur'an interpretation, it secures the sustained progress of Muslim culture.

According to some Muslim theologians, a critical analysis of the Qur'an is a privilege only for those who are worthy of it. Egyptian scholar Yusuf al-Qardawi, despite his commitment to free thinking, maintains: "We should not tolerate the situation when *ijtihad* can be employed by anyone who might wish it, for it will bring about anarchy and discord."[6] He argues that an ignorant mob should be barred from interpreting the Qur'an, which is a preserve of the chosen. Theologians cite prominent medieval thinkers, who believed that it is necessary to limit the number of those entitled to independent thinking. Their motives are easy to understand, as education standards were relatively poor in those days. Since then, the situation has greatly improved: Total literacy and easy access to higher education have given everyone a strong foundation for individual study of the Qur'an in its original or translated versions.

Islam's original language, Arabic, has been gradually giving way to national languages. This is right and proper, as the Lord listens to our hearts and innermost thoughts, which our native language can best help us to put into words. Malaysian theologian Syed Muhammad Naquib al-Attas introduced the notion of a Muslim language, which is the "basic vocabulary of Muslim theology"[7] common to the languages of most Muslim nations. Indeed, words of Arabic origin abound in the Tatar language. Their prevalence in religious terminology spares most of the Tatar faithful the need to learn Arabic. Further infiltration of Arabic religious terms into the national languages seems inevitable in the 21st century.

Islam is often judged by its rites and rituals, which were laden with vital social functions, particularly in medieval Arabia. Presently, a lot of norms have lost their meaning. For example, the ban against making images was introduced in the context of the fight against idol-worship. Today, nobody needs to destroy statues of Buddha as the Taliban did to exhibit their loyalty to Islam. Savagery is not compatible with Islam, nor can blind worship please Allah. The Prophet Mohammad says: "Allah does not approve of unnecessary fanaticism and extremes in expressing one's faith."

Rituals do not serve as a criterion for distinguishing between believers and nonbelievers. Imam Abu Hanifa an-Numan ibn Thabit stated that "We should not take people to be believers or nonbelievers judging from what we hear them accept or reject based on their religious norms and ceremonies. If we meet strangers, whom we only know attend mosque and pray the way we do, with their faces directed to the Qiblah, we assume they are believers.*** We think that what we see gives us enough grounds to decide whether someone is a believer or not. Yet for Allah, such a person may well be as good as a nonbeliever. We may contend that someone is unfaithful based on outward deficiencies in his faith, while for Allah, this person may well be a true believer."[8] Anyone who says "There is no other god except Allah, and Mohammad is his Messenger," immediately passes as a believer. It must be remembered that the observance of rites and rituals strengthens one's faith but does not necessarily testify to that person's candor.

There is an evolution occurring in the perception of religion: The focus tends to shift from religion as a social institution to religion as one's private affair. People increasingly resent any intrusion into their privacy, as well as infringement of their freedom of conscience.

Being righteous means assimilating cultural values, educational values and finally, the values associated with civilization. The Prophet Mohammad states: "There is a way to everything. Knowledge opens the way to paradise." Acquiring knowledge is a moral imperative for every Muslim. A true Muslim is a well-educated person who respects learning and engages in it. The aspiration to know one's self, the world and the Universe is but a reflection of a thirst to know the Truth – i.e., Allah. The Holy Book says: "Allah comprehends all things in (His) Knowledge" [65:12]. Allah comprehends all things because Allah is the Universe itself. Thus, delving into a science or other knowledge brings us closer to the Lord, who does not seek blind worship, but the fruit of humans' labor. The Prophet Mohammad taught: "To him who obtains scientific knowledge in the purpose of transferring it to others, God will grant the salvation of 70 saints." It would be wrong to dismiss the importance of Muslim prayers recited five times a day. But it would be equally wrong to concentrate on rites at the expense of learning. Both extremes are alien to Islam.

In the light of the Qur'an, the faithful are not slaves to Allah. They possess the freedom of choice and follow religious precepts voluntarily. Islam is the religion of a free person.

There is no mediator between man and the Lord. In the words of the Prophet, "The whole world was made a place for prayer." The clergy and the community are mere assistants or tutors. When the Lord calls upon the faithful on Judgment Day, there will be no imam, nor mufti, nor community, nor anyone else to intercede. "Then guard yourselves against a day," it is written in the Qur'an, "when one soul shall not avail another nor shall intercession be accepted for her, nor shall compensation be taken from her, nor shall anyone be helped (from outside)" [2:48].

Islam calls for justice, but this is unthinkable without equality between the sexes. The Qur'an's verses in the *surahs* "Women," "Light" and "Allies" make women unequal in rights. They date from the Medina period. At that time, the attitude toward women codified in Shariah law was the most progressive. Nowadays, these verses look anachronistic.

The Qur'an recognizes man's precedence over woman on the condition that man provides for her security and supports her [4:34]. In a society where the woman is protected by social institutions, as well as enjoying the opportunity of becoming economically independent, the grounds for inequality cease to exist. In the Middle Ages, it was the man's lot to earn bread through hard physical labor; women were in a vulnerable position and required the protection of Shariah law. But the division of labor according to sex is disappearing in the contemporary world.

Muslim legislation on marriage, which permits polygamy, inheritance rights, as well as divorce, places women at a distinct disadvantage. Equality of the sexes is a prerequisite for justice, which is the essence of Islam. All people are born equal and free, regardless of their physiology, origin, race, language, religion or country.

The Qur'an's verses that were transmitted to humanity in the Meccan period make no distinction between the rights of men and women. This principle must be built into the Shariah law of the 21st century. The legal status of women in a given society is a sure indicator of its viability.

Islam is a tolerant creed. The Qur'an says that there is one God but many religions. Their rites are the most conspicuous ingredient that makes them different from each other. If we put aside the Medina verses, which addressed the needs of the Muslim community in a hostile environment, the Qur'an's tolerant disposition toward anyone doing good is obvious. The Qur'an states: "Those who believe [in the Qur'an], and those who follow the Jewish [scriptures], and the Christians and the Sabians – any who believe in God and the Last Day, and work righteousness, shall have their reward with their deity;

on them shall be no fear, nor shall they grieve" [2:62]. Being among the faithful is preferable in the eyes of the deity. But the precept of doing good is paramount and incumbent upon every human being.

While safeguarding the monotheistic tradition, the Prophet Mohammad urged respect for other faiths. Islam does not claim that only their faithful have an exclusive right to God's gifts. Allah endows all nations and all people without exception, for He is merciful and compassionate. Musa Bigiyev, a prominent theologian, wrote: "So that not a single poor thing feels passed over by this endless mercy and the wide-open gates of His boundless charity remain open to people, I declare that the whole of humanity will be saved." According to Bigiyev's theory of God's absolute mercy, the deity's grace embraces all His creatures, regardless of their faith: "Our Lord! Thy Reach is over all things, in Mercy and Knowledge" [40:7]. This verse proves that the Lord shows His mercy not only to Muslims, but to everyone.

All faiths have known periods of bellicosity in their history: Muslims imposed caliphates by the sword; European Christians set out on crusades; Catholics and Protestants fought each other with fanatic enthusiasm. But now the sword is sheathed. We are to discern the call for good and mercy in every faith. This unifies humanity into the *umma* – the single community. Today, international norms take precedence over the interests of individual countries and communities, and Shariah law needs to be brought into conformity with them.

Those who expect to find favor with God by waging war on non-Muslims are wrong. They are playing into the hands of terrorists, who have no insight into the Qur'an. Everyone who does good and has faith is acceptable to the Lord, who says: "Whoever works any act of righteousness and has faith – his endeavor will not be rejected: We shall record it in his favor" [21:94].

The events of 9/11 triggered a surge of Islamophobia throughout the world, although terrorism has no religious notion behind it. The gap between Christians, Jews and Muslims is threatening to grow into a chasm. Only liberal and unorthodox Islamic values can unite the divided world. As a stepping stone of liberal thinking, *ijtihad* can provide a key to rapprochement between the West and the East. The commitment to personal freedoms, education, science and social progress constitutes the common ground for the European and Muslim cultures.

Notes

1. The numbers of Qur'an *surahs* and *ayats* are indicated in brackets; the source of the English versions here is the Qur'an translation by Abdullah Yusufali (first published 1938).

2. This and other quotations from the Prophet Mohammad in this article come from various *hadiths* (sayings) recorded by his companions and passed down through the generations. Thus, many *hadiths* have multiple versions.

3. Haydar Bas. *Makalat*. Yaroslavl, 2000, p. 161. (In Russian.)

4. The traditions developed by Muslims in the North Caucasus differ from those prevalent among Muslims in the European part of Russia and in Siberia.

5. Musina, R. N. "Ethnoconfessional Processes in the Republic of Tatarstan." In *Islam and Christianity in the Dialogue of Cultures at the Turn of the Millennium*. Kazan, 2001, pp. 261-264. (In Russian.)

6. Al-Qardawi, Yusuf. *Modern Ijtihad: From Disorder to Order*. Iman, Kazan, 2001, p. 67. (In Russian.)

7. Naquib al-Attas, Syed Muhammad. *Introduction to the Metaphysics of Islam: An Outline of Islam's Key Concepts*. Moscow-Kuala Lumpur, 2001, p. 36. (In Russian.)

8. Al-Numan ibn Thabit, Abu Hanifa. *Treatises*. Moscow, 2001, p. 55. (In Russian.)

ISLAM AS WE SEE IT

Aleksei Malashenko

*Russia's attitude to Islam and Muslims also fits into the gen-
eral context of xenophobia that in the first half of the 1990s
was considered a relic of post-totalitarian thinking; 10 years
later, however, it has turned into a core element of the public
consciousness.*

Russian society holds two contradictory attitudes toward Islam. On the
one hand, according to Nikolai Silayev: "The myth about the 'mysterious East,' characteristic of Western Europe, never really materialized
in Russia: The East has always been considered endemic to Russia."[1]

On the other hand, notions of the "mysterious East" do exist in
the Russian mindset. Suffice it to consider the many Arab fairy tales,
the harems, and the India of Afanasy Nikitin – not to mention Japan
and China. And if the Tatars did not pose as a mystery, the peoples
of the Caucasus and Central Asia certainly did. The Muslim East has
always been exotic, even despite its close proximity to Russia.

Islam has always been perceived as something alien to Russia on
the subconscious level: Muslims live primarily abroad – in the arid
Middle East, Afghanistan and Central Asia.

This article originally appeared in *Russia in Global Affairs* Vol. 4, No. 4, 2006.

This alienated view of Islam was largely promoted by official Soviet propaganda that divided Islam into "foreign" – i.e., aggressive, politicized and occasionally used as a slogan (jihad) in the liberation movement – and "Soviet Islam," which was associated with "backward old men" and "weak women," and seen as a feudal relic. Needless to say, even then, some intelligent functionaries in the party apparatus and especially in the State Security Committee (KGB) realized that Islam in the Soviet Union proved extremely resilient, retaining its functions as a regulator of social relations. But to reiterate, "Soviet Islam" was not identical to "their Islam," while the religious identity of Soviet Muslims was regarded as marginal – doomed to extinction.

In the late 20th century, following the disintegration of the Soviet Union and under the influence of growing contradictions within the Muslim world, Europe and the US, as well as internal conflicts in Russia, "Russian" Islam began to be increasingly identified with the Muslim world, with all its strengths and weaknesses. This holds true especially for the North Caucasus – a border area that is part of Russia and part of the Muslim world at the same time.

Muslims are perceived as alien or friendly depending on the specific political situation. The war in Chechnya caused the North Caucasus, in the public mindset, to move further from Russia and closer to the Islamic world. Tatarstan, with its thousand mosques, Islamic University and resolve to adopt the Latin script, is also shifting closer to the world of Islam. Boris Yeltsin's famous slogan, "Take as much sovereignty as you can swallow," became a strong incentive for Muslims to turn away from Russia.

The division of Islam into "alien" and "native" remains to the present day and is especially characteristic of the new official ideology, although today there is a somewhat different emphasis: The qualifier "alien" is applied to Islamic fundamentalism (Wahhabism) as opposed to "native," or traditional Islam, which maintains a separation of religion from politics and is engaged in purely religious affairs.

The great majority of Russians judge Islam by:
- the actions of religious extremists
- conflicts involving Muslims
- radical statements by Muslim politicians and spiritual leaders
- an influx of immigrants

Very few people have opened the Qur'an, but practically everybody reads newspapers and watches television, where there are reports of Muslims involved in bomb attacks, wars and special operations in the North Caucasus, and in news reports, Muslim spiritual leaders utter banalities.

There are several common stereotypes associated with Muslims: a head-shaven, bearded man with an automatic rifle; a terrorist wearing a facemask; a crooked businessman. It is noteworthy, however, that none of these negative stereotypes are associated with the Tatars, who, for the most part, especially in urban areas, are either close to or indistinguishable from the Slavs in their lifestyle and mentality. The Russian man on the street seemingly ignores the Tatars' Muslim identity: They are just neighbors whom everyone has long become used to. "Scratch a Russian, find a Tatar," as the saying goes. But no matter how hard you may scratch an Orthodox Christian Russian, you will never find a Muslim.

The perception of the Islamic world has been aggravated by the 9/11 tragedy, terrorist attacks in Russia and in Europe, and the bellicose rhetoric of Muslim politicians. There have been other "incidents" as well, such as the destruction of ancient Buddha statues by the Afghan Taliban (2001), the murder of Dutch film director Theo Van Gogh (2005), the prosecution of an Afghan citizen for converting from Islam to Christianity, and so on.

Pro et Contra

In Russia, as everywhere, public opinion is influenced, above all, by crimes committed by Muslims, which are played up in the media. But while criticizing the media, politicians and other public figures for their negative image, it should be noted that Muslims themselves provide cause for their negative perception in the public mind.

Even without the benefit of a magnifying glass, it is obvious that Russians have ample grounds for complaints against immigrants from Muslim countries and regions. Meanwhile, attempts by Muslim spiritual leaders to cast Islam as a "world religion" are treated skeptically. First, imams and muftis are usually not eloquent enough to convince the public that they are right. Second, as freedom of expression is suppressed, judgments made in the media receive little credence, as was the case with Soviet propaganda. Third, the deeds of Islamic radicals belie Islam's purported peace-loving nature in the public eye.

Furthermore, Russia has been fighting Muslims for almost two decades now with little break. Thus, the enemy in the Russian mindset is associated with the Afghan *mujahedeen* and Caucasus militants. The present generation of war veterans can rightfully call themselves the "veterans of Muslim wars."

Russia's attitude toward Islam and Muslims also fits into the general context of xenophobia that in the first half of the 1990s was considered a relic of post-totalitarian thinking; 10 years later, however, it has turned into a core element of the public consciousness. Whereas in 1989, some 20% of the population showed signs of xenophobia, by 2001 the share rose to 50%. According to Lev Gudkov, a well-known philosopher and sociologist, judging by its level of xenophobia, Russia has surpassed even Austria, the most xenophobic country in Europe.

A poll conducted by the All-Russia Center for the Study of Public Opinion on Social and Economic Questions (ARCSPO) in March 2002 showed that Russian levels of xenophobia were the highest with respect to people from the North Caucasus (43.3%), followed by Central Asia (38.7%) and then the Arab countries (30.3%). The percentage dropped to 12.6% for Belarussians, Moldovans and Ukrainians. Some 73% of Internal Affairs Ministry officers were biased against non-Russian immigrants.

It would seem that on the issue of immigrants, Russia is in the same league with most European countries. For example, according to *The Wall Street Journal* (Dec. 10-12, 2004), Europeans expressed discontent with the presence of Muslims in their countries (75% of Swedes, 72% of Dutch, 67% of Danes and Swiss, 65% of Austrians and Belgians, 61% of Germans, 56% of Finns, 48% of Spaniards, 44% of Italians, 39% of Britons and 35% of Greeks). Yet it should be borne in mind that not so long ago, Muslim immigrants in Russia were Soviet citizens or are still Russian citizens; they speak Russian and can easily adapt to Russia's cultural environment. Muslims in Russia are "strangers among their own," while the older generation of immigrants share the same mentality with Russians. This may bring them closer to the "host nation," but it can also be an additional source of irritation: "We used to be in the same boat," some Russians seem to be saying, "but now you are crowding us out, living off us, and getting rich in the process."

Whereas in the past, xenophobia was mostly dominated by anti-Semitism, now its principal target are people from the south – 70% of them being Muslims. Aleksei Levinson has noted that "Caucasus-phobia" sometimes affects as much as two-thirds of the population.

According to a 2004 poll conducted by the Yury Levada Center, Chechens evoked a negative reaction from 52.3% of respondents, Azeris from 29.2%, and Jews from only 11%.[2]

Jews fought anti-Semitism mainly by leaving the Soviet Union and Russia or, contrary to xenophobic expectations, they integrated into Russian culture, asserting themselves as part of Russia's new elite while preserving their ethnic-religious identity. Muslims are not leaving or integrating; instead, they are painstakingly guarding their religious identity, and they have extensive experience with resistance, including armed resistance.

So, cautious and even negative attitudes toward Islam have a strong basis. When asked "Which religion is more alien (hostile) toward Russian Christian Orthodoxy: Islam or Catholicism?" 50.1% of respondents said Islam, whereas only 12.3% cited Catholicism (Levada Center, 2002). It may be recalled that in a 1994 poll, only 16.5% of respondents said they held a negative opinion of Islam.

A negative view of Islam is also cultivated through the dissemination of biased comments by Islamic politicians and spiritual figures. These individuals talk about the inevitable Islamization of Russia, in addition to prospects for creating an Islamic state, which opposes marriages between Muslims and "infidels," and so on.

Xenophobia toward domestic enemies is inseparable from xenophobia toward foreign enemies, but "Americanophobia" is fundamentally different from Islamophobia. The Americans are not feared: They are envied and their lifestyle is imitated. I would describe this as a national inferiority complex, because it affects the attitude of one nation that not long ago was a superpower to another nation that is still a superpower. There is no inferiority complex with respect to the Muslim world, although there is a certain measure of irritation over the fact that the former little brothers in need of assistance – Arabs, Afghans, Indonesians and Central Asians – have suddenly grown up and started acting independently. This is incomprehensible, and it inspires fear. Military experts and advisers who worked in the Near East find it hard to understand how the Algerians, Egyptians, Iraqis, Saudis, Yemenis and others, who had great difficulty studying the military art, were able to produce so many professional fighters (*mujahedeen*) who caused so much trouble for their former Western and Soviet mentors.

For most Russians, however, relations with the Islamic world are a very low priority. When asked "What countries should have priority for Russia in the long term?" only 1.8% of respondents said Muslim countries, with 40.2% giving priority to the CIS countries, 26.2% to Western Europe and 7% to China.

On the other hand, Russians do not view Muslim countries as a threat to Russia. In a poll conducted in the late 1990s, when pollsters asked people to name states hostile to Russia, respondents in the 17-26 age group mentioned the US (16.9%), Chechnya (13.1%), Japan (8.1%), Afghanistan (5.7%), Iraq (2.9%), Turkey (2.6%) and Iran (2.1 %); respondents in the 40-60 age group gave the following answers: the US (24%), Chechnya (8.5%), Japan (10.1%), Afghanistan (8%), Iraq (1%), Turkey (1.6%), and Iran (2.1%).[3]

Islam in Print and Electronic Media

At the end of the last century and the start of this one, media outlets substantially contributed to a religious revival. They helped increase the ranks of believers, shaping their religious identity and encouraging them to observe religious rites. Although this mostly applied to Russian Christian Orthodoxy, Islam was also given some support, but rather cautiously. Whereas the revival of Orthodoxy was encouraged by the state, Islamic revival was permitted.

The relatively rapid formation of Islam's negative media image in the 1990s was due to a rise in nationalism among Muslims and the ethnic/political conflicts that erupted in the late 1980s, with the conflicting sides often invoking Islam to justify their cause. Starting in the 1990s, Islamic slogans started to be exploited by terrorists. These factors could be described as objective.

The main subjective factor was that the difficulties that had arisen in relations with Muslims quickly evolved into an "Islam scare." The Islamic factor was blown out of proportion (in the mid-1990s, the war in Chechnya was often referred to as a "conflict of civilizations"); the fundamental concepts of Islam (especially *jihad*) were distorted; and extremist ideology was extrapolated (purposely or through ignorance) to the entire Muslim tradition. Many Islam-related publications were linked to wars, terrorist attacks and armed conflicts.

Here are just a few typical newspaper headlines: "Islamic Wolves Kill Russian Soldiers"; "Muslims Besiege the Kremlin"; "Chechen Whores Blow Up Moscow"; "The Sword of Islamic Revolution Forged in London."

Here is an example of a "model" text: "In the theater center on Dubrovka, not only terrorists and commandos, but also Allah and Christ came to blows. Both suffered a devastating defeat" (*Moskovskiye novosti*, No. 45, 2002).

Russian television also contributed to Islamophobia, and more specifically to Caucasus-phobia. Individuals with a clearly non-Russian appearance are principal actors in such television shows as "Criminal Russia," "Man and Law" and "Emergency Report." A comparison of Russian-made films with European and US films shows that among those standing up to evil in the Western productions, there are many non-European faces – Africans, Arabs, Chinese and Southeast Asians, for example. However, in Russian films, exclusively "blond fellows with a Nordic character" fight against the enemy.

The Islamophobia component in crime reports and thrillers is not the result of malicious intent, but rather an attempt to assess the global situation, adapt to the public mindset and boost ratings. On the other hand, cultivation of the enemy stereotype has long been part of the government's political agenda, even if implicitly. In the past decade, this enemy image has become associated with the international terrorist (i.e., the "evil Muslim"). This was followed, at the start of the 21st century, by the restoration of the archetype of the US imperialist, allegedly linked with the Islamic extremist.

Even more worrisome is that there are virtually no shows on Russian television that provide an honest and truthful account of Islam outside of politics, the "conflict of civilizations," and so forth. There is a pressing need for objective information.

It is also remarkable that in the wake of high-profile terrorist attacks in Russia, no attempt has been made to check the rise of negative perceptions toward Islam. After the 2004 bomb attacks in Spain and France, local authorities repeatedly warned the public that anti-Islamism was unacceptable. US President George W. Bush, who in the wake of 9/11 inadvertently used the word "crusade," deployed an extensive damage-control effort, talking in favorable terms about

Islam and emphasizing the need to distinguish between terrorists and Muslims.

Almost nothing of the kind happened in Russia. While I do not think that Russian politicians and media outlets should slavishly copy European and US experience, the fact that Islam remains terra incognita for Russian television must cause some concern: This vacuum tends to be filled with crudely apologetic or, on the contrary, provocative Islamophobic material.

Islam in Fiction

The Russian people do not form their impressions only by watching television and reading newspapers; they also learn something about Islam from books. The problem is that the noble characters in the works of Pushkin, Lermontov and Tolstoy have been replaced in Russian pop culture by thugs and sadists.

The Russian classics did not idealize "persons from the Caucasus," but they did not turn them into beasts justifying their deeds with references to Islam. Those old books aroused genuine interest in Islam and its followers; there was no Islamophobia there. According to Yakov Gordin, "the classics and their contemporaries did not see an inseparable wall between two apparently irreconcilable worlds."[4] The general attitude at that time was: Russia as a great empire was "doomed" to victory, while its adversary was doomed to submit and adapt to it. The empire can afford to be magnanimous toward its new future subjects. This prospect looked fairly optimistic from the 19th century.

Today, by contrast, the situation looks murky, to put it mildly. Aleksei Yermolov, Pavel Tsitsianov and Mikhail Vorontsov were the past conquerors of the Caucasus. However, considering the tactics being employed by Army and police generals today, the word "thug" would seem somehow more appropriate. Meanwhile, the differences between the Russian and the Caucasus Muslim traditions represent an insurmountable wall.

Public opinion is becoming increasingly aware of this wall. And popular literature, primarily thrillers, provides ample evidence of this awareness. There are series of works where the antagonists are represented by "persons from the Caucasus" and where their religious identity is described with references to jihad, the Qur'an, "infidels," Allah, etc. " 'Wahit will avenge us,' he said in a hoarse voice. 'The whole of Russia will be shaken by the hand of Allah!' "[5] This is a good example of the "clash of civilizations" made simple.

Actually, thrillers only touch on Islam superficially, as if to remind readers yet again that murderers and sadists profess this particular religion. Islam is a de rigueur characteristic of antagonists. It is noteworthy that more and more often, standing behind the backs of Islamic terrorists and extremists are Western secret services, but as of lately, also Georgians and Ukrainians.

A case in point is *Dzhakhannam*, a thriller novel by Yulia Latynina, a political journalist. The book's cover, which shows a split crescent and a Muslim rosary, with one of its beads shaped in the form of a bullet, bears all the hallmarks of Islamophobia. The novel attempts to make a separation between the Chechen and Russian criminal underworlds, which live according to their own distinct laws, even though they occasionally cooperate.

In these various fictional tales, the Islamic, Caucasus-Islamic and Western-Islamic threats are primitive but at the same time multifaceted. There are recurring storylines in the Russian version, but also in US and European variety. There is an attempt to carry out a terrorist attack using nuclear weapons (e.g., Daniil Koretsky's *Kod vozvrashcheniya* [The Code of Return]). In yet another doomsday scenario, Chechen Wahid, a character from Aleksandr Prokhanov's book *Gospodin geksagen* [Mister Hexogen][6] also threatens to blow up nuclear power stations, missile silos and chemical plants. Yulia Latynina is only slightly less bloodthirsty than her contemporaries: The terrorists in her thriller only want to blow up a storage facility with 3,500 metric tons of hydrogen sulfide.

The threat of a nuclear apocalypse is present not only in fiction, but is constantly discussed by serious experts, many of whom are convinced that it is only a matter of time before terrorists get their hands on nuclear weapons. This is a Catch-22 situation: The danger of an "Islamic apocalypse" is taken for granted; it is reflected in pulp literature, which inspires the fear of Islam. This shreds the fabric of interreligious accord, which in turn affects the global political situation. In the end, all these factors can serve to justify preparations for a no-holds-barred "ultimate" war.

Unlike the 19th century, modern literature generally caters to people with a "passive mind" who are tired and stressed out. They take everything they read for granted. Few readers will take the time to analyze a thriller. This is fertile soil for cultivating a Caucasus-Muslim enemy stereotype.

The Islamic theme, however, is not limited to thrillers. In the past few years, it has also entered sci-fi literature with an element of political philosophy. All story lines here evolve against the backdrop of total Islamic expansion that some authors see as an apocalypse and others as geopolitical machinations, possibly with a favorable outcome for Russia.

A "classic" Islamophobic novel in this category is *Mechet Parizhskoi Bogomateri* [The Notre Dame de Paris Mosque] by Yelena Chudinova.

Chudinova describes the triumph of Islam in Paris in the middle of the 21st century. In "Sharia France," women have to wear the hijab. One street is called Osama. Those who refuse to convert to Islam live in five ghettoes, while practicing Christians are forced to recite their prayers in catacombs and face death by stoning if discovered. When they learn that the French Muslim authorities are going to destroy the ghettoes, the "non-Muslim" survivors revolt and in the end blow themselves up in the Notre Dame de Paris Cathedral, which in the last few hours before the destruction regains its Christian identity.

The Muslim community ostracized Chudinova's novel, but the critics missed one important passage that proves the author cannot be dismissed as a "zoological Islamophobe." She believes that one of the causes of what happened in France, as well as in entire Western Europe, was that the enlightened Muslims who settled in the Old World were caught unawares by their wild and fanatical religious brethren. It is this fear of "wild Islam" that breeds Islamophobia, sustaining the concept of the clash of civilizations.

In Chudinova's novel, Russia survived because it had just barely managed to close its borders to "Euro-Islam." Following this logic, Russian (Tatar) Islam also saved Russia by its strong immunity to "wild Islam." But for the average reader, *The Notre Dame de Paris Mosque* will only strengthen hostility toward and hatred of Islam, while a more enlightened reader will replace Paris with Moscow and tremble in horror.

Mikhail Veller, Chudinova's ideological soulmate, sends a disturbing message that Muslims' ultimate objective is to destroy the Christian world. "They [Muslims] are stronger in spirit. They are ready to sacrifice more. They sacrifice themselves every day, destroying all those they consider to be their enemies. They are ready to destroy all of us.*** They are ready to destroy our culture."[7]

Veller's plan to fight terror is impressive: "All terrorists are Arab Muslims. So if all Arab Muslims are destroyed, there will be no terrorism. Its technological capacity today enables the white civilization to start and win an all-out war with no holds barred." This passage needs no commentary, except that the author might be reminded that not only Arabs but also Avars, Dargins, Kabardins, Russians, Tajiks, Uzbeks, Uighurs, Chechens, Americans and many other nationalities carry out terrorist attacks.

Vladimir Mikhailov's *Variant-I* (Moscow, 1999) rolls out a whole landscape of a futuristic world. Its storyline is phantasmagoric: Tsarevich Alexei survives the 1917 execution of the tsarist family and ends up in Iran, where he and his offspring succumb to the charms of Islam. In 2045, some international forces (primarily Muslim, but also Israeli) attempt to restore the monarchy and bring it to power in hopes of making Russia an Islamic state.

The concept of the future is represented through the eyes of Mikhailov's characters. Here are some of their judgments:

"Russia needed money and allies to compensate for what it had lost at the first stage after the disintegration, and it found even more than it looked for – in the Islamic world."

"There is a pressing need for consensus with the Persian Gulf countries by establishing an international oil monopoly."

"Nuclear weapons may be transferred to some of our Muslim allies."

"Islam unites everything; it is more comprehensible to the average believer than the Holy Scripture."

"Soldiers who profess Islam will never waver."

What impact will this book have on the average reader? Mikhailov uses a potent word in reference to the Islamic world: "Islamida" – apparently to emphasize the omnipotence of this world. But this "Islamophilia" spooks the Russian reader, eventually turning into Islamophobia.

Yury Nikitin builds a similar concept into his books, *Yarost* [Rage] and *Imperia zla* [Empire of Evil]. According to art critic Leonid Fishman, they present an "Islamic project" that can be summed up as "ideological revenge." A union with Islam is proffered as the only way of saving Russia. Thus, Russians become the "new *shahids*" (martyrs, those who suffer for the sake of principle) and ultimately defeat the West.

It is noteworthy that both Mikhailov and Nikitin wrote their novels before 9/11. Presumably, after the tragedy, the idea of Russia forming a united front with Islam can no longer evoke an unequivocally positive response from the reader. Nevertheless, such views remain, and, amid growing anti-American sentiments, are still relevant.

Most of the books with an Islamic theme that I have read have one thing in common: Today, the Russian state is unable to protect its citizens against violence. It is corrupt and weak, while its officials collaborate with the adversary and are part of the mafia. Needless to say, the aforementioned books are ephemeral, with plots and heroes that are easily forgotten. But their judgments, which shape the reader's image of Islam and Muslims, remain in memory.

***

The main cause of Islamophobia lies in reality – in the events that are unfolding both in Russia and in the world at large: conflicts in the North Caucasus, the rise of nationalism in Russia's "Muslim republics," migration, and international and domestic terrorism. The main sources of fear are largely personified in the "evil Chechen" and the "evil Arab."

But the "Islamic threat" is not so much reality as a perception of reality. Cultivated in the media, reflected in artistic forms, and blown out of proportion by politicians and clerics, it has become part of the Russian mass consciousness. This refers to the Islamic, not Islamist threat, which really exists. The difference between these two concepts did not begin to be appreciated until recently – due to the efforts of certain politicians, experts and journalists. As for Muslim immigrants, the general irritation at their presence has little to do with religion. Against this backdrop, books like *The Notre Dame de Paris Mosque* look especially provocative.

This article has placed an emphasis on the negative perception of Islam. Yet I would like to draw the reader's attention to the fact that some of the aforementioned figures could have a different interpretation: Only 26% of respondents said that Islam was an alien religion,[8] while about half did not see it as an aggressive religion.[9]

We must realize, however, that it is unlikely that the negative perception of Islam in Russia will be reversed in the foreseeable future, especially since many factors outside Russia influence this attitude. Everyone is interested in stopping the rise of Islamophobia, not least Muslim themselves, who should also be more cautious and circumspect, and not speak, for example, about the inevitable "Islamization" of Russia.

Notes

1. Silayev, Nikolai. "Obyatiya tsivilizatsii" [Embraces of civilizations], *Expert*, February 13, 2006, http://expert.ru/expert/2006/06/rossiyskiy_islam_60544/.

2. "Etnicheskaya situatsiya i konflikty v stranakh SNG i Baltii: Yezhegodny doklad Seti etnologicheskogo monitoringa (2004)" [Ethnic Situation and Conflicts in CIS countries and Baltics: Annual Report by Ethnology Monitoring Network (2004)], Moscow, 2005, pp. 43-44.

3. Serebryanikov, V. "Antimilitaristskiye tendentsii massovogo soznaniya v Rossii i na Zapade: baza kultury mira" [Anti-militarist trends in conventional wisdom in Russia and in the West: World Culture Base], *Kultura mira: ot utopii k realnosti* [World Culture: From Utopia to Reality]. Kazan, 1999, p. 141.

4. Yakov, Gordin. *Kavkaz: zemlya i krov* [Caucasus: The Land and the Blood]. St. Petersburg, 2000, p. 338.

5. Koretsky, Daniil. *Kod vozvrashcheniya* [The Code of Return]. Moscow, 2006, p. 26.

6. Prokhanov, Aleksandr. *Gospodin Geksogen* [Mister Hexogen]. Moscow, 2002, p. 196.

7. Veller, Mikhail. *Kassandra* [Cassandra]. St. Petersburg, 2002, p. 169.

8. Verkhovsky, A. "Religioznaya ksenofobia: sovremenniye tendentsii" [Religious Xenophobia: Current Trends], Riselet-Poslaniye, 2004, 8(75), p. 2.

9. http://thames2.alfa.fake/levadad/QueryView.aspx

THE ISLAMIC STATE: ALTERNATIVE STATEHOOD?

Vasily Kuznetsov

Despite all the obvious weaknesses of the Islamic State as a state-building project, it is very attractive to a certain number of people living in the region. This attraction stems not from the confessional nature of the state itself, but from the seeming authenticity of the Islamic State.

In 2015, an alternative model of statehood for the Middle East region became a widely discussed topic. While the ideas of various alternative projects appeared quite often in the 20th century (in connection with the establishment of the State of Palestine, the Kurdish problem, the Third International Theory of Muammar Qaddafi, etc.), they occupied a marginal place and hardly ever came close to realization (suffice it to recall Abdullah Ocalan's idea of democratic confederalism).[1] However, the rapid strengthening of the Islamic State (ISIS) and its exoticism seem to create the impression of a sudden emergence of a real alternative.

This article originally appeared in *Russia in Global Affairs* Vol. 13, No. 4, 2015. It is a shortened version of a paper written for the Valdai International Discussion Club and co-authored with Palestinian researcher Valid Salem. The full text is available at: http://ru.scribd.com/doc/288169093/Valdai-Paper-32-The-Islamic-State-An-Alternative-Statehood.

ISIS formed in 2006 from the merger of 11 factions of Iraqi Al Qaeda that were little known before 2013. The organization comprised only a few thousand people during the initial years of its operation – mainly former soldiers and officers from Saddam Hussein's army. The organization's activities were at the time aimed against the Americans and the new US government that had pursued a tough lustration policy to remove the Baath party and the entire old elite from the political space.

The radical transformation of an ordinary jihadist group was associated, first, with the escalation of the Syrian conflict, which destabilized the situation in Iraq by way of "transfusion" across the border and, second, with the rise in the spring of 2011 of Abu Bakr al-Baghdadi, who set a course for the organization's self-financing through robbery, expropriation of property owned by "infidels," racketeering, bootlegging, etc.

ISIS became widely known in the summer of 2014, when militants seized Mosul and started launching aggressive attacks in Iraq and Syria.

As of late 2015, ISIS controlled territory in Syria and Iraq comparable in size to the UK, with a population of 8 million people.[2] Tens of thousands of militants fight for ISIS (according to some sources, 80,000 to 100,000 or more)[3] from various countries of the world, including over 1,700 from Russia[4] (unofficial data suggest that this figure is much higher).[5]

The question of the Islamic State's nature clearly remains open; however, there are certain prerequisites that allow it to be considered a state rather than just a new version of a jihadist organization, and much has already been said and written about it by now. Nevertheless, the following two questions remain most relevant: (1) What kind of project does ISIS propose (if any) and (2) can ISIS prove effective at solving key statehood-related problems in the Arab countries – i.e., can it solve the nation-building problem, overcome the fragmented nature of societies and harmonize institutional development?

It must be noted, though, that even if it fails to solve these problems but succeeds in overcoming the obvious manifestations of the region's current statehood crisis, it could well be defined as a temporarily successful project, despite all its barbarity and cruelty.

The Islamic State Project

In proposing its own state-building project, ISIS continues the Salafi tradition, urging the Muslim community to return to the time of the Prophet Muhammad and the rightly guided caliphs. While this general Salafi idea has always been quite popular in the Arab and Muslim world, different thinkers and religious and political leaders have given it radically different interpretations.

Unlike the Muslim Brotherhood, Tunisian Ennahda, Hamas, and other Islamist organizations that seek to build their ideologies on a combination of Islamic values, nationalist ideas and democratic principles (it should be recalled that Hamas came to power through democratic elections), ISIS, just like Al Qaeda that produced it, occupies a fundamentally anti-modernist and anti-Western position. Therefore, analysis of the project that the Islamic State is proposing suggests referring to the early Muslim statehood model and identifying its key elements.

The problem is that there are two ways in which statehood, as applied to Arab Muslim political history and culture, can be understood.

In one respect, it can imply the real statehood that existed in the region in the precolonial period. This "real" statehood in the Arab Muslim world was of a twofold origin: On the one hand, it was engendered by Muhammad's religious call and, on the other, by the Arab Muslim conquest in the 7th-8th centuries and the need to control the conquered territories. The ambiguity of this origin affected the structure of the Arab Muslim state and the sources of its legitimacy, as well as its political identity. In one sense, it was an Islamic state for Muslims whose main institutions were established by Muhammad and the rightly guided caliphs; the caliph's power was religiously justified; and the non-Muslim population (mainly, Jews and Christians) that was considered "protected" (*dhimmi*) had its own jurisdiction and paid special taxes. In another sense, it was an ethnocratic state: in the Umayyad period, it was Arab; in the Abbasid period, it was Arab-Persian and Arab-Turkic, etc. Its rulers actively used historical mythology to justify their claim to the caliphate, and they relied on tribal and ethnical groups in exercising their power.

In addition to the combination of religious-ideological and ethnic tribal elements, real Arab Muslim statehood was characterized by active naturalization and transformation of public administration practices in conquered and neighboring nations (primarily, Byzantium and Iran), their rethinking and gradual sophistication of the political system.

Finally, this real statehood was distinguished by the generally secular nature of institutions (to the extent any existed) and public administration methods.

Naturally, the last statement does not imply the secularity of the state but means the emancipation of real political power from its religious origins. Since approximately the 10th century (the Buwayhid period), the Abbasid caliph had reserved the exclusive function to legitimize the power of real rulers – at first, Buwayhid *amir al-umara* (commanders) and, later, Seljuk sultans.

At the same time, it can imply the concept of Islamic statehood, to which ISIS, in fact, refers. This concept, developed in works of Muslim legal scholars, was not, in its main part, intended to describe the existence of political reality and was not a result of it. For the thinkers who developed it, it was not about teaching the ruler how to rule better (for this purpose, a genre of "mirrors for princes" – *specula principum* – was used) and not about explaining the power phenomenon, in which philosophers were interested, but about describing a righteous state as it had been meant by the sacred texts of Islam. It is no coincidence that the key work devoted to Islamic statehood, *Al-Ahkam as-Sultaniyyah* (The Laws of Islamic Governance), was written by al-Mawardi as late as the 11th century, when a single caliphate no longer existed.

It appears that today one can identify several elements of the Islamic statehood concept that have the most significant impact on the project proposed by ISIS and explain its differences from the idea of the nation-state: *umma, imam, dawla, bay'a* and *jihad*.

First, the Islamic State is not a nation-state because an *umma*, in its medieval meaning, is not a nation. As noted by Palestinian and Egyptian thinker Tamim al-Barghouti, "the physical existence of individuals is called an *umma* when these individuals have an image of themselves as a collective, and when this image is guiding them to do things in certain ways distinct from others." Thus, in contrast to a nation, in its "biological" sense, an *umma* is not a natural phenomenon. But nor is it an imaginary community resulting from the socioeconomic development of society, in contrast to the "social" meaning of a nation. An *umma*, which implies spiritual and ideological affinity, is not determined by its settlement territory, nor its numerical size (Prophet Ibrahim was initially an *umma* just by himself), nor its political organization. If the sense of nationhood requires the acquisition of statehood, the *umma* will need political arrangements solely out of practical necessity, but the absence of the state will not result in its degradation or disappearance.

However, above all else, an *umma* is a community following its imam, whose function is fundamentally different from that of the leader of a nation-state: "The imamate is to replace the prophet in the defense of faith and the administration of the world (*ad-dunya*)," al-Mawardi wrote in the 11th century.

The imam (in Sunni theory) is neither a sovereign nor a legislator nor a judge. He is rather a coordinator whose aim is to watch over the observance of interpretations of the sacred texts recognized by the community of religious and legal scholars; an administrator; a teacher; and a role model for Muslims following him along the path of faith and, thus, forming an *umma*. It is for this very reason that the absence of the imam weakens the *umma* and renders it incomplete.

In political terms, al-Mawardi identifies 10 main functions of the imam, and this list largely corresponds to the entire Sunni tradition. Most of these functions, although requiring political action, have religious justification or designation: to ensure religious lawfulness, to apply punishments established by God to defend the rights of believers, to protect the House of Islam (*Dar al-Islam*), to fight those who refuse to become Muslims, to collect taxes (in accordance with the Islamic Sharia), to appoint believers and law-abiding men to official posts, to manage the *umma*, and to protect faith. In addition, there are two purely administrative duties: to secure border regions and to determine the treasury revenue and expenditure in a reasonable manner; and one purely religious – to support religion.

In the Sunni tradition, the imam may not be elected, but should be either appointed directly by his predecessor or the community of religious scholars, or should seize power.

Although the imam is the leader of an *umma* rather than a state (*dawla*), he, in fact, acts within the framework of the latter.

However, the Islamic State is not a state per se, also because a *dawla*, in its medieval sense, is actually not a state. A *dawla* is a secular organization of the *umma* from which it receives its legitimacy. In the classic period of Islamic history, to which the spiritual sentiment of ISIS refers, *dawla* meant primarily a dynasty, not a territory. A *dawla* is an initially temporary and sufficiently flexible establishment that is not territorial and is not characterized by sovereignty because, as it belongs to God, it is delegated by God to the *umma*, by the *umma* to the imam, and by the imam to rulers of lower ranks. As a result, a *dawla* constitutes a polity, or a potestary system that is, in principle, multileveled and capable of organizing itself based on the network principle. Thus, for example, the Abbasid Caliphate was a *dawla* (in fact, it was called the "Abbasid *dawla*," not caliphate), as were its constituent kingdoms of Tulunids and Tahirids. Volga Bulgaria, which had no actual connections with the caliphate, was also viewed by Baghdad as part of this *dawla*, because it was the Abbasid caliph who was the source of its legitimacy.

In the modern world, a *dawla* is not usurped by ISIS. In a certain sense, the southern regions of Libya controlled by Hezbollah, the Palestinian territories controlled by Hamas, and internal areas of the "great" Sahara controlled by nomadic tribes all constitute a *dawla* in the medieval meaning of the term. Having considerable political independence, they certainly weaken nation statehood in the region.

A critical element of ISIS statehood is the *bay'a*, an oath of allegiance given by certain social groups and individuals to the imam. It is the *bay'a* that ensures the connection between the *umma* and imam and his real sovereignty. Furthermore, the *bay'a* exists in modern Arab monarchies, ensuring traditional legitimacy of rulers.

As for *jihad*, in accordance with the ideas of Al Qaeda in Mesopotamia described in their well-known document "Our Ethos and Our Program," and following the radical Salafi tradition, it is understood as armed combat with those who refuse to convert to Islam, being a personal duty of each Muslim and one of the principles of religion (*Usul ad-Din*). Therefore, a refusal to engage in jihad results in *takfir*, an accusation of apostasy.

Thus, the political order proposed by ISIS should be free *a priori* from certain weaknesses of the existing model of statehood. In theory (but not in practice), ISIS may not have problems with the incompleteness of the nation-building project because it rejects the very idea of nationhood. It also seems unable to have problems with its legitimacy deficit and sovereignty because its legitimacy comes from God and its sovereignty covers the entire Muslim *umma*. As for institutional development, the fragmented nature of society and other problems faced by modern states in the region, they are questions of political practice rather than religious theory.

Model Implementation

Seeking to establish firm control over territory, ISIS has to earn the loyalty of the local population and, hence, perform robust social activities (pay salaries, conduct charitable campaigns, build infrastructure, perform law-enforcement duties, etc.). The fact that ISIS brings – although very cruel and distorted but still understandable – order based on well-known rules ensures that it will receive support from the (surviving) population tired of anarchy and the chaos of war.

Social activities force ISIS to improve the structure and methods of administration. Thus, al-Baghdadi was proclaimed caliph; he has two deputies and a cabinet of ministers; and the rulers of 12 vilayets are subordinated to him. The active participation of former officers from Saddam's elite enables the organization's leaders to use their administrative experience.

At the same time, religious elements occupy a considerable place in the management structure: the Consultative Council (*shura*), which verifies that the administration's decisions comply with Sharia principles, as well as the Sharia court and the Council of Muftis.

Many modern ISIS government institutions have a religious interpretation. For example, ISIS social services are managed by the Department of Muslim Services. On the whole, it can be said that in the process of its institutional establishment as a state, ISIS synthetizes elements of a nation state and the archaic nature of Islam, which make it neo-modernist.

While in institutional terms, such synthesis helps create a certain imitation of real statehood, it creates new controversies in other terms.

Thus, the idea of territorial statehood (in Syria and Iraq) in the Islamic State is naturally coherent with the non-territoriality of a *dawla*, because many jihadist groups all over the world have declared themselves subjects of caliph al-Baghdadi and ISIS branches. While the nature of relations between the Islamic State of Iraq and Syria and its branches is not quite clear, they can be described within the paradigm of the *umma-dawla* relationship and, in a completely Western manner, as franchising.

The duality of the territorial identity of ISIS results eventually in the split of the organization into pragmatists oriented toward strengthening the political entity in a limited territory and romanticists pursuing indefinite expansion. However, such a split can hardly be viewed as a factor weakening ISIS, because the organization has an evident opportunity to export romanticists to ISIS branches all over the world.

The archaic and modern values are combined in state-building in a bizarre way, too. On the one hand, Islamic egalitarianism – the idea of *umma* unity – forces ISIS to seek to prevent the ethnic and tribal heterogeneity of society in the territory it controls (naturally, after all infidels have been eliminated). On the other hand, solving the problem through confessionalism creates new dividing lines.

All these bizarre and quite modernist entwinements are supplemented by the Islamic State's active informational activities aimed at spreading the organization's influence in the world.

Thus, today the Islamic State is only able to address the problem of external manifestations of the statehood crisis – to restore institutions and renew the socioeconomic contract between society and the state, reinforce its sovereignty over limited territory, and solve border-related problems. However, it is obvious that none of these problems has been fully solved or can be solved within the framework of the model that is being built.

The created institutions and the economic basis of the social contract, exotic as they are, may provide a solution for the time of jihad and continuous expansion; however, they must be revised in order to maintain the day-to-day activities of a normal state. Of course, there is a certain irony of history here, because to achieve this, ISIS members would have to repeat the path of the Umayyads and early Islamic statehood in general, which halted expansion during the Abd al-Malik Caliphate. At that time, as is known, the inability to adapt resulted in the Abbasid revolution and the split of the caliphate.

Moreover, it is not quite clear how the sovereignty issue is being addressed today. The *bay'a* is still a rather weak instrument of reinforcement for partially modernized societies. It is clear that, at first glance, the ISIS government can control a certain (and considerably large) amount of territory; however, it is unknown how substantially and tightly it controls it. It makes the proclamation of sovereignty even more doubtful, given that the state is not recognized by the international community (since it has been recognized as a terrorist organization).

As for borders, territorial and administrative order, network structures, franchising systems and non-territorial nature, this certainly all sounds very romantic. However, in practice, one can speak of a true Islamic State only on Syrian and Iraqi territory. For other territories, it is rather some kind of brand with a unique situation in each individual case. For example, in Libya, ISIS is essentially a convenient form of self-presentation and consolidation of several small tribes. In fact, the unity of the Syrian and Iraqi area also raises many doubts, partly because of Iraqi domination in the ISIS administrative structure.

Finally, the situation in ISIS is even worse when it comes to addressing profound statehood problems. The idea of a united Islamic nation is certainly poetic; however, it can be attractive only to a limited number of enthusiasts, mainly from the Western Islamic pseudo-*umma*, but it takes no account of the existing regional identities, which, in real social practice, are usually more important than confessional ones. Furthermore, insofar as it relates to the Syrian and Iraqi population, they are forced to join ISIS to avoid horrible conditions of war and simply because they have no choice. The situation is the same with young people from many Arab countries who join ISIS not to fight for religious ideas, but because of disappointment with their own states. "There is no justice, no freedom, and no future" are words one can hear from young people in the poor regions of Tunisia who have decided to join ISIS, where they think they can find all the above. In this discourse, freedom and justice are understood quite specifically – as freedom from humiliation and alienation by the state.

These young people believe that ISIS provides an opportunity to overcome social and political fragmentation, that ISIS elites do not usurp power and are authentic. However, in practice, this [opportunity] has so far been achieved solely through repression and genocide of social groups, while the need for development, strengthening sovereignty (if ISIS survives all other "ifs") and institutions will require a stronger repressive system torn off from society to an even greater extent than in other Arab countries. So ISIS will most likely have difficulty overcoming the fragmented nature of society.

Regarding institutions, ISIS is creating governmental institutions, but civil ones are completely nonexistent. Such a situation can continue only during war.

Nevertheless, despite all obvious weaknesses of ISIS as a state-building project, one cannot deny that it is very attractive to a certain number of people living in the region. By all appearances, this attractiveness is associated not with the confessional nature of the state itself –and certainly not with the cruelty of its policy – but with its aforementioned appearance of authenticity.

Notes

1. Ocalan, Abdullah. *Democratic Confederalism* (trans. International Initiative, 2011). London, Cologne: Transmedia Publishing Ltd., http://www.freeocalan.org/wp-content/uploads/2012/09/Ocalan-Democratic-Confederalism.pdf.

2. See, for example: Di Giovanni, Janine, Leah McGrath Goodman and Damien Sharkov. "How Does ISIS Funds Its Reign of Terror," *Newsweek*, Nov. 6, 2014, https://www.newsweek.com/2014/11/14/how-does-isis-fund-its-reign-terror-282607.html.

3. See, for example: Gartenstein-Ross, Daveed. "How Many Fighters Does the Islamic State Really Have," *War on the Rocks*, Feb. 9, 2015, https://warontherocks.com/2015/02/how-many-fighters-does-the-islamic-state-really-have/.

4. Artemyev, Aleksandr and Polina Khimshiashvili. "Pochti gosudarstvo: kak ustroena ekonomika i politika islamskikh boyevikov" [Almost a Nation: How the Economy and Politics of Islamist Militants Work], *RBC*, Oct. 7, 2015, https://www.rbc.ru/politics/07/10/2015/56154f5b9a7947106fa743d7.

5. See, for example: Gusovsky, Dina. "Russian fighters are joining ISIS in record numbers," *CNBC*, Dec. 9, 2015, https://www.cnbc.com/2015/12/09/russian-fighters-are-joining-isis-in-record-numbers.html.

PART ONE

1.3. Energy and Natural Resources

OIL PRICES: ACTION STRATEGY NEEDED

Andrei Baklanov

We need a substantial strategy of pricing policy and implemen-tation mechanisms to avoid emotional shocks every time oil prices drop. The fuel market should be more controllable, bal-anced and fair, as Russia's national interests demand.

Russian policymakers and economists are concerned about the pos-sible dire consequences of a sharp drop in oil prices. I would like to share some little-known facts showing that the price component has always been the weakest point in Russian energy policy, and propose some measures that may help overcome this trend, which is danger-ous to Russian interests.

In 2000-2005, as Russian ambassador to Saudi Arabia, the world's largest oil producer, I represented my country at meetings of the Secretariat of the International Energy Forum in Riyadh and had permanent contacts with Saudi and other foreign specialists to discuss energy issues.

During those discussions, I was often asked to explain why Russia – a country highly regarded globally for its bold, large-scale energy projects and record-fast development of large oilfields in re-

This article originally appeared in *Russia in Global Affairs* Vol. 13, No. 1, 2015.

mote areas – was so inconsistent and inert in devising measures to influence pricing on the energy market. I believe the question was warranted by solid reasons, which, regrettably, are still valid today.

I will refer to my own experience. In the late 1960s, I was involved in the work of an economic group at the Soviet Embassy in Egypt, a key Arab state in the Middle East. In this capacity, I was probably the first Russian official tasked with looking into the intricacies of the complex game played by the Organization for Petroleum Exporting Countries (OPEC) and its recently established (1968) Arab counterpart – the Organization of Arab Petroleum Exporting Countries (OAPEC).

These countries, acting primarily in the interests of oil producers, have already recognized the need to reach compromises and take into account the views of other major players on the energy market. They have signaled their readiness to work in closer contact with us, notably with regard to energy prices.

Simultaneously, those countries made it clear that they wished we would "play by the rules." In fact, oil producers did not like Russia's approach of supplying oil to Warsaw Pact countries at nearly half the world price. The Arabs also drew our attention to the fact that universally acknowledged market mechanisms did not regulate a considerable segment of the global energy trade. Thus, prices could be negotiated and even reduced without consideration of objective criteria.

I agreed with those Russian economists who called for establishing a permanent interaction channel with OPEC and OAPEC, and practically and substantially coordinating our policy. For a long time, however, government officials arrogantly declined these proposals, reasoning that we should not bind ourselves to "group commitments." At the same time, they did acknowledge the need to explore OPEC's plans.

The Soviet Union held to this ambiguous and inconsistent position for years. Indeed, there seemed to be no grounds for revising it. At that time, oil prices did not cause any concern, and the outbreak of hostilities in the Middle East in 1973 only strengthened the belief that "everything was well on track." Nobody wanted to hear about the increasing volatility of oil prices.

Unexpectedly for most politicians and economists, the situation that developed on the hydrocarbons market in 1983 vindicated the arguments in favor of devising measures to protect the market from price fluctuations. In several months in 1983, oil prices plummeted by one-third from the 1980 level. The measures OPEC implemented were insufficient. The organization needed agreements with other large oil producers, including the Soviet Union.

Under these conditions, OPEC representatives stepped up "exploratory" contacts with the Soviet Union in late 1983 to see if it was possible to coordinate pricing policy in the interests of oil producers. I was directly involved in those contacts.

I was on temporary duty at the Soviet Embassy in Great Britain at the time. At the instruction of the Embassy administration and Ambassador Viktor Popov, I joined the ongoing consultations. Essentially, the proposals forwarded to the Soviet Union were simple: OPEC wanted full-fledged negotiations on energy market problems with the aim of making substantial, long-term decisions.

All proposals were reported to the Soviet government, yet again the response was in no way interested or justified. The alarming signals from oil prices were ignored. No decisions were made in response to overtures from Saudi Arabia in 1982-1984 regarding the restoration of diplomatic, trade and economic ties, and the transition to a coordinated oil policy.

The tragic consequences of this short-sighted policy appeared several years later, as world oil prices plummeted to around $27 per barrel in 1985, and still lower ($14 to $15) in 1988, which admittedly was one of the reasons for the collapse of the Soviet Union.

A belated decision was made to launch closer consultative ties with OPEC, but our country made almost no attempts to secure a more predictable situation in the energy market. In 2000, Saudi Arabia proposed establishing a new organization – the International Energy Forum (IEF). The initiative was based on the quite rational principle of representation in the IEF of all countries interested in a stable market, both major producers and large consumers, as well as energy transit states. Our country's support for the bid was largely declarative.

Norway's representative, Arne Walther, was the first IEF secretary general. His country boasted the most rational system of control over the energy sector and, as many experts acknowledge, was consistent in taking measures to ensure the predictability of the oil market. I used to meet Walther regularly and attend functions at IEF headquarters. My general impression was that the organization had great potential, although it was poorly used.

At the first stage of its operation, the IEF made a sizable contribution to the development of an energy security concept. During a bilateral meeting in August 2005, Walther voiced the idea that Russia should make the issue a priority during its upcoming Group of Eight presidency. Additionally, this question was raised at a subsequent meeting with Saudi Arabia's King Abdullah.[1] It should be noted that Russian-Saudi relations were on the rise at the time, and high-level consultations on various aspects of energy policy were envisioned in one of the agreements signed during King Abdullah's historic visit to Moscow in September 2003 and his talks with Russian President Vladimir Putin.

The Russian government reacted positively to the proposals, and "energy security" became one of the three key themes of Russia's G-8 presidency. Regrettably, no further action resulted from that international cooperation. In recent years, a worsening political situation has frustrated practical results in forming a new balanced and predictable energy market.

Overall, a retrospective view of the history of Russian pricing policy is not inspiring. Russia lost many opportunities, and the consequences of the feeble and inconsistent approach toward this sector were sometimes dramatic. However, the situation has improved recently, although sweeping stabilization proposals have not yet become systemic.

What Could Be Suggested?

First, we should give an honest answer about what the current oil price is and consider the specifics of the energy market in general. If we do not, then we will face unpleasant surprises comparable to the 2008 crisis. In my opinion, the current energy market is a product of unhealthy and inflated market indicators. It was only in 2000-2003 that the price corridor was more or less justified (at $22 to $28 per barrel). Later, prices surged to $60 and then over $100 per barrel. Needless to say, there were no reasons for a three- to four-fold increase in prices in the past decade.

With that in mind, the "speculative" component of the oil price currently reaches a record 30% to 50%. Who is the interested party?

On the surface, the beneficiaries are oil producing countries. But the issue is more complex. It seems the years when the oil market was governed by Western monopolies (the so-called "Seven Sisters" – five American and two European companies) have taken their toll. The system still exists where megaprofits are de-facto shared among leading oil producing countries and Western states. Sharing takes place through the acquisition of US securities or those of other countries. Therefore, the purported "national heritage foundations" in Arab countries are sometimes just a cover for such schemes.

I believe this system is what Saudi oil and gas leaders and experts had in mind when they claimed that the bulk of megaprofits was appropriated by "profiteers" from the US and other Western states that actually give the green light to unjustified oil price hikes or de-creases – depending on which is more advantageous.

Today's oil price corridor should be $52 to $58 dollars per barrel. Let us include an additional $10 to balance expenditures on the development of new oilfields in remote areas in the Far North and offshore. In any case, the final price should not exceed $68 per barrel.

Second, it is important to move toward creating oil reserves, perhaps through a large international stabilization reserve fund of hydrocarbons.

Third, Russia should change its indifferent attitude toward the International Energy Forum, which drafts recommendations on how to synchronize the interests of various countries and ensure the stable and predictable development of the energy market.

At the same time, the IEF should receive help in overcoming inertia in its operation and move from participating in events held by various national and international agencies to taking independent actions in the interests of creating a new global mechanism for energy pricing. Oil prices should be based on a rationale. Exorbitant prices are dangerous for the future of oil-producing countries, because they stimulate the search for alternative energy sources.

Fourth, it is necessary to develop a common approach to setting an optimal and conciliatory "oil price corridor." Additionally, countries should work toward a new type of energy market that is predictable, reliable and stable.

Thus, we must take dynamic action. Work according to this guideline is just beginning, and a lot of time has been lost. Let me again refer to my own experience. On returning from my second assignment in Saudi Arabia, I agreed to publish my forecast in the journal *Neft Rossii* [Oil of Russia].[2] In that article, I offered an analysis of the energy market and some proposals that include the aforementioned positive features. The article stirred some interest, but few of the proposed measures were implemented.

It is time we finally start acting. We need a substantial strategy of pricing policy and implementation mechanisms to avoid emotional shocks every time oil prices drop. The fuel market should be more controllable, balanced and fair, as Russia's national interests demand. This is necessary for Russia to play a more significant role in the modern world and global economy.

Notes

1. Both Walther and King Abdallah specifically expressed their commitment to transform the energy market into more transparent, predictable and consistent mechanism. They voiced their concerns about this task particularly in conjunction with arrangements and holding of the G-8 summit in St. Petersburg in 2006. During my personal meetings with them, they confirmed their willingness to include discussion of energy security issues at the G-8 Summit in the context of ensuring the normal operation of the world economy. However, we did not relay these intentions to the media, since it was not clear whether the topic would be on the summit agenda. Naturally, it was a rather delicate issue for both King Abdullah and Walther. However, all ended well: Energy security was one of the key topics of the summit. Moreover, as noted at the Feb. 20, 2019 Valdai Club meeting (http://valdaiclub.com/events/own/middle-east-new-stage-valdai/), the topic of energy security was analyzed in depth and detail during preparations for that 2006 summit.

2. Baklanov, Andrei. "Uzkoye mesto globalnoi ekonomiki" [Bottleneck in the Global Economy], *Neft Rossii*, No. 6, 2007, http://www.oilru.com/nr/169/3877/.

OLD GOALS, NEW TASKS

Aleksandr Novak

In view of the accelerated development of new technologies and potentially low energy prices, the struggle for energy markets will intensify. No matter in what areas energy cooperation may develop in the future, its main task will be attracting investment, technologies and human capital to the Russian fuel-energy sector.

Energy cooperation is a key area of Russia's international activity. It helps Russia develop mutually advantageous trade relations and ensure energy security for itself and its partners. Implementing international projects strengthens the positions of Russian companies on markets that interest Moscow, improves expertise that is important for the economy, and raises the general level of competitiveness of the Russian fuel-energy sector.

In addition, international energy cooperation helps Russia achieve major foreign economic policy goals:

- creating common energy markets within the Eurasian Economic Union;

This article originally appeared in *Russia in Global Affairs* Vol. 14, No. 4, 2016.

- creating legal and political conditions in Europe for uninterrupted transit of Russian energy resources;
- developing a transport infrastructure that will reduce transit risks and ensure the competitiveness of Russian energy resources;
- enhancing the efficiency of economic integration with Asia-Pacific countries and increasing energy supplies to the growing Asian markets;
- promoting Russian interests in preparing final documents of high-level multilateral forums.

These objectives determine the agenda and continuity of Russia's foreign energy policy. However, the current transformations and uncertainty in markets create new challenges for the country and pose problems that need to be resolved promptly and efficiently. This article discusses Russia's views on, and responses to, major challenges to the world energy sector.

In Search of Market Balance

The main challenge stems from changes in the basic mechanisms and conditions for achieving a stable balance in energy markets that were caused by overinvestment in industries during the period of high oil prices and by the explosive development of technologies. Competition in all areas has sharply increased, and energy prices have plummeted, which has led to reduced investment activity and upset the long-term producer-consumer relationship. High competition enhances the role of advanced technologies that can reduce the cost of energy production in the future. The new situation stimulates broader use of short-term financial instruments and their manipulation. Market uncertainty attracts more and more new players who resort to dumping practices to seize market niches or, if they have political levers, exert direct pressure on consumers. In the short term, these practices have led to the overproduction of energy resources in the world market and reduced the role of producers. In the medium term, they can cause a major shortage of energy resources due to underinvestment in the industry.

A new market balance will come, anyway. The question is: How will Russia's position in the most important markets change then?

This is a major issue for the country, because the fuel-energy sector continues to play a crucial role in the Russian economy (the sector's share in Russia's gross domestic product in 2015 stood at 27%). Energy markets will remain important to the world economy, too, for a long time yet: According to a recent forecast by the International Energy Agency, as well as Russian estimates,[1] the world will remain hydrocarbon-dependent during the next 20 to 30 years and the demand for oil and gas will continue to grow, although not as fast as in the past few decades.

But before answering the question of how the position of the Russian fuel-energy sector will change in the world, we should analyze the conditions in which it will have to develop. The most important long-term trends are:

- Hydrocarbons will retain their lead in the energy markets in the coming decades. Their share in the world energy balance will decrease due to the spread of renewable energy technologies and the reduction of their cost, but quantitatively the consumption of hydrocarbons will keep growing. This is due to the motorization of developing countries (where cheap vehicles with internal combustion engines will for a long time be more popular than electric cars) and the electrification of new regions: 1.5 billion people in the world still have no access to electricity.
- Technological progress in the extraction of conventional hydrocarbons, which makes previously economically unattractive deposits profitable. The development of new deposits will allow importing countries to build up their own hydrocarbon production.
- The growing excess refining capacity (oil refining capacity utilization is 85% worldwide and 80% in Europe). Oil refineries have started moving closer to consumers – in particular, to Southeast Asian countries. Processing depth and the quality of oil products will play an increasingly important role in world trade.
- Growing availability of liquefied natural gas. Over the past 15 years, LNG sales in the world have doubled (from 18% to 36%), and during the next 10 years, they

could exceed pipeline gas sales. Obviously, this will lead to a diversification of suppliers in key markets – in China and Europe – and will increase competition in the world gas market, including for Russian producers.

- A possible emergence of another "black swan" in the innovative technology market. Many countries are working to improve energy storage technologies and the extraction efficiency of hard-to-recover reserves like methane hydrates, and to develop new types of engines – for example, hydrogen engines. These breakthrough technologies could completely change the configuration of the world energy industry.

In the short term, energy markets will remain under pressure. The oil market has been hit by one of the most protracted oil slumps. It was triggered by the overproduction of oil due to technological progress and overinvestment during the period of high oil prices, as well as by an expected slowdown in the global economy and a gradual strengthening of the dollar.

In the medium term, oil prices will be regulated by the cost of extraction of marginal resources. Now it is shale oil, with a ceiling price of $50 to $60. In the future, technological progress may reduce the cost of shale oil production, and more expensive resources in deep-water shelves or bituminous sands will become marginal. Nevertheless, the potential of certain types of deposits and the cost of their extraction remains to be seen.

Natural gas markets have also been hit by oversupply. Demand has been growing more slowlythan expected, and production has proved resistant to low oil and gas prices.

Similar processes are taking place in the world coal market, where the decreasing cost of production and renewable energy technologies have pushed prices down. Competition is growing in power engineering, including the nuclear power industry, where players widely use political lobbyism, restrictions on access to financial markets, and artificial preferences in favor of renewable energy technologies. So, as we can see, power engineering, like the entire global economy, is witnessing increased competition, and the situation is only becoming more pronounced. Meanwhile, Russia must compete with producers that have advantages in accessing financial resources and technologies.

Russia as a Competitor

Despite the objectively difficult situation in international markets, Russia is now one of the most competitive producers of hydrocarbons in the world. This is due to the prime cost of its staple exports, the country's geographical location and the technologies it uses. This is well illustrated by Russian oil and gas companies that, unlike many of their competitors, continue to earn money in the extraction sector and increase production, which explains the continued interest among international investors.

In 2015, Russia retained leadership in gas supplies to world markets (20% [rising to 25% in 2018 – *Ed.*])[2] and regained first place in supplies of liquid hydrocarbons – crude oil (12%) and oil products (9%).[3] Russia's draft Energy Strategy to 2035[4] provides for further development in many areas, specifically the following:

- Russia will remain a leading producer and exporter of oil, gas and condensate. Oil output will not fall below 525 million [metric] tons. The output structure will change in favor of hard-to-recover resources, and offshore and Arctic reserves. In addition, the oil recovery factor at existing oil fields will increase. These changes will require widespread introduction of new extraction technologies, and the development of services and import substitution.
- Russia will continue to modernize its oil- and gas-refining and chemical facilities to increase processing depth (the depth of oil refining is to be increased from 72% to 90%, which will allow for the production of motor fuels of higher environmental standards) and enter foreign markets with new groups of goods.
- Pipeline infrastructure will be developed to diversify destination regions and it will include, first of all, the Eastern Siberia-Pacific Ocean (ESPO) oil pipeline and the Siberian Might, Nord Stream 2, and South/Turkish Stream gas pipelines. Supplies to Eastern consumers will increase substantially (sales of crude oil and oil

products on Asia-Pacific markets will double), while supplies to the West will stay at the same level, on average. The share of the Asia-Pacific region among buyers of Russian gas, including LNG, will increase almost tenfold. Russia expects a fivefold increase in its LNG production by 2035, which will allow it to increase its share in world LNG trade to 15%.

The Energy Strategy envisions reducing the energy intensity of the economy by a factor of 1.6 by the year 2035. Measures that are to be taken to this end include reducing specific fuel consumption for electricity production and energy consumption by fuel and energy facilities. Renewable energy sources will play an important role in these efforts. This sector will develop to form scientific and industrial expertise in this important sphere. By 2035, the installed renewable energy capacity is to reach 7.9 GW, and electricity production by renewable energy power plants will grow by a factor of 10.

The energy sector will see inevitable structural transformation – an increase in investment in innovations, modernization of production, the creation of high-performance jobs, and growth in economic and energy efficiency. There are plans to change the balance between state regulation and market mechanisms in favor of the latter, which will increase the efficiency and quality of the energy sector.

Technological development of the fuel-energy sector and import substitution will enable Russia to export not only fuel and energy but also energy services and technologies. Russian companies already operate in all regions of the world (45 countries), participating in the extraction and processing of energy resources, building generation and infrastructure facilities, and supplying power equipment.

In addition, Russia has for many years been a world leader in the export of nuclear power technologies. It has extensive expertise in building hydroelectric and thermal power plants and competitive know-how in solar power engineering. The latter includes high-efficiency cascade heterojunction solar cells with efficiency of more than 40%.[4]

Russia is increasing supplies of power equipment, including turbines. Russian companies are involved in the construction of all types of energy infrastructure, and Russia trains power engineering specialists for other countries. All these efforts will be continued.

Experience, knowledge and know-how are an important advantage. But, considering the aforementioned challenges, Russia can cash in on this advantage in international energy markets only through concerted efforts of various departments, diplomatic agencies, intergovernmental commissions and offices of Russian energy companies.

Priorities of Energy Cooperation

What priorities should Russia set for energy cooperation at the present stage? First of all, Russia should involve foreign partners in all stages of the production chain – from the extraction and transportation of energy resources to their deep processing, electricity generation and marketing (for example, sales through retail gas station networks or trading operations), including in third countries. A similar approach should be taken to Russian companies abroad. They should be allowed to not only supply energy resources but also process, market and sell them to end consumers, as well as create energy infrastructure. Russia should also actively use asset swaps based on the principle of reciprocity to broaden its presence in the markets of interest to it.

Russia will increasingly use the practice of swap contracts for the supply of LNG and crude oil. However, the liberalization of LNG trade does not mean that Russia will give up its unified export channel policy for pipeline gas.

In the interests of promoting development and investment, Russia needs to extend the localization of high-tech production and power engineering services in the country. Key priorities in these efforts are to increase the export of power engineering technologies and expertise, as well as to implement projects jointly with leading companies in third countries.

The main principles of bilateral and multilateral energy cooperation are consistent development of mutually advantageous partner relations in this sphere, customized approaches and the protection of Russia's basic interests. Let me briefly list the main areas of Russia's policy.

In multilateral cooperation, Russia seeks to continue and strengthen interaction with various organizations, such as the Organization of the Petroleum Exporting Countries (OPEC), the Gas Ex-

porting Countries Forum (GECF) and the Association of Southeast
Asian Nations (ASEAN). It has many shared interests with the BRICS
countries (Brazil, Russia, India, China, South Africa), and there is a
great potential for cooperation with them. The BRICS members have
many similar economic problems, including dependence on high-
tech imports. Russia has proposed boosting economic cooperation,
creating joint R&D projects and promoting high-tech products of
the fuel-energy sector. There are good cooperation prospects within
the framework of the Shanghai Cooperation Organization Energy
Club (including, the promotion of the Silk Road project). In Eurasia,
the main objective is the formation of common energy markets, including resolution of the resource and transit pricing issue.

Politics vs. Markets

Despite the sanctions on Russia and the growing politicization of
Russia's relations with the European Union, the EU remains Russia's key partner. Moscow is ready to resume cooperation that was
disrupted from 2014 to early 2016 by policies of the EU and the
US – naturally, on the basis of equality, noninterference in internal
affairs and respect for mutual interests. Three years ago, Russia and
the EU signed a roadmap on energy cooperation until 2050, aimed
at creating a Pan-European Energy Space. However, no progress has
been achieved since then. Moscow's EU partners obviously seek to
politicize their cooperation with Russia.

Let me cite a few examples. The problem of using the OPAL gas
pipeline has not been solved to this day. The South Stream project
has been abandoned under pressure from the European Commis-
sion. Several countries, especially Poland and the Baltic states, have
launched a campaign against the construction of Nord Stream 2. At
the same time, we are witnessing active support from Brussels and
Washington for competing projects, such as the Trans Adriatic or
Trans-Caspian gas pipelines. Poland, Croatia, Greece and the Baltic
states are being pressured into building LNG receiving terminals for
American natural gas that cannot compete in price with Russian gas.
By the way, the LNG terminals already built in Europe now operate
at only 30% of capacity, which proves their economic inexpediency.

Here is one more example. Negotiations on a unified energy
system that would encompass Russia, Belarus, Latvia, Lithuania and

Estonia have been frozen since the summer of 2013. Meanwhile, this issue is very important for guaranteeing energy security for northwest Russia and its Kaliningrad Region (the Baltic states account for 40% of the transmission capacity between the power systems of central and northwest Russia). In this situation, Russia needs to ensure autonomous power supply to Kaliningrad Province.

Nevertheless, there are no significant barriers (including the so-called Third Energy Package) to full-scale restoration and development of energy cooperation, if it is based on market principles rather than politicized considerations. Nord Stream 2 is precisely such a market-based, commercial project, but its implementation is impeded by politicians. Another package of documents on energy security, published by the EC in early 2016, is aimed at further centralization of powers in the energy sector at the EC level. If the documents are adopted, it will be able to administer contractual relations in the field of energy supply based on the "security of supply" principle in a given member state, region or the EU as a whole. Meanwhile, the EC has not yet established criteria for assessing the impact of agreements on the security of gas supplies within the EU, nor has it determined the consequences of such an assessment. Obviously, this can hardly be called a market approach and, given the recent events, it may expectedly be anti-Russian.

The EU's anti-market and anti-Russian moves also include attempts to force Gazprom to change the terms of gas supply contracts by relocating gas transfer facilities and waiving take-or-pay requirements, and plans to introduce mandatory coordination with the EC of all energy agreements, including nonbinding documents (declarations, memoranda, etc.), between EU members and third countries even before they are signed.

Nevertheless, there are many opportunities for the development of energy cooperation with the EU: The focus should be on developing direct contacts in "nonfrozen" areas, including at the regional level, and the creation of more favorable conditions for cooperation in the future.

Constructive interaction with partners in the GECF on the issues of balance between environmental safety and power engineering, and the popularization of natural gas as an environmentally friendly and affordable fuel, may have a positive impact on relations with the EU. There is great potential in joint expert forums, R&D and projects. Cooperation with Asia-Pacific and other Asian countries is acquiring greater importance. Russia's key partners are China, Japan, Vietnam, India and South Korea. These countries are interested in increased Russian energy supplies as they seek to reduce their dependence on hydrocarbons from the volatile Middle East.

The markets of China and India are the fastest growing in the world, and one of Russia's main tasks is to broaden the presence of its companies there. Cooperation with these countries could encompass many areas: In addition to increased oil supplies via the ESPO pipeline and agreements on LNG sales to China and India, investors from the two countries are showing great interest in various projects in Russia (Vankor, Eastern Petrochemical Company, Verkhnechonsk, and Yamal LNG) and providing access to projects on their own territories (Essar in India and Tianjin oil refinery in China). There is also great interest in some Russian technologies. Chinese and other partners are ready to cooperate regardless of the US sanctions. The multibillion-dollar funding of Yamal LNG and the laying of an underwater power cable from Taman to the Crimea are illustrative examples of that.

The Middle East is another key area. Oil-rich countries – Iran, Iraq and others – are of great interest to Russian energy companies, which could participate in restoring and developing the oil and gas extraction and processing infrastructure there. Russia sees a very high potential for cooperation with all countries in the region. The tasks facing the Gulf countries are in many respects similar to those facing Russia. These include economic diversification and import substitution. Well-coordinated efforts will make the Middle East a promising market for Russian industries and will help strengthen ties with the region for years ahead.

Power engineering is a key area of cooperation with countries in Africa and Latin America, where Russian companies participate not only in developing resources but also in building electrical grid infrastructure and power generation systems.

***

No matter in what areas energy cooperation may develop in the future, its main task will be to keep attracting investment, technologies and human capital to the Russian fuel-energy sector. In view of the accelerated development of new technologies and potentially low energy prices, the struggle for energy markets will intensify. Russia should use its advantages to benefit the development of its energy sector and overall economy as much as possible.

Notes

1. Sources for the statistics quoted include the International Energy Agency's World Energy Outlook 2015, https://www.iea.org/publications/freepublications/publication/WEO2015.pdf; and the Russian Federation's Energy Strategy to 2030, https://minenergo.gov.ru/node/1026.

2. International Energy Agency. *Key World Energy Statistics 2016*, p. 11, http://large.stanford.edu/courses/2017/ph241/kwan1/docs/KeyWorld2016.pdf.

3. RF Energy Strategy to 2030 (see [1] above).

4. See: https://minenergo.gov.ru/node/1920.

5. "Prognoz nauchno-tekhnologicheskogo razvitiya otraslei toplivo-energeticheskogo kompleksa Rossii na period do 2035 goda" [Forecast of the scientific and technological developments of Russia's fuel and energy complex up to 2035], Russian Federation Ministry of Energy, 2016, https://minenergo.gov.ru/node/6366.

WATER AND PEACE

Anastasia Likhachova

The only strategic response to the global water challenge and international competition for water is to use water more efficiently by redistributing water intakes and introducing new water use technologies. Importantly, these measures do not require redistributing water flows among countries.

In early May 2016, a week apart, Russia's Minister of Agriculture Aleksandr Tkachov and presidential economic adviser Sergei Glazyev talked about exporting Russian fresh water. The minister made a radical proposal to export surplus water from hydroelectric power plants in the Altai region to China's Xinjiang via Kazakhstan.[1] Glazyev took a more market-oriented approach. He proposed "collecting, purifying, treating and exporting fresh water."[2] In former years, Moscow's ex-mayor Yury Luzhkov[3] also proposed exporting Russia's water resources, and in December 2013 the Economic Development Ministry considered the idea, too.[4] Now this idea has emerged in a different context, but its essence is the same: to get a lot of money without much effort by selling natural resources that cost the country nothing.

This article originally appeared in *Russia in Global Affairs* Vol. 14, No. 3, 2016.

Global competition for water is growing significantly, and countries rich in water resources will be in an advantageous position. However, the water problem has moved from the level of local crises to the level of a global strategic challenge. This transition plays a fundamental role in the development of real competition. Today, trade in raw water – for example, projects to divert Siberian rivers or build a water pipeline from Lake Baikal to China – is sale without any added cost, with unpredictable environmental effects and a potentially strong corruption element, as the cost of this valuable strategic resource will only keep growing.

Adaptation to the Global Water Challenge: Virtual Water and Quasi-Colonization

In the near future, international relations will face a new long-term problem, when changes in water distribution in river basins will be caused not by the actions of individual countries located upstream but by objective processes that will be difficult to control: population growth, changes in people's consumption habits, urbanization and increased water intake in agriculture. In these circumstances, countries will have no choice but to jointly adapt to these problems, since not even military actions would be able to reverse these trends.

Even if there are no acute international conflicts over water resources in the future, direct consequences of water scarcity will have a profound impact on all major spheres of human activity. Processes already underway precipitate changes in the structure of leading and emerging economies, and provoke large-scale migrations to areas with more water resources. According to estimates by Viktor Danilov-Danilyan, director of the Russian Academy of Sciences' Institute of Water Problems, the number of "water refugees" in the world may reach 500 million by 2030, that is, in less than 15 years.[5]

At the regional level, humankind has significantly redrawn the water resources map: There are more than 57,000 reservoirs and dams in the world and over 300 of them could be defined as giant ones,[6] and irrigation canals divert water hundreds of kilometers away from rivers into steppes and deserts. Countries located downstream strongly react when countries upstream begin to divert water. Egypt has repeatedly expressed readiness to take any measures to prevent the construction of the Renaissance Dam in Ethiopia; Uzbekistan does not rule out a war with Tajikistan over the Rogun Dam; and Syria, prior to the civil war, protested the construction of each new dam in Eastern Anatolia, Turkey. Meanwhile, even at the national level, manipulations with raw water per se are no longer enough to adapt to global water challenges.

Unlike diverting rivers, which even theoretically would benefit only a limited number of countries, efficient use of fresh water provides ample opportunities to the whole world. Resources for extensive growth have been exhausted in many countries. Water scarcity will be the main resource constraint for development, both economic and social, for all countries, except for Brazil, Russia and Canada, and there are no possibilities for reversing trends that stimulate demand for water – the demographic boom, the high-protein diet shift and urbanization. We can only speak of adaptation to these processes and attempts to mitigate them.

Therefore, the only strategic response to the global water challenge and international competition for water is to use water more efficiently by redistributing water intakes and introducing new water use technologies. Importantly, these measures do not require redistributing water flows among countries.

Physically replacing water is possible only at the regional level and in disparate volumes. Any analogy with oil makes sense only if we speak of transportation methods, because the amount of exported oil is far smaller than the amount of water needed to produce goods. On a global scale, redistributing water intakes largely means redistributing the production and sale of not water per se but water-intensive goods: food, energy, industrial goods and biofuels. Academician Danilov-Danilyan gives a very graphic example: The cultivation of grain exported to countries in North Africa and the Middle East requires an amount of water equal to the annual flow of the Nile.[7] In other words, we can say that there are two rivers in the region: the real Nile and the "virtual" Nile. Obviously, it is impossible to provide such amounts of food without international trade in virtual water and technologies.

Virtual Water

The virtual water concept, proposed by professor and water management expert John Anthony Allan in the early 1990s,[8] is based on water consumption statistics and the idea that in most cases, people use water not directly but as a production resource. Allan defined virtual water as "the amount of water embedded in food or other products." According to this concept, countries that have limited water resources can and should purchase water-intensive products from countries where the relative value of water is lower. Thus, water resources will be used most effectively.

In this economic formula, some countries have already found sources to strengthen their international position (for example, Brazil and Argentina have entered Asian markets and are now among the leading meat suppliers in the world; and Jordan has almost completely switched to importing water-intensive grain from the US and has thus significantly relieved water stress in rural areas),[9] while emerging Asian giants are adapting the main areas of their state policies to this formula. This concept did not herald any new form of water trade, but it has had a major impact on water use policies by providing graphic answers to fundamental questions: What is the relative value of water and how can it be adequately calculated in the economy and trade? Net virtual water exporters are North American countries, as well as Argentina, Thailand and India. Net importers are Japan, South Korea, China, Indonesia and the Netherlands.[10]

It is noteworthy that although China is one of the largest food exporters, the volume of its imports, especially meat imports, is so great that the amount of imported virtual water exceeds all exports. The Netherlands is among importers for a different reason. The country has highly efficient agriculture and diligently uses every meter of its land. That is why it grows crops with low added value, preferring to buy fodder from other countries and specialize in animal husbandry and horticulture. Thus, in quantitative terms, the Netherlands is, indeed, a net importer, but in terms of money, the country receives substantial income as an exporter of products in which water has maximum added value.

To get a better idea of benefits from conscious trade in virtual water, let us look at statistics for various countries, provided by the Water Footprint Network.[11] For example, producing one [metric] ton of soybeans requires 4,124 cubic meters of water in India, 2,030 cu.m. in Indonesia and 1,076 cu.m. in Brazil. The average world figure is 1,789 cu.m. If we take the production of meat, its water footprint varies even more: Producing one ton of beef requires 11,681 cu.m of water in the Netherlands, 21,028 cu.m in Russia, and 37,762 cu.m. in Mexico. The average world figure is 15,497 cu.m.

Rice and wheat, the main consumers of water in agriculture (rice accounts for 21% of the total water footprint of grain production, and wheat accounts for 12%), also require varying amounts of water in various countries: Producing one ton of rice takes 1,022 cu.m. of water in Australia and 3,082 cu.m. in Brazil. The water footprint of one ton of wheat varies from 619 cu.m. in the Netherlands to 2,375 cu.m. in Russia. This gap is due to varying levels of efficiency of agricultural technologies, and various water management techniques and climates. Therefore, efficient water use is becoming a very important source of competitiveness.

Trade in virtual water is now the main platform for international competition for water resources, which allows countries to directly impact foreign food, energy and industrial markets and, at the same time, sell their own water resources with maximum added value. The importance of this platform will keep growing with the relative appreciation of fresh water. All countries recognize the political importance of the food problem, and no one doubts the possibility to directly influence food markets through water resources as one of the main factors of agricultural production. An embargo on Russian grain exports in the summer of 2010 and the ensuing bread price hikes were one of the catalysts of the Arab Spring in Egypt. Moreover, not only trade but even just water metering is an important production factor. Studies have shown that control over fresh water sources has become key to the Islamic State's control over vast territories – and over economic activities across the region.[12]

Quasi-Colonization

Over the past 20 years, tens of millions of hectares of land have been sold or leased in developing and, especially, the least developed countries to grow food, procure wood and produce biofuels.[13] These practices have been described as "quasi-colonization," and they include large-scale purchases or leases of land abroad to export food and goods produced there to one's own country and only then to sell them to third countries. According to John Anthony Allan's estimates, these practices now account for "90 percent of all land transactions in Africa and 80 percent in the world."[14] All these businesses are highly water-intensive, and studies confirm that the availability of sources of fresh water is becoming a determining factor in leasing and purchasing land abroad.

Although foreign direct investment has always existed, today we can speak of a new phenomenon: agro-colonization. Land grabbing has become a widespread practice since the early 2000s. What is the main difference between land grabbing and ordinary investment? Land grabbing is accompanied by unequal distribution of income between local communities and investors, and by the export of crops to investors' countries of origin, rather than to the local or international market. This factor explains the high attractiveness to land grabbers of countries where property rights are inadequately protected and there are unstable political regimes. In such cases, income distribution primarily benefits investors (the "colony's" share is in government officials' incomes). They deplete natural resources and have no incentives to adopt long-term strategies for using the land they have leased or even purchased. Although most of these land lease agreements are concluded for terms of 50 to 99 years, they cannot be viewed as a solid basis for long-term cooperation, considering the instability of political regimes in most African countries.

Whereas in the early 1960s, hundreds or thousands of hectares of land were leased, today this figure has reached millions of hectares; land transactions for plots smaller than 10,000 hectares are not even included in statistics of relevant NGOs. Exact figures are hardly available, but in 2008 in Africa alone, the minimum area of such "colonies" was estimated at 34 million hectares: the size of Finland or two Uruguays.[15] The highest concentration of new farmlands is in sub-Saharan countries where people suffer the most from hunger and thirst.

According to tentative and announced agreements, the area of farmland leased by foreign companies in the basin of the Nile, Africa's longest river, will increase to 10 million hectares within the next few years.[16] Ethiopia is the "leader" of the new colonization: since 2008, the Ethiopian government has leased 3.6 million hectares of land to investors from India, China and Saudi Arabia, and plans to increase this figure by another 7.5 million hectares in the coming years. Sudan and South Sudan have concluded contracts for irrigated farming for a total of 8.3 million hectares. Uganda plans to irrigate an additional 1 million hectares of land.[17] Although contracts do not bind investors to engage in farming, prospects for fully exploiting these lands are minimal. According to estimates by the Food and Agricultural Organization, the Nile's irrigation potential is not more than 8 million hectares,[18] irrespective of when the leased land will be developed. Obviously, the river's waters will not be enough even for five countries in its basin (Egypt, Sudan, South Sudan, Ethiopia, and Uganda) which plan to irrigate 8.6 million hectares; meanwhile, the Nile's water resources are shared by eleven countries. Cameroon, Senegal and Niger also actively participate in the competition for foreign lessees. Small tropical countries do not fall behind, either: More than 40 African states are involved in large-scale land lease transactions.

The first "colonizers" were the Persian Gulf states, which back in 1973, during an oil crisis, were faced with a threat of a grain embargo by the US. However, their small populations and large revenues from oil exports, and the favorable situation on world food markets, allowed them to diversify suppliers. The food crisis of 2008-2010, when major food exporters, such as Russia, Argentina, India and Vietnam, limited their export of grain and other products, exacerbated the food security issue and provoked large-scale agro-expansion by Saudi Arabia, the United Arab Emirates, Qatar, Bahrain and Kuwait. Their most attractive targets were countries in Africa (especially Mozambique, Sudan and South Africa) and Southeast Asia (Thailand and Laos – primarily for growing rice, fruit and vegetables).

The Asian giants, China and India, in a bid to adapt to the growing needs of their populations and the growing water shortage, actively joined in the colonization in the 2000s. Although both countries lease land in Southeast Asia, Latin America and even Eastern Europe, the bulk of their investment is made in Africa, where, according to the GRAIN international organization, they invest in multibillion-dollar projects.[19] Japan, Korea and Singapore also actively participate in the new colonization. Developed countries, however, prefer to do business with countries where property rights are better protected and lease land mainly in BRICS countries: China, Brazil and South Africa.

According to estimates shared by Prof. David Zetland of Leiden University, two-thirds of present-day transactions in Africa are made by large agro-holdings, and the other third by financial investors and sovereign wealth funds.[20] It should be noted that developing and developed countries pursue different goals: The former want guarantees for their food security, while the latter seek to ensure high yields for their investors. Therefore, investors who want to reap maximum profits are interested in higher prices. After the food crisis of 2008-2010 and the ensuing growth of prices for basic food commodities, Western institutional investors (particularly pension funds) have been playing an increasing role in this segment.

For those who are interested in the food security of their own country, the amount of available food is the decisive factor. Therefore, the costs of growing food may even exceed the market average: Control over supplies remains the main aspect.

Today, only four companies dominate the food market, and all of them are in the jurisdiction of Western countries (the owners of these companies are among the most influential members of US and West European elites). These companies are Archer Daniels Midland, Bunge, Cargill and Louis Dreyfus. They control 70% to 90% of basic food commodities. The food and territorial expansion of developing countries clearly demonstrates their desire to revise the existing system in global food markets and strengthen their national food sovereignty not by extracting valuable resources (land, water and energy) from the national economy but by using the farmland and water resources of poor producing countries.

Some experts view the direct investments of developing countries, above all China, in leasing and purchasing land in Africa and Latin America as an attempt to challenge the hegemony of Western powers in virtual water trade. Economic competition has acquired a political dimension: Control of virtual water is becoming a source of power and influence.

Virtual Water in Industry and Power Engineering

Since agriculture is very important for developing and the least-developed countries, they pay less attention to trade in virtual water as the water footprint of industrial products. However, the added value of water is much higher in this case. Meanwhile, the water intensity of an industry may differ substantially in various countries, and this difference is even greater if we calculate the amount of water used in energy production. The industries using the greatest amounts of water are petrochemistry, metallurgy, pulp and paper production, and power engineering. As a result, available sources of fresh water become a major restraint for the growth of water-intensive industries in developing and the least-developed countries, even despite the presence of specialized resources.

The development of shale gas production offers a good example of how water can become a resource constraint for the economy. This technology requires much water, without the possibility of its reuse. The absence of reserve fresh water resources is viewed as a major limitation for shale gas production in China, and many experts believe this factor was among the informal arguments during Russian-Chinese negotiations on a gas contract, held on May 21, 2014.

Trade in virtual water as the water footprint of foodstuffs or industrial products has become global. At the regional level, virtual water is more important in terms of energy, which may be hydropower, thermal or nuclear power. The construction of hydroelectric dams is becoming one of the most common causes of acute international conflicts over water resources. At the same time, the sale of electricity to third countries is the best guarantee of stable water use in the international water basin.

It often happens that the export of electricity from a hydroelectric power plant, the construction of which was strongly denounced by other countries in the basin, helps to remove or alleviate international tensions. China, for example, pursues this strategy on the Mekong River, while the purchase by Kazakhstan of hydropower from Kyrgyzstan (on the Chu and Talas Rivers) is the only successful example of water-energy barter trade in Central Asia. Ethiopia, which is building a coalition to revise Nile water quotas and is planning to build Africa's largest dam, uses cheap electricity export as leverage in negotiations with neighbors. The high cooperation potential in power engineering is due to the fact that, in this case, both the country upstream and an importing country downstream are interested in establishing a water discharge regime and water intake quotas.

Building dams gives upstream countries significant political leverage, allowing them to "blackmail" neighbors by threatening to restrict water and electricity supply, which directly impacts not only on agriculture but also industries and infrastructure.

Water Use Potential in Russia's International Strategy

Russia is the world's second largest country in terms of renewable water resources. It has Baikal, the largest freshwater lake in the world.

Russia has more than 120,000 rivers that are at least 10 kilometers long; their total length is 2.3 million km. Russia's renewable water resources are estimated at 4,202 cubic kilometers. Seventy-one percent of this amount belongs to the Arctic Ocean basin; 14% belongs to the Pacific Ocean basin; 10% to the Caspian Sea basin; and only 5% to the Black, Azov and Baltic Sea basins combined. Surface inflows from surrounding countries account for only 185 cu.km., or 4.5% of all renewable water resources in Russia.[21]

Although water supply in Russia's southern and southwestern regions is much smaller than in Siberia (2,000 cu.m. vs. 120,000 to 190,000 cu.m. per capita a year), it is still almost twice as big as that in the Mekong basin (about 1,000 to 1,100 cu.m.) and it exceeds the world average (1,370 cu.m.) by 50%. Russia's water infrastructure is believed to be the longest in the world, and the country is a world leader in terms of number of dams: More than 300 large dams and over 3,000 small and medium-sized dams were built in Russia in the 20th century.[22]

This wealth is undoubtedly a strategic asset, which Russia uses only tactically. Russia does not have a position of its own on the international water agenda.

Table 1 shows water withdrawal by sector for countries with the largest annual water intake. India, China and the US are the top three leaders: Their high demand for water is due to their huge populations (2.9 billion people) and their leading economies (4th, 2nd and 1st places in the world, respectively). Russia is 10th in this list.

Russia's annual water intake is 66 million cu.km., which is a mere 1.5% of the country's renewable resources. Russia has a nonstandard sectoral structure of water intake: Industry accounts for 60% of water intake, of which 80% (30.5 million cu.km.) goes to power (predominantly nuclear power) engineering; agriculture accounts for only 20% (as most Russian regions do not use irrigated farming and advanced technologies); and another 20% is used for municipal water supply – Russia is among the world's top 10 water consumers in this respect and is even ahead of Japan, with 19%.

In terms of the "profitability" of water in the economy, the situation is as follows. The Japanese economy is the most efficient at using water: Each used cubic meter contributes $55.7 to the country's GDP. The US is second with $23.5. Figures for other countries range from $0.6 (Pakistan) to $8.6 (Mexico). In Russia, each cubic meter of

TABLE 1. Water withdrawal by sector for countries with the largest annual water intake, average for 2000-2012 (cubic kilometers per capita)

Country	Water intake, cubic km/yr	Share of water intake in renewable resources, %	Water intake, cubic km per capita/yr	Public utilities, %	Industries, %	Agriculture, %	Population, 2012, mln people	$ to GDP/cubic m
India	661	45.7	575	7	2	91	1,148	1.2
China	545	19.4	417	10	21	69	1,344	4.5
US	477	16.9	1,605	13	46	41	312	23.5
Pakistan	176	72.0	1,099	4	2	94	177	0.6
Iran	92	71.7	1,313	6	1	93	75	1.4
Japan	90	20.9	706	19	18	63	128	55.7
Indonesia	113	5.6	496	12	7	82	242	2.1
Mexico	77	18.9	719	14	9	77	115	8.6
Philippines	80	16.7	931	8	10	83	95	1.5
Russia	66	1.5	461	20	60	20	143	5.7

SOURCES: Worldwater.org, databank.worldbank.org, FAO AQUASTAT

water earned $5.7 in the 2000s. Water profitability in China is only slightly less than in Russia ($4.5), while its water intake is eight times as large as that of Russia. However, reserves for increasing the efficiency of water use in the Russian economy have not only a financial but also a commodity dimension.

As for the productivity of agriculture (specifically water in agriculture), there is great potential for growth: According to La Via Campesina, an international peasants' movement, if the productivity of Russian small private farms extends to the entire sector, the annual productivity of agriculture would increase sixfold![23] By way of comparison, such extrapolation in Kenya would only double productivity, and in Hungary, it would increase it by 30%. The high water intake in the municipal sector is due to the inefficiency of outdated systems and high water losses. Since 2009, the Russian government has sought to overcome this backwardness by proposing several initiatives aimed at modernizing water supply and water treatment systems. However, these programs have not reached their goals yet, although efforts are being made at both the federal and regional levels. Foreign investors, too, have begun to show interest in this sphere, but their activity is largely limited by institutional barriers, the nontransparency of the tariff-setting system, and inefficient management of the existing water canal system.

Paradoxically, Russia is one of the few countries in the world where the water factor is not felt by society as a structural factor. As a result, Russia occupies a disproportionately small place in the global virtual water market, considering the possibilities it has. Russia's average net export of virtual water is 4.2 billion cubic meters a year, whereas that of Canada, which has similar climatic and hydrological conditions, is 12.5 times larger, standing at 52.5 billion cubic meters.[24]

The bulk of Russia's net exports go to the Middle East and North Africa, where it traditionally sells its grain. It is only in these regions that Russia plays an important role as a guarantor of their food security, and in some cases political security. The aforementioned embargo of 2010 was one of the factors that caused the Arab Spring in Egypt.

Meanwhile, Russia may also have similar influence in Asia-Pacific countries, as China, the Association of Southeast Asian Nations (ASEAN) countries (which become increasingly dependent on China), and developed Asian countries – Japan and Korea – are interested in importing Russian foodstuffs. The demand for external sources of food security exists in all countries of the region: China, ASEAN, Japan, and Korea have already taken measures to this effect. In 2014, China published the No. 1 Central Document, in which the Chinese Communist Party Central Committee prioritized the strengthening of national food security and support for agriculture amid a worsening environmental situation.[25] ASEAN has four-year food security plans, and it has adopted the ASEAN Integrated Food Security Framework and the Strategic Plan of Action on Food Security.[26] The Japanese Cabinet in 2010 adopted a new Basic Plan for Food, Agriculture and Rural Areas, which set the goal of increasing the food self-sufficiency ratio from 40% to 50% by 2020.[27] Korea, which imports more than 90% of its food, attaches primary importance to agro-colonization. The country leases more than 1 million hectares of land, nearly half of all arable land, in Madagascar, and more than 300,000 hectares in Mongolia. In all, Korean food-importing conglomerates operate in 16 countries.[28]

As of 2014, however, Russia has been a net importer of virtual water as the water footprint of foodstuffs from the Asia-Pacific (imports exceed exports by a factor of four and amount to 5,277 million cu.m. in transactions with nine major trading partners).[29] Even if we add industrial products, the virtual water trade balance would improve only with some of these countries.

Russia can significantly improve its position in the Asia-Pacific if it acts as a guarantor of the region's food and water security. Over the post-Soviet years, the area of irrigated farming in Russia has decreased by more than 20%.[30] Considering the possibility of bringing new areas into high-technology farming, we can say that more than 30 million hectares of land in the country are now misused. Meanwhile, over the same years, the worldwide average area of arable land per capita has decreased by 50%.[31]

Regional hydropower markets also remain largely untapped in Russia. Increasing hydropower export to China would be a necessary step for effective management of the common international basin.

The aforementioned initiatives have obvious limitations, such as low population density in areas east of the Urals, poorly developed infrastructure, and harsh climatic conditions. Russia could use the experience of Canada and Australia, which have vast territories (the world's second and sixth largest, respectively) and relatively small populations but have built high-tech economies based on access to unique natural resources.

***

Strategic opportunities for Russia lie precisely in the market of global and regional trade in water-intensive products, as Russia has the greatest potential in agriculture and water-intensive industries amid the growing shortages of water, arable land and energy in both developed and developing countries.

It would therefore be advisable for the government to gear its policy in certain regions toward attracting strategic foreign investors capable and willing to introduce advanced technologies in agriculture, rather than producing only virgin raw materials for processing abroad. This practice has been relatively effective only in the European part of Russia. Exports to several Asia-Pacific countries would be an indispensable prerequisite for effective development of water-intensive industries in Siberia and the Russian Far East. Only then could we speak of using water resources as a strategic political resource.

Notes

1. "Tkachov: Rossiya mozhet eksportirovat v Kitai pshenicu i presnuyu vodu" [Tkachov: Russia may export wheat and fresh water to China], *Regnum*, May 3, 2016, https://regnum.ru/news/economy/2127744.html.

2. "Sovetnik Putina uvidel dokhody byudzheta v vode" [Putin's adviser discovered budget income in water], *Lenta.ru*, May 5, 2016, https://lenta.ru/news/2016/05/05/glaziev/.

3. Luzhkov, Yury. *Voda i mir* [Water and peace]. Moscow: Moskovskiye Uchebniki, 2008.

4. "MER: Rossiya mozhet stat eksporterom presnoi vody" [Ministry of Economic Development: Russia may become a net exporter of fresh water], *MK.ru*, December 25, 2013, https://www.mk.ru/economics/2013/12/25/964294-mer-rossiya-mozhet-stat-eksporterom-presnoy-vodyi.html.

5. Danilov-Danilyan, V.V. "Globalny vodny krizis i rol Rossii v ego razreshenii" [The global water crisis and Russia's role in its resolution], *Geopoliticheskiye issledovaniya*, 1(1), 2009.

6. "Questions and Answers About Large Dams," *International Rivers*, https://www.internationalrivers.org/questions-and-answers-about-large-dams.

7. Danilov-Danilyan, V.V., *op. cit.*

8. Allan, John Anthony and Allan, Tony. *The Middle East water question: Hydropolitics and the global economy*. London and New York: I.B. Tauris, 2002.

9. UNCTAD Statistics, https://unctad.org/en/pages/statistics.aspx.

10. Mekonnen, M.M., and Hoekstra, A.J. *National water footprint accounts: the green, blue and grey water footprint of production and consumption*. (Value of water research report series 50). Delft, the Netherlands: UNESCO-IHE, 2011.

11. The Water Footprint Network, https://waterfootprint.org/en/.

12. Mazlum, İbrahim. "ISIS as an Actor Controlling Water Resources in Syria and Iraq." In Oktav, Ö., Parlar, Dal E., Kurşun, A., eds. *Violent Non-state Actors and the Syrian Civil War*. Springer Publishing, 2018, 10.1007/978-3-319-67528-2_6.

13. Allan, John Anthony, ed. *Handbook of land and water grabs in Africa: Foreign direct investment and food and water security*. Routledge, 2012.

14. *Ibid.*

15. Zetland, D. and Möller-Gulland, J. "The political economy of land and water grabs," *PERC Research Paper*, 12-21, 2012.

16. "Squeezing Africa Dry: Behind every land grab is a water grab," *GRAIN Report*. 2012, http://www.grain.org/article/entries/4516-squeezing-africa-dry-behind-every-land-grab-is-a-water-grab.

17. *Ibid.*

18. "Irrigation potential in Africa: A basin approach," *FAO*, 1997, http://www.fao.org/docrep/w4347e/w4347e00.htm.

19. "Squeezing Africa Dry," *op. cit.*

20. Zetland, D., *op. cit.*

21. FAO Aquasat, http://www.fao.org/nr/water/aquastat/countries_regions/RUS/.

22. *Ibid.*

23. Vidal, J. "Hungry for land," *The Guardian*. May 28, 2014, http://www.theguardian.com/environment/2014/may/28/farmland-food-security-small-farmers.

24. Mekonnen, M.M. and Hoekstra A.J., *op. cit.*

25. "No. 1 Central Document targets rural reform," *Xinhua*, http://news.xinhuanet.com/english/china/2014-01/19/c_133057121.htm.

26. ASEAN Integrated Food Security Framework; Strategic Plan of Action on Food Security in the ASEAN Region, http://www.gafspfund.org/sites/gafspfund.org/files/documents/cambodia_11_of_16_regional_strategy_asean_integrated_food_security_framework.pdf.

27. Key Points in the Basic Plan for Food, Agriculture and Rural Areas, www.maff.go.jp/e/pdf/basic_plan.pdf.

28. Allan, John Anthony, ed., *op. cit.*

29. Likhachova, Anastasia and Makarov, Igor. "Virtual water of the Russian Far East for Asia-Pacific: Local Efficiency Vs Regional Sustainability," *WP BRP Series: International Relations*, 2014.

30. FAP AQUASTAT, Country Profile, http://www.fao.org/nr/water/aquastat/countries_regions/RUS/index.stm.

31. Likhachova, Anastasia, Savelieva, Alina and Makarov, Igor. "Daily Bread and Water," *Russia in Global Affairs*, 8(3), 2010, pp. 82-93, https://eng.globalaffairs.ru/number/Daily-Bread-and-Water-15003.

PART TWO

Tactics and Interactions: Falling Into the Same Traps

PART TWO

2.1. Countering Terrorism

LEARNING TO FIGHT INTERNATIONAL TERRORISM

Anatoly Adamishin

The former cold war enemies are still more preoccupied with the tug-of-war between themselves than with combating the new threats. How many more times will we repeat the same mistakes in choosing our priorities?

The main fact about international terrorism is a sad one: The civilized world is losing its war against terrorism despite its seemingly overwhelming superiority. This conclusion is shared by most policymakers and analysts. It is backed by the huge and snowballing number of victims. The cold-blooded murder of children in the Russian town of Beslan has imparted a new, more ominous dimension to terrorism. Yet, the international community is far from united in the face of this new threat. I would even say it still has a somewhat carefree attitude toward it. "Terrorist acts are inevitable, as they are an age-old weapon used by the weak in their struggle against the strong," some politicians reassure themselves. "Terrorism cannot be defeated, just as it is impossible to eradicate evil." However, this postulate, which rather belongs to the domain of psychology, can hardly apply to what is now described – for the sake of brevity rather than accuracy – as

This article originally appeared in *Russia in Global Affairs* Vol. 2, No. 4, 2004.

international terrorism. No doubt, it is a unique phenomenon that has become an integral part of the present stage in the development of civilization, described – again, for the sake of brevity – as globalization.

Lesson 1

The common struggle against international terrorism is impeded by the vagueness of the enemy: It often has no face. Moreover, there is an influential view that declaring war on international terrorism, as the US has done, was a mistake. Proponents of this view argue that there is no globalized terror because it has no national or territorial basis. There are so-called regional terrorisms that have almost no links with one another, they say. Behind these organizations are various political forces pursuing various goals such as separatism, transnational organized crime (usually in the form of drug trafficking) and religious extremism. Each force has its own reasons for resorting to terrorism. What link is there between, for example, the Irish Republican Army, the Corsican separatists and Japan's Aum Shinrikyo sect? They have no common headquarters coordinating their terrorist activities. Or take Al Qaeda, which seeks to take credit even for bombings it has had no hand in. It is political motivation that each time predetermines the suitable ways for neutralizing terror. But war, as a universal means, always leads to one country invading another and, consequently, to a fierce rebuff of the invaders and collaborationists. The times of colonialism and neo-colonialism are over.

The rationale of such reasoning is difficult to dispute. But it is also obvious that the aforementioned categories of terrorism intertwine in real life, forming various kinds of combinations, with one type of terrorism prevailing over another. This is what is happening in Kosovo, for example. It is possible that the trend toward separatism there will create a very negative precedent.

Or take Afghanistan. There, the counterterrorist coalition has carried out an operation against Taliban extremists that is believed to have been quite successful. At the same time, however, no decisive blow was delivered against the drug barons. The coalition lacked an orderly approach, and the drug business was not suppressed. Now, together with its revival, the Taliban is reviving, too. Incidentally, a very large part of the 3,000 metric tons of opium[1] produced in Afghanistan each year is trafficked to other countries via Russia.

It is true that terrorism is a method. But when, in the contemporary world, it is widely used to suppress intellect and distort human consciousness en masse, it is already more than just a tool. It is an ideology, now proliferating around the world.

In light of these facts, is there a danger of overlooking the merger of separate terrorist groups into an army, even if this is done by non-traditional methods? And how much time remains before such an army is controlled, if not from one, then several centers? This army could simply be inspired by such an idea, which is now beginning to prevail more and more over local considerations. Where there is a common idea, sooner or later there will appear a common strategy, and this strategy is taking an increasingly distinct shape. Radical Islamism has been coming into the foreground ever more confidently. Its recent strikes at Russia and at the unity of its multiethnic population were delivered with strategic accuracy.

The theory of regional terrorism has yet another shortcoming. In practice, it prevents people from uniting into a single front against the unseen yet very dangerous enemy. Deflecting the threat away from oneself and causing it to turn against someone else looks more attractive than struggling against this threat jointly: "If this does not concern me directly, I can sit it out and save myself." Hence the advances made to "semi-terrorists" and the tolerant attitude toward various kinds of foundations and associations that provide money and shelter to criminals. Double standards – old as the world – flourish amid such practices and only serve to abet terrorists. There have even been cases when terrorists' demands were fulfilled. If the choice is made in favor of a policy of appeasement (a kind of 1938 Munich Pact of the 21st century), then the chances for losing the war against terrorism will increase. A large proportion of Europeans are simply unwilling to take part in it, considering it someone else's war.

This dilemma can be resolved by taking steps along two avenues. First, the UN should speed up its analytical efforts to find a generally acceptable definition for international terrorism. The India-proposed draft of a Comprehensive Convention on International Terrorism could help achieve accord on this issue.

On the other hand, time is pressing, and it is not necessary to wait until all countries come to an agreement on the definition of terrorism – a highly politicized problem closely linked to national-ism. A wide range of measures have already been worked out for in-ternational interaction in combating terrorism, and these measures must be used without delay.

Lesson 2

The former cold war enemies are still more preoccupied with the tug-of-war between themselves than with combating the new threats. Each new terrorist act causes them to make certain steps toward each other, both bilaterally and multilaterally (within the frameworks of the UN, the Group of Eight, NATO and the Euro-pean Union). A short time later, however, their zeal for cooperation subsides and they return to their accustomed mutual mistrust. Both parties provide justifications for their actions, of course, but how many more times will they repeat the same mistakes in choosing their priorities? Hopefully, after the Beslan tragedy, the enthusiasm for cooperation will not decrease among the parties.

During the cold war era, it was unscrupulous methods that pro-moted the spread of Islamic jihad. In those times, as a French jour-nalist put it, the US struck a deal with the devil known as Muslim extremism. This was done to the detriment of its relations with more moderate circles, with the only intention being to harm the Soviet Union. Unfortunately, many of those who advised Ronald Reagan at that time have not quit big-time politics but have joined the ranks of the neo-conservatives in the US. Similarly, some critical words could be said against Russia, too.

The old differences between Russia and the West have been coupled with differences inside the Euro-Atlantic community. Washington gives priority to the war against Islamist terrorist groups and countries supporting them or giving them shelter. Europeans argue that terrorism can be stopped with "soft force," by combining political and policing methods and using military force only as a last resort. Russia, which is waging its own war in Chechnya, ini-tially gravitated toward the European approach. This was graphically manifest in its appraisal of the US's actions in Iraq. Now, however, Russia has toughened its position.

In 2002, I wrote in *Russia in Global Affairs*: "The former enemies in the cold war must become seriously aware of the fact that their very survival depends on their ability to address new dangers." These words, perhaps, are even more important today, especially if we add the words "and allies" to the word "enemies." Stopping the discord within the civilized community has become an imperative.

The best way to unite the approaches of various countries is for them to engage in practical work coordinating their counterterrorist efforts. Russia, the US, the EU and its individual members, Japan, India, China and Israel must display the political will that would allow them to proceed to a basically new level of cooperation.

In practice, they may take the following measures:
- establish closer and more trusting relations between their special services;
- agree on mutual supplies of modern equipment and armaments (Russia, with its huge territory and extensive transportation systems, including pipelines, desperately needs to overhaul its counterterrorist defenses);
- expose and shut down channels of funding to terrorist organizations;
- carry out joint operations to hunt down and detain terrorists;
- take military measures, including the joint training of troops (moreover, the allies may wish to consider building joint bases and forming joint special forces).

The US and Russia should set an example of such alliance-like cooperation; they have advanced along this path farther than many other countries. The two countries have set up a special high-level counterterrorism working group that has already held more than a dozen fruitful meetings. Russian-US achievements also include some successful field operations. But this is not enough. The two countries' efforts are impeded by their mutual inability to concentrate on what is most important.

The US and Russia need to stop complaining about how difficult one partner is for the other, as well as publicly lecturing each other – not because Russia and the US do not need this, but because these complaints and didacticism are producing an unwanted effect. The parties seem to forget that there has emerged the most dangerous common enemy since World War II. In those times, the members of the anti-Hitler coalition had many disagreements with each other (suffice it to recall the heated debates about the need to open a second front), suspected each other of attempting to enter into separate negotiations with the Nazis, and adhered to diametrically opposed ideological values that formally ruled out any coexistence of socialism and capitalism on the earth. However, the main result of World War II – the defeat of Nazi Germany – was achieved owing to the joint actions of many countries, above all the Soviet Union and the US.

Terrorism has already become a horrible monster, and the international community has yet to find an antidote against the monstrous "discovery" of suicide bombers. The terrorists' inventiveness, severe discipline, mafia-style methods of influencing the population and relatively inexpensive operations all serve to increase the destructive effectiveness of their activities. And it is horrible to even imagine what would happen to the world should terrorists achieve their long-cherished goal of acquiring weapons of mass destruction. The very thought must certainly cause world leaders to cast aside trifling issues in order to ensure the reliable protection of nuclear, chemical, biological and other weapons from criminals. In this context, Russia needs real help from its Western partners, above all the US. So far, this help (about $780 million a year)[2] does not nearly correspond to the scale of the task of destroying weapons and preventing their seizure.

Lesson 3

The international community should amend its counterterrorism legislation by coordinating national laws as much as possible to create a homogeneous legal framework. At present, national counterterrorism laws vary significantly, especially regarding the principles of extradition. A legal environment where any terrorist act is inevitably punished has not yet emerged.

Furthermore, the international community has yet to define situations where the use of outside force to stop genocide and human rights violations in a given country would be justified. One of the main questions concerns the legal basis and mechanism for implementing such measures. Moreover, the very principle of sovereignty must be rethought, because its former absolute character has become archaic. The new agenda must also include the possibility of establishing international trusteeship over states whose governments are unable to fulfill their functions.

Lesson 4

Since the current struggle is for people's minds, especially the minds of the younger generation, it is vital that the international community strengthen the climate for the total rejection of terrorism. This absolute evil cannot be justified by political, religious or other reasons; there cannot be "good" or "bad" terrorism. There must be no room for neutrality or appeasement in the struggle against terrorism, and the international public at large must be rallied against terrorism. Civil societies in various countries must play a decisive role in these efforts.

Lesson 5

It is of paramount importance to distinguish religious fanaticism, which sometimes acquires inhuman forms, from religion per se. This refers, above all, to Islam. Analysts who have begun to harken back to Europe's past experience of fascism, only dressed in Islamic clothing, are mistaken. Italian Fascism and German Nazism developed within the frameworks of their national borders, while Islamic extremism is just a small part of the fairly civilized Muslim world. Also mistaken are those who argue that Islam does not accept modern economic development and is a stranger to democracy. Indonesia, Turkey and Malaysia provide good indications that reforms in the Islamic world are possible. This is a common civilizational task.

The view that we are witnessing a clash of civilizations must be dispelled. This requires modernizing the vast Muslim world and redressing injustices, such as the Israeli-US persecution of Palestinians, which is viewed as a crusade against the Islamic world. There will be little hope for deliverance from the plague of terrorism unless peace is established in the Middle East.

Islam should not be demonized; instead, people must learn to separate the wheat from the extremist chaff. Also, Al Qaeda must not be made a spokesperson for all oppressed Muslim. Radicalism is baneful in any religion and, unfortunately, there have been many occasions when Judaic and Christian fundamentalists, too, behaved as if they alone knew the ultimate truth and must affirm it whatever the cost – even by the sword.

Lesson 6

Military actions alone, however inevitable under certain circumstances, cannot solve the problem. Developments in Iraq and Chechnya have shown that such actions only aggravate it. Politics cannot completely entrust its mission to war. The approaches of both the US and Russia need major revision.

Meanwhile, the difficult problems of inequality, backwardness, instability, the decline of many countries, drug trafficking and many other plagues of the contemporary world are now knocking at the door of humanity. When will the international community find time to begin draining away this nutrient medium of terrorism?

Lesson 7

Organizational frameworks are required for coordinating states' efforts to uncover and eradicate international terrorist networks.

The world, which has left the state of relative stability of the cold war era (sometimes described as negative stability), is now passing through a zone of turbulence; it is unstable and uncontrollable, which encourages a struggle for control over it.

These developments again bring the UN into the limelight as the only universal forum, as the keeper of international law, and as the organization (i.e., its Security Council) authorized to address issues of war and peace. It should be admitted, though, that the UN is not coping with this task. In the fundamental issue of preventive war against Iraq, the Americans simply ignored the Security Council, thus damaging themselves and the international organization. Yet, the UN, too, bears part of the blame, because it should not live according to a charter that was drawn up 60 years ago. The vacuum in international rules, filled by unilateral actions, must be removed in a legal way – by jointly developing new norms of conduct.

Major UN member states seem to have come to understand that this organization must be reformed. Yet efforts in this field are experiencing no progress. Along with providing new impetus to the UN's restructuring, the international community should set up a special international organization to help countries cope with the new challenges and threats. Although there already is the Counter-Terrorism Committee of the UN Security Council, it is largely engaged in monitoring the fulfillment of UN resolutions, of which there are already quite a few. The new special organization must enable countries to promptly react to a wide range of challenges – from preventing terrorist acts to dealing with their aftermath.

The problems the international community is facing in combating this invisible and merciless enemy are colossal. Yet technically they are surmountable. Presently, what countries are lacking most of all is the awareness of the danger, and political will. It is time that we begin to learn from our own – occasionally tragic – mistakes.

Notes

1. "Afghanistan Opium Survey 2003," October 2003. *United Nations Office on Drug and Crimes*, p. 6, https://www.unodc.org/documents/crop-monitoring/ Afghanistan/Afghanistan_survey_2003_full_report.pdf.

2. US State Dept., Press Release, Nov. 17, 2004, https://2001-2009.state.gov/p/ inl/rls/prsrl/spbr/38352.htm.

A NO-COMPROMISE WAR

Yevgeny Satanovsky

Islamists are not waiting for concessions from the Russian Federation or any other country they are fighting. They simply want to destroy the country and its citizens: atheists and believers, Muslims and non-Muslims.

Is Russian society prepared to counter terrorism? This question begs an answer every time Russian politicians, experts, journalists or ordinary citizens discuss – in diplomatic or crude language, in informal conversations or in front of TV cameras – the past events in Beslan, Budyonnovsk and Moscow. There are many oppressive factors that create fertile ground for political analysts and consultants to make various kinds of apocalyptic forecasts: confusion, xenophobia, a readiness to point an accusing finger at anyone (even at professionals who save people's lives), and mutual mistrust between the authorities and the population, including Muslims and non-Muslims, Russians and non-Russians.

Three components can, if acted upon simultaneously, provide a positive answer to the aforementioned question: an understanding of exactly what is happening, readiness for action and an ability to make

This article originally appeared in *Russia in Global Affairs* Vol. 3, No. 1, 2005.

adequate decisions as new situations arise. The main thing here is to understand what Russia has come up against. Who are its enemies and allies? What moves should it make to endure the trial by terrorism? What actions should it not take under any circumstances?

The Offensive of the 'Green International'

First, it must be said that contemporary terrorism has come to stay – for decades rather than years. We must learn to live with this evil, treating it like, say, an epidemic or a traffic jam. Apart from special systems that make up a large part of contemporary civilization, there are sets of rules, known to everyone since childhood, that help a person to survive a car crash, for example, or avoid getting ill. If a person does fall ill, he or she needs the knowledge of how to treat the condition. Not all people observe these rules, and those who do not have only themselves to blame. The survival of a country that has faced terrorism largely depends on how soon these rules are worked out and become part of the national culture.

Israel's experience is very indicative in this respect. The Palestinian leadership planned the Al-Aqsa Intifada, which included the unprecedented use of suicide bombers, to inflict a defeat on either Israeli society or the Israeli Army. It was expected that, with losses estimated at 1:3, Israel would simply cease to exist; the number of Israelis wishing to leave the country would exceed the number of immigrants and the natural population growth. Moreover, the Palestinians expected a retaliatory strike from the Israeli Defense Forces, which would result in the death of tens of thousands of people. Such losses could allow Palestine to accuse Israel of using excessive force. This could result in the deployment of a European Union peacekeeping force, as was the case in Yugoslavia.

However, none of those scenarios has actually taken place. Although the ratio of Israeli losses amounted to 1:2, Israeli society united; Israeli leftists, who were consistent allies of Yasser Arafat, suffered a crushing defeat in parliamentary elections; the Israeli Army implemented the tactics of targeted elimination of terrorist leaders. Israel continued to live and develop despite the terror. This provides a good example for Russia to follow.

The politically correct words that terrorism knows neither nationality nor religion are effective at stopping ethnic or religious paranoia, but they are not right per se. Terrorists operating on Russian territory cannot be called the Basque separatist group ETA, the Irish Republican Army, the Maoist-Trotskyist guerillas from Southeast Asia or Latin America, the Red Brigades from Italy, or the Aum Shinrikyo sect from Japan. The suicide bombers killing Russian civilians have a direct relation to the Green International. This informal military-political association is redividing power in the Islamic world and seeks to influence Muslims beyond its boundaries. It is striving to extend its influence on the outside world as much as possible through aggressive religious, ideological, political and territorial expansion.

Terrorist acts can be committed by people of any nationality. However, the war that has been going on in the North Caucasus for the last 10 years has caused the Russian population and international observers to associate Russian terrorism almost exclusively with developments in Chechnya. The Green International could currently be much more involved in the war against Russia if it had not dissipated its forces and resources among numerous "fronts" of the new jihad, in particular in Iraq. This is particularly true as the core of Islamist terrorist organizations comprises Afghan Arabs who have been in a state of war with Moscow since 1980. In the Caucasus, Islamists, who have a 25-year-long record of guerilla warfare and terrorist acts, have revived the tactics that were used in Afghanistan in the 1980s. When committing terrorist acts, they employ Palestinian suicide-bomber "technologies." The practice of mass hostage-taking has also been borrowed from foreign experience.

Russia's Main Line of Resistance

According to the logic of the leaders and participants in the terrorist war against Russia (waged in the name of the neo-Salafist teaching known as Wahhabism), Russian Muslims, including local leaders, religious figures and the civil population, must either obey its dogmas or be destroyed. That is why they are priority targets for Islamists. It is Russian Muslims, primarily representatives of the ethnic elite, including Vainakhs (Chechens and Ingush), that may become Russia's main line of resistance in the war against the terrorist threat. This line of resistance could eventually include a terror warning system.

Xenophobia and the activities of anti-Caucasus and anti-Muslim groups, including skinheads, only play into the terrorists' hands and help them consolidate their position. The problem is that, despite the constant rhetoric of "proletarian internationalism" in Soviet times, the probability of serious ethnic conflicts has persisted in Russia for decades. The Central Committee of the Soviet Communist Party played the role of supreme arbiter in ethnic relations. No one could have imagined back then that this arbiter might eventually disappear; and when it ceased to exist, the system collapsed.

Russia has always been populated by hundreds of nationalities and ethnic groups practicing different religions, speaking different languages and preserving their own ways of life. Russia is therefore destined to remain a multiethnic state, and the issue of "the national pride of the Great Russians" is now as acute as it was in Lenin's times. The Soviet nationalities policy was imperfect, bad in many respects and sometimes even horrible, but at least it did exist. The 1990s saw a period of general disillusionment with the past and the emergence of numerous local nationalisms in place of the single nationalities policy; this change weakened the country. The understanding of one's neighbors inside a common house could have been a foundation of a solid civil society. This, however, requires direct people-to-people contacts or a permanent information flow that would provide citizens with truthful, positive and appealing information about the country's peoples and religions.

The main question is how to prevent the substitution of traditional Islamic institutions in Russia with Wahhabi structures without turning any restrictions on them or their activities into some sort of a struggle against Islam. Over the last decade, Russia has become an open society with a high degree of religious freedom where differences between the population and the state have been largely resolved. However, this freedom has fostered the emergence of foreign political-religious groups in the religious sphere whose influence has been steadily growing. Russian society has long been discussing whether the activities of these organizations are useful, harmful or dangerous. However, it must be admitted that the only area where society and the state have encountered a direct military-terrorist threat is from adherents of Islam. Loyalty to any state that does not live according to Sharia law runs counter to membership in the Islamic *umma*, as interpreted by Wahhabis. Their views contrast with those who adhere to the dogmas of Christianity or the postulates of Judaism, where the law of the country is law.

This also refers to any nation-state, even if it is populated by Muslims. A Chechen state that does not live according to Sharia law – in its Salafist interpretation – is illegitimate in the eyes of the Islamist community. Political dialogue with Chechen separatist leaders could be a tool for resolving tactical tasks, yet it cannot solve the problem of terrorism, since The Green International views Chechen politicians only as temporary allies. In other words, Chechnya is only part of a future Islamist caliphate, and terrorism exists as the main means for building it. The Wahhabization of Muslims studying at Islamic universities across the Arab world and participating in the *hadj*, which is mandatory for every Muslim, is a serious challenge for Russia. It is fair to say, though, that no country in the West, none of the Arab monarchies and none of the secular authoritarian regimes in the Islamic world have been able to solve this problem.

Noble Rebels or Vagrant Bandits?

The double standards the present political establishment applies to terrorists are the rule rather than an exception. Politicians support national liberation movements – as long as they exist in someone else's country. International organizations have become a tool of the struggle waged by the Third World, largely controlled by Islamists, against the "golden billion." The liberal-minded intelligentsia defends the rights of the oppressed without noticing that the struggle of the "noble rebels" has turned into the destruction of the civilian population by armed bands, while the banner of "multiculturalism" is carried by religious fanatics. There are no exceptions here. Russia's Foreign Ministry and the US State Department, with perseverance worthy of a better application, are developing the "peace process" in the Middle East, which in reality is yet another war in the region. Europe is becoming Islamized, while its leaders pursue anti-Russian and anti-Israeli policies that seek to appease the leaders of terrorist groups based in European capitals. The UN, whose ineffectiveness has prompted loud calls for its renewed role, has for many years been unable to solve a single question it has addressed. The tough statements by the Russian leadership, issued after the tragedy in Beslan, sum up the realities of international politics today: "If you're drowning, you're on your own."

The support of allies and the consolidation of society play a significant role in combating terrorism. Comparing the present danger of terrorism now confronting Russia to World War II is no exaggeration. In the 1980s, the Soviet Union failed to defeat Afghan Islamists who were supported by the West. Today, the West is no longer an ally of the Islamists, yet, at the same time, it has not become Russia's ally. Russia, which is now halfway between the past and the future, is trying to establish order on its territory. This is occurring while the system of power is still being formed and civil society is still in the initial stages of construction. Russia, weakened by 15 years of reforms, is extremely vulnerable, and this vulnerability is further aggravated by the illusions of the political elite.

Conservatives oppose a union with the West, mainly with the US. They somewhat correctly point to the opportunistic nature of Western policies, while pinning hopes on a multipolar world. It is unclear, however, why Russia's relations with, say, India, and especially with China, should have a more solid foundation than Russia's relations with the Group of Seven countries. Furthermore, why should a "new Entente" be more preferable for Russia than a union with the US? The Islamists have proven themselves enemies of all the aforementioned partners of Russia. More difficult is the issue of Russia's relations with the Islamic (above all, Arab) world. The domestic lobby, which acts in the interests of those countries, relies on its recollections of past relations that were established in the 1960s through the 1980s. They are inspired by myths from the Islamic community's ideological arsenal, such as blaming Mossad and the CIA for the 9/11 events, as well as the suggestion that the Western coalition occupied Iraq at Israel's request.

The former Soviet satellites in the Arab world have reoriented themselves to the West; they only cooperate with Russia because they cannot make a bargain with the West. They are using Russia as a bargaining chip in this relationship. The wars in Afghanistan and developments in Chechnya have turned Moscow into a bugbear for the Islamic world. This world despises Russia less than it despises the US, yet it does not consider Russia a force to fear or reckon with. Events in Qatar proved that. Secular regimes and moderate monarchies in the Islamic world are ready to partner with Russia to combat their own Islamists, but they do not want to generate tensions inside their countries. Thus, they avoid taking any actions against anti-Russian forces on their territory. Russia's dialogue with the Organization of the Islamic Conference and similar organizations does nothing to solve the problem. In the eyes of the Islamists, it only confirms the illegitimacy of these organizations, encouraging terrorism rather than stopping it. From the viewpoint of the Islamists, a country courting the Islamic world only because it is weak and unable to put up efficient resistance demonstrates weakness.

Repeating the clichés of the international community, which describes terrorism as a "weapon of the poor," liberals have come to believe that the war in Chechnya was caused only by its economic state. Thus, they advocate terminating all military actions against militants as a necessary condition for protecting the local population's rights. This pacifism is praiseworthy, but theories have no relation to reality: Terrorism is a tool for redistributing power, and it is being used by educated, formerly middleclass men. They use the redistribution of economic aid in favor of "vagrant bandits" (common not only in Sudan, Algeria or Palestine, but also in Chechnya), just as any ceasefire (*hudna*) is used for taking a rest and regrouping forces before resuming hostilities.

The financial and organizational support of Islamist terrorism, and the recruitment of new members, is carried out not only by the Islamic countries, but also from the territory of those states being attacked by the Islamist community. Organizations operating under the brand name Al Qaeda and their allies have taken root in the US and Great Britain, and successfully use the Western banking system to replenish their resources. It has been proven that funds of the EU and other sponsors of the Palestine National Authority are being spent on organizing terrorism. Experts argue that a large part of the money used by terrorists in Chechnya is of Russian origin and comes from funds allocated for Chechnya's reconstruction. Corruption is an ally of terrorists: be it a border guard letting in cars and trucks without following appropriate inspection and verification procedures (for a bribe, of course), or officials milking the national budget.

Coordinating federal and local authorities' efforts is a must for building a counterterrorism system. It is no accident that the Beslan tragedy is viewed as an attempt to extend the Chechen conflict into the entire Great Caucasus and turn the region into a civil war zone, uncontrolled by the federal center.

Reacting as a New Situation Arises

Counterterrorism experience gained by the West and Russian special services over the last few decades – particularly with regard to
hostage-taking, negotiations on their release, etc. – has not proven to
be very useful when dealing with terrorists of the new type: fanatic
suicide bombers. Many experts say that the chances of surviving a
terrorist act committed by a suicide bomber are higher for those who
are ready for an immediate reaction and action, be it an attack or
escape. A high number of potential terrorist acts have been thwarted
in Israel in recent years by such people: waiters, and bus and taxi
drivers with a military service record who immediately reacted to
some imminent danger. Many of the children who escaped from the
school in Beslan when it was seized by terrorists saved their own
lives, unlike some of their schoolmates who followed classical recommendations and did not resist the terrorists.

Another factor that helps counter terrorism is the coordination
of the actions of professionals and authorities, and public support
of these actions. Even professionals cannot work miracles. That is
why the Israeli special forces, when planning a counterterrorism
operation, assume in advance that the death rate among hostages
will be 100%. This approach helps them avoid mistakes that are
caused by the wish to save everybody. Unfortunately, nothing can
ever guarantee the rescue of all hostages. Exceptions to this rule are
very rare, and in those cases involving "mega-terrorism," which Russia has now encountered – and Israel encountered much earlier – it
is virtually ruled out.

Unlike geographically small Israel, the counterterrorism system
in Russia cannot be made uniform throughout the country. Large
and small towns, major industrial centers, villages and special-purpose facilities need their own plans to counter suicide bombers or
groups of terrorists, many of whom are armed and trained every bit
as well as national special services. These plans must consider local
conditions, the state of infrastructure, seasonal weather changes, the
specificity of the local nationality and proximity to combat zones.

At the same time, the main indicator that Russian society understands the problem it faces can be witnessed by its degree of
consolidation, which is similar to the degree of consolidation Israelis or Americans have displayed during their national tragedies.

Countering terrorism cannot be the job of the state or special agencies and organizations alone. Without the participation of broad segments of the population, all counterterrorism efforts would be doomed – if not to defeat, then to the infinite repetition of terrorist acts. How Russian citizens can unite to form a community capable of withstanding an outside threat while keeping its foundation intact is a special subject. I would only like to comment here that at least in two countries of the contemporary world, Britain and Israel, the years-long struggle against terrorism has affected civil freedoms and society's self-perception to a minimal degree.

The most important factor, perhaps, that can help Russia discover the mechanisms for efficiently combating Islamist terror is understanding its nature. Islamists are not waiting for concessions from the Russian Federation or any other country they are fighting. They simply want to destroy the country and its citizens: atheists and believers, Muslims and non-Muslims. Islamists do not consider these individuals to be people and are ready to sacrifice their own lives and the lives of their relatives for a victory in the new jihad, which, in its senseless cruelty, has far exceeded the jihad of the Prophet's times. When fighting such an enemy, compromise is senseless, and the only efficient strategy is to destroy the terrorists before they strike. Creating a mechanism that makes this possible will bring victory.

DEMOGRAPHY AND TERRORIST THREATS

Anatoly Vishnevsky

The problem is not rooted in Islam; it is rooted in the intractable economic and social problems facing the majority of third-world countries. Moreover, the problem is exacerbated by unprecedented population growth and an inevitable transformation of demographic processes.

Some may find the notion of a link between demography and terrorism strange. Is this idea plausible or far-fetched?

The import of my reflections is that the demographic component of what we now call international terrorism (although I am not sure that this is an accurate definition of what is happening today) is very important, yet I certainly do not mean to assert that demographic events and processes alone fuel terrorism. Nevertheless, understanding the essence of global demographic processes has made it possible to foresee the present growth of terrorist threats long before they became a stark reality of our world today.

This article was first published in Russian in *Nezavisimaya gazeta*, Dec. 22, 2015.[1] The English version subsequently appeared in *Russia in Global Affairs* Vol. 14, No. 2, 2016.

The 'Third World' of Alfred Sauvy

From a global perspective, the most obvious link between demography and terrorist threats is the so-called population explosion – i.e., the significantly increased birth rate in the world after World War II. Demographers foresaw a "demographic tsunami" 50 to 70 years ago.

The world's population has always grown very slowly. In the early 19th century, the Earth's population for the first time approached one billion people. In the 18th century, enlightened Europeans argued about whether the European population was growing at all, but by the end of the century it was already clear: It was – and faster than usual. At that time, Thomas Malthus proposed curtailing population growth. However, during the next 150 years, the problem of population growth did not feature prominently in the global agenda, although the world population increased by another 1.5 billion people over that time.

It was only after World War II, when the population of developing countries began to grow rapidly, that signs emerged of potential threats related to demography. Demographers were, perhaps, the first to realize that. It was French demographer Alfred Sauvy who coined the term "Third World" to distinguish this world of rapid population growth from the other two worlds – capitalist and socialist – where nothing like that was happening.

At that time, not everything was clear. In 1950, the world population was 2.5 billion people. According to the first postwar UN forecast (1951), the number of people in the world was expected to increase to 3.3 billion by 1980. Actually, the population exceeded this forecast already in 1965, and in 1980, the number of people on the planet grew to more than 4.4 billion. Nevertheless, in the early 1950s, there were those who understood that unprecedented population growth in the Third World posed a great danger. Sauvy warned that "this ignored, exploited and scorned Third World, like the Third Estate, wants to become something too."[2] This phrase hints at a possible revolt of the Third World – it was no coincidence that it mentions the "third estate" and alludes to a line from "The Internationale:" "We have been nought, we shall be all!"

The reasons for the population explosion were very simple. After World War II, the achievements of modern medicine in the developed world began to spread to developing countries, which led to a rapid decline in mortality rates there. The reproductive behavior of people remained the same and birth rates were high. Fertility and mortality rates went out of balance, but restoring the balance meant reducing birth rates.

Birth rates in Europe used to be high, too, but starting in the 18th century, death rates declined slowly and gradually, and birth rates had enough time to adapt to changes in mortality. However, Europe failed to immediately restore the balance and prevent a population explosion of its own in the 19th century. But this explosion was much weaker. In addition, Europe got rid of much of its excess population by sending great numbers of people to the New World. Given the rate of decline in mortality in developing countries, a special demographic policy needed to be adopted to accelerate a decline in birth rates.

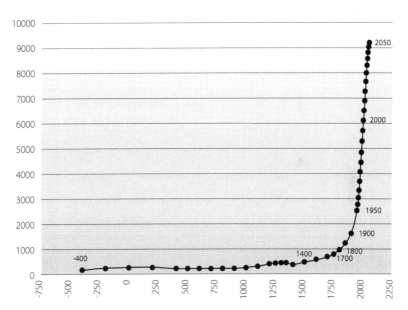

FIG. 1. World population growth from 400 BC to 2050 – UN forecast (mln people)

SOURCES: Jean-Noël Birabin. The History of Human Population from the Very Beginnings to the Present Days // Demography: Analysis and Synthesis. Elsevier, 2006. Vol. III, p. 13; UN Department of Economic and Social Affairs, Population Division (2015). World Population Prospects: The 2015 Revision, DVD Edition.

Demographers and politicians, including leaders of developing countries, grew increasingly aware of the need for a new policy.

However, traditionalist societies resisted those efforts. There was also no unanimity in the two worlds that were particularly threatened by population growth in the Third World.

In particular and contrary to its own interests, the Soviet Union opposed programs designed to reduce birth rates. Here is an excerpt from a typical speech by a high-ranking Soviet official (1969): "On Dec. 10, 1966, 12 states – India, Malaysia, South Korea, Tunisia, Sweden, Yugoslavia, etc. – signed a declaration on the need for a family planning policy. David Rockefeller exerted much effort to collect signatures under this declaration.*** Rockefeller's efforts on the family planning issue are understandable: Large-scale implementation of this policy would bring capitalist monopolies huge profits from the sale of contraceptives.*** The Soviet government, after a thorough discussion of this issue, including at the Academy of Sciences of the USSR, decided not to join the Declaration and stated that purely demographic methods of regulating population dynamics are not essential."[3]

The US position was initially more sober. In 1974, the US National Security Council drafted a memorandum on the implications of worldwide population growth for US security and overseas interests that clearly identified possible threats: "…[W]orld population growth is widely recognized within the (US) Government as a current danger of the highest magnitude calling for urgent measures.*** Population factors are crucial in, and often determinants of, violent conflicts in developing areas. Conflicts that are regarded in primarily political terms often have demographic roots. Recognition of these relationships appears crucial to any understanding or prevention of such hostilities.*** Where population size is greater than available resources, or is expanding more rapidly than the available resources, there is a tendency toward internal disorders and violence and, sometimes, disruptive international policies or violence.*** In developing countries, the burden of population factors, added to others, will weaken unstable governments, often only marginally effective in good times, and open the way for extremist regimes."[4]

However, the US position was also inconsistent. During the Ronald Reagan administration in the 1980s, conservative views prevailed in Washington and were reflected in the activity of American opponents of abortion, although abortion as a family planning tool played a less significant role after the "contraceptive revolution." The

US stopped supporting international family planning programs. But now its position was less important, because increasingly more politicians in developing countries realized the need to reduce birth rates, and those countries adopted corresponding policies.

I will not go into detail about how various countries sought to solve this problem. Everyone is familiar with the experience of China, a country that pursued a strict demographic policy and achieved a fast decline in birth rates, albeit with some unfavorable demographic consequences. Although less well known, Iran's experience is also very instructive.

What 'American Fascism' Sought to Achieve

I was honored to meet with Russian President [Vladimir Putin] during his first term in office. I showed him a list of countries that, according to a UN forecast, could overtake Russia in terms of population. He immediately noted that Iran could be among the first to do so. It was a forecast from 2000, and now we know that it did not materialize and is not likely to happen. Why?

At about the same time, I read the following text on a Russian Orthodox Church Web site: "The Iranian shah was a great friend of the US.*** He launched an active family planning policy in his country. The Ministry of Education revised school curricula, issued new textbooks that now included information on sex and contraception, and retrained teachers to teach sex education. Thousands of highly paid healthcare workers sought to prevent 'unwanted children.' *** But later, the shah was overthrown, and Ayatollah Khomeini fired all family planners, together with their American sponsors. But, alas, those were only isolated cases. One has to admit that, on the whole, American fascism has won."[5]

Apparently, the victory of "American fascism" in this text meant the spread in developing countries of family planning and birth control practices – i.e., the very type of demographic behavior that prevails in all developed countries, including Russia. But if the authors of the text were informed about what they had written, they would have to admit that Iran was where "American fascism" scored its largest victory (after China).

A year after the Islamic Revolution, Ayatollah Khomeini approved the use of contraception in a *fatwa* in 1980. The *fatwa* approved the birth control "as long as the mother and child were not harmed and abortion was excluded."[6] In 1989, Prominent Iranian demographer Mohammad Abbasi-Shavazi wrote: "In December 1989, the Iranian government radically reversed its policy and launched a new family planning program. The latter, according to figures, seems to have been very successful, since the contraceptive prevalence rate (CPR) rose from 37 % in 1976 to about 75% in 2000; in rural areas, the CPR rose from 20 % in 1976 to 72 % in 2000 and in urban areas from 54 % to 82%."[7]

Very soon, birth rates in Iran began to decline rapidly, but it was not the only Islamic country to achieve that. Many people still view Arab Middle Eastern countries as an outpost of high birth rates, but this is already history for most of them. In the 1950s, Israel was the only country in the region with relatively low birth rates. At the beginning of the 21st century, birth rates in Israel were already higher than in most of the countries in the region, with the lowest birth rates registered in Iran.

Birth rates have been decreasing in most developing countries, even in Africa, although the decline there has been very slow. Overall, population growth rates in the third world are gradually slowing, which provides grounds to confidently predict the end of the population explosion, although not until the end of the 21st century.

World Asymmetry

But even with this relatively optimistic prospect, the world's population is expected to increase to 9 billion people by 2050 and to 11 billion by the end of the century. Clearly, constant population growth has radically changed global demographic trends and therefore the geopolitical situation. These changes have diverse and very serious consequences – economic, environmental, and others – but I would like to focus on the emergence of an unprecedented demographic asymmetry in the world today, because answers to global economic, environmental or political challenges will have to be found in conditions of this asymmetry.

From Fig. 2, we can see that the bulk of the world population has always lived in countries we now call developing. Yet until the middle of the 20th century, the share of developed countries increased and reached approximately one-third of the world's population, after which it began to decrease. According to forecasts, the population of developed countries will fall below 12% of the total population by the year 2100.

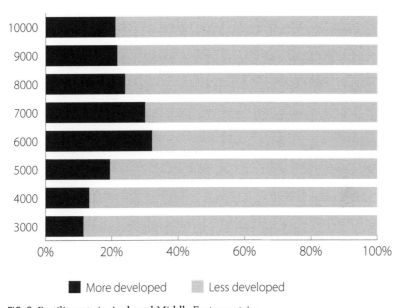

FIG. 2. Fertility rate in Arab and Middle East countries

Fig. 3 shows the present and future unevenness in population growth rates in the world and in developed countries, including Russia. The demographic mass of developing countries in the Global South already hangs over the countries of the Global North, whose population is barely increasing. And this overhang will keep growing.

This expanding demographic asymmetry is coupled with territorial unevenness (see Fig. 4), not to mention economic asymmetry, and a huge gap between the rich demographic minority and the poor majority. Russia belongs to the demographic minority but pretends not to notice.

The dramatic changes in the ratio between demographic masses are very important per se. but changes are taking place not only in the ratio of populations, but also in the balance of power. The economic or military power of developed Northern countries is currently greater than that of developing countries of the Global South, but life does not remain still. Increasingly, we hear that China is competing with the US for the title of the world's No. 1 economy. Of course, if we speak of per capita income, China is still far behind the US. But if we speak of the aggregate income of that country with a population of 1.4 billion people, and of the possibility for concentrating enormous resources in the hands of the state, then its economic and military potential looks very serious.

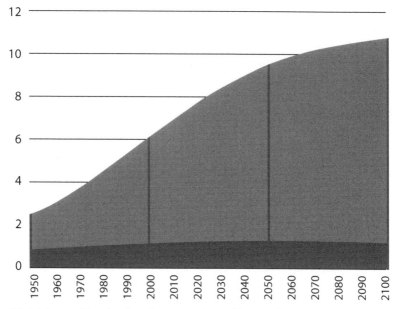

FIG. 3. More and less developed countries in world population

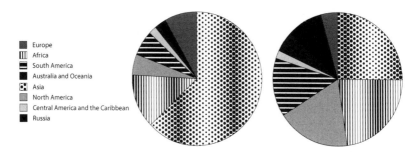

FIG. 4. Disparity in population/territory ratios in major regions

All these factors will have a huge impact on the destiny of our world in the 21st century. What will this impact be? And what place will countries in the "demographic majority" take in this world?

A Bit of Geopolitics

Oddly enough, our habitual system of views, apparently rooted in the Soviet era, does not assign an independent place to developing countries. The Soviet ideological mythology was based on the idea that the 20th century was mainly about the "transition from capitalism to socialism" and the ensuing confrontation between the First and Second worlds. The other, or Third World, was vaguely described in terms of "national liberation revolutions" and "the elimination of the colonial system," without clarifying what could be expected of these societies comprising billions of people that had not even reached the stage of capitalism. Many still believe that no one on this planet except Russia, the US and Europe should have a say in the fate of these nations. Vladimir Zhirinovsky expressed this idea in a simple-minded way in his book "The Last Thrust to the South": "We should agree***to divide the whole planet into spheres of economic influence and act along the North-South axis. The Japanese and Chinese should extend their spheres of influence downward, toward Southeast Asia, the Philippines, Malaysia, Indonesia, and Australia. Russia projects its influence to the South: Afghanistan, Iran and Turkey. Western Europe – also to the South: the African continent. And finally, Canada and the US – again to the South: the whole of Latin America.*** We would concentrate our economic ties mainly on Afghanistan, Iran and Turkey as long as these countries exist***and until they become part of the Russian state."[8]

Let me note parenthetically that the population of the countries Zhirinovsky proposed incorporating into Russia now stands at 190 million people. If they become part of the Russian state, it would cease to be Russian. The point, however, is not Zhirinovsky's fantasies, but that we (and not only Zhirinovsky), while identifying ourselves as part of the Global North, still believe that we will continue, as before, to give orders to the Global South. However, the real future of third-world countries depends not on us, but on objective laws of development and the real challenges to which these countries will have to respond and determine their own development trajectories.

We have never realized that these trajectories may pose potential risks not only to the vicious West, but also to blameless Russia. We still view the world as "North-centric" and believe that its destiny is decided in international confrontation within the North; for example, in the confrontation between Russia and the US. At the same time, the rest of the world plays the role of extras, dependent on the outcome of this confrontation. This view may have been justified in the first half of the 20th century, but no longer.

Three-quarters of Russian territory are in Asia, where it has the longest border, and we will certainly have the biggest [demographic] problems there. To see this, just look at Fig. 6, which shows the ratio between the populations of Russia and the whole of Asia. Asia's population already exceeds 4 billion people, and by 2050, it will reach 5 billion. Russia's population in its Asian part is less than 30 million. To hear some Russian geopoliticians talk, one might think there is no task more important to Russia than to lock horns with the US and Europe. Meanwhile, Asia and Africa are repeatedly making themselves felt.

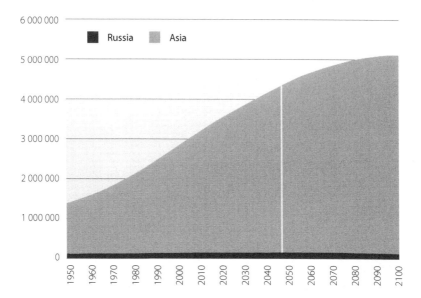

FIG. 5. Population in Russia and Asia; actual and as forecasted by the UN (1,000 people)

How predictable are relationships between the global demographic minority and the global demographic majority? This largely or even decisively depends on how third-world countries cope with their internal problems.

The Difficult Path to Modernization

Most third-world countries are poised to begin or have embarked on the path of modernization in the hope of catching up sooner or later with the developed countries, which are now way ahead of them. This catch-up modernization at first seems to be instrumental: Developing countries borrow Western technologies, pharmaceuticals and weapons, while trying to preserve, at least partially, traditional social relations, values and norms. But attempts to combine the modern and the traditional always fail. Traditional attitudes and the traditional system of values succumb to the new social conditions: the spread of the power of money, population migration to cities and universal education. Unprecedented demographic changes are another – and major – part of the new reality.

Demographic behavior is always very closely connected with the main existential human values like life, death, birth, sex and interaction between the sexes. The attitude to these values forms the basis of any culture, is reflected in views of good and evil, of what is acceptable and unacceptable, and is codified in religious norms and secular laws.

It is hard to imagine more profound changes in all these fundamental aspects of life than those that are required by one of humankind's greatest achievements – the unprecedented decline in mortality.

For example, consider how the role of women has changed. Europe has already forgotten about women's traditional positions but in Islamic countries, these issues are still relevant. Should women get an education? Should they be allowed to drive a car? Should they be allowed to vote? Should they be allowed to hold government positions? Can they have the same rights as men? All these issues are still topics of discussion.

But if we must recognize and approve of family planning and low birth rates, then we cannot avoid a chain of unavoidable consequences affecting the entire system of traditional norms that have for centuries regulated the private and family life of an individual, the institution of marriage, relationships between parents and children and between husband and wife, the family and social roles of men and women, and family values. The new demographic conditions give women more freedom. Nothing can stop radical changes in their position in family and society.

Whether we want it or not, this is just one example of how demographic innovations are becoming one of the sharpest wedges splitting the traditional order.

Demographic changes affect virtually everyone. All families almost simultaneously are involved in these changes and begin to feel or at least understand that life requires that people forsake much of what they thought was sacred even yesterday. New moral norms and rules of conduct are needed, and values should be reassessed. It took Europeans centuries to reassess their values, but societies in developing countries do not have that much time now. Changes are accomplished within the lifetime of one generation.

When faced with a stream of rapid and profound changes (and demographic changes are only part of this stream, albeit a very important one), few countries manage to avoid difficulties during the transition period, including a sharp conflict within culture and society, an identity crisis, a cultural split, and the emergence of fanatical supporters of the new and no less fanatical defenders of the old.

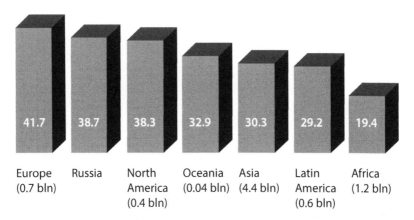

| Europe (0.7 bln) | Russia | North America (0.4 bln) | Oceania (0.04 bln) | Asia (4.4 bln) | Latin America (0.6 bln) | Africa (1.2 bln) |

FIG. 6. Median age of the population of major regions

This is a very painful period for any society. It finds itself at a crossroads, which one African anthropologist figuratively described by quoting two conflicting African proverbs: "It is better to destroy a village than destroy a custom" and "When the river changes direction, the crocodile follows it."

Changes, including demographic ones, occur in societies that have already been affected to various degrees by modernization. Such societies are already in motion and have begun to move away from a patriarchal order toward urbanization. Various intermediary and marginal social groups are emerging that are semi-rural and semi-urban. Those groups are semi-literate and are experiencing a cultural identity crisis and split. Neither men nor women are content with the old ways any longer, but they are not ready to fully accept the new ones, either. So they are at a crossroads. The absence of any solid ground makes them very susceptible to simplistic "fundamentalist" ideas, which they think will help them get rid of their cultural split and become their own selves again.

There are billions of such people.

The situation is further complicated by one more demographic factor: the population of most developing countries is very young.

The so-called median age of the Russian population is 39 years. This means that half of Russians are younger and the other half is older. In Syria, half of the population is under the age of 21, and in Nigeria half of the population is younger than 18 years.

A huge number of young people and teenagers, whether partly educated or not educated at all, who do not see any prospects for the future, and who grow up in poor and marginalized societies, are easily susceptible to manipulation through catchy slogans that require no understanding but blind faith.

Looking for Culprits

Russia's population stood at 101 million in 1950 and was already at 144 million (without the Crimea) in 2015; thus, the population grew by less than half. Over the same period, the population of Nigeria increased from 39 million to 182 million people, or 4.5-fold over 65 years because of an unprecedented decline in death rates. Infant mortality in Nigeria has since decreased from 201 in 1950 to 76 per 1,000 births (Russia's level in 1955), while birth rates have decreased very little – from 6.4 to 5.7 births per woman. According to a UN forecast, Nigeria's population may reach 500 million people by 2050.

The huge problems posed by rapid population growth for Nigeria are clear. In fact, Nigeria knows how important economic, social and demographic modernization is to the country. Modernization can help minimize or even prevent growing tensions and stop the continuing population explosion. However, in demography, like in other spheres, modernization generates huge conflicts. One of the reasons is the cultural split that always accompanies a transition from the old to the new, especially if the transition is fast.

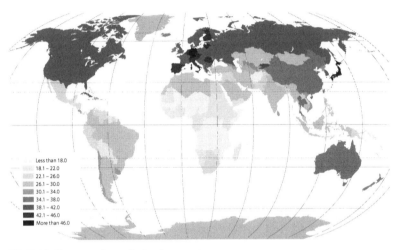

FIG. 7. Median age of population by country

The main sources of cultural conflict are in the very development of these countries, which changes the habitual situation (generally to the benefit of society). Yet as a rule, defenders of the old order do not recognize the internal nature of the conflict and seek its origins in an imported "contagion," a foreign conspiracy or the activities of foreign agents, thus forming the image of a hated foreign enemy. Most often, this enemy is the West. This is not a geographical term, but a symbolic designation of everything that accompanies modernization and does not fit into the system of traditional values inherited from past eras.

This is an old story. The dispute is well known between Slavophiles and Westernizers in 19th-century Russia. Nikolai Danilevsky wrote that "the struggle with the West is the only remedy against our Russian cultural ailments."[9] But Slavophiles were disciples of Germans, who also fought with the West – only the West for them began west of the Rhine. Oswald Spengler's best-known book is called *Der Untergang des Abendlandes* (The Decline of the West). So it is little surprise that slogans calling for struggle against the West are written on banners of fighters against their own "cultural ailments" in Asia or Africa.

As traditionalism wanes, the protection of traditional values from external enemies has enormous mobilization potential, which is usually in higher demand in societies with more unsolved economic and social problems. Poor and underdeveloped countries with a fast-growing population abound with such problems. Acute problems, the absence of alternative ways to solve them, and faith in mobilizing slogans bordering on fanaticism lead to the radicalization of broad social strata. Let me repeat, this is happening in countries where half of the population is under the age of 20.

They definitely know against whom to direct their radicalism. If women – at least some of them – want to hold a higher position in the family and society than in the past, it is not because new demographic conditions are making the life of a woman constantly giving birth meaningless nor because they open completely different prospects for her, but because this desire is inspired by Western ideas, Western education, etc. And Western education is a sin.

The expression "Western education is a sin" in the Hausa language (one of the African languages) sounds like "Boko Haram," the name of a terrorist group in Nigeria that for years has been terrifying the population in the country's northeast. In 2014, the group attacked a secondary school and kidnapped 270 female students, declaring that "the girls must leave school and get married." This was just one of dozens of terrorist attacks in which Boko Haram has killed large numbers of people. In January 2015, Boko Haram burned 16 towns and villages in northern Nigeria, and in March 2015, the group pledged allegiance to the Islamic State (IS) and began to refer to itself as the "West African Province" of IS.

Not surprisingly, terrorist groups in Islamic regions are disguised in Islamic garb. However, the problem is not rooted in Islam. The Khmer Rouge, who committed more atrocities than ISIS and also hated the West, were not Muslims. But the median age of the population of Cambodia in the 1970s, the years of Pol Pot's genocide, was 17 to 18 years.

The problem is rooted in the intractable economic and social problems facing the majority of third world countries. Moreover, the problem is exacerbated by unprecedented population growth and an inevitable transformation of demographic processes.

Migration: Pressure and Opposition

As clearly seen in Fig. 3, the picture of the growing "demographic overhang" shows that the question of potential pressure from the Third World (Global South) on the "golden billion" (Global North) and the possible consequences could (and should) have been raised 50 years ago. This pressure may be due to different reasons and may take various forms.

Perhaps the most obvious is migration. Migration has played a very important role in population redistribution throughout human history. Until World War II, the largest migrations of the recent past were from Europe overseas – to new countries in the Americas or Oceania, or to the overseas colonies of European countries. However, after the war, the direction of migration flows changed, and Europe turned from a source of migration into a recipient of migrants.

At first, the influx of migrants into Europe did not draw much attention, but gradually anxiety began to grow. The scope of migration was not immediately understood. Only with time did concern over migrant waves enter public consciousness in European countries and even the US, the traditional haven for immigrants. Active opponents of immigration appeared, and attitudes toward immigration became a tool in domestic politics. Recently, British demographer David Coleman introduced the notion of a "third demographic transition"[10] to denote a phase in global demographic changes when the scale of migration flows from third-world countries begins to threaten the existing ethnocultural and even political identity of the populations of developed countries receiving migrants.

The question is how awareness of this threat makes it possible to prevent it. The entire range of discontent with growing immigration – from the academic position of Coleman to the radical slogans of European far-right politicians – only leads to all sorts of suggestions about how countries accepting immigrants should treat them.

But what difference do these suggestions make for countries from where the migration pressure is coming? After all, they are interested in the migration of their citizens – at least for economic reasons. According to World Bank estimates (which are likely incomplete), the amount of money transferred by migrants to developing countries increased from $18 billion in 1980 to a staggering $436 billion in 2014. Emigration provides at least one outlet for overpopulated countries experiencing job shortages and provides a glimmer of hope to young people who cannot find a niche for themselves at home.

We see people from poor African countries trying to cross the sea in rickety boats, risking their lives and often dying to reach wealthy Europe. And even this is a difficult problem to solve. Are we capable of resisting pressure from the other side and stopping migrants?

Migration pressure is the most obvious, albeit spontaneous, form of pressure of the demographic majority on the demographic minority. But there may be more organized, state forms of pressure.

The average Russian is not rich, but Russia is a rich country with the largest territory in the world. It has vast arable lands, which are in short supply in much of the rest of the world. Russia has rich fresh water resources, while neighboring China badly needs such resources. Who can guarantee that someday China will not demand that we share our resources with it? After all, is water not a gift from above that cannot belong to one country? Of course, arguments like these do not exist in international law, but is international law always followed? We have some other natural resources that other countries might like to have, too.

Russia will not hear such claims from Europe, but why not from Asia? They know that we belong to the global minority, from which we somehow are trying to fence ourselves off. On the contrary, I believe that we should cling to the global minority, because all major problems that Russia may confront stem from Asia.

Asia is where we are hearing the first sounds of a coming storm that we now call terrorism.

The 'Mutiny War' of Colonel Messner

Let us consider migrations from which no country can fence itself off. All countries in the world turned into communicating vessels long ago. Russia now receives the bulk of its migrants from Asia – namely, from its "soft Central Asian underbelly" – a phrase sometimes at-tributed to Winston Churchill. Most migrants may have peaceful intentions, and I am confident that this is so, but one cannot rule out the existence among them of those with radical ideas coming from the Third World. How can we prevent their spread and especially implementation in Russia? This applies to all developed countries accepting migrants.

Migrations, even large-scale ones, are common in world history, but this does not mean that all major migrations were peaceful. On the contrary, often they took place as military invasions and con-quests. For instance, the Migration Period bore little resemblance to the peasant resettlement in 19th-century Russia, and the name of Attila still evokes terror. The military campaigns of Genghis Khan, the Arab conquests, and Ottoman expansion into Europe were also types of migration.

Many things recur in history, although not in the same way. Even assuming that the pressure of the "demographic overhang" on the demographic minority acquires a military dimension, this will not be the raids of horse-riding archers or the trenches of Stalingrad. It will be something else.

Of course, groups emerge from time to time like the Taliban or IS that call themselves states and try to establish their own order in a particular area, but this happens inside the Third World and does not seem to pose an immediate threat to developed countries. Who would dare attack 21st-century military heavyweights possessing nuclear weapons, ballistic missiles and all kinds of state-of-the-art armaments?

But this does not mean that they cannot be attacked. Moreover, we see that they are increasingly becoming targets of what we now call terrorist attacks. It is hard to name a country with a high mili-tary potential – ranging from Israel to the US and Russia – that has not been subject to terrorist attacks, and these attacks are becoming more frequent. In almost all cases they can be traced to the Third World.

In fact, these are not just individual acts of terror, which have always taken place in history and had a specific goal – regicide, political revenge, intimidation, etc. Instead, this is a special kind of warfare waged by the weak against the strong, using available means. But this only seems like weakness because the attackers are relying on unlimited human resources and the boundless fanaticism of their soldiers.

This factor could have been foreseen, too, in order to prepare for this war, rather than for a past war, which is what peacetime generals always do.

Few people in Russia know the name of Yevgeny Messner, a colonel in the Imperial Russian Army who lived in exile and disgraced himself by collaborating with the Nazis. But today his name should be remembered because he foresaw the nature of future warfare. In his book *Mutiny, or the Name of the Third World War*,[11] Messner wrote that in a future war, "hostilities will be held not on a two-dimensional surface, as before, and not in three-dimensional space, as it has been since the birth of military aviation, but in four-dimensional space, where the psyche of warring nations will be the fourth dimension." Messner called this kind of warfare "mutiny war."

I do not know whether Messner thought of future demographic changes when writing his book. Most likely he did not. But I do not doubt that these changes have created additional and substantial prerequisites for a global "mutiny war." Our attempts to respond to the challenges of this war using aerospace forces show that we are not ready for it.

Notes

1. http://www.ng.ru/stsenarii/2015-12-22/9_demography.html?PREVIEW_SECRET_KEY=d919701ef3962ceeacd78eb48ed57131 (Part I) and http://www.ng.ru/scenario/2015-12-22/13_demography.html (Part II).

2. Sauvy, Alfred. "Trois Mondes, Une Planète" [Three Worlds, One Planet], *L'Observateur*, Aug. 14, 1952, n. 118, p. 14.

3. Podyachikh, P.G. "Dopolneniye k dokladu 'Dve tendentsii rosta chislennosti naseleniya: dve problemy' (o roli demograficheskoi politiki v regulirovanii rosta naseleniya)" [Addendum to the report "Two trends in population growth: two problems" (on the role of demographic policies in population growth control)], Moscow, Central Statistics Administration of the USSR, 1969, p. 17.

4. "Implications of Worldwide Population Growth for US Security and Overseas Interests," *National Security Study Memorandum* (NSSM 200) (THE KISSINGER REPORT), Dec. 10, 1974, https://pdf.usaid.gov/pdf_docs/PCAAB500.pdf.

5. Originally published in: Medvedeva, Irina and Shishiova, Tatiana. *Spetsmissiya Antikhrista* [Special mission of the Antichrist]. Moscow: Algoritm, 2009.

6. Aghajanian, Akbar. "Family Planning and Contraceptive Use in Iran, 1967-1992," *International Family Planning Perspectives*, 20 (2), June 1994, p. 67.

7. Mehryar, A.H. et al. "Iranian miracle: how to raise contraceptive prevalence rate to above 70% and cut TFR by two-thirds in less than a decade?" Paper presented at the IUSSP conference, Salvador de Bahia, Brazil, August 18-24, 2001; cited in: Mohammad Jalal Abbasi-Shavazi. "The fertility revolution in Iran," *Population et Sociétés*, 373, November 2001, p. 1, https://www.ined.fr/fichier/s_rubrique/18837/publi_pdf2_pop_and_soc_english_373.en.pdf.

8. Zhirinovsky, Vladimir. *Posledny brosok na yug* [The last thrust to the South]. Moscow: 12CT, 1996, https://litresp.ru/chitat/ru/%D0%96/zhirinovskij-vladimir/poslednij-brosok-na-yug/1.

9. Danilevsky, Nikolai. *Rossia i Yevropa* [Russia and Europe], 1869.

10. Coleman, David. "Immigration and Ethnic Change in Low-Fertility Countries: A Third Demographic Transition," *Population and Development Review*, 32(3), September 2006, pp. 401-446.

11. Messner, Yevgeny. *Myatezh – imya tretyei vsemirnoi* [Mutiny, or the name of the Third World War]. Buenos Aires, 1960.

PART TWO

2.2. À la Guerre Comme à la Guerre (Military Analysis)

WARFARE AGAINST THE RULES

Aleksandr Golts

The Pentagon has said that the Iraq war marked a "revolution in military affairs." However, Russian generals tend to ignore the importance of this "revolution." Their attitude is rather easy to understand: Any unbiased analysis of the US military actions would call into question Russia's current program for military development, its concept of military reform and most of its plans concerning the combat deployment of its Armed Forces.

The heads of the Russian military, specifically Defense Minister Sergei Ivanov and Chief of the General Staff Anatoly Kvashnin, assert that the lessons of the recent Iraq war are being thoroughly analyzed. On previous occasions, they said the same things about the US campaigns in Yugoslavia and Afghanistan, and for one reason or another, the analysis by the Russian military led to one conclusion: The Americans were lucky to have confronted a weak opponent. For example, NATO secured victory over Yugoslavia because of the latter's lack of air defense weapons and Moscow's indecision; similarly, it defeated the Taliban in Afghanistan because Pakistan had stopped rendering it support and blocked the Afghan-Pakistani border.

This article originally appeared in *Russia in Global Affairs* Vol. 1, No. 3, 2003.

Today, as before, the Russian military alleges that the Americans won a "fixed war" over Iraq by bribing the generals of the Iraqi Republican Guard. This summer, this particular idea was reiterated by most speakers at an enlarged meeting of the Academic Council of the Academy of Military Science. Leading Russian military experts have also focused on criticizing US foreign policy and Washington's attempts to build a unipolar world. The military aspect of the problem per se was obviously of secondary importance. "In terms of military art, the Iraq campaign does not allow us to draw any far-reaching conclusions, for we have not witnessed any serious war against a strong opponent," said Army Gen. Makhmut Gareyev, president of the Academy of Military Science.

The reluctance of Russia's top military personnel to conduct an in-depth analysis of the ongoing profound changes in modern warfare (described as a "revolution in military affairs" by the Pentagon) is rather easy to understand: Any serious analysis of the changes would shake Russia's current military development program, its concept of military reform and most plans concerning the combat deployment of its Armed Forces.

The Enemy We Choose

The US campaign in Iraq is significant for Russia for two interrelated reasons. First, it is the second time, after the Afghan campaign, that the American military has chalked up a victory that, according to Russian strategists, could not have been won. The main point is that in both engagements, they carried out combat operations on the enemy's territory and were opposed not only by the standing army, but also by paramilitary formations that were expected to wage a large-scale guerilla war. At the outset of the Iraq operation, just as at the start of the Afghan campaign, Russian generals predicted that the Americans would become entangled in a protracted and bloody war. Obviously, they based their conclusions on their own experience – the war the Soviet generals lost in Afghanistan and the one the Russian generals are presently failing to win in Chechnya. Both in Afghanistan and in Iraq, the US commanders deployed a ground force that was smaller than the one the Russians had in Chechnya (slightly over 30,000 troops were engaged in the Afghan campaign and some 114,000 troops in Iraq). They did not shell either Kabul or

Baghdad with heavy howitzer artillery, yet they still emerged from battle victorious.

Second and most important, it would be no exaggeration to say that the Iraq campaign has fiercely tested the plans of Russia's General Staff for repelling a hypothetical, large-scale act of aggression. For the first time in the past decade, US forces were engaged in a war that, according to the Russian General Staff, would be typical of a strategy implemented by any potential adversary.

Russian military scholars failed to properly address the strategic situation that emerged in the second half of the 1990s. At this time, it became apparent that the US had secured the advantage of overwhelming air superiority and sought to maintain its predominance through large-scale air operations, thus, essentially eliminating the need for grand ground operations. At some point, the Russian General Staff decided that in its scenarios the "enemy forces" should play a give-away game against Russia's forces. The scenarios of all the latest Russian strategic exercises, beginning with the West-99 exercise, assume that any opponent will necessarily engage in ground operations that would, it is believed, result in heavy losses.

Another alternative response to a large-scale air campaign would be initiated through a demonstrative air-to-ground nuclear cruise missile attack against uninhabited or scarcely populated areas on enemy territory. It is assumed that such a demonstration would force the enemy to halt its offensive and sit down at the negotiating table. Yet it is not clear how Russia's strategic bombers would be able to approach an attack line in the face of the opponent's overwhelming air superiority. Until recently, these scenarios were rather hypothetical and had only indirect relevance to the actual situation.

However, in case of the Iraq war, the US president made it clear that the US would have to eventually abandon the strategy of sustained air attacks and launch ground operations once the campaign commenced. The point was that massive bombardments were not conducive to a war strategy whose declared purpose was the "liberation of the Iraqi people" as opposed to their wanton destruction. Furthermore, having failed to obtain an international mandate from the international community for its military operation in Iraq after months of bargaining, the US did not have enough time to gain absolute superiority over the enemy before the scorching summer season set in.

That was the primary reason why the US attacked Iraq using a fairly small force. The 400,000-troop Iraqi Army faced slightly more than 100,000 US troops. The US 3rd Mechanized Division bypassed large Iraqi formations and dashed for Baghdad. The Iraqi generals could have taken advantage of this situation and struck the rear units of US troops, while the latter's overstretched lines of communication offered lucrative targets for subversion. This is precisely what the Russian military recommended the Yugoslavs do during their defensive campaign.

At a conference held by the Russian Defense Ministry in the summer of 1999, Army Gen. Makhmut Gareyev also accused the Yugoslavs of being passive: "It is worth remembering how Soviet Naval aviation, although suffering huge losses, kept launching air strikes on Berlin in 1941. Always and everywhere it is necessary to impose contact land battles against the enemy." The same criticism was voiced rhetorically toward the Iraqis by Gen. Gareyev: "Did the Iraqis blow up bridges and other installations or lay minefields along the routes of the enemy advance? Did they erect barricades, pole obstacles, dig antitank ditches and set ambushes in their cities, desperately defending each house the way we did in Stalingrad?"[1]

It looks like the answer to the question of why the Iraqi defense system collapsed like a house of cards is not as simple as the alleged betrayal of the Iraqi generals.

'Fog of War' Cleared Away

Saddam Hussein's Army has disappointed all who had relied on its stubborn resistance and dreamed of "ordinary Iraqi peasants shooting down US combat helicopters by the dozens." Like the Taliban, the Iraqis displayed passivity and defeatism, which is difficult to explain. Even though the Americans enjoyed complete superiority, the Iraqi military had the opportunity to carry out so-called asymmetric actions, such as subversions and attacks against overstretched communication lines. When several Marines from a US maintenance company got caught in an ambush and were taken prisoner, President Bush called it the gravest day in the three weeks of operations. It proved to be the most successful operation of the Iraqi Army. Who knows how things would have evolved had such incidences occurred with much greater frequency. But they never did.

However, the central point should not be the passivity of the Iraqi resistance, but the fact that a battle was waged between two fundamentally different armies: one doomed to defeat and the other destined to win, because one of them was still anchored to the industrial century, whereas the other was high-powered with information technologies; the difference proved to be no less than the difference between the Spanish conquistadors and the Incan Army.

With each new war, the US Armed Forces have made wider use of the latest achievements in information technologies. For many centuries, the military strategy relied on a singular maxim: To hold down the enemy's forces and deprive them of maneuverability, the attacker should control as much of the combat-stricken territory as possible. According to Jane's Defence Weekly, an authoritative British magazine, today an army's task is not to seize territory but to obtain as much information about the battlefield as possible.

On this point, the Americans have truly displayed their success. First in Afghanistan and then in Iraq, the Pentagon constructed a huge multilayered Integrated Information and Control System comprised of reconnaissance and communications satellites, U-2 reconnaissance aircraft, E-8 Joint STARS target acquisition system aircraft, E-3 AWACS early warning system aircraft, and RC-130 tactical reconnaissance aircraft. Furthermore, the Americans made use of 10 different types of unmanned air vehicles, ranging from the high-altitude Global Hawk to the collapsible Dragon Eye. Using these advanced technologies, the forward headquarters of the Central Command stationed in Doha (Qatar) exercised a real-time surveillance of the entire Iraqi territory. Even during the most severe sand storms, the Iraqis failed to elude overhead reconnaissance; their attempts to concentrate their reserves and initiate strikes at the rear of the US forces were regularly foiled. (There were several such attempts, namely from the surrounded city of Basra, near En-Nasiriyah, on March 21-22 and west of Kerbela on March 27.)

The US "revolution in military affairs" has, in fact, cleared "the fog of war," as Carl von Clausewitz, a distinguished military theorist of the past, described the insufficient knowledge about the opponent's plans and maneuvers. The greatest achievement of the Integrated Information System is that it is constructed on not only the vertical plane but also the horizontal plane. As a result, vital reconnaissance information concerning the location of the opponent is transmitted not only to the military command center but also directly to land-based units and combat aircraft; therefore, it takes no more than 12 minutes to hit a target after the information has been acquired. According to the US Air Force Command, over 500 air attacks hit targets after in-flight retasking.

High-precision weapons, which, according according to U.S. defense officials, accounted for approximately 70% of all the munitions used during the Iraq war,[2] were part of the information and attack system; their implementation made it possible to immediately launch attacks against detected targets. The information system allowed US generals to conduct online video conferences with commanders at all levels and to make decisions practically within seconds. The Doha-based headquarters received real-time information concerning the operations of all friendly troops, irrespective of their size, for which purpose they were fitted with special equipment.

Precise knowledge of the battlefield situation, along with the capability to instantly respond to sudden developments, produces a profound psychological effect on the adversary. Enemy commanders start to imagine that their opponent is almighty and all-knowing and can foresee or even direct their actions, while the rank-and-file develop something like schizophrenia; they get the terrifying feeling that enemy airplanes are hunting them personally. Combat experience demonstrates that such operations lasting three or four weeks are enough to make even such battle-hardened fighters as the Taliban abandon their positions and flee.

Another major innovative aspect of the US strategy is the marked increased in troop mobility. In the past, the capability of the US to quickly respond to a crisis in Europe or Asia may have been due to a network of major bases where large contingents of forces were stationed. They were designed to not only contain the first strike, but also provide conditions for disembarking and deploying US forces overseas. There were no such bases around Afghanistan, while during the Iraq operation, Turkey, as is well known, did not permit the Americans to deploy their forces from its territory.

The Pentagon has demonstrated that what it requires today is only temporary and fairly small bases to store the required heavy weapons. Such depots, for example, were established in Kuwait in advance, and the only remaining task was to airlift the military personnel of the 3rd Mechanized Division. In fact, the 173rd Airborne

Brigade, as well as the Marine Expeditionary Brigade, acted without a preliminary deployment and launched a hasty attack in northern Iraq.[3] According to the new US norms, a brigade should be deployable to any point of the globe four days after it has received the order; a single division is given five days, while a five-division task force is given one month. By the designated time, carrier-based Naval task forces, Marine Expeditionary Forces and Air Force units should be deployed near the conflict.

Such a high level of mobility provides for an unprecedented speed of operation and initiative on the battlefield; the adversary simply has no time to respond to the fast changes in the situation. Gen. Tommie Franks, who led the general planning of the Iraq operation, told his officers to stop reminding him of US exposed flanks. He said the US troops were advancing so fast that the Iraqis would not be able to find out where their flanks were.

Finally, as in all recent US military campaigns, Special Operations Forces played an important role in Iraq. The strength of the Green Berets, Naval Special Warfare Forces and Delta teams operating in Iraq numbered more than 10,000. During the first days of the war, they seized control of the oil fields, thereby denying Saddam the chance to destroy them. That would have resulted in an environmental disaster like the one in Kuwait in 1991. They subsequently guided US and British planes to critical targets.

The Americans also succeeded in providing the enemy with strategic misinformation. After announcing the "crisis of their advance in the desert" on April 4, they did not suspend their offensive but bypassed the Iraqi defensive line near Kerbela. More than 40 million leaflets were dropped on Iraq before the first attack on 20 March, and another 40 million plus were dropped during the campaign.[4] Psychological warfare specialists even succeeded in sending messages to the mobile phones of some Iraqi generals,[5] calling on them to surrender; the smartest generals hurried to accept the offer they could not refuse. However, it is evident that attributing the US victory in Iraq to the bribing of Saddam's generals would be the most primitive explanation.

Pointless Mobilization

Russian generals simply cannot allow themselves to offer an explanation for the changes in modern warfare; otherwise, they would be forced to admit that Russia is not prepared to face the challenge of the "revolution in military affairs" evolving today.

Inside the Russian military, the phenomenon is not being perceived in its entirety; at most, only a few aspects of it are being given worthy consideration. Hence, reactions to the situation are only very fragmentary. Currently, most attention is being paid to the ever-increasing role of space communications and reconnaissance systems. As a result, the development of the Space Forces has been declared a priority of the country's military reform, with abundant funds being allocated to the construction of a space satellite force. In 2004, the number of defense communications and reconnaissance satellites is expected to exceed 70. Col. Gen. Aleksei Moskovsky, in charge of military-technical policy for the Russian Defense Ministry, claims that space communication and reconnaissance equipment will enter service with military companies, platoons and squads as early as next year. Yet one has to wonder who will operate these technologies. Enlisted personnel, less than half of whom have high-school educations? Or will it be the pilots, whose flying time totals no more than 10 to 12 hours per year?

Reducing the essence of the revolution in warfare to the use of new technologies is certainly nonsensical. Only a totally different army, which the Russian generals are reluctant to build, can efficiently use them. Recently, the Russian government passed a federal program for transitioning some military forces to a contract system. It would seem that the Defense Ministry, despite the limited funds available to it, should take all of the necessary measures to acquire at least a few more or less combat-ready formations. Unfortunately, this is not the case. The military department has succeeded in pushing through the bizarre idea of a "mixed army," with the bulk of its forces made up of draftees. The General Staff insists that national security can be maintained merely by retaining millions of reservists and mobilizing them en masse in case of emergency.

Beginning with the West-99 exercise, Russia's strategic maneuvers have necessarily provided for mobilizing reservists. Initially, only regiment-level personnel were called up. In 2002, the mobilization of 7,500 troops (an equivalent of a reinforced brigade or a peacetime division) and their deployment over several thousand kilometers was presented by Defense Minister Sergei Ivanov as major achievement for Russia. But in practical terms, there seems to have been little sense in that move. Given the Defense Ministry's permanent shortage of funds necessary for training its service personnel, there is no sense in trying over a two-week period to "refresh the military skills" of those who lost them a long time ago.

Russia's top military experts argue that waiving full conscription will lead to a considerable reduction in the number of reservists, and the government will not be able to call up 6 million to 8 million soldiers in case of a large-scale war. Yet, they ignore the fact that the strategic reserves of weapons, clothing and foodstuffs needed for a multimillion army were exhausted a long time ago. The present state of affairs in the Russian defense industry does not allow it to produce the required amount of weapons and clothing.

To stake the security of the country on full mobilization means retaining the Soviet-era model of military planning, which plays into the hands of Army commanders but is not in the best interests of Russia. Constructing the Russian forces around the model of a mass army means leaving intact the ugly structure of the officers' corps. In such a model, there are actually more colonels than lieutenants, because an army that has divisions of reservists naturally needs scores of commanders. This model does not require a real reform of the military, since mass army personnel only require basic military skills. Moreover, this model allows for reducing the training time of officers to four years, thereby depriving them of the opportunity to receive a higher education. Also, "mobilization production facilities" have to be maintained, which prevent industrial enterprises from operating effectively. If the call-up model is left intact, the General Staff does not have to substantially change its defense strategy. If so, there is no need to reform the Armed Forces at all; instead, Russia's economy, and its social and education policies should be adapted to the Soviet model of the army.

It goes without saying that this option has nothing to do with the vital needs of the state with regard to its national security. Now that the war in Iraq is over (with Soviet military advisers having stayed with the Iraqi Army since the early 1960s), it becomes perfectly clear that the mobilization model will fail to work. Such armed forces were built around Napoleon's idea, true for the epoch of industrial wars, when he commented that "on the winning side are large battalions." Both in 1812 and in 1941, Russia won its victories not only because of its nationwide patriotism, but also because the draft system allowed the Army to be continuously replenished with fresh forces. In such a mass army, a soldier or an officer is destined to die in the very first battle, and there is no need to spend funds on their comprehensive training – they just need to be trained in the most elementary skills. Initiative is alien to such soldiers and they are expected to execute orders without reasoning.

However, when no orders are given, soldiers completely lose control of the situation, which often happens during counterterrorist operations, when they have to act in small teams. The Americans fight with small teams purposefully and seek to destroy the enemy's communications infrastructure during the very first minutes of operation. Commanders who have been trained for a long time to execute orders without reasoning are more likely to flee than to prepare counterattacks when they receive no orders. This, in my view, is the real explanation for why the Iraqis were so passive and why the Russian military prefers to explain the success of the US military in terms of a "fixed war." Strategic assumptions that our potential adversary, which has air superiority, can be expected to get bogged down in bloody land battles appears to be built on sand. In order to force the Americans to engage in such battles, a totally different level of troop training is needed.

There was one reported case of poor intelligence information leading the forward detachment of the US 3rd Infantry Division into a tank ambush that had been carefully prepared by the Iraqis. The Iraqi tanks fired only a single salvo, and missed. That is how low their level of their combat training was. They did not have a second chance.[6]

Notes

1. Gareyev, Makhmut. "Tainiye pruzhiny irakskoi voiny [Hidden springs behind the war in Iraq]," *Krasnaya zvezda*, July 18, 2003, http://old.redstar.ru/2003/07/18_07/2_01.html.

2. Pangyanszki, Jennifer. "Lessons learned from new-era warfare," *CNN*, April 19, 2003, http://edition.cnn.com/2003/US/04/19/sprj.irq.lessons/.

3. "Airborne Operations – Recent," *GlobalSecurity.org*, https://www.globalsecurity.org/military/ops/airborne4.htm.

4. Collins, Steven. "Mind games," *NATO Review*, Summer 2003, https://www.nato.int/docu/review/2003/issue2/English/art4.html.

5. *Ibid.*

6. Faruqui, Ahmad. "Saddam Hussein as Tactician," *Daily Times*, Oct. 30, 2018, https://dailytimes.com.pk/316219/saddam-hussain-as-tactician/. See also: https://bbs.stardestroyer.net/viewtopic.php?f=22&t=18086.

WINNING A WAR WITHOUT LOSING THE PEACE

Aleksei Arbatov

Is there anything in common between the armed conflicts in Chechnya, Afghanistan and Iraq? The answer is that practically everything is different: their history, their nature, the composition of the conflicting parties and their goals, the legal basis, the social and political consequences, etc. Yet there are some points that permit us to compare these conflicts and even learn some vital lessons from them.

Is there anything in common between the armed conflicts in Chechnya, Afghanistan and Iraq? The answer is that practically everything is different: their history, their nature (internal or external), the conflicting parties and their goals, the legal basis, social and political consequences, etc. Yet there are some points that permit us to compare these conflicts and even learn some vital lessons from them.

The military operations in Chechnya and Iraq (launched in 1999 and 2003, respectively) have not put an end to the resistance of local armed groups nor have they brought about social and political stability. Moreover, in Iraq they have transformed the conflicts into protracted guerilla warfare that involved large-scale international ter-

---

This article originally appeared in *Russia in Global Affairs* Vol. 3, No. 1, 2005.

rorism (Islamic State) and the escalation of armed conflict. Armed opposition in Chechnya was eventually suppressed through the establishment of a personalized totalitarian regime based on stringent Islamic rules and supported by huge financial donations from Russian federal budget, which does not look like a long-lasting solution. In contrast, the operation in Afghanistan (2001-2002) did in fact defeat the armed forces of the Taliban and Al Qaeda and lay the groundwork for stabilization and restoring peace. Those efforts had every chance for success, but the US campaign in Iraq diverted resources from Afghanistan, undermined the authority of the UN, split the antiterrorist coalition and inspired the Taliban and Al Qaeda to seek revenge.

Lesson 1

When statesmen and politicians, sitting comfortably in their luxurious air-conditioned offices, decide to send young soldiers into the line of fire, in mud and blood, from where they may well return home crippled or in coffins, these decision-makers must be absolutely sure that all other means of solving the problem have been exhausted and that the military option is the last resort. This is their supreme moral duty. This was the case with Afghanistan, when it had become unquestionable that Al Qaeda was responsible for "Black September" of 2001 and all attempts to get the Taliban to repudiate terrorists had failed.

In 1999, Russia launched the Chechen campaign following bomb attacks on apartment buildings in Moscow and Volgodonsk, and the Wahhabi insurrection in Dagestan. However, the federal center launched a full-scale military operation against Chechnya without making other attempts to settle the conflict. For example, many politicians and military commanders proposed fencing off the rebellious Chechen Republic along its administrative borders, or along the borders and the northern bank of the Terek River. There were suggestions of combining these measures with special operations, pinpoint strikes against the insurgents' infrastructure and troops, forming an internal armed Chechen opposition to the regime, and other such moves. However, Moscow chose another way that it thought would be more resolute and expedient. The result is obvious: Casualties among federal troops alone had exceeded 20,000 killed and wounded.[1] The following series of terrorist acts, which culminated in the monstrous tragedies in Moscow theater and Beslan, demonstrated that there is still a long way to go before stability is achieved in the Caucasus.

Iraq provides an even more graphic example. Today, there is already documented proof that the White House made the decision to launch a military operation against Iraq back in the spring of 2002.[2] All subsequent political maneuvers regarding US allies and Russia, as well as the diplomatic gambits at the UN, were only a "seasoning" for the use of force. Not long ago, the number of American casualties in Iraq exceeded 1,000, and the end of the Iraqi quagmire is nowhere in sight.

Lesson 2

In cases like those mentioned above, maximum legitimacy (legal basis) and clarity of a military operation's purposes are paramount. Perhaps politicians proficient at manipulating the law do not need such substantiating elements. However, these are necessary conditions for such operations to receive the support of public opinion inside the country going to war, as well as of the international community. Such support, serving as a strong political base, provides high morale to soldiers going into combat and makes them confident that their cause is just and they will not be treated as outcasts after returning home.

These conditions are also important because they help regulate relations between troops and the local population, minimizing inevitable frictions. Finally, theyare a major factor in undermining the morale of the armed resistance.

The unanimously adopted UN Security Council resolution on the use of force in Afghanistan accomplished all these tasks. The resolution was a product of the international community's unity and laid the foundation for a broad antiterrorist coalition of many countries united by a common goal. (In the autumn of 2001, according to some reports, the formerly invincible Taliban forces were demoralized and scattered.)

The Russian government did not declare a state of emergency in Chechnya in either of the two military campaigns there, even though by law the Armed Forces could be used inside the country only in a state of emergency. There was the same uncertainty about the goals of the operation and the acceptable methods for conducting it (during his first term in office President Vladimir Putin expressed his amazement at the scale of destruction in Chechnya's capital, Grozny). This lack of clarity largely predetermined the mixed reaction to the campaign on the part of Russian political quarters, the mass media and the international community.

Perhaps there are forces with malicious plans for dismembering Russia, as President Putin declared after Beslan. However, this "admixture" by no means determines mainstream sentiments among the Russian liberal opposition, nor public opinion in the US and Western Europe. There is a persistent inclination of the powers that be to blame their policy mistakes on foreign and domestic enemies. This, however, does not help correct those mistakes and only leads policy deeper into deadlock.

For example, without a clearly formulated state-of-emergency regime, all issues regarding relations with the local population were addressed at the level of regiment commanders (as seen from the case of Col. Yury Budanov, who was accused of raping and killing a young Chechen woman), company commanders or even private soldiers. Without clear-cut legal regulations, it is difficult for the population and soldiers to understand what they can and cannot do – at this point, the Kalashnikov assault rifle becomes the law. Soldiers cannot distinguish peaceful civilians from militants, while militants have ample opportunities to organize sneak attacks against federal troops; this exposes the peaceful population to retaliatory attacks by federal troops, which in turn causes the victims of those attacks to join the militant ranks. (It is no coincidence that the estimated number of active Chechen militants has for many years remained about 2,000 to 3,000,[3] despite the continuous casualties inflicted by federal troops.) The federal troops, operating in an environment of corruption and constantly being stabbed in the back, regard all Chechens as potential traitors and enemies. Thus, they lose a sense of the purpose of their actions and the meaning of their sacrifices.

Russian law stipulates that a state of emergency needs parliamentary approval every two months. This provision seemingly restricts the freedom of action of the executive branch. In reality, however, as shown by the two Chechen campaigns (especially the second, in which troops and law-enforcement agencies were given a free hand), such freedom does not necessarily make policy more effective. That is why democratic procedures are needed: They help check the effectiveness of a given policy and conformity between the goals and the means. They help reveal mistakes before bloody upheavals break out.

A preliminary detailed and open parliamentary discussion of military and political plans in connection with the introduction of a state of emergency might have kept the government from rushing into war and offered alternative strategies, such as a blockade. In any case, this precaution would have made it possible to thoroughly check the condition of troops, law-enforcement agencies and special services, to enhance their readiness and prevent corruption. This would have prevented the inadequacy of troops and security agencies four years later, during the Moscow Theater and Beslan nightmare.

The use of force by the US in Iraq was not based on a resolution of the UN Security Council, which alone is authorized to sanction any use of force, save in cases of lawful self-defense (Art. 51 of the UN Charter). Perhaps Washington viewed efforts to reach consensus in the Security Council as a long, dull and unnecessary diplomatic procedure that would tie its hands and prevent it from effectively using its colossal military power to quickly solve the problem.

The untenable American arguments in favor of war, which failed to influence the positions of most UN Security Council members, doomed the US policy to catastrophe. Washington has never been able to prove any link between the Saddam Hussein regime and terrorists – because there was no such link. Nor did Iraq possess weapons of mass destruction. All it would have taken to reach that conclusion was to broaden UN weapon inspections headed by prominent UN diplomat Hans Blix. Washington's real goal –forcefully implanting a pro-American ("democratic") regime in a politically immature and ethnically and religiously diverse country like Iraq – was simply hopeless. Equally unattainable were plans to open world markets to Iraqi oil amid guerrilla and terrorist warfare. Neither objective would have been approved by the Security Council had Washington openly declared its goals. And had Washington not ignored the issue of the legitimacy of its policy and refrained from taking military action in circumvention of the UN, the US would have been saved from its greatest failure since the Vietnam War.

The American Army went to Iraq with half of the US opposed to the military campaign; public opinion was the same throughout Western Europe, Russia and almost the entire Islamic world. After completing the military phase of the operation quickly and professionally, American soldiers encountered growing resistance from the Iraqi population, on whom they had intended to bestow "democracy." The Army ceased to understand its purpose for being in the country and the meaning of its mounting losses. Troop morale began to fall while armed resistance and terrorism rose. Eventually Iraq (and later a large part of Syria) fell under Iranian domination – a much unexpected and highly negative result for the US interests in the region.

Lesson 3

The strategy of fighting nonstate military groups (rebels, insurgents, guerrillas) is not a matter of simply killing as many militants as possible but rather of depriving them of support among an overwhelming part of the peaceful population in the conflict zone. Otherwise, the indiscriminate use of force and harsh "preventive" measures against civilians will only cause them to side with the enemy, thus providing it with fresh forces.

It is much easier to prevent peaceful citizens from taking up arms than to make them lay arms down later. It is better to let 10 militants escape than to kill one peaceful civilian. It is even justifiable to permit additional risks for government soldiers in order to avoid excessive casualties among innocent civilians. In the final analysis, this strategy will pay off, as there will be fewer people who will have the desire to shoot, take hostages or become suicide bombers.

The selective use of force, combined with efforts to win over the local population, is the main way to win such wars. This method helped suppress the resistance of the Taliban and Al Qaeda in Afghanistan[4] (prior to the war in Iraq) quickly and with minimal losses. Ignoring this method or being unable to use it effectively in Chechnya and Iraq has led to a blind course with constant upsurges in the horizontal (geographical) and vertical (scale of violence) escalation of armed clashes and terrorist acts.

Lesson 4

This lesson considers the importance of relying on local forces. In Afghanistan, the forces of the Northern Alliance were organized, armed and trained in record time. They bore the brunt of the ground combat – the most difficult type of combat that may involve the greatest number of clashes with the local population. Russia, together with some other countries (Tajikistan, Uzbekistan and Iran) under its influence, played a great role here. The US and its allies conducted limited ground operations and provided largely air, missile, artillery, logistical, and command and communications support. The enemy, for its part, failed to use the fierce ground battle to kindle religious discord (all the parties to the conflict were Muslims). Great efforts were made to prevent ethnic hostilities: The anti-Taliban coalition made every effort to win over the Pashtuns, who comprised the core of the Taliban, and offered them high posts in the postwar political system of Afghanistan.

In Chechnya, in November 1994, Moscow also attempted to rely on internal opposition to the Dzhokhar Dudayev regime. However, after initial failure, instead of better preparing itself and continuing this strategy, Moscow decided to take everything upon itself. It relied on the bragging of its military leaders (Pavel Grachev, the defense minister at the time, boasted that his federal troops could defeat the insurgents "with one paratroop regiment within two hours").[5] The result was dismal: Over a decade the conflict developed into religious and ethnic enmity and a terrorist war without boundaries or moral limits.

In Iraq, the US Army and its "coalition of the willing" also took everything upon themselves. At first, they scored a brilliant military victory, but eventually they became bogged down in an endless guerrilla and terrorist conflict with an increasingly radical Islamic and nationalistic tinge.

Lesson 5

This lesson relates to postwar stabilization. Until the armed resistance is suppressed, there should be no rush to form a local government just to shift the war burden onto its shoulders. Whenever such a government is involved in a domestic and transborder armed conflict, it is fully dependent on outside armed forces, yet it does not control these forces at all. That is why it is incapable of gaining the support of the bulk of the local population and therefore assuming a policy of restoring peace.

Moreover, a dependent regime will inevitably create more division in society, even among more moderate local circles, and increase the influence of the radical opposition. Such a regime creates additional difficulties, since it attempts to pursue its own policy (often a repressive one) yet leaves it up to the army to address the consequences. Foreign troops and law-enforcement agencies must necessarily involve such a regime and its police into their operations, and thus they constantly run the risk of information leaks, treachery and being stabbed in the back. Furthermore, a newly established regime will do all it can to impede negotiations even with the moderate part of the armed opposition. This only aggravates the conflict and thwarts any dialogue.

Lesson 6

If the conditions arise for forming a local government, this must be done not according to imported rules but in consideration of local traditions and the level of society's social, political and economic development. This is better initiated from the rank-and-file and representative bodies of power, rather than from higher levels of government, including executive structures. There should also be no hurry to organize local armed forces, since the new authorities must coexist with the foreign armed forces and law-enforcement agencies.

In this respect, the policy pursued in Afghanistan was mostly successful, whereas the operations in Chechnya and Iraq have been largely plagued by mistakes and failures.

Lesson 7

This lesson concerns what is perhaps the most difficult issue: negotiating with terrorists. During a hostage-taking crisis, some countries (e.g., Italy) conduct such negotiations. Others (e.g., Israel) do not, and in these places the terrorists do not take hostages but simply use suicide bombers to kill innocent citizens.

There must be no doubt that if it is impossible or very risky to free hostages by force, then negotiations must be conducted. Even if this may damage the prestige of the state and encourage more hostage-taking, there can be only one moral principle here: If the authorities, with all their law-enforcement and security agencies supported by taxpayer money, are unable to protect their citizens from terrorists, then they must save them by any possible means. Then, the officials who allowed the hostage-taking and consequently damaged the state's prestige by their concessions should either resign or improve their operations to guarantee that such events do not happen again. For those who value the state's prestige more than the life of hostages, there is a noble way out of the quandary: These officials can offer themselves to the terrorists in exchange for the hostages (surely the terrorists would eagerly accept such an offer) and then, after staking their own lives instead of the lives of others, they can take the position of repudiating any "deals" with terrorists.

As for more general negotiations aimed at achieving a peaceful settlement of terrorist-prone conflicts, such negotiations are necessary if the armed opposition cannot be suppressed by force and if the conflict tends to escalate. There are three criteria for choosing counterparts to the negotiation process: First, they must have reputations that have not been sullied by organizing or participating in terrorist acts, and second, they must enjoy support among the local population. Lastly, they must be able to control a large part of the militants to make them lay down arms on certain terms.

The analogies recently drawn by President Putin between Aslan Maskhadov and Osama bin Laden[6] are not quite correct. Bin Laden can rather be compared to Shamil Basayev, with whom no one proposed holding negotiations. On the other hand, parallels can be drawn between Maskhadov and, say, former Iraqi foreign minister Tariq Aziz (included on a "black list" by the Americans and subsequently imprisoned by them) or the late Palestinian leader Yasser Arafat; granted, any such analogies are imperfect.

The main issue is not, of course, legal aspects (in this respect, the conflicts in Chechnya, Iraq and Palestine are completely different), but rather the dynamics of an armed conflict with a clearly terrorist bent combined with the sensitive issue of negotiating with the enemy. When the involvement of a certain opposition leader in terrorism or other crimes is a mute issue, settling the negotiations issue requires enormous state will and political skill. And in this respect, neither the US nor Israel has any grounds for lecturing Russia about which examples it should follow. Both of them have quite a poor record.

In Afghanistan, a peaceful settlement following the military operation would have been impossible without negotiations or the involvement in the process of Pashtun leaders, including those who were closely linked with the Taliban but who had not compromised themselves by collaborating with Al Qaeda.

Lesson 8

The eighth lesson seems to be purely technical, but is actually political. Unless the boundaries of an armed conflict zone are sealed, waging operations against militants and terrorists is like trying to draw water with a sieve. If the boundaries are porous, guerrillas can freely enter the area, deliver supplies and carry out attacks, and then elude pursuit by escaping across the border. Once they are beyond the border, they can rest, reorganize and "share experiences." Worst of all, open borders help militants escaping retaliation to put peaceful civilians in harm's way of retaliatory strikes and thus cause them to join their ranks. This is one aspect of the political question concerning the border issue.

There is another aspect, too. Sealing off a conflict zone is not only a problem of resources, well-trained troops (e.g., border guards), equipment and legislation (for example, using border troops on Chechnya's administrative borders required amendments to the Law on the State Border of the Russian Federation): It is also an issue of relations with adjacent countries – i.e., establishing an antiterrorist coalition on the basis of settling a wide range of disputes concerning interstate relations.

In Afghanistan, this concept worked – with Russia's active participation – when various rather hostile neighboring countries (such as Iran, Pakistan, China, Tajikistan and Uzbekistan) united in a general front and closed their borders to the Taliban and Al Qaeda. On the other hand, the US campaign in Iraq fragmented this coalition and made the Afghan borders mostly open; this led to the *mujahedeen* stepping up their activities and infiltrating the country.

In Chechnya, all administrative boundaries, except for the southern border with Georgia, remained open to the movement of militants, while Russia's relations with adjacent countries – Azerbaijan and especially Georgia – left much to be desired. Along with the absence of a legal regime such as a state of emergency, Chechnya's porous boundaries were the greatest obstacle to an effective policy against the guerrilla units and terrorists that would involve both military and political actions to deprive the militants of the peaceful population's support.

In Iraq, Washington was so confident of its military superiority that it did not bother to consider such a "trifle" as Iraq's borders. Moreover, neighboring Iran and Syria were included by Washington in the "axis of evil" and named as prospective targets for US attacks. This factor guaranteed these countries' unwillingness to cooperate. Thus, Iraq has become a veritable Mecca for terrorists from around the world who come and go across open borders quite freely, greatly reducing the effectiveness of US military and political efforts.

Lesson 9

Before launching operations of this kind, it is important to give considerable thought to postwar settlement. Such an approach justified itself in Afghanistan (at least before the war in Iraq started and bogged down). In some sense the second Chechen campaign and, to an even greater extent, the US invasion of Iraq demonstrated that it is possible to win a war and yet lose the peace; this fact makes a mockery of even the most brilliantly conceived military operations. Without a well-conceived and realistic plan for restoring peace that includes relying on nonhostile local forces, starting a war is imprudent, no matter how much military superiority one may possess.

Lesson 10

This concerns the new nature and role of terrorism in such conflicts. Many factors have removed the border between domestic and international terrorism, such as the modern exchange of information and transportation facilities, enormous revenues from drug trafficking and transborder crime, and the availability of almost any kind of weapon from state arsenals and the black market. Terrorism has acquired development dynamics of its own and rests on the foundation of global organization and finance. Today, terrorism freely "flows" from one conflict to another (Chechnya – Palestine – Syria – Iraq – Afghanistan – Indonesia – Kashmir) and creates its own ideology, strategy, arsenals, recruitment and training bases, professional cells and networks, as well as PR infrastructure.

Accordingly, the goals of terrorism have also changed. Today, they are no longer asserting the rights of ethnic and religious minorities or social groups, even if this is what is proclaimed in public. The main goal of international terrorism now is maintaining and expanding its "habitat" – namely, ethnic and religious conflicts, extremism of any kind, and disruption and chaos in "failing" states (where it is easier to take refuge and recruit fighters).

Terrorist organizations no longer seek to force states to address religious, ethnic, social or political problems, even on the terms of the extremists. On the contrary, terrorist acts, apart from shock effect, are now aimed primarily at preventing any peaceful settlement by provoking the public to oppose "negotiating with terrorists." It is no coincidence that there is an uptick in terrorism whenever a negotiating process is about to begin or when political stabilization prospects emerge (Chechnya, Palestine, Kashmir).

These factors suggest the following conclusions concerning Chechnya, Iraq and Afghanistan. First, when a state uses force against terrorism, the latter may be successfully suppressed (as was the case in Afghanistan before the reckless operation in Iraq was launched). However, if there are no terrorists in the conflict zone, and if the popular slogan of combating terrorism is simply used to achieve other purposes, then terrorism raises its head and enters the conflict zone just as an infection attacks an open wound.

Worse, using the banner of combating terrorism to achieve other, even quite virtuous and lawful goals inevitably discredits the right strategy for countering terrorism, fragments the international antiterrorist coalition, undermines practical efforts in this field, and destroys the unity of society in individual countries.

In Chechnya, the original goal was not combating terrorism but ending militant ethnic separatism – and a large-scale military campaign was not the best method for solving that problem (as the first catastrophic operation of 1994-1996 showed). In Iraq, the military operation was aimed at overthrowing the reviled Saddam regime and obtaining access to Iraqi oil. In both cases, terrorism later emerged in the social environment destabilized by war as a secondary phenomenon and expanded in the manner of a self-fulfilling prophecy.

Second, it would be wrong to call the peaceful settlement of conflicts a condition for snuffing out terrorism. Of course, conflicts must be stopped, because they are not only a breeding ground for terrorism but a source of many other woes. One must bear in mind, however, that a peaceful settlement per se no longer guarantees the cessation of terrorism. It is an essential but not the only condition for combating terrorism. That is because terrorism can simply "flow" into another conflict or provoke it. Furthermore, terrorists will make every effort to thwart any peace process. Thus, peace will hardly be achieved without the most resolute measures to suppress terrorist organizations and their accomplices.

Third, considering the global nature of terrorism, the war against it will be successful only if it is waged on a multilateral, international basis. To this end, countries must totally abandon the practice of applying double standards: No goals, even the noblest ones, can justify terrorist methods. No rights of nations or religions can be recognized if terrorist outrages are committed in their name. No geopolitical or economic interests can justify any tacit support of terrorism. It is not permissible to hunt for Al Qaeda activists around the world and simultaneously provide political asylum to Chechen militant leaders; or denounce Chechen terrorism while justifying Palestinian or Iraqi terrorism; or accuse Syria of assisting Palestinian terrorists and yet turn a blind eye to Pakistan's support of the Taliban who survived the operation in Afghanistan (or of Kashmir terrorists).

The civilized world has all the requisite material and intellectual resources and capabilities to successfully combat terrorism. Yet so far it lacks the most important components: unity, mutual confidence and readiness to abandon double standards and sacrifice secondary political and economic interests for the main common goal.

Notes

1. The official number of losses announced by the Russian Ministry of Defense press service was as follows: "Between 1 October 1999 and 23 December 2002, the total loss of life of the federal forces in Chechnya amounted to 4,572 people killed and 1,549 injured." RIA Novosti. "Ubitykh v Chechne voennykh podshchitali [Soldiers killed in Chechnya have been counted]," *RIA Novosti*, Feb. 17, 2003, https://ria.ru/20030217/322058.html. Other sources estimate much higher losses for the same period: up to 9,000 Defense Ministry military personnel alone killed; see http://www.demoscope.ru/weekly/2005/0211/analit02.php#_FN_28. The counterterrorist operation in Chechnya was called off in April 2009, and data on losses between 2002 and 2004 were somewhat vague, although they amount to 1,000 more federal military personnel killed: "Ot Dagestana do Moskvy cherez Grozny [From Dagestan to Moscow via Grozny]," *Kommersant*, Aug. 8, 2004,

https://www.kommersant.ru/doc/494117.

2. See, for example: Bob Woodward. *Plan of Attack*. New York: Simon & Schuster, 2004. Woodward would claim that the ultimate decision to attack was taken on Jan. 11, 2003. Yet, as F. Gregory Gause later pointed out in his book *The International Relations in the Persian Gulf* (Cambridge: Cambridge University Press, 2009, p. 228), "During the spring of 2002 . . . intensive military planning began, with Gen. Franks visiting the White House to brief the President every three or four weeks." He elaborated: "A briefing paper for a July 2002 meeting among British Prime Minister Tony Blair and his foreign policy and security ministers, leaked to the London *Times* in 2005, stated that Great Britain agreed to a regime change strategy in Iraq that included the use of military force at the April 2002 Bush-Blair summit in Crawford, Texas." (*Ibid.*, p. 229).

3. In fact, estimates of active militants in Chechnya varied greatly during the second Chechen war (1999-2009). The estimates ranged from as many as 30,000 "trained militants" in the first year of the campaign to several hundred by 2005. In 2001 through early 2004, estimates fluctuated between around 600 and 5,000 active militants; see "Ot Dagestana do Moskvy cherez Grozny [From Dagestan to Moscow via Grozny]."

4. There is ongoing debate over the best strategy to deal with militant groups like the Taliban and Al Qaeda. Apparently, no "golden rule" exists; see, for example, a 2009 discussion among experts on this point: https://www.cfr.org/expert-roundup/six-experts-negotiating-taliban.

5. Grachev said this during a TV interview in November 1994 after a failed assault on Grozny by pro-federal Chechen forces (then in the opposition) backed up by Russian regular soldiers recruited by the Federal Counterintelligence Service. Later, Grachev confirmed his outburst, but insisted that his words were "taken out of context." See: "Grachev opravdyvaetsya [Grachev offers excuses]," *Argumenty i fakty*, May 17, 2000, http://www.aif.ru/archive/1638848.

6. Barakhova, Alla. "Poslednyaya zhertva terakta [The last victim of a terrorist attack]," *Kommersant-Vlast*, Nov. 18, 2002. https://www.kommersant.ru/doc/351340.

A PROVING GROUND FOR THE FUTURE

Ruslan Pukhov

Whereas the short conflict with Georgia in 2008 resulted in a radical reform of Russia's Air Force, the participation of Russian military aviation in the Syrian campaign will have even more far-reaching effects, since the experience acquired during it is immeasurably greater.

Russia's air operation in Syria is the most spectacular military-political event of our time. In its post-Soviet history, it is the first time that Russia's Armed Forces were deployed and extensively used in real combat conditions beyond the boundaries of the former Soviet Union. The Syrian campaign is the largest engagement of the Russian Air Force since the war in Afghanistan, and is unparalleled in the history of Russian and Soviet aviation in terms of the complexity and intensity of warfare, and the remoteness of the area of operations.

Russia's capability to maintain a very high sortie rate for a long period of time and the absence of combat and operational losses (except for a Su-24M frontline bomber shot down by the Turkish Air Force) came as, perhaps, the biggest surprise to observers, especially abroad. This indicates that the Russian air group's combat activities

This article originally appeared in *Russia in Global Affairs* Vol. 14, No. 2, 2016.

in Syria have been well organized at all levels, and that the Russian Aerospace Forces meet modern requirements.

The situation stands in stark contrast to Russia's actions in the five-day conflict with Georgia in August 2008. Although confronted by a weak enemy, Russian aviation lost seven combat aircraft in four days (including a Tu-22M3 long-range bomber), and another four aircraft were seriously damaged. Most of these losses were caused not by the Georgian military but by "friendly fire." For example, the 368th Assault Aviation Regiment, stationed at Budyonnovsk, had three Su-25s shot down and another two damaged, and later written off, in only 86 sorties. The loss rate was one aircraft per 17 sorties, which corresponded to the worst periods of the Soviet air campaign against Nazi Germany in 1941. On the whole, Russian Air Force operations in August 2008 were poorly coordinated and lacked effective interaction with ground forces.

During the seven years that have passed since then, the Russian Air Force (renamed the Aerospace Forces on Aug. 1, 2015) has progressed rapidly in all areas, ranging from technical equipment and organization to control and combat training.

Reform of the Russian Air Force

The Russian Air Force became the centerpiece of the military reform that started in 2008, and has changed profoundly since then. The reform was necessitated by many long-standing problems in this branch of the Armed Forces. Organizationally, the prereform structure of the Air Force was formed in 1997-2000, during the previous large-scale consolidation and disbandment of regiments in the Air Force and the Air Defense Forces, which themselves were merged into one branch. The transfer of Army aviation to the Air Force in 2003 had no major impact on the overall situation in the branch. By the beginning of the reform, in the fall of 2008, the Air Force and the Air Defense Forces were a formidable force – but only on paper. The two branches had some 2,800 aircraft and helicopters, and about 100 air defense battalions.[1] In reality, however, the Air Force, like the whole of the Russian Armed Forces, was plagued by problems, and its actual combat potential was very low.

One of the main problems facing the Air Force before 2008 was its great technological backwardness caused by a 15-year pause in purchasing new hardware. Supplies of new aircraft and helicopters dropped sharply in the first few years after the Soviet Union's break-up and decreased to zero in 1994-1995. So, even the newest aircraft were at least 15 to 20 years old by 2008.[2] Most aircraft and air defense systems were even older. Over the years when there was no replacement of material, aircraft and weapon systems became physically and morally obsolete, and exceeded their life span.[3] The serviceability rate by 2007 did not exceed 40%.[4] Without new aircraft and modern airborne weapons, the Russian Air Force was stuck in the mid-1980s.

Structural Reforms

The main aspects of the reforms in Russia's Air Force and Air Defense Forces in 2008-2012 were as follows:

- Changing the air army-air corps (division)-air regiment structure established in 1938 to an air base-air group structure, and gradually reducing the number of air bases. By 2012, following a series of reorganizations, a system had been created in which the few remaining air bases (eight in the Air Force, not counting Army aviation) had an umbrella structure comprising several air groups, each based at its own airfield.
- Reducing the strength of the Air Force by getting rid of obsolete equipment. Simultaneously, the number of home bases was also reduced.
- Some tactical air defense units and Naval aircraft were assigned to the Air Force and the Air Defense Forces.
- As part of broader military education reform efforts, the military education system was centralized and downsized.
- Four Air and Air Defense Forces commands were established for the four new military districts set up in 2010. Tactical Air Force units were assigned to the new military districts (strategic commands), and the role of the Air Force Major Command was reduced.
- The Air Defense Forces were reorganized and reduced; Aerospace Defense brigades were established as the main formations of the Air Defense Forces.

- Finally, a new branch of the Armed Forces was created: the Aerospace Defense Forces.

By the end of 2012, the Air Force and the Air Defense Forces looked different: They were much more compact and had matching available resources. The reduction of the Air Force personnel and a steep increase in defense spending helped to intensify combat and flight training, improve logistical support and raise pay for personnel. Finally, in 2009, after a 15-year pause, the Air Force began to be supplied, in increasing volumes, with new aircraft and armaments.

However, not all decisions made during the creation of a "new look" for the Armed Forces were deemed optimal. In November 2012, Defense Minister Anatoly Serdyukov was replaced by Sergei Shoigu, and Air Force reform entered a new stage.

In 2013-2015, the main purposes of the reorganization of Russia's Air Force and Air Defense Forces were as follows:

- restoring, as of Dec. 1, 2013, the air division-air regiment structure (it should be noted, however, that in fact this was done by renaming existing air bases and air groups)
- restoring Army aviation regiments and forming Army aviation brigades
- restoring armies within the Air Force and the Air Defense Forces in 2014-2015, instead of commands (while preserving their structure)
- partially changing the deployment of Air Force units and expanding the airfield network
- partially returning Naval aviation to the Navy
- decentralizing the military education system and restoring the system of independent flying schools
- reorganizing brigades of the Aerospace Defense (Air Defense) Forces into air defense divisions
- reorganizing, as of Aug. 1, 2015, the Air Force into the Aerospace Forces.

In addition, in 2014, for the first time since the late 1980s, Russia began to build up the strength of its Air Force units by forming new combat regiments. This process started in the Crimea, where the new 27th Mixed Air Division was formed from several new regiments. Subsequently, several new air regiments were formed in other Russian regions. For the first time in almost 30 years, the Russian Air Force began to increase its strength.

Procurement of New Equipment

The procurement of new aircraft was a priority of the state armaments program for 2011-2020 (SAP-2020), approved on Dec. 31, 2010. Total spending for the program equals 20.7 trillion rubles, of which 19.4 trillion rubles are to be allocated to the Defense Ministry. Of this sum, 4.7 trillion rubles will go toward purchasing new aircraft. The program provides for the acquisition of more than 600 planes and 1,100 helicopters for all branches of the Armed Forces.[5] So far, the program has been consistently implemented within the Air Force.

The result was a rapid increase in aircraft deliveries to the Armed Forces. For example, in 2000-2008, the Defense Ministry received only four combat aircraft,[6] but in 2009 alone, the Air Force purchased 33 combat and combat-capable trainer aircraft. It must be noted, though, that 31 of them were MiG-29 SMT/UB fighters returned by Algeria.[7] In 2010, manufacturers began to deliver series-produced combat and combat-capable trainer aircraft ordered by the Defense Ministry. The Armed Forces received 19 to 21 aircraft in 2010; 24 to 28 in 2011; 35 in 2012[8]; 51 in 2013; 102 in 2014; and 91 in 2015.[9] In 2016, about 100 aircraft are expected to be supplied.[10]

The Defense Ministry has signed contracts for building 387 combat aircraft for tactical and Naval aviation (12 Su-27M3s; 20 Su-30M2s; 80 Su-30SMs; 129 Su-34s; 98 Su-35Ss, 20 MiG-29SMT/UBs, and 24 MiG-29KR/Kubrs) and 101 Yak-130 trainer/combat aircraft. Of these, it has already received 234 aircraft (12 Su-27M3s; 24 Su-30M2s; 56 Su-30SMs; 74 Su-34s; 48 Su-35Ss; six MiG-29SMT/UBs; and 24 MiG-29KR/Kubrs) and 79 Yak-130s.[11]

In addition, the Russian Air Force has received one new strategic bomber, a Tu-160,[12] and four long-range surveillance and reconnaissance aircraft (two Tu-214ONs[13] and two Tu-214Rs[14]).

The top priority for Russia's combat aviation is the creation of a Prospective Airborne Complex of Frontline Aviation (PAK FA) – the T-50 fifth-generation fighter. Since 2010, five prototypes of the T-50 have been built and are now undergoing testing, and another four prototypes are to be tested in 2016. In all, 14 experimental and preproduction T-50 prototypes, and 12 series-produced T-50s are set to be produced before 2020. Their mass production will begin in the next decade.

After 2020, Russia expects to see the first results from two other programs to build completely new aircraft – a Prospective Airborne Complex of Long-Range Aviation (PAK DA, a new strategic bomber)[15] and a Prospective Airborne Complex of Transport Aviation (PAK TA, a heavy transport aircraft).[16] Until then, Russia intends to resume the production of the Tu-160M2 modernized strategic bomber, and to transfer the production of the Il-76MD-90A modernized military transport aircraft from Tashkent to Ulyanovsk. Thirty-nine Il-76MD-90As have been ordered for the Defense Ministry, and there are plans to procure Il-78M-90A aerial refueling tankers based on them.[17]

Another key purpose of the reform was the modernization of the fleet of combat aircraft. By 2020, the upgrade program is to cover up to 100 Su-27 fighters, 150 MiG-31 fighters, 200 Su-24M tactical bombers and their reconnaissance versions (Su-24MR), 180 Su-25 assault aircraft, 30 Tu-22M3 long-range bombers, and 60 Tu-95MS and Tu-160 strategic bombers. The Air Force has also begun to modernize the A-50 airborne early warning and control aircraft. Simultaneously, work is underway to develop a new generation of this type of aircraft, the A-100.[18]

Modernization has been going particularly rapidly in Army aviation units. Over the last few years, the Defense Ministry has received more than 100 new helicopters per year. Contracts have been signed for the delivery of over 450 new Mi-28N, Mi-35M and Ka-52 combat helicopters, of which more than 250 have already been delivered. New transport helicopters of the Mi-17 series are purchased on a constant basis. The Defense Ministry has also procured[19] new Mi-26 heavy transport helicopters and more than 70 Ka-226 and Ansat light helicopters.[20] Starting in 2012, a wide range of new guided air weapons has been purchased for the Air Force, including RVV-SD and RVV-MD air-to-air missiles.

Much attention is given to the development of unmanned aerial vehicles (UAVs). At first, the Defense Ministry purchased a large number of Russian-made light, short-range UAVs and some Israeli-made tactical UAVs, and licensed production of the latter was started. Simultaneously, Russia launched extensive programs to develop various types of long-range UAVs with a takeoff weight of one to five metric tons, although practical results will apparently be available only by the end of the decade, upon which it will be decided whether they can be made operational. Also, Russia has begun developing jet-powered attack drones.

In all, given the current procurement plans, Russia's Air Force and Naval aviation may have up to 1,500 combat aircraft by 2020 under the best-case scenario:

- up to 130 bombers (16 Tu-160s; 50 Tu-96MSs; and 70 Tu-22M3s)
- up to 820 fighters (12 T-50s; 100 Su-35s; 200 Su-30SMs; 20 Su-30M2s; 100 modernized and new Su-27SM/SM3s; 120 nonupgraded Su-27s and Su-33s; 150 upgraded MiG-31s; 36 MiG-35s; 50 MiG-29SMTs; and 24 MiG-29KR/Kubrs)
- up to 350 strike and reconnaissance aircraft (150 Su-34s; and 200 upgraded Su-24Ms and Su-24MRs)
- up to 180 ground attack aircraft (modernized Su-25SMs/Su-25UBs).

This will mean that the Russian Air Force will continue to rank second in the world after the US Air Force in terms of combat capabilities.

Problems

However, there are serious problems complicating the reform and functioning of the Air Force, such as:

- instability of the organizational structure in recent years, caused by continuous reforms since 2008;
- unconfirmed effectiveness of the existing structure, where the bulk of the Air Force is subordinated to operational-strategic commands (military districts); in particular, it remains unclear whether this may lead to the regionalization of air power instead of its concentration;
- unclear status and development prospects of the newly formed Aerospace Defense Forces;

- largely outdated methods of using the Air Force at operational and tactical levels; lack of experience in conducting major modern air operations while meeting aggressive enemy counteraction;
- shortage of modern airborne weapons, which is likely to continue for a long time;
- weakness of modern surveillance and target acquisition assets – in particular, the absence of targeting pods in the Air Force;
- insufficient maturity of many new types of modern aircraft coming into service is likely to remain an issue for a long time;
- a large number of outdated aircraft in the Air Force, which causes maintenance, service life, flight safety, and other problems;
- weak long-range UAV and attack drone capabilities are unlikely to be improved in the near future.

Russia's Air Operation in Syria

With all its strengths and weaknesses, Russia's Aerospace Forces surprised many by intervening in the war in Syria. The operation was the first major practical test for Russia's overhauled and reborn military aviation. It would be safe to say that it has successfully passed this test.

I will not focus on political problems raised by Russia's military intervention in the Syrian war, as they have been widely discussed in recent months. I will only note that in military-political terms, the main problem concerning the Russian operation in Syria is its ambiguity. On the one hand, the official goal of the campaign is to fight the Islamic State (ISIS), which emerged from the civil wars in Syria and Iraq, threatens to reshape the map of the Middle East and has become an overt terrorist state entity. On the other hand, it is obvious that one of the main goals of the Russian intervention in Syria is to support Syrian President Bashar Assad. Russia seeks if not to drastically improve the military status of his regime (which is hardly possible), then at least to consolidate its military and territorial positions, which will create prerequisites for achieving a peaceful settlement in Syria and dropping the issue of Assad's exit as a precondition for settlement.

Although the presence of the Russian air group in Syria will obviously continue for months, it is vital that Russia not get involved in a protracted war, minimize its own losses by all means, carefully and flexibly choose "political" targets for air strikes, avoid a military confrontation with Western military powers in the region, and finally, make a timely exit.

The operation in Syria is of paramount importance for Russia's Aerospace Forces, which have for the first time gained experience conducting a broad offensive campaign involving various types of aircraft in coordination with ground forces and foreign partners (Syria, Iran and Iraq). Equally valuable, and unique for the Russian Armed Forces, is the experience of deploying and supporting an expeditionary air group at a considerable distance from the national territory.

Russia's air group in Syria was deployed at the Hmeimim air base (which had earlier been used by Syria's sea-based helicopters) near Latakia in September 2015. Initially, the group included 12 Su-24M tactical bombers (M2 and Gefest-T upgrades), 12 modernized Su-25SM and Su-25UB attack aircraft, four new Su-34 tactical bombers, four new Su-30SM multirole fighters, one IL-20M1 reconnaissance aircraft, 12 Mi-24P combat helicopters, and five Mi-8AMTSh military transport helicopters.[21] All the planes and helicopters arrived with their crews from various combat units of the Aerospace Forces – i.e., the air group was manned by ordinary pilots flying in-service aircraft.

Later, the group was enhanced. On Dec. 6, 2015, four more Su-34 tactical bombers were sent to Syria from Russia,[22] and on Jan. 30, 2016, the group received four Su-35S multirole fighters, which had just entered service in Russia.[23] The Su-24M bomber, downed by a Turkish fighter jet on Nov. 24, was replaced by a bomber of the same type that arrived at the Hmeimim air base in January 2016. By February 2016, the total number of Russian combat aircraft in Syria had reached 40. The helicopter group had been increased, too: Four new Mi-35M combat helicopters and several Mi-8 transport helicopters were delivered to the base in late 2015.[24]

On Nov. 17, 2015, Russia's Aerospace Forces group at Hmeimim air base was renamed a special-purpose air brigade, with its headquarters also controlling aircraft operating against targets in Syria from the territory of Russia. The Russian air group in Syria has been commanded by Maj. Gen. Aleksandr Maksimtsev.[25]

Russia has deployed a large ground force to defend the Hmeimim air base – initially 1,500 and now possibly 3,000 troops, including units of special forces, the 810th Naval Infantry Brigade of the Black Sea,[26] the 7th Air Assault Division from Novorossiisk, and several units of the ground forces.[27] The group has T-90A main battle tanks,[28] various types of armored vehicles, and 152-mm Msta-B towed howitzers.[29] To defend the airfield from air attacks, modern air defense weapons have been deployed, including Buk-M2 surface-to-air missile systems, and Pantsir-S gun/SAM systems. In late November, this group was reinforced with an S-400 air defense battalion.[30]

The Russian military group is supplied by air – via Iran and Iraq – by Il-76 and An-124 military transport aircraft, and by sea – by the Navy's large landing ships and auxiliary and transport vessels, which constantly shuttle between Novorossiisk or Sevastopol and the Syrian port of Tartus. Because of intensive traffic, this sea route has been called the "Syrian Express." Military transport aircraft are also widely used. Between September and December 2015, An-124 aircraft of the Aerospace Forces made 113 flights to Hmeimim and delivered 10,200 metric tons of cargo.[31]

A special feature of the Russian air operation in Syria is the large-scale use of precision-guided air-to-surface weapons. In particular, Russia for the first time used KAB-500S precision-guided bombs with a satellite-aided guidance system. Yet, unguided air munitions continue to play the main role in destroying terrorist targets. But as Mi-24P and Mi-35M combat helicopters and Su-25SM attack aircraft use unguided missiles, they inevitably come under fire from low-altitude air defense systems used by rebels and Islamists.

By the beginning of February 2016, the total number of sorties made by Russian aircraft in Syria reached an estimated 6,600. The limited air group conducted intensive operations with up to 100 sorties a day, and increased their number to 150 by the end of November (including those made by aircraft from the Russian territory).[32] On Oct. 7, 2015, Russia's operation in Syria involved Navy ships for the first time. The missile ships *Dagestan, Grad Sviyazhsk, Veliky Ustyug* and *Uglich* fired Kalibr precision cruise missiles from the Caspian Sea to hit targets some 1,500 kilometers away. In all, they launched 26 missiles against 11 targets in Syria.[33] Later, Kalibr missiles were fired from the same ships on Nov. 20 (18 missiles) and from the *Rostov-on-Don* diesel-electric submarine (Dec. 8, four missiles). During the three attacks, 48 Kalibr missiles were launched.[34] This was the first time the Russian Navy used this weapon.

On Nov. 17, 2015, Russia for the first time since the beginning of the operation in Syria used its Tu-160, Tu-95MS and Tu-22M3 long-range aircraft. Tu-95MS and Tu-160 aircraft took off from the Engels airfield in Saratov Region, and Tu-22M3 aircraft flew out of the Mozdok base in North Ossetia. This was a truly historic day for the Russian Armed Forces: Tu-160 and Tu-95MS strategic bombers, which had never participated in combat operations before, received the baptism of fire.[35]

During their combat missions in Syria, Tu-160 aircraft use modern Kh-101 cruise missiles; Tu-95MS aircraft use Kh-555 cruise missiles (a conventionally armed version of the Kh-55 missile); and Tu-22M3 bombers use free-fall bombs.[36] In all, Russian long-range aircraft have made 187 sorties to Syria from the Russian territory. Tu-95MS and Tu-160 aircraft have launched 97 cruise missiles.[37]

Undoubtedly, the attacks by sea- and air-launched cruise missiles against targets in Syria were not a military necessity but a purely military-political demonstration of the Russian Armed Forces' capabilities.

To support long-range bombers, Su-27SM and Su-30SM fighters were used with in-flight refueling. Since December 2015, the A-50 airborne early warning and control aircraft has been operating in Syrian skies to control the airspace. It may also serve as a flying command post. The aircraft makes flights from the Mozdok airfield.

Some Results and Assessments of Russia's Air Operation in Syria

The Russian air group's activities have not yet led to the defeat of ISIS or the Syrian opposition. However, it is obvious that Russian air attacks do have a slow but real effect and are gradually tipping the balance in favor of the Syrian government forces, which have moved from strategic defensive to offensive operations – largely tactical so far.

Despite the unprecedentedly intensive combat actions, Russia's air group has not yet suffered combat or noncombat losses. The only exception was the Su-24M2 tactical bomber shot down by a Turkish F-16 fighter jet in an incident near the Syrian-Turkish border on Nov. 24, 2015. Russia's Mi-8AMTSh helicopter, sent to find and rescue the pilots from the crash site, was attacked by pro-Turkish rebels and destroyed after an emergency landing. Those have been the only losses of Russian aviation during the Syrian campaign.

Russia's Aerospace Forces have for the first time in their history used precision-guided weapons in relatively large amounts, including new KAB-500S precision-guided bombs with a satellite-aided guidance system. For the first time, conventional cruise missiles are used in military operations, including new Kh-101 air-launched missiles, modified Kh-555 missiles, and sea-launched Kalibr missiles. In addition, Russia actively uses UAVs, both domestic and Iranian-made, for reconnaissance, fire adjustment, target designation and evaluation of strike effectiveness during the air campaign in Syria.

In general, the Aerospace Forces have demonstrated an unprecedentedly high level of combat and operational readiness, and their capability to conduct highly intensive combat operations far from the Russian territory. The absence of combat and operational losses during the air campaign is impressive.

On the other hand, the effectiveness of combat actions is rather moderate. Apparently, the attacks have inflicted less damage on the rebels than expected, and the Syrian government Army has been slow in exploiting the effects of the air strikes. The interaction between the Russian Aerospace Forces and Syrian government forces on the ground leaves much to be desired. Russia's air support for ground troops does not appear to be quite effective. On the whole, the Aerospace Forces' operation has demonstrated the limits of air power – something Western powers encountered earlier, too.

Despite the obvious progress, the technological level of Russia's Aerospace Forces in the Syrian campaign matches that of the US Air Force during Operation Desert Storm of 1991. In other words, they are far behind US and, generally, Western military aviation. With respect to precision-guided weapons, Russia uses mainly munitions with satellite-aided guidance in Syria. This type of guidance has certain limitations, including in terms of accuracy. KAB-500S bombs, which weigh 500 kg, and cruise missiles are often too powerful to be used against typical targets in this war. Russian aviation has few (if any) high-precision weapons for use against moving, small-sized and well-fortified targets.

Russian aviation is experiencing an acute shortage of target designation assets for precision-guided weapons. The only exception is the Platan electro-optical targeting system used by new Su-34 tactical bombers. Russian UAVs do not have target designation capability, either. Russia's Aerospace Forces still do not have targeting pods, which have been used by Western military aviation for the last 25 to 30 years.

Apparently, the effectiveness of Russia's combat actions in Syria is limited mainly by deficient reconnaissance capabilities, rather than a lack of aircraft or weapons. Russian aviation urgently needs specialized reconnaissance aircraft, UAVs with a wide range of equipment and a long-range capability, and efficient space-based reconnaissance systems. There is also a complete lack of drones with strike capabilities. Also, Russia has not yet sent its new Mi-28N and Ka-52 combat helicopters to Syria due to their insufficient maturity.

Despite these inadequacies, Syria has become a perfect proving ground for trying out new tactics and new weapons of Russia's Aerospace Forces on a large scale. Russia has for the first time used its most advanced Su-30SM and Su-34 (and now also Su-35S) aircraft, cruise missiles, precision-guided weapons, and UAVs, and practiced intricate forms of interaction among various forces. Russia's Aerospace Forces have been gaining rich combat and operational experience. The operation in Syria seems to have cost Russia relatively little so far.

Whereas the short conflict with Georgia in 2008 resulted in a radical reform of Russia's Air Force, the participation of Russian military aviation in the Syrian campaign will have even more far-reaching effects, since the experience acquired there is immeasurably greater. One result will be more intensive development of the Aerospace Forces in the next few years.

Notes

1. Barabanov, Mikhail. "Kuda letit rossiiskaya aviatsia" [Where does the Russian air force fly], *Kommersant-Vlast*, 33, Aug. 25, 2008, https://www.kommersant.ru/doc/1014592.

2. Lavrov, Anton. "Reformirovaniye Voyenno-vozdushnykh sil Rossii" [Reforming the Air Force of Russia]. In Barabanov, Mikhail, ed., *Novaya Armiya Rossii* [New Army of Russia]. Moscow: Centre for the Analysis of Strategies and Technologies, 2010, p. 56, http://militera.lib.ru/science/0/pdf/sb_new-army.pdf.

3. Frolov, Andrei and Barabanov, Mikhail. "Tysyacha samoletov k 2020 godu" [One thousand warplanes by the year 2020], *Voyenno-promyshlenny Kuryer*, Oct. 22, 2012, https://vpk-news.ru/articles/12848.

4. Barabanov, *op. cit.*

5. Frolov and Barabanov, *op. cit.*

6. Barabanov, Mikhail. "Po samoletam plany grandiozniye" [Huge plans for the aircrafts], *Voyenno-promyshlenny Kuryer*, Jan. 15, 2013, https://vpk-news.ru/articles/13976.

7. "VVS Rossii kupili zabrakovanniye Alzhirom istrebiteli" [The Russian Air Force bought fighter jets rejected by Algeria], *Lenta.ru*, Feb. 9, 2009, https://lenta.ru/news/2009/02/09/fighters/.

8. Various sources differ slightly. See: Barabanov, Mikhail. "VVS Rossii poluchat popolneniye" [The Russian Air Force is being replenished], *Periskop.2. Novosti OPK i VTS Rossii*, March 18, 2011, http://periscope2.ru/2011/03/18/2800/.

9. Barabanov, Mikhail. "Po samoletam plany grandiozniye," *op. cit.* See also: Kramnik, Ilya. "VVS Rossii v ozhidanii kachestvennogo perekhoda" [The Russian Air Force: expecting a quality transition], *Novosti VPK*, Jan. 11, 2013, https://vpk.name/news/82201_vvs_rossii_ozhidanie_kachestvennogo_perehoda.html.

10. See updated information at: "Postavki boevykh samoletov v Vooruzhenniye Sily Rossii v 2016 godu" [Supply of combat aircraft to the Russian Armed Forces in 2016], Oruzhiye Rossii Information Agency, March 22, http://www.arms-expo.ru/news/vooruzhenie_i_voennaya_tekhnika/postavki_boevykh_samoletov_v_vooruzhennye_sily_rossii_v_2016_godu/.

11. Author's calculations from various sources.

12. "Ocherednoi Tu-160 posle modernizatsii postupil na sluzhbu Minoborony Rossii" [The next Tu-160 joined the fleet of Ministry of Defense of Russia after modernization], Tupolev company official announcement, Jan. 28, 2016, http://www.tupolev.ru/tu-160-after-modernization.

13. "Tu-214ON (Open Skies) Reconnaissance Aircraft," *Airforce Technology*, https://www.airforce-technology.com/projects/tu-214on-open-skies-reconnaissance-aircraft/

14. "Strategic Reconnaissance Aircraft Tu-214R. Sources and data collection" (in Russian). *Voyenno-tekhnicheskii sbornik Bastion*, 2012-2018, http://bastion-karpenko.ru/tu-214r/.

15. "PAK DA cherez desyat let" [PAK DA in ten years], *Voyenno-promyshlenny Kuryer*, Aug. 14, 2012, https://vpk-news.ru/articles/9166. See also: " 'Tupolev' zavershil proektirovaniye novogo bombardirovshchika" [Tupolev has completed the design of a new bomber], *Lenta.ru*, April 10, 2014, https://lenta.ru/news/2014/04/10/pakda/. See also: Mikhailov, Aleksei. "Bombardirovshchik pyatogo pokoleniya budet dozvukovym" [Fifth-generation bomber will be subsonic], *Izvestia*, March 4, 2013, https://iz.ru/news/545925.

16. "PAK TA: noveishii transportnyi samolet dlya rossiiskoi armii" [PAK TA: The newest transport aircraft for the Russian Army], *Militaryarms.ru*, Nov. 20, 2018, https://militaryarms.ru/voennaya-texnika/aviaciya/pak-ta-novyj-transportnyj-samolet/.

17. Peshkov, Aleksandr. " 'Ilyushin' planiruyet narastit vypusk Il-76MD-90A v blizhaishiye 5 let" [Ilyushin plans to increase the output of IL-76MD-90A in the next 5 years], *Tvzvezda*, Feb. 21, 2019, https://tvzvezda.ru/news/opk/content/2019221152-f87pp.html.

18. "Perspektivny rossiisky samolet-zapravshchik vperviye podnyalsya v

vozdukh" [A promising Russian refueling aircraft made the first flight], *Interfax*, Jan. 25, 2018, https://www.interfax.ru/russia/597067.

19. For updated data, see, for example: "VKS Rossii zakhoteli poluchit 700 istrebitelei" [Russian Aerospace Forces want 700 fighter jets], *Lenta.ru*, Dec. 15, 2016, https://lenta.ru/news/2016/12/15/fighters/; and https://topwar.ru/25204-primernyy-kolichestvennyy-sostav-vvs-rf-k-2020-godu.html.

20. Author's calculations from various sources. See, for example: "Minoborony poluchit pochti 150 udarnykh vertoletov Ka-52 'Alligator' do 2020 goda" [Ministry of Defense will receive almost 150 Ka-52 Alligator attack helicopters by 2020], *TASS*, June 24, 2014, https://tass.ru/politika/1275689. See also: Hackett, James. "The Military Balance 2016," *International Institute for Strategic Studies*, 2016.

21. See: "Gruppirovka VKS v Sirii. Kolichestvo i kachestvo" [Russian Aerospace Forces group in Syria: quantity and quality], *Voennoye obozreniye*, Oct. 5, 2015, https://topwar.ru/83643-gruppirovka-vks-v-sirii-kolichestvo-i-kachestvo.html. See also: "Noveishiye Su-35 perebrosheny v Siriyu" [The newest Su-35s have been relocated to Syria], *Voyenno-promyshlenny Kuryer*, Jan. 31, 2016, https://vpk-news.ru/news/28981.

22. O'Connor, Sean. "Russia deploys additional Su-34s to Syria," *Jane's Defence Weekly*, Dec. 10, 2015, https://world-defense.com/threads/russia-deploys-additional-su-34s-to-syria.3358/.

23. "Chetyre istrebitelya Su-35S perebrosheny v Siriyu" [Four Su-35S fighters have been relocated to Syria], BMPD Livejournal Blog, Jan. 31, 2016, https://bmpd.livejournal.com/1710222.html.

24. See: Azanov, Roman. "Boyevoye kreshcheniye Siriei" [Baptism of fire in Syria], *TASS*, Sept. 28, 2018, https://tass.ru/armiya-i-opk/5616784.

25. "Operatsiya rossiiskikh VKS v Sirii" [Operations of Russian Aerospace Forces in Syria], *RIA Novosti*, Dec. 30, 2015, https://ria.ru/20151230/1350483631.html?in=t.

26. Krymova, Yulia. "V Sevastopole nagradili vernuvshikhsya iz Sirii morpekhov" [Marines returned from Syria were honored in Sebastopol], *Rossiiskaya gazeta*, Dec. 28, 2015, https://rg.ru/2015/12/28/reg-kfo/morpehi-anons.html.

27. Solopov, Maksim. "Vezhlivy kontingent: skolko v Sirii rossiiskikh voennykh" [Polite expeditionary force: How many Russian troops are there in Syria], *RBC-News*, Oct. 1, 2015., https://www.rbc.ru/politics/01/10/2015/560d472d9a7947ed7fa0540d.

28. "T-90A v Sirii" [T-90A in Syria], *BMPD Livejournal Blog*, Nov. 13, 2015, https://bmpd.livejournal.com/1576223.html.

29. "Rassledovaniye: rossiiskiye voenniye nachali ispolzovat'v Sirii gaubitsy i tanki" [Investigation: Russian Army began using howitzers and tanks in Syria], *Znak.com* Internet newspaper, Nov. 16, 2016, https://www.znak.com/2015-11-16/rassledovanie_rossiyskie_voennye_nachali_ispolzovat_v_sirii_gaubicy_i_tanki.

30. "Tri eshelona zashchity: kak ustroena zenitnaya raketnaya oborona na aviabaze Hmeimim" [Three layers of defense: how the anti-aircraft missile defense at Hmeimim Air Force Base works], *TASS*, Feb. 12, 2016, https://tass.ru/armiya-i-opk/2650477.

31. Valangin, Anton. "An 124 ustanovil rekord v Sirii" [An-124 sets record in Syria], *Rossiiskaya gazeta*, Feb. 3, 2016, https://rg.ru/2016/02/03/an-124-rekord.html.

32. See also: Lee, Robert. "Voenniye aspekty rossiiskoi operatsii v Sirii" [Military aspects of Russia's operations in Syria], *Nezavisimoye voennoye obozreniye*, Jan. 15, 2016, http://nvo.ng.ru/wars/2016-01-15/8_aspects.html.

33. "VMF Rossii vperviye primenil krylatiye rakety bolshoi dalnosti v boyu" [Russian Navy used long-range cruise missiles in battle for the first time], *Rambler-news*, Oct. 7, 2017, https://news.rambler.ru/middleeast/31558528-udar-po-ig-v-sirii-stal-pervym-sluchaem-primeneniya-rossiyskih-tomagavkov-v-boyu/.

34. "Korabli Kaspiiskoi flotilii udarili 18 krylatymi raketami po pozitsiyam boyevikov v Sirii" [Caspian Flotilla ships fired 18 cruise missiles at militant positions in Syria], *TASS*, Nov. 20, 2015, https://tass.ru/armiya-i-opk/2459199.

35. Sevastyanov, Mikhail. "Operatsia VKS v Sirii: Rossia obrela stretegiyu i opyt distantsionnoi voiny" [Russian Airspace Forces operation in Syria: Russia gains remote war strategy and experience], *RIA-Novosti*, Sept. 30, 2016, https://ria.ru/20160930/1478181962.html.

36. "VVS Rossii sushchestvenno narastili…" [Russian Air Force markedly intensified…], RF MOD official announcement, Nov. 18, 2015, https://function.mil.ru/news_page/country/more.htm?id=12066265.

37. "VKS Rossii v Sirii za 100 dnei vypustili 97 krylatykh raket po IG" [In 100 days Russia's Air Force in Syria fired 97 cruise missiles at ISIS], *RIA-Novosti*, Nov. 15, 2016, https://ria.ru/20160115/1360093250.html.

THE LIMITS OF CAPABILITIES

Prokhor Tebin

An analysis of the Russian Navy's involvement in the Syrian campaign suggests two conclusions. The first is rather optimistic: The Russian Navy has begun to recover after a long period of decline. The second is less comforting: The Navy is already facing a shortage of ships of almost all major classes.

Russia's military operation in Syria has demonstrated a high level of combat readiness of the Russian Aerospace Forces and positive results of the military reform in general. This issue was discussed in detail in Ruslan Pukhov's article "A Proving Ground for the Future" [see above in this volume – *Ed.*]. Media and expert attention to the Aerospace Forces' actions is not surprising as this branch of the Armed Forces plays the main role in the Russian campaign against the radical Islamic State (IS). Yet, equally important is the role played by the Russian Navy. It is interesting to analyze how its actions in Syria characterize the current state of the Russian Navy, especially as it continues its mission in the Eastern Mediterranean amid the partial withdrawal of the Russian force from Syria.

This article originally appeared in *Russia in Global Affairs* Vol. 14, No. 3, 2016.

Between Nuclear Holocaust and Humanitarian Assistance

The routine tasks of the Russian Navy at present can be classified into three main groups.

First, the Navy, which includes ballistic missile submarines, participates in maintaining strategic stability between Russia and the US. General purpose forces provide combat stability to ballistic missile submarines, while the latter are an instrument of nuclear deterrence against the US and NATO.

Second, general purpose Naval forces serve as nonnuclear deterrence against potential enemies. Reliance on nuclear missile submarines would only significantly limit the capabilities of the country's leadership in the event of a conflict with some major sea power. The presence of advanced nonnuclear deterrence forces helps avoid an unnecessary escalation of a conflict and raises the nuclear threshold. This is especially important, since in many scenarios of conflicts between great powers the parties have limited political goals. The use or threat of the use of nuclear weapons in such situations is impossible or unreasonable, and a party that does not have sufficient conventional deterrence forces has a losing position.

And third, the Navy also has peacetime missions – humanitarian operations, assistance to diplomatic efforts, and the struggle against terrorism and other nontraditional threats to national security. In addition, the third group of tasks includes participating in local and low-intensity conflicts. The Russian operation in Syria largely belongs to this category. But its implementation requires nonnuclear deterrence, as well.

As part of the Syrian operation, the Navy has been:
- Ensuring supplies of weapons, military equipment and other cargo to the government of Syria (the "Syrian Express"), and supplies to the Russian ground force by sea. These efforts involve landing and auxiliary ships, including civilian vessels that were recently purchased for this purpose and assigned to the Navy.
- Ensuring the sustainability of supplies to Syria, controlling the air and underwater situation, and protecting the Hmeimim air base, as well as the supply and maintenance base in Tartus from the sea. These operations are being performed by the Russian Navy's

Mediterranean Task Force.

- Attacking targets with long-range sea-launched cruise missiles (SLCM). According to official information from the Defense Ministry, SLCMs were used three times: on Oct. 7[1] and Nov. 20,[2] 2015 from surface ships of the Caspian Flotilla (44 missiles in total), and on Dec. 8, 2015 from the Rostov-on-Don submarine, which was located in the eastern part of the Mediterranean (four missiles were reportedly fired).[3]

An analysis of the Russian Navy's involvement in the Syrian campaign suggests the following two conclusions. The first one is rather optimistic: The Russian Navy has begun to recover after a long period of decline in the 1990s and early 2000s. The second conclusion is less comforting: The Navy is already facing a shortage of ships of almost all major classes. Overcoming this shortage requires the commissioning of new ships, and at a faster pace than the decommissioning of Soviet-built ships.

Sea Bridge

The Russian Navy began to deliver various kinds of cargo to the Syrian government in 2012. The reason is clear: Unlike the civilian fleet, the Navy enjoys the right of extraterritoriality, which, for example, makes the inspection of its cargo legally impossible. Also, the Navy's weapons and marines serve as additional insurance against various contingencies.

Between 2013 and September 2015, large landing ships of the Russian Navy made over 200 voyages to Syria.[4] The "Syrian Express" provided useful experience to sailors and shore-based personnel who ensured technical serviceability of the ships. For example, the *Novocherkassk* large landing ship carried out 10 combat missions and covered 30,000 [nautical] miles over 170 vessel-days.[5] Another large landing ship, *Aleksandr Shabalin* of the Baltic Fleet, was on continuous combat duty at sea for 392 days, from the end of 2012 to the beginning of 2014, and covered about 47,000 miles over 283 vessel-days.[6]

Delivering supplies to Syria required using almost all large landing ships. Each year, nine or 10 ships were used for that purpose. In all, 16 out of 19[7] large landing ships in service with the Russian Navy were involved, which put a great strain on the Navy. The average age of Russian large landing ships is 34 years. The oldest ship is 50 years old and the youngest is 25 years old. Unfortunately, the Navy may receive only two new large landing ships (Project 11711) in 2016-2017. There is still no clarity about how the fleet of landing ships will be modernized after that.

The bulk of the missions (about 60%) were carried out by Black Sea Fleet ships. Capt. Aleksandr Plokhotnyuk, chief navigator of the Black Sea Fleet, said in March 2016 that the time spent by the fleet's ships under way increased quickly between 2013 and 2015 – from 272,000 nautical miles in 2013 to 544,000 miles in 2014 and to 767,500 miles in 2015.[8] According to available information, the increase was due to the ships' participation in the "Syrian Express" operation.

The traffic intensity increased with the start of the Russian Aerospace Forces' operation in Syria. According to the commander of the Russian force in Syria, Col. Gen. Aleksandr Dvornikov, Russian ships made more than 80 voyages from September 2015 to March 2016.[9] The delivery of supplies for the Russian force and the Syrian Army required the use of tankers and other auxiliary ships. The shortage of landing and specialized transport ships forced the government to purchase second-hand civilian ships.

Using civilian ships under a military flag and in military-political interests is reasonable and justified in terms of cost-effectiveness – especially in a scenario similar to the Syrian one, where a military flag neutralizes most political and legal risks and where there is no real and immediate military threat. There is a hypothetical threat from Turkey's powerful submarine fleet, but Project 775 and Project 1171 large landing ships are as vulnerable to submarines as civilian ships.

The "Syrian Express" experience is an argument in favor of creating a body within the Russian Navy that would be similar to the US Military Sealift Command and would control ships delivering cargo in the interests of the Defense Ministry in times of peace and war. These ships include both newly built or second-hand ships, and ships on long-term lease. Crews are largely civilian, and the number of military personnel can be reduced significantly, down to a small group of marines per ship.

The Mediterranean Squadron

The creation of a Naval task force in the Mediterranean, subordinate to the Black Sea Fleet commander, began in the spring of 2013 when a squadron of Pacific Fleet ships set off for the region. The squadron's composition constantly changed and included, at various times, ships from all fleets and flotillas of the Russian Navy, among them the *Pyotr Veliky* nuclear-powered heavy missile cruiser and the *Admiral Flota Sovetskogo Soyuza Kuznetsov* heavy aircraft carrier. During the Aerospace Forces' operation in Syria, the composition of the task force was more or less the same: the *Moskva* missile cruiser and several other surface warships, plus "Syrian Express" ships and various types of auxiliary vessels. In addition, the task force apparently included submarines, but this information is classified. Nevertheless, after submarine-launched cruise missiles were fired, it became known that they were fired by the *Rostov-on-Don* submarine.

In January 2016, the *Moskva* cruiser in the "Syrian squadron" was replaced by its sister ship – the *Varyag* missile cruiser of the Pacific Fleet. According to Capt. Plokhotnyuk, the *Moskva* covered 40,000 miles during its three combat missions in 2015.[10] The *Moskva* and later the *Varyag* were the core of the task force that provided support to the Aerospace Forces and landing ships. They ensured air, antisubmarine and antiship defense, and controlled the airspace and the entire task force. It should be noted that supporting the Aerospace Forces in Syria initially was not among the Russian Navy's tasks. However, after Turkish troops shot down a Russian bomber, the *Moskva* cruiser sailed to the coast of Latakia, and an S400 surface-to-air missile system was deployed on the ground.

The choice of the *Moskva* and the *Varyag* was not coincidental. In fact, they were the only combat-ready ships capable of performing such missions. A third cruiser, *Marshal Ustinov* (Project 1164), and the *Pyotr Veliky* are undergoing shipyard overhauls. The average age of these four ships is 27 years. In 2018, the Navy expects to receive the *Admiral Nakhimov* heavy missile cruiser, with the *Pyotr Veliky* taking its place in the repair dock. Soviet-built large antisubmarine ships and destroyers now in service with the Russian Navy cannot serve as the flagship of the Mediterranean Task Force. Further modernization of the small fleet of large surface ships depends on the implementation of the program to build a new-generation destroyer. Project 22350 frigates can also perform air defense functions but can hardly serve as the flagship of a task force for a long period of time.

The situation with other ships in the task force is a little better. Near the Syrian coast, the *Moskva* was accompanied by various Soviet-built ships, including the *Smetlivy* destroyer (commissioned 47 years ago). In March 2016, the Black Sea Fleet received the *Admiral Grigorovich* frigate (Project 11356) and is expected to receive two more ships of this project soon. Due to Ukraine's decision not to supply gas turbines for these ships, Russia has abandoned plans to build three more frigates of this type. On the one hand, this may be for the better: Project 11356 ships have been a forced and temporary solution because these ships are obsolete. On the other hand, this raises the issue of building a series of multipurpose surface warships. Russia is now building Project 22350 frigates, but slowly, due to their high cost and complexity.

The situation is much better with submarines. Six new Project 636.3 submarines, such as the *Rostov-on-Don*, can drastically reinforce the Black Sea submarine fleet. In addition, their construction can be continued in the interests of other regional fleets of Russia.

Long Arm of the Fleet

The event that attracted particular attention from observers was the active use of new long-range sea-launched 3M14 Kalibr cruise missiles. Andrei Kartapolov, head of the Chief Operations Administration of the Russian Armed Forces' General Staff, said that the decision to fire the missiles was made after Russian intelligence detected several important targets of militants that needed to be destroyed immediately.[11] Nevertheless, the use of the cruise missiles was required not so much by military necessity as by the desire to test and demonstrate Russia's new capabilities.

These missiles were largely deployed on Project 21631 missile corvettes in service with the Caspian Flotilla. For a long time, some experts questioned the advisability of building these ships armed with such powerful missiles, as well as the active rearmament of the flotilla in general, which in the early 2000s received the first four ships armed with Kalibr missiles. The Syrian campaign clearly showed the wisdom of this decision: Now flotilla ships have 32 launchers for long-range cruise missiles with an operational range covering the entire Caucasus and large parts of Central Asia and the Middle East. These are the areas where threats to Russia's national security are most likely to emerge, and particularly from international terrorist organizations.

The relatively cheap Project 21631 BuyanM class missile corvettes, which are not covered by the Intermediate-Range Nuclear Forces Treaty, have a major advantage: They can be easily redeployed using Russia's inland waterways. Instead of long voyages from one fleet to another, which is not safe in wartime, missile corvettes can move easily and relatively quickly – for example, from the Caspian Sea to the Baltic or Black Seas or to the Northern Fleet's area of responsibility.

In December 2015, the Black Sea Fleet received two Project 21631 missile corvettes that should partly compensate for the curtailment of the Project 11356 frigate program.[12] In all, the Navy expects to receive nine BuyanM class ships. In addition, Russia has begun to build Project 22800 missile corvettes, which will have better seaworthiness than the BuyanM and will be capable of operating on the high seas. The first two of the planned 18 Project 22800 ships have already been laid down.[13]

Thanks to missile corvettes, Russia will receive up to 27 new ships, capable of carrying over 200 cruise missiles, within a short period of time and at a reasonable price (compared to the construction of larger and technologically more sophisticated multipurpose ships). In addition, almost all newly built ships, including Project 11356 frigates and Project 636.3 submarines, will be armed with Kalibr missiles.

There is an important point here. The possibility of firing sea-launched cruise missiles from closed water areas, such as the Black or Caspian Seas, depends on the permission of third countries to use their airspace. In the case of the Caspian Sea, Russia had such permission, and the missiles flew through the airspace of Iran and Iraq. Using cruise missiles against targets in Syria from the Black Sea would have been impossible because of Turkey's position. Perhaps, this was why the *Zelyony Dol* missile corvette of the Black Sea Fleet was dispatched to the Mediterranean in February 2016. In August 2016, the ship, and her sister-ship *Serpukhov* were reported to have fired cruise missiles at targets in Syria.[14]

Transforming Quantity into Quality

In the 2010s, the bulk of funds allocated for the shipbuilding program was used to finance two major projects: the construction of Project 995/995A strategic missile submarines and Project 885/8851 nuclear-powered multipurpose attack submarines armed with cruise missiles. These submarines are to become the core of Russia's Naval nuclear and conventional deterrence force in the future. However, the experience of the Syrian campaign suggests that Russia should speed up the construction of other types of ships as well. Otherwise, in 15 years, the Russian Navy will be unable to carry out even one operation similar to the Syrian one. Shipbuilding priorities are as follows:

- the construction of ocean-going multipurpose surface warships (destroyers under the Leader program), capable of acting as the flagship of a Naval task force in the oceans and providing active nonnuclear deterrence;
- the construction of a large number of relatively cheap sea-going patrol ships;
- the modernization of the fleet of Soviet-built landing ships;
- the creation within the Navy of a department in charge of sealifts; and
- the formation of a fleet of transport vessels.

Special mention should be made of two more classes of ships, the need for which became evident during the Syrian campaign. These are multipurpose landing ships and aircraft carriers. The Russian Navy needs at least two aircraft carriers. The current operation would hardly have been possible without access to the Hmeimim air base. Another factor of major importance was that the air base was located away from the area of hostilities, and that there were no immediate threats to it from the ground or air. The maintenance base in Tartus made it possible to supply the Russian force quickly and sufficiently.

Attacks from the air and the ground, interruptions in supplies to the air base, or simply the absence of a suitable and available airfield would have made the Russian Aerospace Forces' operation much more difficult or even impossible. Strategic aircraft and sea-launched cruise missiles could not fully replace frontline aviation. An aircraft carrier could be the only alternative for the entire duration of the operation or until the required ground air base was created. Russia's only aircraft carrier, *Admiral Flota Sovetskogo Soyuza Kuznetsov,* was not involved in the Syrian campaign, but the ship and its aircraft have rather modest capabilities to combat coastal targets.

The results of Russia's military involvement in Syria (more than 9,000 air sorties over five and a half months) are comparable with the capabilities of one US Nimitz-class aircraft carrier. For example, during the operation in Afghanistan in 2002, aircraft deployed aboard the USS Theodore Roosevelt aircraft carrier made more than 10,000 sorties over five months.[15] While the force at the Hmeimim air base is capable of continuing the operation indefinitely, an aircraft carrier can intensively participate in an air campaign for not more than four to six months.

Finally, Mistral-class amphibious assault ships would be useful in an operation like the one in Syria. They could play an active role in transporting cargos and troops, and serve as command ships, hospital ships or carriers of large helicopter groups. Combining a Mistral-class ship as a command ship and a Project 22350 frigate as an air defense ship could ensure effective actions by a Naval task force in the absence of a full-fledged flagship. However, the Russian Navy has not received the *Sevastopol* and the *Vladivostok* amphibious assault ships. Therefore, it would be expedient to develop and build a series of landing platform docks, similar to the *Rotterdam* LPD of the Royal Netherlands Navy. Compared to Mistral-class ships, they would have smaller displacement and reduced air capabilities, and would be cheaper. Developing and building full-fledged amphibious assault ships with large displacement is hardly expedient in the short term, given the aforementioned needs of the Navy.

Notes

1. "Vstrecha s glavoi Minoborony Sergeyem Shoigu" [A meeting with the head of MOD Sergei Shoigu], Official site of the President of Russia, Oct. 5, 2015, http://www.kremlin.ru/events/president/news/50458.

2. "Raketniye udary Kaspiiskoi flotilii porazili boyevikov IG v tryokh provintsiyakh" [Caspian fleet missile strikes hit ISIS fighters in three provinces], *Interfax,* Nov. 20, 2015, https://www.interfax.ru/world/480610.

3. "Iz Rossii s podderzhkoi" [From Russia with support], *TASS*, https://tass.ru/spec/syria.

4. Shishkin, Aleksandr. "Letopis 'Siriiskogo ekspressa' " [Chronicles of the 'Syrian Express'], *Navy-korabel blog*, Oct. 18, 2017, https://navy-korabel.livejournal.com/173427.html?fbclid=IwAR04QEEb9YIIbyC_iWA7L_JFV0KTVtq BldabhXmsuTGC7GXBdocrgyFx5Wg.

5. Pasyakin, Vladimir. "Intervyu s glavnym shturmanom Chernomorskogo flota" [Interview with the Chief Navigator of the Black Sea Fleet], *Novosti Sevastopolya*, Jan. 23, 2016, http://sevnews.info/rus/view-news/25-yanvarya-Den-shturmana-Voenno-Morskogo-Flota-Intervyu-s-glavnym-shturmanom-Chernomorskogo-flota/24043.

6. Marchenko, Igor. "Official Department. From the Decree of the President of the Russian Federation on conferring military ranks of the highest officers to servicemen of the Armed Forces of the Russian Federation," *Morskoi sbornik*, No. 3, 2014, pp. 5-33.

7. Shishkin, Aleksandr, *op. cit.* This assessment, naturally, did not include LLS *Ivan Gren,* which joined the Northern Fleet on June 20, 2018.

8. Pasyakin, Vladimir, *op. cit.*

9. Dvornikov, Aleksandr and Gavrilov, Yuri. "Siriya: russky grom" [Syria: Russian thunder], Interview with the Commander of the Russian Army Group in Syria Aleksandr Dvornikov, *Rossiiskaya gazeta*, March 23, 2016, https://rg.ru/2016/03/23/aleksandr-dvornikov-dejstviia-rf-v-korne-perelomili-situaciiu-v-sirii.html#ac955904/16964/10.

10. Pasyakin, Vladimir, *op. cit.*

11. "Minoborony: rakety 'Kalibr' porazili obyekty IG v Sirii s tochnostyu do tryokh metrov" [Ministry of Defense: 'Kalibr' missiles hit ISIS targets in Syria with an accuracy of three meters], *TASS*, Oct. 7, 2015, https://tass.ru/politika/2326051.

12. "Maliye raketniye korabli 'Zeleny Dol' i 'Serpukhov' voshli v sostav VMF" [Missile corvettes 'Zeleny Dol' and 'Serpukhov' became part of the Navy], *BMPD LiveJournal blog*, https://bmpd.livejournal.com/1625091.html.

13. "Perviye dva korablya proekta 22800 'Uragan' i 'Taifun' voidut v stroi v 2017 i 2018 godakh" [Uragan and Taifun: First two ships of the 22800 project will be put into operation in 2017 and 2018], *Novosti VPK*, Dec. 24, 2015, https://vpk.name/news/146804_pervyie_dva_korablya_proekta_22800_uragan_i_taifun_voidut_v_stroi_v_2017_i_2018_godah.html.

14. "Primeneniye krylatykh raket 'Kalibr' v siriiskoi kampanii. Dosye" [Kalibr Cruise Missiles Engagement in Syria Campaign: A Profile], *TASS*, Nov. 22, 2017, https://tass.ru/info/4751516. See also: Russian Defense Ministry Web site on Kalibr launches, Aug. 19, 2016, https://function.mil.ru/news_page/country/more.htm?id=12093238@egNews

15. Lambeth, Benjamin S. *American Carrier Air Power at the Dawn of a New Century.* RAND, 2005, p. 28.

PART THREE

The Middle East as a Factor of World Order
(and Disorder)

PART THREE

3.1. The Arab Spring: Democracy and Revolution

REVOLUTIONS AND DEMOCRACY IN THE ISLAMIC WORLD
Yevgeny Satanovsky

With the growing presence of China, India and Iran, the com-
position of players and the alignment of forces in the Middle
East in the 21st century will look more like those in the 17th
century than in the 20th. This conception fits perfectly with the
theory of historical cycles, although it may appear disappoint-
ing if looked at from the standpoint of Paris, London, Brussels
or Washington.

All revolutions are caused by abuses of power, but the consequences of any of these revolutions are worse than any of the
abuses that caused them. – A long (and well) forgotten truth.

Tunisia, Egypt and Libya pose a stunning paradox. The revolutions
there, which have already caused a domino effect and put the entire
system of checks and counterbalances in the Arab world on the brink
of collapse, have been lauded not only by Iran and Al Qaeda, but also
by a number of Western politicians, above all the US president and
secretary of state. French President Nicolas Sarkozy's refusal to grant
asylum to run-away Tunisian President Zine el-Abidine Ben Ali,

This article originally appeared in *Russia in Global Affairs* Vol. 9, No. 1, 2011.

who had for decades served as a stronghold of Paris's interests in the Maghreb, and his unexpected U-turn on Muammar Qaddafi could still be attributed to confusion, or to some "old scores," obscure to the general public. But the appeals from US President Barack Obama and US Secretary of State Hillary Clinton, who in the midst of riots, looting and antigovernment protests demanded that Egyptian President Hosni Mubarak immediately turn on the Internet, ensure the smooth operation of foreign media, enter into a dialogue with the opposition and start the transfer of power, went beyond the bounds of what is not only reasonable but acceptable. Washington has once again demonstrated that it has neither allies nor clearly understood interests in the region.

America's Irreparable Mistakes

The frank, outright betrayal of the main partner of the US in the Arab world (as Mubarak had fancied himself until recently) admits no plausible explanation from the practical viewpoint. The "liberal opposition" under Muhammad el-Baradei, who urgently flew to Egypt with the intention to "take over," and whose influence in the country amounts to nothing, has no chances whatsoever. Unless, of course, one leaves aside the possibility that the ex-head of the International Atomic Energy Agency may be used as a cover-up, doomed to be disposed of as soon as he becomes redundant. Statements by the Muslim Brotherhood suggest that the first thing they will do as soon as they rise to power will be to reconsider the Camp David deal, and their own past provides few grounds for optimism. The ambitions of another potential challenger for the Egyptian presidency, Secretary-General of the League of Arab States Amr Moussa, are incommensurate with the capabilities of the military junta that has taken power in Egypt and is gradually getting rid of members of the inner circle of ex-president Mubarak, starting with just-appointed Vice-President Omar Suleiman, who concentrated enormous power in his hands until quite recently.

The American leadership's "shot to the foot" is hard to explain. To do so, one would have to earnestly believe the conspiracy theory that the US is seeking to establish "controlled chaos" worldwide, for which it will support any protest movement and stage all sorts of "color revolutions," irrespective of who these may be for or against.

Another alternative is to suspect that the governments of the US and some European countries briefly went insane (after a few days, their rhetoric did begin to change after all). One gets the impression that the Western leaders in critical situations choose to follow not the voice of reason, or public or personal obligations, but some latent instinct. That instinct prompts them to hail – even to the detriment of their own countries, themselves and the world order in general – any turmoil under the slogan of "striving for freedom and democracy," wherever it may occur and whomever of their allies it may harm.

The sort of conclusions leaders of countries in the region from Morocco to Pakistan without exception have drawn from this is easy to guess. Anyway, the Israelis who have so far thought that the Obama administration's biased attitude toward the government of Israeli Prime Minister Benjamin Netanyahu is rooted in the encounter of the American populist theory with the Middle Eastern realities that have torpedoed it, in anti-Israel lobbying and in personal animosity, all of a sudden began to realize that things are much worse; there is a system at work.

Within this system of historically incorrigible mistakes committed successively by US presidents, Jimmy Carter in 1979 forced the Shah of Iran, Mohammed Reza Pahlavi, to give up the confrontation with Ayatollah Khomeini. The Islamic revolution in Iran, unopposed, attained victory, triggering a long chain of consequences for that country, the region and the world, one of which was the deployment of Soviet troops in Afghanistan.

Carter's successor, Ronald Reagan, supported not only fanatical *mujahedeen*, but also the creation of Al Qaeda under Osama bin Laden. Suffice it to recall Dr. Najibullah, a general of the KHAD (the analogue of the Soviet KGB in the Democratic Republic of Afghanistan), who, with support from the West, could have become no worse a leader in Afghanistan than Soviet KGB Gen. Heydar Aliyev would become in Azerbaijan and Internal Affairs Ministry Gen. Eduard Shevardnadze would become in Georgia. Instead, Shiite political Islam in Iran received a worthy neighbor and rival – the Sunni terrorist Green International. The presidency of George H.W. Bush was too short to contribute to the strengthening of radical political Islam to any significant extent. He merely fought the Persian Gulf War to weaken the regime of Saddam Hussein, but he did not eliminate it at that very brief historical moment when that move could have gained support from all regional players and yielded minimum benefit for extremist organizations.

Bill Clinton preferred to turn a blind eye to Pakistan's newly acquired nuclear capability and overlooked the "black nuclear market," organized by the father of Pakistan's bomb, Abdul Qadeer Khan. He supported the adventure of Israeli leftists that brought Yasser Arafat to the Palestinian territories, and backed the Pakistani secret services' operation to promote the Taliban to the position of the leading military and political force in Afghanistan. It was Clinton's Middle East policy that led to the Al-Aqsa Intifada in Israel and the mega 9/11 terrorist attack in the US.

President George W. Bush, trying to tidy up Clinton's grave Middle East legacy, cleared Iraq as a base not only for Al Qaeda and other Sunni radicals, but also for such a radical Shiite group as the Iranian-backed Mahdi Army. Iran, when its dangerous neighbor Saddam Hussein was deposed and hanged, was given a free hand to realize its imperial ambitions, including nuclear ones, and it is rapidly growing into a regional superpower. Attempts by Iran's liberal President Mohammad Khatami to mend relations with Washington after the US Army captured Baghdad were rejected, which paved the way to power for Iranian "neocons" and President Mahmoud Ahmadinejad. In Afghanistan, neither the Taliban nor Al Qaeda were defeated. Their leaders Mullah Omar and Osama bin Laden, respectively, were on the loose and could not be found, but the US administration, as represented by Secretary of State Condoleezza Rice, set out to democratize the region in earnest.

As a result, Hamas became the leading military and political force in Palestine, and, having unleashed a civil war, seized the Gaza Strip. Pro-Iranian Hezbollah gained a firmer foothold in Lebanon; the Muslim Brotherhood won nearly 20% of the seats in the Egyptian parliament; and Pakistani President Pervez Musharraf, quite successful at fighting the Islamists, and the Army he led ceded power to the corrupt clans of Bhutto-Zardari and Nawaz Sharif. A country with an arsenal of dozens of nuclear warheads is now controlled by people behind the Taliban and the Abdul Qadeer Khan conspiracy.

Finally, Barack Obama "corrected" the policies of his predecessor and made a politically reasonable but strategically disastrous decision to withdraw troops from Iraq and Afghanistan and reconciled himself with the Iranian nuclear bomb, which would undoubtedly bring down the nonproliferation regime. Attempts to put strong pressure on Israel, going beyond all the "red lines" in that country's relations with the US, made Jerusalem certain that its friends in the current administration are more dangerous than most of its enemies. Despite the unprecedented cooling of relations with Israel, the flirtation with the Islamic world, which began with Obama's "historic speech" in Cairo, has not yielded the expected dividends. The popularity among Muslims of the US under Barack Obama's leadership is best seen in the Egyptian media's response to that speech: "Away goes a white dog, and along comes a black dog."[1]

The US president's support of a version of Egyptian democracy that incorporates Islamic radicals will, among other things, open the door to the de-Christianization of Egypt. Copts, who make up 10% of Egypt's population, are already largely limited in their rights by the authorities, despite their continued demonstrations of loyalty, and remain a welcome target for terrorists. Their future in a new "democratic" Egypt is unlikely to be any better than that of their neighbors – the Christians in Palestine, which over the years of Arafat's and his successor's rule lost much of its once large Christian population.

The stubborn backing of the corrupt and illegitimate regimes of Hamid Karzai in Afghanistan and Asif Ali Zardari in Pakistan; the inability to influence government crises in Iraq and Lebanon; the leaking of hundreds of thousands of classified documents through WikiLeaks; the lack of coordination among the State Department, the Pentagon and the intelligence services; a string of resignations of high-ranking military officers; and the unprecedented public criticism they have piled on the civilian authorities – all of this prompts suspicions about a systemic crisis, and not only in Middle East policy but in the American government as a whole.

Obama's idea of a nuclear-free zone in the Middle East and movement toward the "global nuclear zero" (both strongly supported by Saudi Arabia), are directed equally against Iran, which has violated the Nonproliferation Treaty (NPT), and Israel, which has never been a party to it. That these initiatives stand no chance of being implemented is not the sole problem – they completely ignore Pakistan, although the risk of the Pakistani nuclear arsenal being handed over to Saudi Arabia and perhaps to someone else is no less realistic than prospects of the emergence of a nuclear Iran. Saudi Prince Turki al-Faisal's decision to throw his weight in favor of Barack Obama's nuclear initiatives in Davos at the end of last January is full of innuendo. The father of the Saudi intelligence services is not only known as the architect of Al Qaeda, but is also suspected of involvement in staging the 9/11 attacks in the US and the hostage-taking crisis at a theater in Moscow in the autumn of 2002. Against this backdrop, the hasty and ill-considered statements addressed to Hosni Mubarak provided fresh evidence that the US in the Middle East (North Africa and Western Asia) relies on theory, not practice; ignores realities in its pursuit of a phantom "democracy" (just as the Soviet Union once pressed for building phantom "socialism"); and mercilessly and mindlessly betrays allies for the sake of theoretical dogmatism.

Democracy, Middle East Style

It is generally accepted that democracy is the best and most advanced form of government. The relevant quote from Winston Churchill is commonplace. The right of the people to rise in revolt against tyranny, a pillar of the Western political establishment for the past few centuries, remains a holy shrine, and both Washington and Brussels react to any encroachment on it as a heresy as blasphemous as any hint of doubt about the infallibility of the Pope. The discrepancy between the democracy theory and its implementation in real life is not a matter of analysis in most of the modern world. Worse still, the "international community" (to be more precise, the politicians, political analysts, political strategists, experts and journalists who belong to the inner circle that not only calls itself the "international community" but also fancies itself to be the only one) remains unaware of that discrepancy.

One can postulate some Middle East policy axioms. Francis Fukuyama's predicted "end of history" has not taken place, in contrast to Samuel Huntington's "clash of civilizations." In any case, no Western-style democracies are anywhere in sight in the Middle East, and the chances some may emerge in the coming decades are slim. The region is ruled by monarchies, authoritarian dictators or military juntas. All of them appeal to traditional values of Islam, as long as Islam does not question the legitimacy of sovereign power. The republican regimes in the Middle East may imitate Western governments to the tiniest detail, but this imitation of European parliamentarianism fails the test of tolerance. The rights of ethnic and religious minorities exist as long as the supreme leader or ruling group intend to use them for their own purposes and to the extent allowed at the "top," while sexual minority rights do not exist even in theory. In contrast to the Western community, the rights of the majority do not involve the protection of minorities, and even in the absence of arbitrariness and tyranny, they give the majority an opportunity to oppress and destroy minorities physically. Political neo-Salafism welcomes this, and all of theorists' references to the tolerance of Islam are in fundamental conflict with real practices, including contemporary ones.

Any democratization and strengthening of parliamentarianism in the region, wherever it may be initiated and whoever may lead it at the initial stage, eventually results in the strengthening of political Islam. Nationalist and liberal secular parties and movements may be used by Islamists only as temporary, casual allies. The Islamization of political life can be gradual and involve the use of parliamentary methods (the way it happened in Recep Tayyip Erdogan's Turkey), or revolutionary ones (as was the case in *Rahbar* Khomeini's Iran), but it is inevitable.

The era of secular states, whose founders saw Islam as a historical argument in favor of secession from the parent countries, and not as a routine practice mandatory for all, is drawing to a close. The costs of this may be small or they may be great. Various Islamist groups appeal to the values of various eras, from those of extreme barbarism to relatively moderate periods. Some of them are prepared to maintain relations with the West, to the extent these ties may be useful to them, while others are initially disposed to severing all ties. In some countries, the Islamization of public and political life proceeds alongside the preservation of public institutions, while in others it eliminates them. Each country differs from the others in terms of the tribal factor's impact on the situation, or the influence of religious brotherhoods and orders. But all movements, without exception, that have seized power or teamed up with the authorities and will be shaping regimes in the Middle East in the future have some shared features.

These movements are firmly opposed to letting Western values take root in the territories under their control; they struggle with Westernization and at the same time spread to the West the "values of the Islamic world" inside the closed ethnic and religious enclaves that have been growing in the European Union, the US and Canada under the slogans of the theory and practice of "multiculturalism." The most notorious manifestations of this trend were the "Paris intifada"; the Danish "cartoon scandal"; the fight against Christmas symbols in British municipalities; attacks on "anti-Islamic" politicians and public figures, and assassinations of some of them in the Netherlands; the pan-European "war of minarets"; and the attempt to build a mosque on the site of the 9/11 tragedy in New York. Despite statements by politicians like German Chancellor Angela Merkel and British Prime Minister David Cameron to the effect that multiculturalism has exhausted itself, the spread of radical Islamism in the West has already gone too far, and the momentum of this process is far from easing. The growth of conservative, anti-immigrant political and popular movements in Switzerland, Austria, Belgium and other European countries is a natural reaction, but it is also a belated one. In the meantime, the Islamists have successfully used the antiglobalization movement, human rights agencies and international organizations, including the UN, to achieve their strategic aims.

Consolidation Against Israel

Israel is one of the main targets of modern political Islam, of all its sects and trends. The struggle against Zionism is not just the sole goal that unites the Islamic world, but also the main achievement of that world on the international stage. As a result, there is an exaggerated attention of the international community, including the political establishment and the media, to the relationship between the Israelis and the Palestinians. The exclusiveness of the Palestinian problem is deeply ingrained in the public mind, not only in the Islamic world, but also in the West; although, perhaps, it is the least acute one in the chain of conflicts in the region. For the sake of creating a Palestinian state, many are eager to defy economic, political and demographic realities, and also common sense – as witnessed by the string of recognitions by a number of Latin American and European countries of the hitherto nonexistent Palestinian state within the 1967 borders.

Israel is watching, waiting, getting ready for war and distancing itself from current events in the region, so as not to provoke a conflict. The country's leadership is aware that the security situation is returning to the days that preceded the Six-Day War. Any evolution of the authorities in Egypt and Jordan will be possible only through a cooling of relations with Israel, because for many decades the main demand on the streets in these Arab countries has been the severance of diplomatic and economic relations with the Jewish state. This slogan has been used by all organized opposition groups, from the Muslim Brotherhood to trade unions and secular liberals.

Not only Amr Moussa and el-Baradei, both known for their anti-Israeli sentiment, but any government, will be forced to reconsider Mubarak's legacy in relations with Israel. This will inevitably cause a weakening or cessation of the struggle against anti-Israel terrorism in the Sinai Peninsula, which has the backing of both Sunni extremist groups and Iran. The demonstrative passage of Iranian warships through the Suez Canal came as a symbol of these changes. An end to the Egyptian blockade of Gaza would open a route for delivering medium-range Zilzal missiles, capable of hitting not only the nuclear reactor at Dimona and the US radar in the Negev, which monitors Iranian airspace, but also Tel Aviv and Jerusalem. Support for Hamas from Syria and Iran will intensify, and the Palestinian National Authority (PNA) in the West Bank will grow weaker. All this will dramatically increase the likelihood of terrorist attacks against Israel and of a military operation by the latter not only against Iran, for which Jerusalem has been preparing for several years now, but along the entire border line, including Gaza and the West Bank.

Military operations against Lebanon and Syria are possible if Hezbollah becomes active on the northern border. A war with Egypt would be likely only if Islamists come to power and break the peace treaty with Israel. Any scenarios of hostilities may be possible (depending on whether the US stops supplying arms and spare parts to Egypt), including a strike against the Aswan Dam in case of developments catastrophic for Israel. The situation in Egypt will get dramatically worse in three to five years, when the government of South Sudan, whose independence was confirmed in a January 2011 referendum, will block the upper reaches of the Nile with hydroelectric power plants. These will reduce water runoff toward North Sudan and Egypt, putting the latter on the brink of an ecological disaster made worse by a demographic catastrophe. On March 1,

2011, Burundi – the last, sixth Nile upstream country – joined an agreement on water usage from the Nile River (the Cooperative Framework Agreement). The move ended a decades-long accord between Egypt and Sudan, which claimed 90% of the Nile's flow for the two countries. At the same time, the physical survival of Egypt's population will not be guaranteed if and when the maximum allowable number of residents of 86 million is exceeded (currently Egypt has a population of 80.5 million).[2]

Israel's conflict with the Arab world may be triggered by a crisis in the PNA. A Palestinian state has not materialized to this day. All the improvements in the economy of the West Bank are an achievement of Prime Minister Salam Fayyad, who is in deep conflict with President Abu Mazen. An attempt to overthrow the president by Fatah's former number one strongman in Gaza, Mohammad Dahlan, led to the expulsion of the latter to Jordan. The PNA's chief negotiator, Saeb Erikat, was accused of corruption and dismissed from all activities. Abu Mazen is completely isolated inside the Palestinian elite. Aggressive anti-Israeli actions by the PNA leadership on the international stage stand in stark contrast to its total dependence on Israel's economy and security. The population of the West Bank depends on job opportunities in Israel or in Israeli settlements in Judea and Samaria. Terrorist attacks against Israeli civilians (the killing of a Jewish settler family in the Israeli settlement of Itamar in March 2011 was the latest shocking attack) have exhausted the patience of the Israeli government and provoked the resumption of mass construction of Israeli settlements in the West Bank.

Iran and Others

Without support from Israeli security agencies, the fall of the regime in Ramallah would be a matter of several months. The implications for Jordan could be very severe. So far, King Abdullah II of Jordan has managed to hold back the Palestinian subjects with support from Circassians, Chechens and Bedouins. The change of the prime minister and several other political and economic measures have so far allowed him to avoid the scenario his father implemented in "Black September" 1970 (the suppression of a Palestinian uprising). The situation in Jordan is further aggravated by the factor of Iraqi refugees (700,000), as well as a financial and land scam blamed on

Palestinian relatives of Queen Rania – the Yassin family. In contrast to the years of King Hussein's rule, these days Jordan is facing no danger from Syria or Saudi Arabia, but it remains a target for radical Sunni Islamists. The shift in relations between Jordan and Iran is another alarming signal for Israel.

Iran, along with Turkey, is a leading political and military player in the modern Islamic world, and a successful competitor for influence apart from traditional leaders like Egypt, Saudi Arabia and Morocco. Despite the economic sanctions, Iran is proceeding with work on its nuclear program, and although according to the ex-director of the Mossad, Meir Dagan, it is unlikely to deliver a nuclear bomb before 2015, Iran has accumulated enough fissile material to make five warheads, and by 2020, it may be ready for a limited nuclear war. Immediate dangers from the Islamic Republic of Iran (IRI) are addressed to its neighbors in the Persian Gulf and Israel, which Tehran has consistently promised to destroy.

Speculation about the possibility of Iran striking the EU or the US is untenable. Israeli and US air strikes against Iranian nuclear facilities are unlikely. America can destroy the industrial potential of Iran, but it has no human resources to conduct a ground operation, which would be a must if the Iranian nuclear program is to be eliminated in earnest. Israel does not possess the necessary military capabilities, although the computer virus that hit Iranian nuclear facilities is linked – not without reason – to the confrontation between the two countries.

The power struggle in Iran is about to end in favor of the generals of the Revolutionary Guards, who are sidelining the ayatollahs. The Green Movement of orthodox Islamists and the liberals has suffered a defeat. Although it retained the slogans of the Islamic Revolution, Iran is transforming into a state where ideology will increasingly rely on superpower Persian nationalism. Iran is successfully developing relations with China, Africa, Latin America, Eastern Europe, India, Pakistan and Turkey. In fact, it has shared with the latter spheres of influence in Iraq, whose government coordinates its actions not only with the US, but also with Iran. In the Middle East, Iran's interests stretch from Afghanistan's Herat to Mauritania's Nouakchott (Iran's growing position in Mauritania caused Morocco to sever diplomatic relations with it, while arms supplies to West Africa have complicated its relations with several leading countries in the region).

Tehran avoids direct conflicts with opponents in preference of "proxy wars" fought by its satellites. The Second Lebanon War and Operation Cast Lead in Gaza were Iranian-Israeli wars, and according to some analysts, Iran is also behind the conflict between the Yemeni Hausa tribes and Saudi Arabia. Iran's aggressive stance on the smaller Gulf monarchies relies on the presence of Shiite communities in such countries as Bahrain, Qatar and, to a lesser extent, the United Arab Emirates (UAE) and Kuwait. Iran's only ally in the Arab world is Syria, which, with support from Hezbollah, is gradually regaining control of the situation in Lebanon and continues to supervise Hamas, whose political leadership is headquartered in Damascus. In view of the sanctions imposed on Iran, the future of its gas export to the EU depends heavily on cooperation with Turkey, which will use this situation to its advantage until its interests come into conflict with those of Iran (which will undoubtedly happen in the long run).

When it set the course toward building a "new Ottoman Empire," the Turkish leadership forestalled events to launch gradual Islamization of the country's political and public life. The ruling party forced the Army away from the leverage of power under the slogans of democracy and fighting corruption. It railroaded all the necessary constitutional amendments through parliament and nipped in the bud another military coup. Turkey's economic success allows it to act without regard to the EU or the US. And participation in NATO as the second largest army of the bloc gives it substantial freedom of maneuver, including in Iraqi Kurdistan and in relations with Israel, which grew much cooler after the Freedom Flotilla incident. In the meantime, that country remains split along ethnic lines (the Kurdish question is still relevant), the secular opposition to the ruling Justice and Development Party is strong, and the Army's leadership is in confusion. However, whatever factors (or combinations of factors) may provoke antigovernment unrest, the triumvirate of the prime minister, the president and the foreign minister will retain sufficient resources to implement plans for economic and diplomatic expansion in Africa, the Islamic world and Eastern Europe. Turkey has more reasons than Iran to lay claim to the status of a regional superpower, for which it has the necessary potential that is not overburdened, in contrast to Iran, by any external conflicts.

Syria's stability rests on cooperation with Turkey and Iran, on the condition of better relations with the US and the EU. The Syrian

President Bashar Assad-led Alawite ruling military elite is balancing between Sunni Arabs and Christian Arabs; it is suppressing the Kurds and making use of the business activity of Armenians. However, if the Egyptian Muslim Brotherhood gets a firmer foothold in Syria, one should not rule out unrest of the sort Hafez Assad suppressed only at the cost of great bloodshed in 1982, and that could weaken or even bring down the regime. The latter has strengthened its positions in Lebanon, but the situation inside Syria proper is complicated by the presence of Iraqi refugees (more than 1 million),[3] and to a lesser extent Palestinian refugees (472,000).[4]

Lebanon, after the fall of the Saad Hariri government, is struggling with its own crisis, sparked by a confrontation between the Syrian and Saudi lobbies (the latter bet on confrontation with Damascus and lost). A gradual descent into a civil war is possible, with Sheikh Nasrallah's Hezbollah playing the leading role. Palestinian refugee camps (more than 400,000 people) may spark a conflict again, just as they did in 1975-1978; however, a conflict between Hezbollah and its opponents is more likely.

In the Arabian Peninsula, a catastrophic situation is unfolding in Yemen. The country's breakup looks almost unavoidable after the ouster of President Ali Abdullah Saleh, who had been at the helm in Sana since 1978 and in control of South Yemen since 1990, and may well trigger irreversible processes in Saudi Arabia, which has so far been able to keep protests among the population under control. Yemen is where the interests of Iran and the US, and Qatar and Saudi Arabia have clashed. That country is not only the birthplace of many "global jihad" fighters (Osama bin Laden has Yemeni background), but a real "pot of trouble." The conflict between the president and the tribes, who have united in the opposition organization al-Liqa'a al-Mushtarak and categorically rejected the attempt at a hereditary transfer of supreme power, looks a lot like a similar problem in Egypt. However, the opposition of Shafii southerners and Zaidi northerners, thriving on the anger of the former military elite from the south, ousted from power and stripped of benefits and privileges, is a purely local feature.

Yemen is the first country in the Middle East capable of unleashing a "water war" with neighboring Saudi Arabia (in the near future, Sana will risk becoming the first world capital with a zero water balance), especially since a number of historically Yemeni provinces were annexed by the Saudis in the early years of the 20th century. The glaring poverty of the Yemeni population, heavily armed and in the habit of chewing the local drug khat, is an additional risk factor. It would be a sheer waste of time guessing whether the 25.7 million Saudis, most of whom have never held a weapon in their hands, would be able to resist 23.5 million Yemenis, who have always carried weapons as long as they can remember. The ability of the Saudi elite, whose top rulers are old enough to look like the Soviet Politburo of the late 1980s, to control the situation in a way other than bribing belligerent tribes on the southern borders and the radicals of the "errant sect" inside the country is very questionable. Given the importance of the Bab al-Mandab Strait, the impact on the world energy market of a hypothetical conflict between Yemen and Saudi Arabia, or of a civil war in Yemen, would be equivalent to plugging the Suez Canal. In case Gen. Saleh has no worthy successor and there is no such person in Yemen (in contrast to Egypt), the country will run the risk of turning into a territory of piracy, like Somalia, especially since hundreds of thousands of Somali refugees are already present in its territory.

The consequences of a collapse of the ruling regime in Yemen for Ibadi Oman, where Sultan Qaboos bin Said – a ruler since 1970 who is trying to calm protests against the supreme authority with subsidies and promises of democracy – has no heirs, and for the smaller Gulf monarchies, is anyone's guess. While balancing between the US (which has military bases in Kuwait, Qatar and Bahrain), Britain (which has a presence in Oman) and France (which has announced plans for constructing a military base in the UAE), on the one hand, and Iran (the conflict with the UAE and Bahrain), on the other, as well as Saudi Arabia – all these countries have established an informal relationship with Israel in case of a possible war. Israel-made water purification plants, agro-complexes and safety systems at strategic facilities, carrying logos of foreign affiliates of Israeli firms or no indication of the country of manufacture at all, are as common on the southern coast of the Gulf as Iranian ships in local ports, Iranian bank accounts, and Iranians at local business centers. Oman is in a state of self-isolation, enhanced by the uncovering of an Islamist plot that Muscat has blamed on the UAE.

Kuwait has not yet recovered from the Iraqi occupation of 1990-1991. Bahrain's Sunni dynasty has had to request the Cooperation

Council for the Arab States of the Gulf to send forces to suppress antigovernment protests of the Shiite majority in the country, which are believed – not without grounds – to be encouraged by Iran. The economic crisis has weakened the UAE, particularly Dubai, causing a collapse of the "real estate pyramid," which had been the primary source of its well-being over years. Only moderately Wahhabi Qatar – the holder of the world's third-largest gas reserves, which for decades was the home of Sheikh Yusuf al-Qaradawi, the spiritual leader of the Muslim Brotherhood who is sometimes described as a "Sunni Khomeini" – has been building up its political influence. As a mediator of regional conflicts, it has successfully competed with such giants of the Arab world as Egypt and Saudi Arabia. The Qatari Emir's main weapon in the struggle for dominance in the inter-Arab political scene is Al-Jazeera, whose effectiveness is seen in the ban imposed on it in Egypt, where that TV channel in no small measure contributed to "rocking the boat." But this tool may prove useless if unrest spills over to the territory of Qatar itself. In that case, foreign workers, often exceeding the indigenous populations many times over, and stateless Arab nomads – *bidun* – may turn into the main factor of instability in the Gulf monarchies, including Saudi Arabia.

Another destabilizing factor for the peninsula is its proximity to the Horn of Africa, on the shores of which are the poorest countries ravaged by civil strife and crowded by refugees: Eritrea, Djibouti and piratical Somalia, split into several enclaves, of which Puntland and Somaliland are the largest. Islamists from the Al Shabab movement and other radical groups are the only force that can unite that country, subjugating or eliminating warlords the way the Taliban once did in Afghanistan. That is a frightening prospect, indeed – especially considering the utter failure of the international community to fight the pirates, rampaging in increasingly larger areas of the Indian Ocean. One should not forget about the problem of borders, for their fundamental redrawing will be inevitable after the bloodless breakup of Sudan. North Sudan in the near-term historical perspective may unite with Egypt – particularly in the event of the Islamization of the latter – or disintegrate into separate enclaves. It is no coincidence that the Sudanese Islamist leader Hassan al-Turabi has been repeatedly arrested by the Sudanese authorities.

Unrest in Tunisia, Egypt and Libya threatens to have the most regrettable impact on the situation in Algeria, where a low-intensity civil war has been smoldering since 1992. President Abdulaziz Boute-flika is very old, the conflict between the Arabs and the Berbers re-mains where it was decades ago, and Islamists are still there. Stability in Morocco is in jeopardy, because to Al Qaeda in the Maghreb, the Jewish and Christian holy shrines look just as legitimate as foreign tourists as targets for attack. Mauritania, where the number of slaves is estimated at 800,000, is experiencing a series of military coups and is very receptive to any revolutionary calls.

The civil war in Libya is developing in an unpredictable way, and the involvement of Muammar Qaddafi's African mercenaries is threatening to blow up the continent, especially as quite a few Afri-can countries have been swept by protests like those taking place in the Arab world. This situation poses a special threat to Europe, as hundreds of thousands to several million African and Arab refugees may flood into the European continent. The international military intervention makes the situation increasingly unpredictable.

The sole, albeit poor, consolation in this situation is that the regional upheaval poses no threat to Iraq, Afghanistan or Pakistan. The former two have long been not so much states as territories. As for Pakistan – with Islamists firmly entrenched in the North-West-ern Province and in Punjab, and the Pashtun Taliban rooted in the tribal areas; with the Baluchistan and Sindh separatists; and with the internal strife among the government, the army and the judiciary – Afghanistan alone would be enough for its collapse. After which its formidable nuclear arsenals would emerge on the "free market," which would be a much more significant cause of concern for the in-ternational community than the future of the Palestinian state or the ruler of any single Arab country, even if that single country is Egypt.

And lastly, it should be remembered that the declining influence of the great powers in the Middle East is creating a vacuum, part of which New Delhi will fill in some provinces of Afghanistan. In all other territories of the region, including what is left of Afghanistan, Beijing's influence will soar. As a consequence, the composition of players and the alignment of forces in the Middle East in the 21st century will look more like those in the 17th century than in the 20th. This fits perfectly with the theory of historical cycles, although it may appear disappointing if looked at from the positions of Paris, London, Brussels or Washington.

Notes

1. "Muntazer Al-Zaidi, Who Famously Threw Shoes at President Bush: 'Away Goes a White Dog, Along Comes a Black Dog' – Obama No Different than Bush," *MEMRI*, July 1, 2010, https://www.memri.org/reports/muntazer-al-zaidi-who-famously-threw-shoes-president-bush-away-goes-white-dog-along-comes.

2. Although today the population of Egypt is well over 86 million (almost 95 million, according to the 2017 census), the problem of overpopulation and resource scarcity was widely recognized at the time this article was written, and is recognized now as well (see, for example: Jonathan Abbamonte. "Egyptian Government Pushes for Population Control," *Population Research Institute*, December 5, 2018, https://www.pop.org/egyptian-government-pushes-for-population-control/).

3. "Irakskiye bezhentsy v bedstvennom polozhenii" [Iraqi refugees in disastrous state], *Amnesty International*, June 2008, https://amnesty.org.ru/node/1216.

4. "Palestinian Refugees: An Overview," *Palestinian Refugee Research Net*, http://prrn.mcgill.ca/background/index.htm.

A DIFFERENT DEMOCRACY

Veronika Kostenko, Eduard Ponarin and Pavel Kuzmichov

A majority of people in the Middle East either share extremely conservative views regarding democracy and women's rights, or feel the need for political and social reform and call such aspirations "democracy" – while real knowledge of how democracy works is still rudimentary.

An explicit focus on modernization was a crucial component in the Soviet Union's influence on satellite countries in the Arab world. Yet the global superpower's disappearance from the geopolitical scene facilitated processes that have reinforced a radical agenda in those Arab countries previously dependent on the Soviet Union or oriented toward the socialist system. Despite the spread of higher education, this transformation is particularly noticeable among young people. Their views on human rights and, above all, the position of women have come under the considerable influence of fundamentalists backed by Saudi Arabia and other Gulf monarchies. Although people in those countries seemingly profess a positive attitude toward democracy, a closer look reveals that the Arab understanding of democracy differs greatly from that of the West. Not a single

This article originally appeared in *Russia in Global Affairs* Vol. 13, No. 1, 2015.

244

Arab society can be called an electoral democracy. Moreover, Arab countries lack traditional value-based prerequisites for democratic reform. It is highly likely that all of these countries will remain authoritarian regimes for quite some time.

Discrepant Values

Since the September 11, 2001 attacks, the Arab world has enjoyed the unflagging attention of politicians and researchers around the globe. The mass media have persuaded the public at large to see the region as a den of terrorism; and after the events of the Arab Spring – the wave of unrest and revolutions in the Middle East that started in 2012 – as another destabilizing factor for international politics. Very often the participants in debates about the region lack knowledge about the real situation, which is largely a result of the region's seclusion and scarcity of impartial information about the processes underway.

The first credible data from opinion polls conducted in Middle Eastern countries appeared fairly recently, in 2009, when the Arab Barometer survey,[1] launched in 2006 by an international team of researchers in seven countries in the region, presented its initial findings. The authors of this article – a research group from the Moscow Higher School of Economics – used these data to analyze the attitude of people in Arab countries towards democracy.

In order to understand how the values shared by people in Arab countries are changing, we compared the attitudes of different age groups using a method that has been most effective when earlier statistics are unavailable. Sociologists maintain that political preferences usually form between 20 and 25 years of age. Later, an individual's ideas of politics and society change little, even if those around the individual adhere to a different view. We believe the views of senior citizens represent the public opinion that existed in the country when those citizens were young.

Since the very term "democracy" can be understood differently, we compared the opinions of respondents regarding the desirability of democracy with opinions of women's rights and also whether such countries as Saudi Arabia are democratic or not.

Fig. 1 depicts the average values received for responses to the question "Do you believe that your country is a democracy?" The values range from 1 (a totalitarian regime) to 10 (a democracy). People in Arab societies were asked to assess the level of democracy in their country and also in Israel, China, the United States, Japan, Saudi Arabia, Turkey and Iran.

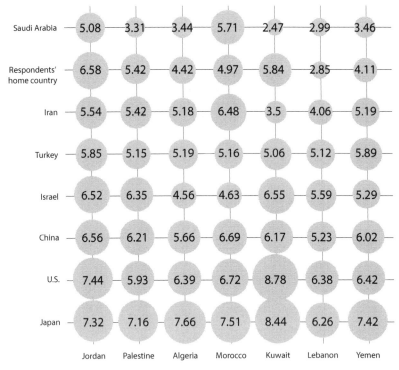

FIG. 1. Level of democracy as rated by citizens of seven Arab societies (numbers and relative sizes of circles around them show the average value for each country)[2]

The figure shows that people in Arab countries quite often rate the degree of democracy in a country not according to formal parameters (free elections, free expression of popular will, separation of powers, reliance on the constitution, observance of human rights, etc.), but by a general positive or negative perception of a country formed by the mass media. For instance, Moroccans consider Saudi Arabia a more democratic society than Turkey, Israel, or even their own country. Incidentally, many trends correspond to the Western perception: in all surveyed Arab societies Japan is seen as a fairly democratic country, while Saudi Arabia receives generally low marks. For this reason, it would be wrong to say that people support democracy in Arab societies. That would entail misreading the real situation in the region.

In order to verify the results of the survey on democracy we analyzed the opinions of respondents regarding a different subject – attitudes towards the position of women in society. Although this issue seemingly concerns a completely different aspect of life, research data confirm that it is directly related to support for democracy. Attitudes toward the position of women reveal the extent to which the declared support for democracy in Arab societies is related to an understanding of basic human rights, without which the concept of democracy appears emasculated. We analyzed attitudes toward gender equality in seven Arab societies using such factors as strength of religious beliefs and support for democracy. We also compared the results using such parameters as gender, age, and education.

Impact of Education and Religious Belief on Support for Gender Equality

In studying the impact of demographic variables, education and religious beliefs on support for gender equality, we used a multiple-linear regression model.

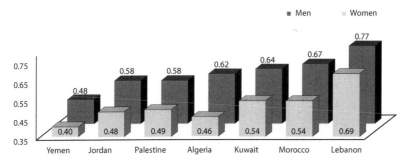

FIG. 2. Support for gender equality in 7 Middle Eastern Arab countries[3]

Formal modeling confirms that women in Arab Middle Eastern countries (and worldwide) are far more inclined to support gender equality than men. The effect of education is also predictable: people with more education tend to support equality far more often. As for distinctions among countries, Lebanon shows the most egalitarian approach toward gender issues, while Yemen appears to be the most conservative country in the surveyed group (in terms of women's real rights Yemen is in last place globally.) As for prodemocracy sentiment, Kuwait is the most liberal country and Morocco is second.

The frequency of reading the Qur'an, used in this research as a benchmark of religiousness, is inversely proportionate to support for gender equality. In other words, the most religious Muslims adhere to the most conservative ideas concerning the position of women in society, which agrees with general global trends.

Statistical analysis indicates that senior citizens in Arab countries are more disposed toward gender equality than young people, which runs counter to trends observed in other countries undergoing modernization. Young people between 25 and 34 tend to profess more conservative views, while the oldest age group (over 65) has the most egalitarian attitude toward gender equality.

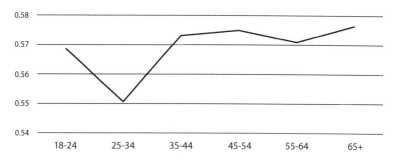

FIG. 3. Attitudes of different age groups toward the position of women in Arab countries (the higher the index, the more liberal the attitude)[4]

This result of the survey is quite unexpected from the standpoint of the modernization theory developed by Ronald Inglehart and Christian Welzel.[5] An analysis of the data gathered by the World Values Survey, a project encompassing hundreds of scholars globally, indicates that older people are more conservative in almost all respects and nearly all societies, while young people tend to be more open to novelties and do not abide by traditional conservative rules and values in all respects as living standards increase. The surprising trend identified in the Middle East deserves special research, but already at this point we can offer several explanations, relying on historical arguments, for this phenomenon.

The region's political history is significant. The political views of the senior generation in Arab countries were shaped during anti-colonial wars in the 1950s and the 1960s. The Arab peoples' struggle for independence from imperial countries was a secular rather than religious movement. Also, pan-Arabism and nationalism – and not pan-Islamism – were the prevailing ideology. A large share of the newly founded Arab states enjoyed the financial and ideological backing of the Soviet Union, which promoted gender equality (the well-known slogan of the "emancipated woman of the Orient") and had its own extensive experience in eradicating the lack of opportunities for women in Central Asia and the Caucasus. Young people between the ages of 15 to 25 absorbed those ideas. The socialization theory postulates that social norms adopted at this age last throughout an individual's life and undergo only slight changes, if any.

As for the most conservative generation (born in the late 1970s and early 1980s), in accordance with the same theory, two historical events may have influenced their attitude toward gender equality. The end of the cold war meant that some societies in the Middle East remained stagnant after Soviet financial support dwindled, and then dried up (as in Yemen for instance). Also, the rapid rise of the international prestige of the United States and its geopolitical allies followed rapidly. Notably, US partners in the Middle East mostly included conservative oil-producing Gulf monarchies. Having at their disposal considerable ideological capital in the Muslim world (the main centers of Islam – Mecca and Medina – are in Saudi Arabia), those countries received an opportunity to translate their extremely conservative views to the entire Middle East via television and a network of theological schools and colleges.

It would be interesting to see how exactly the reinforcement of traditional values among young Arabs correlates with the revolutionary processes that started in the region in 2012. At first glance, these two tendencies appear to contradict each other, because a desire to toss out an outdated, archaic regime usually goes hand in hand with the growth of education and emergence of a generation of young people sharing liberal values. However, as the analysis of available data indicates, despite a growing level of education, young Arabs profess far more conservative views than people of older generations (who are far less educated). To analyze the mutual correlation of these phenomena we used more complex statistical techniques (cluster analysis and negative binomial regression).

Support for Democracy and Gender Equality in Muslim Arab Countries

In order to study the interrelation of support for democracy and gender equality, all respondents were grouped into five categories according to their attitude toward these two issues. The results of this analysis (distribution of respondents by their likes and dislikes in a two-dimensional space) are shown in Table 1. It should be noted that the characteristics of each category are probabilistic and not absolute.

TABLE 1. Attitudes toward democracy and gender equality in seven Arab countries[6]

Attitude to democracy	Attitude to gender equality	
	Good	Bad
Bad	C 18%	A 17%
Good	D 19%	B 13%

NOTE: About 32% of respondents have no specific attitude toward these issues. For that reason, they belong to a central cluster that is not represented in the table.

Cluster A unites people who are equally supportive of democracy and liberally minded about gender equality. They account for about 17% of respondents and mostly include women over 45 years of age. There are few representatives of the generation aged 25-34 in this cluster. One might assume with a high degree of probability that these people have master's degrees and reside in Lebanon or Morocco.

Cluster B represents those for whom gender equality is important, but whose support for democracy is low. This group of respondents makes up 13%. These are people of various age groups, mostly women without higher education. Most representatives of this group live in Jordan, with far fewer residing in Morocco, Lebanon and Yemen.

Cluster C is a group of people who are negative about gender equality, but at the same time support democracy (18% of the surveyed respondents). In this group there are significantly more young men (under 35) with the lowest level of education (including people who are illiterate). There are noticeably fewer people sharing such views in Lebanon, Morocco, Palestine and Algeria.

Cluster D unites opponents of democracy and gender equality; they make up 19% of all respondents. These are mostly young men (under 34 years of age), while those over 55 are practically absent from this group. As a rule, this group has graduated from a secondary or vocational school. Almost none of them have a university education. Such people are represented in all countries, except for Morocco, Kuwait and Lebanon.

The respondents in groups B and C support gender equality and are either negative towards democracy (B) or support it (C). The existence of two large groups with greatly varied opinions explains some of the observations mentioned in the previous section.

Who Supports Gender Equality and Democracy in Arab Societies?

The distribution of countries by cluster is uneven. For instance, the populations of Lebanon and Morocco demonstrate similar trends. Many residents of these two countries form the upper right Cluster A. In other words, their ideas of democracy and gender equality are consistent and liberal, which in value terms puts this group closer to Western Europeans. These countries are represented in other clusters too (except for the most conservative Cluster D), but to a far smaller extent. The people of Lebanon are hardly representative of Cluster C (support for democracy in combination with rejection of gender equality); Kuwait's results are similar to those in Lebanon, but the rates are much lower.

Palestine and Yemen can be put into one group, as opposed to Morocco and Lebanon. These countries are best represented in the lower left cluster (the most conservative). Palestinians are found in the central cluster and Yemenis in the upper left (C). Algeria is somewhat remarkable: It appears both in the lower left and upper right clusters, which points to considerable social polarization.

Support for democracy in the Arab world is related to gender egalitarianism at a very low level (correlation ratio 0.19). In some countries the correlation is positive, while it is negative in others. Statistical analysis has shown that in the surveyed societies there are groups of people who support both democracy and gender equality (approximately 17%); groups also include those who are either proponents of the two or reject both. This observation prompts the conclusion that the understanding of the term "democracy" in the

Arab world is quite different from that in Western societies (where debates on this issue are still underway).

If respondents do not regard equality as part of a democratic system, one should be cautious about statements by many scholars that the majority of people in Arab countries are striving toward democracy, although without much success so far. In reality, we believe that a mere 17% of those surveyed want to live in a democratic country (the term implies liberal democracy, human rights and emancipative values), and not 80%, as Mark Tessler and other researchers of the public opinion in that region claim. These people (represented in our survey by Cluster A) are distributed very unevenly by country; in fact, most of them are in Lebanon and Morocco. A majority of them are women over 45 with higher education degrees. Respondents between 25 and 34 years of age demonstrate a low level of support for gender equality and are practically absent from Cluster A.

This observation shows that a majority of people in the surveyed societies of the Middle East either share extremely conservative views regarding democracy and women's rights, or feel the need for political and social reform and call such aspirations "democracy" – while real knowledge of how democracy works is still rudimentary. Possibly, this explains why the Arab Spring has failed to bring about a transition to democracy in any of the surveyed societies. Since emancipative values are still shared by only a small minority and in very few countries in the region, full-fledged democratic regimes will not likely emerge anytime soon.

The above statistical analysis has revealed a remarkable relationship between age, education and political preferences. In each given age group, more highly educated people share liberal views on the position of women. On the one hand, this indicates that the modernization process in the Arab world is continuing, albeit slowly. So is urbanization, and young people are becoming more educated than older generations. On the other hand, the region is experiencing the reverse trend toward conservatism. Despite a higher level of education, the younger generation is far more conservative than their parents and, in particular, their grandparents. Counter to theoretical expectations, this trend has not been observed anywhere else in the world except in Arab societies. Traditionalist views are especially characteristic of Arabs born between 1972 and 1982.

Notes

1. See: http://www.arabbarometer.org/.

2. Figure designed by the authors based on Arab Barometer Wave 1 data, http://www.arabbarometer.org/survey-data/#waves-grid.

3. Figure designed by the authors based on Arab Barometer Wave 1 data, *op. cit.*

4. Figure designed by the authors based on Arab Barometer Wave 1 data, *op. cit.*

5. Inglehart, Ronald and Welzel, Christian. *Modernization, cultural change, and democracy: The human development sequence.* Cambridge University Press, 2005.

6. This table was created by the authors based on Arab Barometer data. For more details, see: Kostenko, Veronica V., Kuzmichov, Pavel A. and Ponarin, Eduard D. "Attitudes towards gender equality and perception of democracy in the Arab world," *Democratization* 23(5), 2016, pp. 862-891.

LISTENING TO THE MUSIC OF REVOLUTION?

Aleksandr Aksenyonok and Irina Zvyagelskaya

If the international community fails to establish acceptable and understandable rules of international behavior in the context of "revolutionary challenges," the world may slip into a new round of global confrontation, which will be caused not by systemic contradictions but by vain disregard for real common threats.

The late 1990s and the early 2000s were marked by profound changes in geopolitics, the world economy and global finance. The cold war paradigm of international relations seemed gone for good. At the same time, no new rules for the behavior of states had emerged that would apply to the new world order.

The cold war years showed that, for all the ideological, military and political costs, the bipolar system was relatively stable. It helped maintain balance as it imposed quite rigid restrictions on weaker countries in regions (allies or partners of the great powers). There was a universally recognized red line that could not be crossed – i.e., provoking a global clash. Regional forces sought to gain the support of their patron, sometimes not paying due attention to their own

This article originally appeared in *Russia in Global Affairs* Vol. 12, No. 4, 2014.

concerns, but ultimately the fear of unacceptable risks caused the great powers to act together, pressuring regional allies and enforcing restraint in international relations.

The collapse of the bipolar system and the impossibility of complying with the prior rules of the game in a polycentric world made international relations more chaotic. Regional state and nonstate actors began to behave more actively, often guided by the behavior of the US, which was no longer restrained by the other power center. Washington often demonstrated irresponsible policies, not even trying to assess the possible consequences of its actions. It seemed there had come a period of international solipsism, when global players, lost in their own worlds and ignoring the interests of others, started reshaping the Yalta system.

Such notions as sovereignty and territorial integrity, on the one hand, and national self-determination, on the other, which have long been in conflict with each other, are de facto eroding and turning into legal fictions. But these notions should not be viewed as mutually exclusive, either. The right to self-determination can be realized in various forms, for example, within a federal state or as autonomy granted to an ethnic group, which does not violate the territorial integrity of a given state. In practice, however, the growth of ethnic nationalism and the activity of new elites seeking access to power and property have equated the concept of self-determination with secession.

Under the new circumstances, powerful states increasingly often resort to the principles of territorial integrity and national self-determination to justify their "sovereign" decisions, proceeding from their own considerations of political expediency. In other words, they act depending on a specific situation or impulsively react to what they see as the unlawful actions of another actor.

The world is witnessing a clash of two different tendencies: the chaotization of world politics, with selective use of military force, and the objective need for humankind to preserve the hard-built integration ties that suggest a certain degree of financial, economic and, in some matters, political interdependence.

Why is the Fourth Enlargement Wave Ebbing?

The crisis over Ukraine has become the most dangerous episode in a series of conflicts that have taken place in the world over the last quarter century, although the Arab Spring has already sent enough signals to major actors to shun ideology in reevaluating objective trends and to analyze their miscalculations and mistakes. Whereas no one perceived local conflicts of the recent decades in Yugoslavia, Iraq, Libya and even Syria as serious threats to international security (the US's bellicose rhetoric at the UN Security Council in response to Russian vetoes was aimed at enhancing Washington's image at home and abroad), the confrontation on Ukrainian soil has prompted the question of whether the world is sliding into the abyss of another cold war. This time it is a worst-case-scenario cold war, when the conflicting parties are losing the degree of mutual trust and ability to heed each other, which in the years of systemic confrontation, allowed the US and Soviet leaders to undo the most intricate knots of tension.

Why have tensions in Russia-West relations come to a head? The sliding from "strategic partnership" to a new round of confrontation led to the accumulation of an explosive mass of irritating factors, as well as mutual misunderstanding and misinterpretation of each other's motives. The events that led to the conflict over Ukraine had been developing slowly but consistently, moving steadily eastward toward Russia's border and its centuries-old cultural and national habitat.

Whereas tension over NATO's enlargement into Eastern Europe in the late 1990s, which provoked a strong reaction from Russia, subsided over time, the situation began to change rapidly as Western ambitions went as far as the borders of the former Soviet Union. While Russia's ties with Central and Eastern European countries in the last decade were marked by positive trends, the European Union tried hard to draw former Soviet republics into its orbit under the political cover of the so-called Eastern Partnership. Considering the experience of the three previous waves of enlargement, Russia could not consider these developments as anything other than preparations for the subsequent admission of these countries to the Euro-Atlantic alliance (there is an unwritten rule that NATO membership cannot be given to a country that has not gone through the difficult procedure of joining the EU).

Ukraine was placed on this waiting list, just like Georgia and Moldova before it. The West resumed its policy of containing Russia long before the current Ukrainian crisis, disguising it with talk of partnership and the inadmissibility of returning to the struggle for spheres of influence. Among its instruments, it used the strategy of regime change, earlier tested in the Balkans, Georgia and some other transition countries. In Ukraine, however, the West failed to observe democratic decencies. When the regime in Ukraine was replaced by force, with blatant interference of the West, Russia, which until then had held defensive positions, decided it could no longer leave this challenge unanswered. In Russia's public opinion and official strategy, Ukraine means not only national security and cooperative ties, vital to the economies of both countries, but also centuries of spiritual kinship, and cultural and language commonality.

Defense considerations played an important role in the Russian reaction. Recent years were marked by a large-scale anti-Russian campaign in the West under various pretenses. The West toughened its criticism of the social and political systems in Russia, which in turn increased conservative sentiment in Russia as a reaction to abortive rapprochement with the West.

There must be some key link in the entire causal chain of actions and counteractions between Russia and the West. One of these links is fundamental differences in the perception of modern revolutions and the new local or regional threats they cause.

After the end of the era of bipolar confrontation, Central and Eastern Europe, the former Soviet Union and the Middle East were swept by three waves of revolutions, with different balances of pros and cons, and gains and losses. At the turn of the 1980s-1990s, Russia was also involved in the renewal process that was full of internal contradictions, achievements and setbacks. New challenges, such as international terrorism, surges of ethnic nationalism, drug trafficking, transborder crime and immigration, coupled with a global financial crisis, revealed vulnerabilities in the functioning of political systems and market economy mechanisms even in developed countries.

While the communist ideology failed around the world and the evolutionary model of post-Soviet Russia has not yet produced an attractive alternative, serious defects and dysfunctions have been revealed in liberal democracies as well. Many Western experts point to a decline in the quality of democracy in the US and Great Britain, to increasing institutional failures, and the growing number of "defective democracies." The institution of elections, the main element of democratic government, is losing its former value in the eyes of voters, especially young people (only two out of five Britons aged under 30 voted in the 2010 parliamentary elections in Great Britain).

It took a quarter of a century to see that the "end of history" predicted by Francis Fukuyama was not going to happen. Later, analyzing "dramatic changes" in the postindustrial era in his book *The Great Disruption*, he showed convincingly that "history," meaning the victory of liberalism as a perfect state model, is far from over. The period since the end of the 20th century has been marked by a craving for freedom of choice in everything, and decreasing trust in social and political institutions. The democracy established in the West has revealed its internal contradictions, making the messianic ambitions of the majority of the American establishment a naïve exaggeration, to say the least.

The US, whose foreign policy is constrained by ideological clichés, has more than once had to pay for its "interventionism" or idealization of the revolutionary change of political regimes with chaotic moves in the Middle East. Washington made obvious blunders in assessing such a social-political phenomenon as the Arab Spring. The revolutions in Egypt and Tunisia were automatically taken as a universal phenomenon in the victorious march of democracy. They were even compared to the "velvet revolutions" in Eastern and Central European countries. However, soon it became clear to everyone that Arab revolutions cannot be "velvet."

Whereas European countries had the experience of bourgeois-democratic development and built their identities on rejecting communism and viewing the EU as the center of attraction, there were no such reference points in the Middle East – or in most post-Soviet states, for that matter, and Ukraine is no exception.

The national development of the territories where the present Ukrainian state was established by a historical confluence of circumstances has always been influenced by two tendencies: a search for independence and a desire for political and cultural community with Russia, with the latter trend obviously prevailing. Ukraine, which was artificially cobbled together from two different parts after the Soviet Union's military advance in the West in the late 1930s, has remained culturally and politically fragmented to this day. The different historical narratives and national heroes, mentality, patterns of employment, and the alienation from Russia characteristic of people in Western Ukraine – all these factors surfaced after Ukraine became independent. Unfortunately, the Ukrainian political elite has proven unable to achieve national unity: It has exploited the Ukrainian division and traded service to the nation for money and self-interest. The EU's self-confident policy of pressure forced Ukraine into a dilemma that it was unable to resolve by definition.

Pointless Interference

Speaking of nation-building, which has much in common in all countries regardless of regional specificities, one should mention the disastrous experience of the first attempts of bourgeois reforms in the Middle East in the late 19th and early 20th centuries. The political systems of Egypt, Syria and Iraq, patterned after the Western model, failed to take root on Arab-Muslim soil and were swept away in the military coups of the 1950s-1960s. The dramatic changes of the 21st century have also destroyed the myth that the world is developing along the main track from "authoritarianism" to "democracy," which the majority of the US political elite views as a purely American product – a kind of "Protestant fundamentalism."

Young people in Arab countries, like Ukrainian young people, shocked the world with mass calls for a renovation of social foundations, for respect for human dignity and civil liberties, and for social justice. Soon, however, the revolutionary transformation of the Middle East ceased to fit into the democratic context. As developments spun more and more out of control, the Middle East policies of the US and the EU increasingly faced serious difficulties, in many cases becoming hostage to traditional thinking.

The powerful popular unrest in Arab countries was caused by a mixture of social and economic factors. External factors did play a role, but initially an indirect one. At the same time, as the domino effect spread, the West a priori supported opposition forces, the way it used to do in other regional conflicts, ignoring their diversity and contradictions in their political attitudes. Since then, external interference in favor of one of the conflicting parties only increased, while the hope to gain political capital by showing solidarity with the Arab "democratic revolutions" was more and more at odds with the real transformation processes in the region.

The fate of Iraq, which has found itself on the verge of losing its statehood and involved in a religious war, has now caused the West to rethink the harmful effects of the American invasion in 2003. As leading Middle East expert Richard Haass wrote in the *Financial Times* (June 15, 2014), the US policy in Iraq "reinforced sectarian rather than national identities." In the same way as the Suez Crisis of 1956 caused a surge of pan-Arab nationalism, the Western co-alition's war against a Muslim country triggered an unprecedented escalation of violence by radical Islamists and created fertile ground for the rise of Al Qaeda. The delicate balance between the ruling Sunni minority and the Shiite majority, maintained by Saddam Hussein's iron hand, was upset in no time in favor of the Shiites. The attempt to impose Western-style parliamentarianism on Iraq resulted in the emergence of a Shiite regime. Prime Minister Nuri al-Maliki pursued a narrow confessional policy that prevented the inclusive participation of other religious and ethnic groups in the government. Kurds began to actively build their own autonomy, while Sunnis and Christians found themselves left without any po-litical representation. The dissolution of the Army and the Ba'ath Party, which had been the core of Iraq's political system, gave rise to a powerful domestic protest.

Just as much harm was done by the US's active but erratic par-ticipation in the complicated transitional processes in Egypt. After a momentary hesitation, Washington used all its political and in-formational resources to support the Egyptian revolution, forcing Hosni Mubarak to resign. Later, when Islamists had succeeded in riding the revolutionary wave, the US assigned the key role to the moderate wing of the Muslim Brotherhood, which used the new situation to quickly become an influential political party and win parliamentary and presidential elections. Just like during the rise of Islamism in Algeria in the 1990s that evolved into a decade-long civil war, the Americans exerted constant pressure on the Egyptian Army, which led the transition process, forcing it to hand over power to a civilian government, essentially to Islamists. Therefore, the "sec-ond coming" of the Army to power in July 2013 and the removal of democratically elected Islamist president Mohamed Morsi in what cannot be described other than a military coup put the White House in a difficult situation again.

The Army's actions, even if they were a response to the demands of millions of people who had taken to the streets again, did not fit into the antithesis of coup vs. democracy; nor did they look like a movement to defend democracy against "Islamic dictatorship," simply because democracy had never existed in Egypt.

In the Muslim world, which had divided over the attitude toward political Islam, the changes in US policy alienated both supporters of the new military regime and its opponents who supported the Muslim Brotherhood.

Washington also made mistakes in handling the Syrian conflict. Its unconditional support for the motley opposition movement in Syria, in which jihadist organizations linked to Al Qaeda were gaining strength, and the declaration of the Bashar Assad regime as a priori illegitimate made American diplomacy weaker rather than stronger and tied its hands. This made Washington hostage to the exorbitantly ambitious demands of Syrian émigré politicians and their regional sponsors, and complicated preparations for the Geneva Conference. Ultimately, US policy obviously began to play into the hands of terrorism, on which the US had declared war. This became particularly manifest in the summer of 2014, when military successes achieved in Iraq by the terrorist organization the Islamic State (IS) put the Obama administration in a still more delicate situation.

In the short-term historical perspective, the balance of pros and cons of regime change in the Middle East has not been in favor of revolutions. The main reason for the overthrow of governments was their inability to meet the basic social, economic and political needs of society, and keep their promises, although the Arab region in the past decade was developing along the path of modernization and integration into the world economic system. Yet this evolution was much slower than the development of other regions, such as Southeast Asia and Latin America. Second, it failed to solve key growth problems. Economic reforms in Egypt, Tunisia and Syria created a middle class but did not narrow the chasm of wealth inequality. Only a small group of people close to power benefited from the results of the reforms. Representative political institutions underwent only token changes. The democratic façade hid authoritarian rule, which grew increasingly nepotic. The laws of revolutionary chaos came into play when the authorities proved totally incapable of regenerating the political system to broaden citizens' participation in decision-making affecting their vital interests.

Revolutionary Challenges for the Entire World

The transformation of the Arab Middle East is proceeding unevenly, with ups and downs, progress and regression. Nevertheless, we can try to summarize some of the lessons learned from these developments and draw some parallels with crises in other regions.

Revolutions come not only when outdated state and political systems have to be removed. Whereas in Syria, for example, the Ba'ath party's monopoly on power has long become an anachronism and its slogan "Unity, Freedom, Socialism" has lost its former appeal, the 10-year civil war in Algeria was largely the result of ill-prepared reforms and hasty democratization launched in the late 1980s through the early 1990s under the influence of changes in Russia and Central and Eastern Europe.

The crisis of the unitary state model in Ukraine, coupled with corruption and moral decay among the elites, is additional evidence of the need for timely reform. Instead of reform, there was revolutionary chaos, armed conflict in southeastern Ukraine and a humanitarian crisis.

The West took purely formal features, such as the electoral process, for democracy in the Arab-Muslim countries. At the same time, equally or even more important issues were not given due consideration: Can the political force that has won national elections build a society that will meet the hopes of the revolutionary masses? Can democracy be promoted using nondemocratic means? Of course, elections are an important tool of democracy, but absent developed institutions, they cannot guarantee a transition to democratic rule. In societies that do not share common democratic values, the forces that win are the ones that can offer the simplest solutions for the nation's transformation that would be understandable and acceptable to the most conservative and larger part of the electorate. In Palestine, believed to be the most secular Arab society, the 2005 elections were won by the Islamic Hamas movement; and in Egypt, a leading Arab country with a "hybrid regime," power went to the Muslim Brotherhood. The first thing they did was to amend the Constitution in order to stay in power indefinitely.

Does this experience mean that elections are useless in politically immature societies where most people do not understand their own social interest? Obviously, the question should be put differently. Not just elections, but a guaranteed handover of power (as a result of elections) can gradually make the authorities more responsible and nationally oriented.

Developments in Egypt, where two "revolutions" took place over three years, raise the question of whether a military coup can be a catalyst for a return to stable evolutionary development. Both Islamists who resort to terror to restore "constitutional law" and secularists who invited the military to power are grossly mistaken in hoping to build a new Egypt without achieving a national consensus.

Not all winds of change can be explained by foreign interference, yet the way internal conflicts are settled – by force or through a peaceful division of power – plays an important role, as it predetermines whether the postrevolutionary transitional period is smooth. The conflicts in Iraq, Syria and Libya have shown that violence and civil wars, especially if they are supported from abroad or if there is foreign intervention, cause enormous damage to creative efforts.

The experience of most revolutions in the world shows that power is taken not by the forces that stage them but by those who "have caught the wave" with foreign support or by chance. The regime change in the Arab world, which took place under democratic slogans, once again confirmed the relevance of this historical trend. When mass protests began in Arab countries, there were no Islamic slogans in the streets, but eventually Tunisian and Egyptian Islamists came to lead these revolutionary-democratic protests, using their experience of organizational work among the masses, sermons in mosques, and discord in the secular opposition. In fact, the Egyptian revolution experienced two popular uprisings, just as the revolution in Ukraine did. One uprising was moderate, pro-European and directed against the corrupt regime; the other one, radical and nationalistic, transformed the change of power into an armed mutiny, with a hostile attitude toward Russia and the Russian-speaking population of eastern Ukraine.

As the transition period has slowed down in Arab countries shaken by revolutions, in all of them, democratic illusions are giving way to the local, including Islamic, reality. Many Arab political analysts wonder whether their countries are ready for democracy and what development model will take root in the Middle East, where the foundations of the social contract between the state and society have been undermined. All known variants – Egyptian, Turkish, Saudi and Iranian – have been discredited or are losing their attractiveness. "Political Islam" at the present stage has failed. Further progress toward a Western-type parliamentary system is unlikely.

In contrast to the Western political process that developed in societies with structured private ownership relations, the domination of commodity production, and the absence of a centralized government, in Eastern societies the political process has always been the result of the domination of state and communal ownership. In these countries power was the equivalent of ownership, and society was subordinate to the state. Absolutization of the state meant, in particular, that its power did not transform into the welfare of citizens, who remained subjects subordinate to the communal interest merged with the state interest.

Disappointed hopes for rapid improvement of life after the overthrow of the old regimes transform into a desire for a strong hand and order. This phenomenon can be seen in Egypt, where Field Marshal Abdel Fattah el-Sisi, who won the latest presidential election, is viewed by most Egyptians as the "savior of the nation." A strong personality has also emerged in Libya. Gen. Khalifa Haftar, who returned to his country from exile after the revolution began, united part of the Army, tribes and local militias to challenge the transitional government under the banner of fighting Islamists.

The formation of new governments may take long efforts to achieve national consensus under the aegis of a personified political force that has taken the upper hand in political in-fighting, which means the preservation of authoritarianism, and not necessarily in an enlightened form.

* * *

Today, revolutions have become major factors influencing the system of international relations. Obviously, leading world powers may have differing attitudes to them, yet they should be balanced and responsible. Russia and the West can and should avoid a recurrence of crisis situations in their mutual relations. This, in fact, is their historical responsibility. If they could agree on common principles for settling intrastate conflicts that give rise to ethnic, religious or purely political extremism, this would play a positive role.

The nature of modern revolutions has long been a subject of heated discussion. When do domestic affairs cease to be domestic? Does this happen when there is suppression of civil liberties, a disproportionate use of force against mass opposition protests, acts of violence or other violations of human rights and international humanitarian law? Without questioning the basic principle of sovereignty and noninterference in domestic affairs, one should admit that many of these issues have already acquired a global dimension.

If the international community fails to establish acceptable and understandable rules of international behavior in the context of "revolutionary challenges," the world may slip into a new round of global confrontation, which will be caused not by systemic contradictions of the cold war era but by vain disregard for real common threats.

PART THREE

3.2. Prospects for Stability in the Region

DEMOCRACY, INTERNATIONAL GOVERNANCE, AND THE FUTURE WORLD ORDER

Sergei Lavrov

Democracy cannot be imposed from the outside. Attempts to re-
place a ruling regime by force only serve to destabilize the situa-
tion in a given country. Democratic institutions must be formed
on the national basis of a given country, while the international
community must help create favorable conditions for promoting
this process. It must show respect for the existing traditions of
every country and for the choice of ways to develop democracy.

How can international relations be made more systemic and govern-
able under conditions of globalization and the growing interdependence of states? This question, which is not a theoretical one, has
now come into the focus of international politics. An answer to this
question will largely determine how effective the international community will be at countering global threats and challenges like terrorism, the proliferation of weapons of mass destruction, drug trafficking and organized crime. Actually, it will determine whether we
will be able to accelerate the protracted transition from the former
bipolar system of international relations to a new, safer and more
stable world order.

This article originally appeared in *Russia in Global Affairs* Vol. 3, No. 1, 2005.

The 15 years that have passed since the end of the cold war have seen sweeping positive changes in the world. Democracy has been growing in individual countries and in international relations, and there is growing understanding in the world that only free people can ensure economic growth and the prosperity of a state. Civil society is developing around the world, although in different ways, and is playing an increasingly active role at national, regional and global levels.

At the same time, the hopes of some politicians and scholars that a majority of states would adopt democratic values, which would then become a universal regulating principle of international relations, have failed to materialize. On the contrary, these values have become the target of attacks from militant separatism and other manifestations of extremism, which serve as a fertile medium for international terrorism.

There are other factors – promoted under the banner of "defending democracy" – that are impeding the universalization of democratic principles. These include interfering in the domestic affairs of other countries; exerting political pressure on them; and imposing double standards on other countries when assessing their election processes and the state of civil rights and freedoms. Those resorting to such practices must realize that they only discredit democratic values, turning them into bargaining chips for achieving selfish geostrategic interests.

The creation of new mechanisms for ensuring security and stability in the world is impeded largely by the contradictory nature of globalization. On the one hand, this process, albeit far from complete, is taking humanity to a new level of civilizational development in many respects. At the same time, it entails heavy costs, including the increasing developmental gap between states and regions, soaring economic and social degradation, and the growing impact on the global economy of spontaneous market forces that are beyond state control.

These developments increase the amount of unsolved international problems. The disappearance of the negative stability of the cold war era has resulted in the escalation of numerous regional conflicts, both old and new, which have begun to evolve into real or potential sources of terrorism, crime, drug trafficking and WMD proliferation. Poverty, unemployment and mounting tension on a social, economic, ethnic and religious basis, which persist in many regions of the world, create fertile ground for these evils and extremist sentiments.

The international community does not yet have a common strategy for addressing these problems and oftentimes must grope for adequate ways to ensure its security and stability.

Nobody holds a monopoly on the right answers to these questions; the realities of the modern world (global and, at the same time, infinitely versatile) rule out the possibility of such a monopoly – be it on the issue of democracy or international relations. Current developments in the post-Soviet space provide a characteristic example. Russian President Vladimir Putin told a conference of Russian ambassadors in July 2004 that Russia does not have a monopoly on this region. The members of the Commonwealth of Independent States enjoy the sovereign right to form their foreign policies in accordance with their own national interests. That is why no other state or group of states can claim a monopoly on influence. Any attempt to place the CIS countries in a false dilemma ("either with the West or with Russia") would be unnatural, dangerous and irresponsible. No one would gain from a revival of obsolete methods of geopolitical rivalry.

Obviously, the right path to a stable and democratic world order can be found only through a dialogue that would involve not only governments but also parliaments, political parties, analysts, businesspeople and civil society as a whole. The present session of the UN General Assembly has demonstrated that such dialogue is already gaining momentum. The international community has begun to work out general approaches that take into account the views of the international public and are shared by a large number of countries.

First, the recent course of global events proves that any attempt to handle new threats unilaterally is futile. The present developments in Iraq, where the US launched a military operation without UN Security Council approval, illustrate the advantages of a multilateral approach. Eventually, the US began to form a broad international coalition, seeking to include any – even the most insignificant – countries. This coalition was formed to demonstrate the international participation (much of it token) and multilateral nature of US actions. Later, Washington asked the UN to place the postwar restoration of Iraq under its umbrella, and the international community is presently facing the common task of assisting Iraq to stabilize the situation and prevent its disintegration. This can be accomplished through broad inter-Iraqi dialogue aimed at encouraging national accord, and fair elections that would help build truly representative bodies of power reflecting the interests of all groups of the Iraqi population.

Like an overwhelming majority of other countries, Russia believes that the future world order must be based on collective mechanisms for addressing global problems. Whether this will be called a multipolar system or otherwise does not really matter. More importantly, this system must contain as many fulcrum points as possible in order to guarantee its stability. The international community must discover a platform for broad accord and interaction between the main actors on the global arena, including the Group of Eight, the European Union, China, India, Japan and the key countries of Southeast Asia, the Middle East, Latin America and Africa. This platform must rest on mutual confidence and respect for each other's interests in addressing international problems, as opposed to a group of countries invited to join a single nation that has already decided everything unilaterally.

Another aspect of achieving more reliable international governance is improving mechanisms of multilateral cooperation; of these, the UN is undoubtedly the most universal. This organization, which has unique legitimacy and an extensive record of global and regional activities, must be made more effective at crisis management and acquire better-defined criteria for using coercive measures, including force, by a Security Council decision. This subject (discussed in recent years under various names – "humanitarian intervention," "human security" and the "right to protection") is in the focus of the High-Level Panel on Threats, Challenges and Change, established by UN Secretary-General Kofi Annan; the panel includes Russian Academician Yevgeny Primakov. The UN is expected to soon begin discussion of the Panel's report.

Russia maintains that the UN Security Council must avoid applying mechanical approaches when advancing criteria for approving the use of force. Each individual situation must be considered in light of its particular characteristics. There can be no universal formula or simple arithmetic solutions, such as "99 people killed is not quite genocide, but 100 people killed is, so the Security Council must automatically make a respective decision." It is also important that the international community make decisions on its interference in a crisis, especially "preventive interference," based on verified and irrefutable facts rather than conjecture and unsubstantiated accusations, as was the case, for example, with assertions about weapons of mass destruction in Iraq.

Efforts to solve this difficult and topical problem involve scholars, diplomats and leaders from many countries. The success of these efforts will enable the international community to build equitable and multilateral mechanisms for the new world order. These mechanisms could also be applied to regional organizations pertaining to international cooperation. Today, all of them, especially in Europe, are undergoing deep transformation, adapting to the new threats and challenges.

The disruption of the cold war bloc discipline has played a very positive role in this respect. A new, more flexible and mobile structure of international relations is now being formed, and regional integration associations are taking an increasingly prominent place in it. These associations are turning into independent poles of international politics, enabling even relatively small states to influence it. These changes have had an effect on Russia's international ties, as well. This country is building new interaction mechanisms – e.g., the Russia-NATO Council and new partnership institutions with the EU. Russia has established close contacts with the Organization of the Islamic Conference, the Association of Southeast Asian Nations (ASEAN), integration associations in Latin America, and individual countries in various regions, for example, the Persian Gulf, with which it formerly had no dialogue.

But despite these positive processes, the inertia of the bloc approach still persists. An illustrative example is NATO's expansion, which does not correspond with any of the real challenges the European countries are now facing. Furthermore, strange things are happening in the Organization for Security and Cooperation in Europe (OSCE). The OSCE, which emerged when the world was divided into two blocs, was established on the basis of consensus and generally acceptable approaches to cooperation in the areas of security, economics and human rights. It would seem that, now that the bloc system has ceased to exist, the OSCE could fully realize these qualities. In practice, however, and rather paradoxically, this organization is erecting a wall within itself, artificially dividing its members into the NATO and EU members, and the rest. Actually, the EU, especially after its enlargement to 25 members, has emerged as a new political bloc in the OSCE, and its position is evolving in a destructive direction under the influence of some of its new members.

Attempts are being made to restrict the OSCE agenda to solely humanitarian issues and to reduce the latter to the monitoring of democratic processes and the observance of human rights in the post-Soviet space. Thus, the OSCE's work in ensuring security and encouraging economic development is being downplayed. As it turns out, NATO deals with security issues, the EU with economic issues, and the OSCE will only monitor the adoption of these organizations' values by countries that have remained outside the EU and NATO.

This state of affairs can hardly be accepted. Russia, together with its CIS partners, has come out with constructive proposals for reforming the OSCE in order to bring it back to the original concept of balanced and equal cooperation in each of the three baskets.

Finally, the third area in building a new world order is the consolidation of international law. Russia does not view it as dogma, believing that international law, as well as national legislation, must keep up with the times. In particular, the need for new approaches to humanitarian catastrophes shows that international law needs to be amended, and that certain voids within it must be filled. In keeping with the UN Charter, the Security Council can establish new legal norms within its prerogative, as it did when it set up ad hoc tribunals for the former Yugoslavia and Rwanda in the absence of international treaties.

However, after the Security Council fills in dangerous gaps with its decisions, universal international treaties must be worked out by all interested countries. This was how the Statute of the International Criminal Court was drawn up following years of tribunals on the former Yugoslavia and Rwanda. The International Criminal Court makes the establishment of ad hoc tribunals redundant.

In much the same way, the UN Security Council – following the tragic events of 9/11 – adopted special counterterrorism resolutions so that each country would bring its national legislation into line and participate in the international legal regimes for stopping various kinds of support for terrorist activities. In 2004, on Russia's initiative, the Security Council adopted Resolutions No. 1540 and No. 1566, which filled a legal void in the WMD nonproliferation regimes with regard to access to WMD and their components for nonstate actors; the need for a clearer definition of terrorism; and the inadmissibility of states providing safe haven to individuals who support, facilitate or participate in terrorist acts, and protecting them from justice. However, this kind of Security Council decision must be followed up with efforts made on a universal basis. This refers, in particular, to promoting the draft international counterterrorism convention and the Russia-proposed draft convention on nuclear terrorism.

Heated debates are under way on an issue that is closely connected with "humanitarian interventions" – namely, the balance between state sovereignty and the need to respond to crises in any particular country. The search for the right legal solution may take much effort; however, the creation of new international laws, be it through Security Council resolutions or universal instruments, must proceed on the basis of strict observance of generally accepted international norms while these remain in effect.

The dimensions of the terrorist threat present domestic legal problems for countries. One of the most difficult problems is: How does a country effectively combat terrorism without going beyond the frameworks of constitutional, democratic standards? There are no ready-made solutions for such a question. Fundamental democratic values are universal, but each country implements them in its own way, taking into account its traditions, culture and national peculiarities. Likewise, this approach manifests itself in the tactics a particular country chooses for combating terrorism.

When fighting an enemy, it is possible to put oneself in the enemy's position to better predict his actions. However, terrorists have deliberately overstepped all ethical norms; thus, the average person finds it difficult to foresee their next move. This is why all countries facing the terrorist threat are committing inevitable mistakes. To minimize these mistakes, governments must establish a professional and trusting exchange of information and experience. However, when the public appeals to the authorities to "report" why a particular terrorist act was allowed to be committed, it actually harms counterterrorist efforts; such appeals are often made to gain points in domestic or foreign policies.

Russian society, as well as the entire world, was deeply shocked by the terrorist act in Beslan. Russia will continue to wage an uncompromising war against terrorism and defend the country's unity and security. At the same time, Russia will remain a democratic state that respects the rights and freedoms of its citizens. When considering such issues, Russia is open to a mutually respectful dialogue and an exchange of experience; it is prepared to listen to an outside opinion that may not coincide with its own opinions. The only things it cannot accept, however, are arrogance, a didactic tone, double standards and attempts to use the war on terrorism in various kinds of geopolitical games.

To construct a new system of international relations, double standards must be eradicated. It is impermissible, for example, to fight against aggressive separatism and, simultaneously, encourage the independence of Kosovo. It should be understood that such a policy could spark a chain reaction – and not only in the Balkans. Those who argue that refugees should be allowed to return home somehow "forget" about the largest group of refugees in Europe – the 500,000 Serbs.

The real provision of human rights is incompatible with double standards. In its dialogue with the EU, Russia finds it very difficult to prove the obvious and well-documented injustice done to ethnic minorities in Latvia and Estonia. Rolf Ekeus, the OSCE High Commissioner on National Minorities, who recently visited Latvia, proposed yet again specific recommendations to the Latvian government, urging it to speed up the rate of naturalization, ratify the Convention for the Protection of National Minorities, and grant everyone, including so-called noncitizens, the right to participate in the election of municipal authorities. However, these recommendations have never been fulfilled. Paradoxically, a foreigner, say, from Portugal, can come to Latvia and, after living in the country for six months, have the right to vote in the municipal elections. Compare this situation to that of the many people who were born in Latvia and permanently live in a municipal entity yet do not enjoy such rights.

The UN Committee on the Elimination of Racial Discrimination, set up to monitor the implementation of the UN Convention on the Elimination of All Forms of Racial Discrimination, adopted specific observations regarding Latvia that Riga has failed to respond to. Thus, the EU's assertions that Latvia, as well as Estonia, fully comply with the EU's Copenhagen criteria are groundless.

To eradicate double-standard practices, people must change their mentality and relinquish the philosophy of the past epoch. Thus far, not everyone has managed to do that, as shown by the reaction of certain circles in Europe and the US regarding the political crisis in Ukraine. Even before the presidential elections there began, these outside groups sent strong signals that the West would not recognize the outcome of the election if the victory went to a candidate it did not support. When the results of the elections did turn out to be different than they had expected, they immediately spoke of the "invalidity" of the vote and the need to revise its outcome. Those who pose in their own countries as staunch defenders of democracy and law began to openly encourage the Ukrainian opposition, even when some of its leaders actually provoked public disorder and the forceful seizure of power. Statements were made in Europe that "Ukraine must be with the West."

Such methods, when applied toward a sovereign state, may have grave consequences for the situation in Europe, as well as damage democratic values. Democracy must be established within the framework of law rather than by street rallies, which may provoke violence and the division of society.

History proves that democracy cannot be imposed from the outside. Attempts to replace a ruling regime by force only serve to destabilize the situation in a given country. Democratic institutions must be formed on the national basis of a given country, while the international community must help create favorable conditions for promoting this process. It must show respect for the existing traditions of every country and for the choice of ways to develop democracy; these are established by each country on the basis of the fundamental values proclaimed in the Universal Declaration of Human Rights.

As for the fundamental principles of Russia's foreign policy, they remain unchanged. We will continue building our foreign policy as befits a strong, peace-loving and responsible member of the international community, acting through dialogue and partnership, rather than confrontation, even when the most complicated global problems arise in interstate relations. Together with other countries, Russia will make constructive contributions to efforts to increase the governability of global processes and build a fairer, safer and more stable system of international relations.

THE MIDDLE EAST: À LA VERSAILLES OR À LA WESTPHALIA?

Pyotr Stegny

There are two principal development scenarios for the situation in the Middle East. The first scenario concerns postwar settlement à la Versailles – specifically, the division of the Arab territories of the Ottoman Empire, in which the lead was taken by external forces. The second scenario, à la Westphalia, is a protracted and painful process of self-development of a democratic community of nation states.

The Arab Spring, which has been raging in the Middle East for two years, has swept away seemingly irremovable regimes in Egypt, Libya, Tunisia and Yemen. In Syria, where the Ba'athist leadership has preserved its bond with the Armed Forces and law-enforcement agencies, the civil war is escalating with unclear prospects for President Bashar Assad's regime. In terms of the democratic transformation of the region, more has been done during the past two years of the Arab Spring than in the entire history of the independent existence of Middle Eastern countries. However, the process is not yet complete: Democratic change has affected the core of the Arab world and stopped in its periphery – at the borders of the traditionalist

---

This article originally appeared in *Russia in Global Affairs* Vol. 10, No. 4, 2012.

monarchies of the Persian Gulf, which are attempting to bribe their way out of long overdue transformations. Iraq, Lebanon and Algeria are immune to "twitter revolutions," as they had earlier undergone (albeit with varying degree of success) a modernization cycle, including foreign interventions and civil wars. The monarchies of Morocco and Jordan are adapting fairly flexibly to the imperatives of the day and are continuing to make concessions to the opposition. Yet, overall, the impression of the region is not that of a decisive pivot toward democracy nor of integration into global modernization processes.

In addition, the Arab Spring, having begun as a "twitter revolution" of the middle class, has handed power to conservative Islamic forces, from fundamentalist to extremist factions, some of which march under theocratic slogans. The regimes that passed into political obscurity were predictable; they knew and obeyed the rules of the game, and did not cross the "red lines" that determine regional stability. The political positions of the new Islamic elite are rather vague.

In this situation the important question is: Will the Middle East remain a balanced regional system, able to collectively comprehend and defend common interests while staying congruent with global development imperatives? On one hand, the Arab League and the Cooperation Council for the Arab States of the Gulf (CCASG) supported Western armed intervention in Libya and are taking a similar position on Syria; on the other hand, regime change in the course of the Arab Spring has heightened ethnic and religious antagonisms as radical Islamists enter the political scene. The gap between Sunnis and Shiites is widening. It is difficult to know where the interfaith disputes will end and start (with the involvement of actors from outside the region) a struggle for territories, oil and control over energy supply routes. In short, the time has come to consider the options, to look for parallels in global experience, and to probe the obvious and hidden implications of the processes occurring in the Middle East.

Global Context

Within a geopolitical context, the Arab Spring is the second "passionary" (to use Lev Gumilyov's term[1]) shift in the last 50 years in the Middle East. The first shift, which occurred on the wave of the collapse of the colonial system in the 1950s and 1960s, brought

Arab nationalists to power in the leading countries of the region. In general, they successfully used the confrontation between the two superpowers to achieve their postcolonial development goals.

In the subsequent political evolution of the Middle East, three cycles can be observed, each lasting approximately 20 years. The first cycle (which, for the purposes of discussion, began with the 1952 revolution in Egypt) saw a greater part of the Arab world come under the influence of the Soviet bloc, which provided considerable financial and technological assistance to industrializing Arab states (Egypt under Nasser, Syria, Algeria). The Soviet Union supported the Arabs and the Palestinians in their conflict with Israel, and was their main supplier of weapons. The Middle East became a staging area for the military and strategic confrontation between the Soviet Union and the US, which was occurring over the heads of the regional powers.

The situation began to change radically in the early 1970s at the start of the second cycle, when the Soviet Union lost the first technological round of the modernization contest ("powder technologies") to the West. Then the Soviet Union failed to rationally use the abrupt spike in oil prices (which, in essence, was the result of Soviet policies in the Arab-Israeli conflict) to overcome its lag in computer technology.

As a consequence, Moscow gradually lost the initiative in the global competition of the two sociopolitical systems. This process culminated (though to date not fully acknowledged) in Helsinki at the 1975 Conference on Security and Cooperation in Europe. One result was that the Soviet Union, exhausted by the arms race, ceded its role as a guarantor of postwar borders in Europe to the European community, represented by the Organization for Security and Cooperation in Europe, and made substantial concessions on human rights. It is unlikely that the Soviet leadership, which viewed the Helsinki Declaration as its own victory (since it guaranteed Poland's western border along the Oder-Neisse line), could imagine the geopolitical consequences this act would shortly create. The disintegration of the Soviet Union and Yugoslavia became possible (from an international legal perspective) only "under the umbrella" of the Helsinki Accords.

In the regional picture, Moscow's geopolitical retreat displayed an intermittent, uneven character. The West effectively used the inherent contradiction of late Soviet policy, between the ideologeme of the anti-imperialist struggle and its desire to come to terms with a strategic adversary, to assure its victory in the cold war. Afghanistan, Angola, and Mozambique became tragic landmarks on the path to the geopolitical disaster of 1991.

In the Middle East, the growing inconsistency of the "elder brother's" political conduct was seen as the main cause of the existing situation of "neither war nor peace" with Israel. The "negotiated draw" in the Yom Kippur war with Israel (in the sense that it launched Henry Kissinger's "shuttle diplomacy") was used by Anwar Sadat to reorient Egypt's foreign policy toward the US and to sign the 1978 Camp David peace accords with Israel. The Camp David accords triggered a return swing of the Arab policy pendulum toward the West, which, so it emerged, controlled more significant and attractive resources to support modernization. The process slowly developed, with noticeable rollbacks caused by relapses of residual radicalism and mutual mistrust of the parties to the Arab-Israeli conflict.

Largely for this reason, the period after the disintegration of the Soviet Union (or the third 20-year cycle) became a time of lost opportunities for the Middle East. The chances for a peaceful settlement of the Arab-Israeli conflict offered by the Madrid Peace Conference formula and by the Oslo process failed to materialize, and implementation of the "Road Map" almost immediately slid to a halt. By and large, Arab elites were late with reforms and failed to adapt in a timely manner to the political and democratic changes occurring around the globe.

The Arab world found itself on the sidelines of history, and dangerously close to the geopolitical rift between an expanding Europe and an Asia transforming into an influential economic and political player, with rapidly rising China and India at its helm. The "civilizational rift" between Europe and Asia formed a "triangle of instability" of Iran, Pakistan and Afghanistan, where, given the logic of global processes, there concentrated global risks connected to the spread of nuclear weapons and the threat of terrorism. For the foreseeable future, the region will remain a vulnerable point of Euro-Atlantic security – its "soft underbelly," in Churchill's terms. If so, in geopolitical significance, the Greater Middle East is functionally becoming the Balkans of the interwar period, with a corresponding increase of its role in the global environment.

This circumstance largely determined the scope and radical character of the second passionary shift labeled the Arab Spring, which roused the region in 2011. Having begun as a social protest against authoritarian rulers, it transformed in Syria – a relatively successful country according to basic economic indicators – into something fundamentally different. The ongoing events in Syria increasingly resemble a battle on the Iranian borderlands or, if viewed broadly, on the forefront of a new "Eastern frontier" emerging as a geopolitical partition dividing the West from the East. Control over the activities on this frontier will, to a large degree, define the nature of the geopolitical struggle in the 21st century.

The subtexts of the Arab Spring defined the reaction of external players. For the Americans, who without hesitation laid their established regional allies on the altar of democracy, the defining factor was how closely the "twitter revolutions" in the Arab world matched the geopolitical essence – rather than the democratic pathos – of Barack Obama's policy speech in Cairo. [This policy] amounts to incorporating the Greater Middle East into the White House's own idea of a multipolar world under US leadership. Fulfillment of this goal acquired special significance in the [US Democrats'] preelection battle with the Republicans, as it contrasted advantageously with the latter's blunt schemes for the territorial repartitioning of the problematic region in the spirit of Woodrow Wilson.

It is difficult to say to what degree Washington might have predicted the rise to power of Islamists in leading Arab countries. One can surmise that a role has been played by the old American connections, since the time of the Afghanistan war, to moderate and not-so-moderate Islamist factions. The anti-communism of Muslim radicals of the cold war era seemed to guarantee their conformity with the Western value system. Life, however, once again differed from our expectations of it. Young "Green" democracies in the Arab world quickly revealed that they possess their own agendas that do not necessarily correspond with the calculations of US political theorists. The September 2012 assaults on US diplomatic missions that swept across the entire Islamic world and caused alarm in Europe and even Australia, and the murder of the US ambassador in Tripoli indicated a generally disturbing pattern.

Regional Implications

There is grim symbolism in the fact that the anti-American protests began on Sept. 11 2012, the 11th anniversary of the 9/11 attacks in the US. Especially intriguing were the fierceness and scale of the mass protests in defense of Islam, which clearly were disproportionate to the trigger event: a hastily plotted amateurish film that exploded on social networks in the Muslim world. Is it a mutation of the Arab Spring virus that makes victims of both foes and yesterday's friends, or is it a demonstration of power skillfully orchestrated by extremists?

Probably it is both. A third option is also possible. The virtual space generates too many conflicts of a similar type in different countries: Pussy Riot in Russia, the Innocence of Muslims, French cartoons featuring the Prophet. These are the worst type of conflict: collisions not of ideas but of their reflections and clichés (viral strains) implanted into mass consciousness. The issue is seemingly viral social network technologies that infest society with various types of fundamentalism. Moreover, it is difficult to say which mutation – liberal or Islamist – is more dangerous.

Western meandering in the labyrinths of multiculturalism does not simplify the situation. While urging opponents to display tolerance, the West ignores that it imposes on them its own values, which have never coincided with Eastern ethics, and are far removed from the traditional understanding of Christian morality. Demonstrating reluctance or inability to curb its own democratic fundamentalists, the West, according to its reaction to the September popular protests in Islamic countries, simply does not comprehend what kind of genie has been let out of the bottle.

It is worth considering what is at stake: On the wave of resurgent protest sentiment alongside moderate Islamists and the Army, a third force is surfacing in Middle Eastern political life. It is Islamic extremist groups fused by one ideology and acting as a well-organized force. They rely on the moods of the "Arab street" – i.e., a union of the urban poor, farmers on the verge of bankruptcy, lumpen jobless intellectuals, the lower-middle class, dervishes and rural teachers. In short, those who took to the streets of Cairo, Tunis and Benghazi in the first active phase of the Arab Spring.

Fundamentalist Sunni groups of the Salafi and Wahhabi sects, who for a long time remained in the shadow of the relatively moderate Muslim Brotherhood, possess considerable influence on these social strata, particularly after the "self-dispersal" of the leftist, socialist alternative to capitalism in the late 1980s and the early 1990s. They have long experience with clandestine struggle and avoid frontal attacks – at least for now. Their target is not the democracy that brought the Muslim Brotherhood to power, but rather the system being promoted by the West of neoliberal views on family, women's social status and the issue of sexual minorities. Under slogans of returning to Sharia morality, they garnered about 30% of votes in the parliamentary election in Egypt, and their presence is more pronounced now in other countries of the Maghreb and Mashreq. These are the segments (as demonstrated by events in Libya) that show support for Al Qaeda.

The future for Salafis, who idealize a golden age of early Islam, is found in the past, and they view the West as a disseminator of moral degradation. They consider the borders of Arab countries to be a legacy of the colonial era. Their agenda centers on creating the *umma* (or mother nation) on the basis of Sharia teachings. The further course of developments will depend considerably – or maybe even decisively – on how openly and persistently they press this agenda.

The degree of compatibility of moderate and radical Islamist outlooks will determine the outcome of the reciprocal adjustment process now occurring within the new Arab elite. After becoming Egypt's president, Mohammed Morsi left the Muslim Brotherhood, expressed solidarity with the Western (and, to a larger extent, Saudi) position on Syria, issued appeasing statements toward Israel, and then acted as an efficient ceasefire mediator during Israel's Pillar of Cloud operation in Gaza. At the same time, he pushed the military with surprising ease from power, although they remain a powerful force – a state within a state.

Only time will tell how durable the Muslim Brotherhood's positions are. In late November 2012, before the start of their rigid standoff with the judges and secularist groups of society, one would have gotten the impression that the pattern of future Egyptian policy would be defined within the Muslim Brotherhood-Army-Salafist triangle. But the public's reaction to Morsi's attempt to force the adoption of a new Constitution has shown that the balance of forces in Egypt is still far from stable. The internal structure and ideology of the Brotherhood are far from a homogeneous force. The radicals among them, who belonged in the past to its paramilitary wing, are difficult to distinguish from the Salafis. Equally complex is the Army's composition, where enlisted and junior officers come mostly from the Arab streets. Its role in the power hierarchy will depend on whether it remains a counterweight to the Islamists (the Turkish model) or, like in Pakistan, it becomes an object of Islamization itself.

Without going deep into these tricky issues, let us note that the Muslim Brotherhood will most probably seek to make Egypt's state structure something of a mix between the de facto Shiite theocracy in Iran and the Turkish model of Demo-Islam of the Sunni type. In other words, it will ensure a slightly stronger role of religion than in Turkey and a slightly stronger role of the state than in Iran.

The configuration of power in Egypt and other Arab Spring countries will be impacted by the ability or inability of the Muslim Brotherhood to work out effective approaches to a plethora of socially explosive problems: food security, unemployment, demographic imbalances, etc. Their own resources will hardly be sufficient to address these problems; the economy is disorganized and traditional revenue sources, such as tourism, are questionable.

Yet amid a growing global crisis and the aftermath of the wars in Afghanistan and Iraq – the forcible democratization of which largely incited this crisis – there are not sufficient opportunities for the West to prevent the regional situation from descending into uncontrollable turmoil. Hence the emergence of collective formats of financial donations, such as the Deauville Partnership implemented following the May 2011 Group of Eight summit in Deauville, France. Through this project, allocations to Arab countries for "democratic transformation and economic modernization" have totaled $40 billion, which includes $20 billion from the IMF, and $10 billion from each of the Persian Gulf countries and the G-8. However, the money has been allocated only until 2013; there will be difficulties collecting additional donor resources.

If the constitutional crisis passes without serious losses, then the social and economic situation may change for the better to the extent of the "maturation" of the new authorities and their integration into the market. However, the revolutionaries will have to be fed during the transitional period. Considering the dwindling capabilities of "internal sponsors," like the oil-producing countries of the Persian Gulf, an alternative begins to emerge of a financial and economic reorientation toward Asian economic giants, with a corresponding geopolitical repositioning. It is noteworthy that one of Morsi's first official visits was to China.

With regard to foreign policy, the Muslim Brotherhood will most likely appear as successors and, in a certain sense, continuers of the Arab nationalist ideas with which they not only competed but also cooperated. Naturally, they will adapt these ideas to changing regional and global realities. At one time, Gamal Abdel Nasser, in his work "Egypt's Liberation: The Philosophy of Revolution," formulated the concept of three concentric circles, within the framework of which Egypt and Arab nationalists in other countries of the region conducted their foreign policies.[2] The first, small circle included countries of the Arab world, the second, broader circle contained the countries of the Nonaligned Movement (including the Soviet Union and Eastern bloc countries as its allies), and the third circle concerned global policy issues.

There are sufficient reasons to assume that the foreign policy positions of the Muslim Brotherhood will be formulated on a similar pattern. Its foundation will remain the elaboration of a pan-Arab position on a range of regional problems, first and foremost the Palestinian problem. The degree of radicalism will depend on whether the US and Israel will agree to relaunch the Middle Eastern peace process on terms acceptable to Arabs and Palestinians. An increase of the role of pan-Arab organizations, primarily the Arab League, can be confidently predicted, possibly on the basis of a slightly amended Saudi peace initiative.

In the second circle, the Nonaligned Movement, the principal foreign partner of Arab nationalists, will most likely also remain in that capacity for the Islamists (at the August summit in Tehran, Iran was elected chairman of the movement for the next three years). It can be presumed, however, that the Saudis will attempt to shift the emphasis to establishing closer ties with the Islamic world through support of the Organization of the Islamic Conference. In any case, we can expect initiatives directed at increasing the role of Muslim countries in the new multipolar world system that is forming. Most illustrative is the speech made by Mahmoud Ahmadinejad at the last session of the UN General Assembly, where he demanded radical reform of the UN Security Council through an expansion of the rights of the General Assembly. It is entirely possible that, should UN self-reform stall further, Muslim countries and leading Nonaligned Movement states such as India, Brazil and South Africa, may assume the role of gravediggers of the Yalta/Potsdam system.

In general, the Muslim Brotherhood will most likely formulate its global positions on the basis of pan-Arab and Muslim formats. Proof that this tendency is gaining momentum can be seen in consolidated Arab support at an early stage for a Palestinian Authority request to gain observer status in the UN. In a similar vein is their joint position of support for an international conference planned for December 2012 in Helsinki on the nuclear-free status of the Middle East, the agenda of which includes Israel's nuclear potential.

Naturally, the discussion here is not about trends, but the prerequisites for them. The extent to which they will materialize is contingent on a range of factors: the ability of moderate Islamists to attenuate the influence of extremist organizations, the acuteness of animosities within the current Arab world and the behavior of external players. Much will depend on how all parties involved will act concerning the pressing issues of the current Middle Eastern agenda. The three issues are essentially Syria, Iran and the Palestinians.

The Agenda

To begin with Syria, the civil war in this key Arab country is resembling a latent regional conflict. Turkey, Saudi Arabia and Qatar support the opposition of the Free Syrian Army, while Bashar Assad's administration is supported by Iran (according to *The Times* of London, in the past two years, Iran has invested more than $10 billion in Syria[3]). In the sphere of involved external parties, the US and the EU are siding with the Syrian opposition, while Russia and China are thwarting attempts to enclose Damascus in a ring of international isolation, tighten sanctions against it, and, eventually, create a reason for interference.

Reacting to demands of mass protests, Assad changed the government, lifted the 48-year long national emergency, adopted a new Constitution, and introduced more than 200 laws that rendered the nation's political system considerably more democratic. The role of the Ba'ath party has been curtailed, and the authority of executive and legislative agencies has been redistributed. In May 2012, an election on a multiparty basis was held to the People's Council, but the West did not recognize the results, presumably because all the same Ba'athists won. Of course, these steps were compulsory in the context of the fierce armed clashes that swept across the country. The Americans have defined the conditions under which they may intervene. It is understood that the main incentive, though unadvertised, is the policy of the "logistical encirclement" of Iran and its isolation from its allies in the Arab world (destruction of the "axis of evil").

But what will come of the elimination of practically the last secular regime in the Middle East? It can be asserted fairly confidently that the Assad regime will be replaced by a conglomerate of moderate and radical Islamists, as in other countries of the Arab Spring. The only exception is that Syrian members of the Muslim Brotherhood have experience in protracted and fierce combat with the authorities in the 1980s. The period of Islamist transformation of the Middle East will then end. What consequences will it have for regional and global stability?

This is a rhetorical question. The best and seemingly only viable external response to Syria's problems is to not interfere, to give the sides an opportunity to sort out the difficult situation on their own, and to accept the outcome as a reality that must be considered. But the Turks and the Saudis supplying the Syrian opposition with weaponry and volunteers are so deeply entrenched in Syrian affairs that they cannot retreat. The overthrow of the Assad regime has become for them and the West a matter of prestige. At stake is also the issue of regional leadership, since Saudi Arabia, Egypt and Syria would reasonably advance to leading roles in the rejuvenated region after, and if, Assad falls. Under certain circumstances, such a situation could be an alternative to the increasing threat of the Arab world's consolidation "from below," on a radical basis.

Clearly, the situation is not that simple. The Egyptian Muslim Brotherhood is searching for ways to build broader regional alliances. Morsi made his first visits in the region to Riyadh and Tehran, while simultaneously suggesting that the settlement of the Syrian crisis be handled by an "Islamic quartet" of Egypt, Saudi Arabia, Turkey and Iran. It is understood that in today's climate, there are no apparent conditions for such a massive shift of reference. The Saudis not only mistrust the Turks and see Iran as their main rival, but also have serious grievances with the Muslim Brotherhood, whose members were deported from the kingdom after the 9/11 terrorist attacks.

The Iranians supported the Arab Spring everywhere except in Syria, which has further complicated their relations with the Saudis and the Turks.

But who knows what the future will bring. The Arab Spring may hold many more surprises for the world. There might even be a political alliance between the Sunnis and Shiites, perhaps on the grounds of solidarity with the Palestinians. Anti-American street actions brought Sunni and Shiite radicals together in September 2012. This is not a likely scenario, but it is still possible if no urgent steps are taken to draw the Israeli-Palestinian peace process out of deadlock.

There are some signs that certain politicians in Israel have begun to understand this situation. In mid-September 2012, Defense Minister Ehud Barak called on the Israeli government to abandon the occupied West Bank (while maintaining large Jewish settlements and a military presence in the Jordan River valley). Right now, it is only a personal initiative of Barak, which is why it appeared during the run-up to the January 2013 early parliamentary elections. Prime Minister Benjamin Netanyahu, speaking at the UN General Assembly, reiterated Israel's well-known stance of readiness to resume negotiations with the Palestinians without any preconditions (i.e., he effectively rejected Mahmoud Abbas's demand to freeze the construction of Jewish settlements in East Jerusalem during the talks). It is significant that Netanyahu has characterized the new positioning of forces in the Middle East as a "conflict between the Middle Ages and progress." The democratic transformation of the region did not feature in his speech.

Such an approach to the matter more truly reflects the absence of any realistic plan of action in Netanyahu's cabinet than a dangerously simplified treatment of such a complex phenomenon as the Arab Spring. Two years ago, Tel Aviv deliberately torpedoed US Senator George Mitchell's efforts to resume, at Barack Obama's request, Israeli-Palestinian dialogue. Only after the start of the Arab Spring, which considerably complicated Israel's regional positions, did it become clear how timely the US president's efforts were to link the task of democratizing the region with progress on Middle Eastern reconciliation.

However, the chance was lost, primarily because Israel sees Iran and its nuclear program as an absolute priority. Netanyahu regards the possibility of the "Ayatollah regime" obtaining nuclear weapons as an existential threat to the Israeli state. It must be acknowledged that a host of Ahmadinejad's anti-Israeli declarations prove there is a good basis for this perception. The Arab Spring, accompanied by the sweeping rise to power of Islamists, has only amplified Israel's apprehension of Tehran.

The byproducts of such apprehension could be seen throughout August and a greater part of September as Israel seethed with public debate of unparalleled breadth and intensity about what further action to take toward Iran. Netanyahu and Barak, claiming that the Iranian nuclear program was approaching a "point of no return," advocated attacking Iran's nuclear facilities before the US presidential election. A significant number of the Israeli political and military elite, including the chief of the General Staff and the heads of other armed and intelligence services, objected to Israel's striking Iran on its own, without military coordination with and the political support of the US. Obama, however, categorically refused to support the bellicose plans of his strategic ally, saying there was still time for a political and diplomatic solution of the Iranian nuclear problem, while he also reiterated that the US would not allow Iran to have a nuclear bomb.

It was not difficult to predict such an outcome, as Obama clearly did not need a regional conflict with an ambiguous outcome on the eve of the election. Nevertheless, Netanyahu, who is thoroughly familiar with American realities, took this risky step and systematically increased tensions around Iran over the course of two months.

Why? There were many reasons, though the principal one seems to be Israel's understanding, when it found itself at the center of a regional tsunami, that the trend toward the radicalization of the Middle East that revealed itself during the Arab Spring narrows the window of opportunity for active operations in Iran. With a careless action, the region could begin to act like a system with advanced mobilization capacities in the interests of Islamist factions and organizations.

Similarly, this understanding defined the subtext of Israel's November armed operation in Gaza, including its rapidity (compared with the previous Gaza War of 2008-2009). In the better scenario of further developments, a "draw" in the Pillar of Cloud operation may facilitate, by analogy to the Yom Kippur War, a resumption of

Israeli-Palestinian talks, starting with territorial issues and later the entire range of problems about a final status.

The necessity of urgent steps in this direction was manifested in the reaction of European countries to the decision by Netanyahu's cabinet to expand the construction of Jewish settlements in the critically important zones of the West Bank and in East Jerusalem in response to the UN General Assembly's support of a request by the Palestinian Authority to grant it observer status at the UN. Among other things, the renewal of the Arab-Israeli peace process offers the most reliable, if not the only possible, path to preventing the radicalization of the region as a possible outcome of the Arab Spring.

An Attempt at Generalization

The two years of the Arab Spring have occurred during a profound break in the old structures and ideas of the Middle East. This process is not yet complete, either horizontally (as the scope of the countries undergoing modernization will continue to expand) or vertically (as the restructuring of state power in the countries of the victorious Arab Spring continues). New civil uprising cannot be precluded across the entirety of the Arabic East, from Morocco to Saudi Arabia and Kuwait, or, as the Arabs say, from the Ocean to the Gulf. It is possible that they would be less haphazard and more controllable, since they would involve not the overthrow of lifelong leaders and presidents, but the readjustment of already functioning forms of rule in the context of the Arab world's collective search for a new identity.

And, if so, a natural question arises: To what extent will this readjustment and, more broadly, the model of democracy born of the Arab Spring with a clear Islamist component, meet the requirements and expectations of the outside world? The characteristics of Arab democracy are determined by the realities of the Middle Eastern economy, politics and way of life. In other words, the coming to power of Islamists is not an anomaly but a logical consequence of these realities, and the fact that it came as an "anticipated surprise" to the outside world changes nothing essential.

In its second part, the situation is more complex. Clearly, the Arab Spring does not satisfy all the expectations of the outside world, and yet the harmonization of interests is possible, provided there is reciprocal movement toward creating a culture of intercivilizational and interreligious compromise. In this regard, Western countries should not only once more ponder their own votes in the Human Rights Council and in sessions of the UN General Assembly on draft resolutions declaring the impermissibility of the defamation of religions, but also look closely at Russia's experience in reacting legislatively to insults to the feelings of believers and to the desecration of shrines. Otherwise, conflict situations akin to the September anti-American protests across the Islamic world will occasionally arise. In the East, they are the idiosyncratic instinct of self-preservation, a civilizational identifier.

The first general conclusion is that the formation of a new Middle East as a rationally developing system compatible with global trends is possible only on the condition that the West accepts the emerging regional model of democracy and the subsequent adjustments of the existing system for monitoring democratic processes and human rights based on greater consideration of local characteristics.

The second is that the aforementioned cyclic periodicity in the process of social and political modernization of the Middle East indicates that the second passionary explosion in the Middle East, launched by the Arab Spring, considered with a long view, will last through the middle of the 21st century, and will include phases of growth, stabilization and decay, as displayed in the period from 1952-2011.

In the initial, current phase, it is reasonable for external players to fashion their policies on the basis of the long-term strategic principles of this process, and not on changing political situations, like the Sunni-Shiite and Arab-Iranian clashes. Much less should they be based on their conventional ideas about how a new political map of the region should be drawn, in which the arc of ethnic instability in the region stretches from the Western Sahara, to Iranian Azerbaijan, and to the Turkish province of Hatay, formerly the sanjak of Alexandretta. Many good intentions are buried in the minefields of separatism.

Third, there are two principal development scenarios for the situation in the Middle East. We can call them "à la Versailles" (in reference to the repartitioning of Europe after World War I) and "à la Westphalia" (in reference to the Westphalia Peace Treaty of 1648). The first scenario concerns postwar settlement – specifically, the division of the Arab territories of the Ottoman Empire, in which the lead was taken by external forces. The second scenario is a protracted and painful process of self-development of a democratic community of nation-states.

The collapse of authoritarian regimes in the Middle East that has gotten under way during the Arab Spring may become a new stage of a single democratic process. Following in the footsteps of Eastern Europe and the Balkans, the Middle East may join a community of nations whose relations are built on shared values: democracy, respect for human rights and the free market. It may not join if it does not sense a reciprocal movement and a readiness to play by shared rules on the side of other parties in the formation of a multipolar world. The crucial component is an unconditional respect for state sovereignty and a renunciation of attempts to supplant it with policies of political expediency. If Europe, the US and Russia summon enough common sense, political will and responsibility, the situation in the Middle East will be bearable, if not favorable.

Finally, to reiterate the crucial conditions: Yesterday's revolutionaries should be well fed and provided with jobs; Pastor Terry Jones should not decide to burn the Qur'an in public again or make a sequel to *The Innocence of Muslims*. Otherwise, a prophetic statement, made by Russian diplomat and philosopher Konstantin Leontyev on the eve of the Russian revolutions, should be remembered: "The most ominous weapon of a global revolution is the European philistine."[4]

Notes

1. Gumilyov, L. N. *Etnogenez i biosfera Zemli* [Ethnogenesis and the biosphere of the Earth]. St. Petersburg: Kristall, 2001.

2. Abdel Nasser, Gamal. *Egypt's Liberation: The Philosophy of Revolution*. New York: Foreign Affairs Press, 1955.

3. Tomlinson, Hugh. "Tehran Split Over Billions Spent by Spy Chief to Prop Up Assad Regime," *The Times*, Oct. 1, 2012, https://www.thetimes.co.uk/article/tehran-split-over-billions-spent-by-spy-chief-to-prop-up-assad-regime-hjfxlf86bvb.

4. Leontyev, Konstantin. "Sredny yevropeyets kak ideal i orudiye vsemirnogo razrusheniya" [The average European as an icon and a weapon of worldwide destruction]. In K. Leontyev. *Sobraniye sochineniy* [Complete Works], Moscow-St. Petersburg, 1912-1913.

BETWEEN CRISIS AND CATASTROPHE

Yevgeny Satanovsky

By the middle of the second decade of the 21st century, it has become clear that the world is moving toward a balance of power that was more typical of the 17th and 18th centuries, with the appropriate geopolitical adjustments. Western influence, with its opportunities and military capabilities, is decreasing, while the East and the South are rising.

The good thing about our world today is that the spread of information leaves little secret about history. For example, consider the Anglo-Russian Convention signed in St. Petersburg in 1907, which left Tibet with China, put Afghanistan under British rule, and divided Iran between Britain and Russia, giving the latter control over the Caspian Sea. If the October Revolution of 1917 had not taken place, the Great Game would have been over. The Sublime Porte shrank enormously after World War I, Russia acquired new territories in Eastern Anatolia under the Sykes-Picot Agreement (a special provision gave Russia control over the Black Sea Straits), and the US presence in the Middle East was barely noticeable, while Britain and France played a leading role in the region.

This article originally appeared in *Russia in Global Affairs* Vol. 13, No. 4, 2015.

History knows no "ifs." The Ottoman Empire collapsed, but so did the Russian Empire, only to rise again as the Soviet Union; however, the Soviet Union disintegrated at the end of the 20th century, sharing the fate of its rivals, the British and French colonial empires. By the middle of the second decade of the 21st century, it had become clear that the world was moving toward a balance of power that was more typical of the 17th and 18th centuries, with the appropriate geopolitical adjustments. Western influence, with its possibilities and military capabilities, is decreasing, while the East and the South are rising. Russia is trying to find a balance between them. China, India and Turkey are regaining their positions on the international stage, as are Japan and South Korea, which returned to the world's economic elite much earlier.

New actors have emerged, including Latin American countries (specifically Brazil), South Africa, Canada and Australia. These countries have their own niches in the present world order. The US is trying to keep its superpower status as it competes with China and continues to act as the global hegemon, with interests encompassing the entire world. The US still gets involved in one local war after another just to suffer a new defeat and pull out, leaving chaos in its wake. Ukraine has once again become a playing field for a renewed rivalry between the West and Russia. Central Asia is following suit, with the US putting its stakes on Turkmenistan, which sincerely believes that US assistance will protect it from the threat stemming from the south. The US is also trying to expand its influence to other countries in the region, primarily Uzbekistan. Arab countries are destabilized, and the Arab Spring, initially directed against secular regimes in the Middle East and actively supported by Saudi Arabia and Qatar, has developed into a struggle for power between Islamist fighters and the military.

Samuel Huntington was right, Francis Fukuyama was wrong. The war of civilizations is well underway, but no "end of history" or final victory of the liberal Western democracy is anywhere in sight. Globalization will do Europe no good, especially since immigrants from Africa and the Middle East are not going to assimilate and become Europeans, but will adjust Europe to their own standards. Millions of immigrants already live in European Union member states, and tens of millions more are ready to move closer toward European benefits whenever possible. Europe is crawling with all kinds of far-right radicals and Islamists who are turning it into a battlefield rather than a comfortable sanctuary of social democratic liberalism. Europe's balancing between Anders Breivik and Osama bin Laden does not bode well for anyone. If immigration continues at its current rate, indigenous Europeans will barely account for one-third of the EU's population by 2050.

The path Russia is treading and where it leads are separate issues. What are Russia's prospects for development (or degradation) if its historical experience forebodes serious upheavals in the 2030s – or the 2040s at the latest – after the ruling elite changes for natural reasons? In fact, Russia's current problems in the economy, education and other areas vital for the successful functioning of the state appear to be a secret only to the government, which is doing nothing to change the direction of those processes. However, this article is not about Russia (even though it cannot but be mentioned) but about the current situation in and possible prospects for the Middle East and neighboring regions: Africa, Europe, Central Asia and the Transcaucasus. Indeed, everything is interconnected in the world, and these connections manifest themselves faster than before, including the recent past.

This was vividly proved by the refugee crisis Turkey provoked when several hundred thousand people (and the number could reach a million by the end of the year) were directed via Greece and the Balkans to Western Europe, primarily Germany. This is in addition to the endless flow of refugees from Africa and the Middle East who head to Italy through Libya, which ceased to be a functioning state after the removal of the Qaddafi regime. High-ranking UN officials say there are about 60 million refugees in the world and more than 200 million are ready to migrate because of unbearable economic and living conditions in their home countries. In fact, this is only the beginning of a process that may become a new Great Migration for Europe. The author of this article is not ready to believe that European politicians can work out adequate mechanisms for responding to this challenge.

Turkey has pursued several goals in the European immigration crisis. President Recep Tayyip Erdogan had to show ahead of the Nov. 1 parliamentary elections that he could handle the crisis he had provoked by supporting the civil war in Syria and rid Turkey of some of the more than 3 million refugees and immigrants on its ter-

BETWEEN CRISIS AND CATASTROPHE | 297

ritory. Also, he pressured the EU for money to deal with the refugees (which was provided), thus shifting the burden to Europe (mainly to Germany). Finally, he sought to incite NATO's European countries to confront Bashar Assad's troops in Syria (to no avail now that Russian military aircraft have been sent to that country). The situation clearly shows how much the West is vulnerable to the processes unfolding in the Middle East. But let us take a closer look at the details of those processes.

Informal Alliances and Conflicts

The Arab Spring witnessed the fall of authoritarian leaders who ruled their countries for decades. However, those leaders were replaced not with liberal democrats, young people, women, technocrats and human rights activists, but with Islamists. That revolution is running out of steam, as was expected. In Tunisia, the Muslim Brotherhood's al-Nahda party and its allies have lost control of the country after parliamentary elections. In Egypt, the Muslim Brotherhood has been deposed by the military. In Libya, Islamists of all stripes are fighting one another with the support of Saudi Arabia and Qatar (the two Salafi states compete with each other, especially in the Islamic world), while Egypt is backing Gen. Khalifa Haftar and his allies with what used to be Muammar Qaddafi's army. Yemen has become one of Iran's most dangerous regional bridgeheads against the Sunni monarchies in Arabia, even though the Saudis and supporting Arab monarchies are opposed in Yemen not by Iranians, but by the Houthis and former President Ali Abdullah Saleh.

Attempts to remove Assad in Syria have stalled and may as well fail, although Damascus could have been a step away from falling to the opposition due to terrorist attacks backed by Turkey, Saudi Arabia and Qatar had it not been for Iran's support and Russian air strikes. Two military-political and economic alliances have taken shape in the region: one formed by Turkey and Qatar, and the other by Egypt and Saudi Arabia. Military capabilities, industrial potential, and large human resources amassed by Turkey and Egypt as their main strategic advantage complement the financial wealth of Qatar and Saudi Arabia, guaranteeing their security if serious problems emerge. And those problems are more than likely, especially given the adventurist policies Qatar and Saudi Arabia pursued in the early

2010s with the connivance of the US and Europe, which developed a taste for reformatting the Middle East on a whim.

The Turkish-Qatari alliance is based on the similarity of their approaches toward "external support groups." Both countries patronize all segments of the Muslim Brotherhood, including Hamas and the Islamic State (IS), even though each has its own projects, such as Qatar's Ahrar al-Sham or pro-Turkish supporters in Syria. Turkey, however, views the Kurds as the main threat. Kurdish statehood or territorial autonomy in Iraq and Syria may increase separatist sentiment in Turkey's eastern provinces but it definitely cannot threaten Qatar. By contrast, Egypt and Saudi Arabia are working together against their common enemy – the Muslim Brotherhood and IS. But their alliance is not as strong. For the Egyptian military, radical Salafi groups are a natural enemy no different from all other Islamic fundamentalists; for the Saudis, the Islamic militants are allies (with the exception of IS, which has "sold out" to Qatar). And this may trigger a conflict of interest in the near future.

The Egypt-Saudi Arabia axis may face its main test of strength with the commissioning of the four-cascade Grand Ethiopian Renaissance Dam on the Blue Nile River scheduled to become operational in 2017. It will take six years to fill its reservoir, during which time water flow to Egypt will drop by 30% (and subsequently by "only" 20% if no other waterworks are built on the Nile). As a result, electricity production at the Aswan hydroelectric power plant may decrease by 40%, causing an economic and social catastrophe in Egypt given its complex demographic problems. It is doubtful that Egypt will be able to cope with such a problem without massive outside assistance. It is also doubtful that Saudi Arabia will have enough resources to provide such assistance, since it has to commit them to the Arab coalition in Yemen, the fight against Qatar in Libya, the global confrontation with Iran, and support for Syrian groups opposing Assad, let alone the oil price war with the US, which is as wasteful for the Saudi budget as it is for US shale oil producers.

The main questions about the current situation in the Middle East include the following: What course will Erdogan take following the victory of his Justice and Development Party in early parliamentary elections on Nov. 1? How will the situation develop in Afghanistan and the "Central Asian Spring" processes outside it? And what will happen to the Islamist groups now that Russian aircraft have begun bombing their positions? The latter may have the most un-predictable effect on the Salafi monarchical regimes in Saudi Arabia, which has been relying on them in its foreign policy for a quarter of a century, and in Qatar, which has been competing with Saudi Arabia on this track for two decades. In fact, experts see a Qatari trail in the Russian passenger jet crash over Sinai and point to Qatari Foreign Minister Khalid al-Attiyah, just as they clearly saw Saudi Arabia's intelligence service and its heads, Prince Turki bin Faisal and Prince Bandar bin Sultan, behind Al Qaeda's activities.

Turkey's Riddles

Erdogan, known for his explosive and confrontational outbursts and ambitious plans to turn Turkey into a new Sublime Porte, has a chance to retain control over a one-party government and thus can now focus on amending the Constitution in a bid to make Turkey a presidential republic. Indeed, he may succeed.

Likewise, Erdogan may embark on a new foreign policy escapade in Syria, whether in an attempt to carve out a "buffer zone" under the pretext of protecting the interests of the local pro-Turkish popula-tion, to fight the Kurds, or to provide massive support to Islamists in Aleppo, which Turkey historically considers to be in its zone of interests. The first and third options would pit Erdogan against Iran without any prospect of getting US support, and Erdogan knows that. The second scenario would run counter to US plans to attack IS's "capital" of Raqqa, where the Kurds are supposed to act as the main assault force. Turkey's decision to shoot down the Russian bomber, which has triggered a deep crisis in relations with Moscow and put NATO in a sticky situation, testifies to Erdogan's readiness to risk all in a bid to implement his regional strategy.

The US-led coalition can no longer afford a sluggish operation against IS with unclear results and a vague timeframe. Given the Russian Aerospace Forces' successes in Syria, this would be tanta-mount to losing the initiative in the Middle East. Despite the Arab monarchies' support for certain Islamist groups as a "moderate op-position," attempts to use Islamic fundamentalists to remove Assad or counterbalance Iran and the Shiite regime in Baghdad may do their advocates in Western capitals more harm than good. Turkey's and Erdogan's interest in keeping IS as a partner (for smuggling oil, grain, flour and archaeological artifacts; selling arms; and trading hostages) and as an opponent of Syrian and Iraqi Kurds did restrain the antiterrorist coalition, of which Turkey is a member, for some time, but personal animosity between Erdogan and US President Barack Obama has gone too far for the US to ignore any longer.

Blackmail and threats are Erdogan's trademark style, and this has actually isolated him among his NATO counterparts. The "zero problems with neighbors" policy proclaimed by Turkish Prime Minister Ahmet Davutoglu at the beginning of his career as foreign minister has created conflicts with virtually every one of Turkey's neighbors over the past decade. Quarreling with Russia on top of it all would be senseless for Turkey, which is currently locked in a fierce confrontation with Iran over Syria. In fact, Iranian oil and gas exports to Turkey are in danger because of pipeline bombings in eastern Turkey carried out by the Kurdistan Workers' Party. But then, nobody forced Erdogan to break the armistice with the Kurds for the sake of domestic political speculations.

Moreover, no other company would be prepared to build the Akkuyu nuclear power plant in Turkey under the terms offered by Rosatom. Turkey's future as a world energy hub for gas supplies to Southern and Eastern Europe depends entirely on Russia and its South Stream project, transformed into Turkish Stream. But implementing the project will require more than the existing pipelines linking Turkey with Azerbaijan or the Trans-Caspian Pipeline designed to transport natural gas from Turkmenistan to Europe. The latter project, strongly opposed by Russia and Iran, with China vitally interested in its resources, is no more feasible than building gas pipelines to Turkey from the Arabian Peninsula. Qatar, Saudi Arabia and Turkey failed to get Assad to agree with their plans, which essentially triggered the campaign to remove him from power that later became the chief goal of the civil war in Syria.

Fever in Central Asia

"Pipeline wars" in Central Asia are yet to come. Competition for Turkmen gas is growing not only between US-backed Europe, and China, but also between the Trans-Caspian Pipeline and TAPI (Turkmenistan-Afghanistan-Pakistan-India). Turkmenistan's assurances that it has enough natural gas to satisfy all potential consumers have little in common with reality. In the fall of 2015, Turkmenistan replaced Chinese companies with Japanese firms at its giant Galkynysh Gas Field after China refused to provide new low-interest loans to Turkmenistan, which is struggling to fill the budget drained by the Asian Games. Now Turkmenistan has no choice but to be a bargaining chip in a new Great Game.

Attempts to play the same game on all tracks have failed. The policy of neutrality proclaimed by former Turkmen President Saparmurat Niyazov does not allow the US to use the Mary Air Force base in Turkmenistan. Talks on the matter have virtually come to a halt. Turkmenistan has put itself in a tight spot by overlooking security threats from Afghanistan and falling short of expectations in Russia, China and Iran. Kabul has no control either over the Pashtun provinces in the south or over northern regions populated by ethnic Turkmens, Uzbeks and Tajiks. Iran controls areas inhabited by the Hazara Shia people and more or less secures the border in Sistan and Baluchestan, keeping away drug traffickers and militants from the pro-Saudi terrorist organization Jundullah.

The Afghan government cannot protect the border with post-Soviet republics from the Taliban, which split up after the death of its leader Mullah Omar but remains just as dangerous as long as it is supported by Saudi Arabia and Pakistan. The Taliban is also supported by militants and movements sponsored by Qatar and Turkey, some of which have joined IS, including the Islamic Movement of Uzbekistan, other Islamist movements, and parties of Tajiks and Uyghurs. Clearly, the "Syrian troika" – Qatar, Turkey and Saudi Arabia, all of which have strong positions in the region – will automatically support any attempts to destabilize post-Soviet countries in Central Asia and remove their secular regimes, regardless of the degree of their authoritarianism or contacts with the West. There is no doubt that the US and EU will welcome these efforts, simply because they will create problems for Russia and China.

The region's collective security system – be it the Shanghai Cooperation Organization or the Collective Security Treaty Organization – is incomplete without Turkmenistan and Uzbekistan, which are ignoring it and trying to play their own game. The legitimate transfer of supreme power in the Central Asian states is a serious issue. There is no such tradition, unless one counts leadership succession (as in Turkmenistan) or coups (as in Kyrgyzstan). The parliamentary opposition is either not genuine or nonexistent. Corruption is rampant. Pro-Islamic sentiment is strong among the people, and the movements that back it uphold jihad and have close ties with far-right Islamic radicals and their sponsors, inspired by the idea of a global caliphate. The influence of regional elites, criminal clans and drug cartels on the situation in Central Asia should also be taken into account, since it by far exceeds US leverage.

Drugs are a special issue because they are the main source of income for both common people and elites in Afghanistan. The country has turned into the sole producer and supplier of opiates and heroin during the international – but essentially American, despite the UN mandate – occupation and will keep this status under any government. Afghanistan will be helped by Pakistan, which wants to control the situation in Afghanistan with Saudi support (as part of geopolitical competition with Qatar and, to a lesser extent, with Turkey). The alliance formed by Saudi Arabia and Pakistan over more than 30 years of cooperation since their joint fight against Soviet troops in Afghanistan is likely to be strengthened through broader nuclear partnership.

The Nuclear Dimension

Put simply, Saudi Arabia finances Pakistan's efforts to build up its stocks of medium-range nuclear missiles in order to stand up to India and maintain a nuclear balance. But the Saudis always did this before. The only difference now is that after Iran's "nuclear deal" with the US and other members of the P5+1 group, which had long attempted to balance out their interests with that Islamic country, Iran poses a bigger threat to Saudi Arabia with the sanctions lifted. Experts believe that Pakistan will soon provide Saudi Arabia with nuclear weapons, in small amounts but combat ready. Rather than using these weapons against an external threat, Saudi Arabia will need them as protection in an emergency now that the US has shown during the talks with Iran what it really thinks of its old Middle Eastern allies.

Initially, the main, if not the only, purpose of the plan to create a nuclear weapon-free zone in the Middle East was to disarm Israel. But Iran's nuclear program made it senseless, which it actually was from the very beginning for the simple reason that Pakistan, armed with nuclear weapons and closely connected to the conservative Arab monarchies in the Persian Gulf, belongs to South Asia only geographically. In fact, throughout its history, Pakistan has always been an integral part of the Middle East. The nuclear arms race in the region is a natural result of the failed policy of sanctions against Iran and its agreement with the international community, which essentially legitimized its nuclear status. The best solution guaranteeing the security of the entire region would be a nonaggression pact between Israel and Iran. However, in contrast to Israel, Iran is unlikely to take such a step in the foreseeable future.

Israel as such has no claims against its neighbors and wants nothing but its own security. To achieve that, Israel will respond strongly to any attempt to undermine its defense capability, no matter from where such perpetrations come. The appearance of Russian military aircraft in Syria, which prevents Iran from taking it under its full control, is viewed by Israel in terms of positive neutrality. In fact, Israel was the first Western country to begin coordinating with Russia over Syria. This stopped Saudi Arabia's dangerous moves, undertaken in vain for a long time, to draw the Israeli Defense Forces into a war against Iran.

Palestine and Refugees

The last point about Israel concerns the disastrous failure of the Israeli-Palestinian "peace settlement" process. The positions of the sides appeared to be completely and ultimately irreconcilable, which they had always been. Israeli society does not approve of the unilateral concessions made to maintain the illusion of talks, partly because of the terrorist attacks on Israel supported by Hamas leaders in Gaza and the Palestinian Authority in Ramallah. The Palestinians' unwillingness to discuss issues that were supposed to be solved as far back as May 1999 stands in stark contrast to the hopes of the 1990s. Some of the most pressing issues are rampant corruption in the Palestinian Authority and a reluctance to build its own state, even though Israel has not dismantled Palestinian self-government mechanisms to avoid assuming responsibility for the Palestinian Arabs.

The refugee crisis, which includes Arabs, may lead the international community to unify its refugee support programs in the near future, thus depriving Palestinians of their privileges. The situation in Jordan, which borders Iraq and Syria, and in Lebanon is more than precarious. Libya's neighbor Algeria is unstable, with its ruling gerontocracy and elites fighting for power; Sudan is still gripped by civil war despite separation from Juba; Somalia is divided between warring clans; Eritrea has been increasingly leaning on Saudi Arabia and the United Arab Emirates; and Djibouti is drawing support from foreign military bases – all this creates a continuous zone of instability. The same is true of the Middle East's African periphery – Sahara and Saleh – where separatist and radical Islamist movements are destabilizing a large area from Morocco to Mauritania, and a considerable part of Sub-Saharan Africa.

Perhaps the only "good" news about the Middle East is that in contrast to Afghanistan and Pakistan, the Balkans and the Transcaucasus seem to be an oasis of peace. This clearly shows how much the situation in the region has degraded despite (or rather because of) attempts by the US and its allies to "democratize" it. The collapse of the Schengen agreement under the flow of refugees heading to Germany through the Balkans may become, and most probably will become, the beginning of the EU's demise. Turkey and Iran are influencing the situation in the Transcaucasus along with the confrontation between the US and the EU, on the one hand, and Russia, on the other. But the situation in the Balkans and Transcaucasia is relatively stable compared to what it could be. Greece, Serbia or Hungary will most likely disagree with this, but given the problem of slavery in Iraq, Sudan and Mauritania; the genocide of Christians in Syria and Iraq; and the extermination of Yazidi Kurds in Iraq, one can clearly see the difference between a crisis and a catastrophe.

HARASS AND HOLD OUT

Andrej Krickovic and Yuval Weber

US-Russian relations are beginning to resemble a cold war as the US institutes containment policies in preparation for a drawn-out showdown. The issue then becomes who can hold out longer to demonstrate the necessary resolve to get the other side to back down.

Nearly 70 years ago, George Kennan wrote his famous long telegram, later published as "The Sources of Soviet Conduct" in *Foreign Affairs*.[1] Kennan's seminal article integrated material, ideological and historical factors into its analysis, developing a comprehensive and holistic approach to studying the foreign policy of the Soviet Union. Inspired by Kennan's work, this article outlines the structural, domestic and ideational sources of contemporary US policy toward Russia. These three factors reinforce a dominant narrative among US policymakers that sees the US as defending the status quo against Russia's revisionist challenge to the post-cold war international order. They shape the US response to this perceived challenge, preventing the US from seeking an understanding with Russia, but also discouraging it from immediately and forcefully confronting the "Russian threat" – even

This article originally appeared in *Russia in Global Affairs* Vol. 14, No. 2, 2016.

though many powerful domestic constituents are lobbying for this course of action.[2]

Following John Ikenberry's studies of postwar settlements,[3] which identify the parameters and institutions of international order – i.e., the "rules of the game" – we contend that a fundamental disagreement about the genesis of the current international order lies at the root of the current conflict between Russia and the US. From the Russian perspective, the contemporary international order should begin from 1989 and General Secretary Mikhail Gorbachev's efforts to conclude the cold war. In an effort to revitalize the Soviet economy and save the Soviet system by reducing massive defense expenditures and transitioning from autarky to engaging with the international economy, Gorbachev moved boldly to dismantle Russia's political and military dominance in Eastern Europe. The expectation at the time was that internal restructuring would reinvigorate the Soviet Union and that it would continue to play a pivotal role in world politics as a full-fledged partner, instead of a rival, of the US. From the American perspective, the contemporary international order begins specifically with the Soviet Union's collapse in 1991. A new postwar settlement in which Russia does not enjoy any residual rights or privileges and states are free to choose their own alliances and associations replaced the cold war's bipolarity. In a materially unipolar system dominated by the US, this permitted Warsaw Pact members to band with NATO to protect themselves from Russian revanchism. The basic disagreement thus becomes clear: Was the status quo set in 1989, making the US a revisionist hegemon, or was it set in 1991, making Russia a revisionist challenger?

This fundamental disagreement shapes both sides' policies in Ukraine and Syria. From Russia's viewpoint, its actions in Ukraine and Syria are merely defensive responses to serious challenges to its security and national interests created by America's short-sighted and destabilizing foreign policies. In Ukraine, Russia sees itself as acting to defend its vital sphere of influence against encroachment by the West.[4] In Syria, it believes it is preventing further destabilizing "regime change" and addressing the real terrorist threat from ISIS by protecting the lawful and legitimate government of that country.[5] However, this is not how Russia's behavior is perceived in Washington. For Washington, it is Russia's policies that are destabilizing. Russia's actions in Ukraine, in particular its incorporation of the

Crimea, are seen as a grave challenge to the international order and to one of its most cherished and inviolable rules: no unilateral border changes.[6] Similarly, Russia's policy of supporting Bashar Assad in Syria is seen as hindering the fight against ISIS and contributing to the refugee crisis by prolonging the Syrian civil war.[7]

Consequently, many US leaders see Putin's Russia as a revisionist power that is bent on overturning the established order and challenging US global leadership. There are still some voices in Washington calling for a larger bargain with Russia that would avoid a new cold war, toward which the two sides seem to be inextricably sliding. However, as we will show, structural, domestic political and ideational factors all make any such agreement a nonstarter for the American side. Instead, the debate in American policy circles is now focused on how best to deter Russia from its current course and correct its behavior, or failing that, how to isolate Russia and contain its nondemocratic regime.

Structural Factors

Structural factors such as the current balance of power and capabilities between states and their future power trajectories (whether their power is rising or declining) profoundly shape relations between states. Following the cold war, American observers perceive Russia as a declining power that is losing its global and even regional preeminence because it has failed to adapt to a new globalized world where economic and technological advantage trump military and great power politics. The power disparity between the US and Russia is simply too great for Russia to be considered a credible challenger to the international order, and Russia's position is seen to be weakening over time. Accordingly, President Obama has dismissively referred to Russia as a "regional power" and questioned its ability to exert influence internationally, while Senator John McCain has called Russia a "gas station masquerading as a country."

For Russia, the unipolar international structure established in 1991 and the relative diminution of Russian power within it has meant that Russian objections to policies that it believes threaten its most vital interests, such as the ballistic missile shield proposed for Central Europe and NATO enlargement, have fallen on deaf ears. To be taken seriously and to gain the spot at the bargaining table that

Russia believes it earned in 1989, the country has to demonstrate that ignoring its interests and preferences comes at a cost. It thus has to escalate crises and engage in brinksmanship to show that ignoring Russia on questions of world security and order will hurt America and its allies. This kind of strategy may thrust Russia into the limelight, but it is fundamentally contradictory if Russia's ultimate purpose is to gain recognition as a bargaining partner. Escalating and destabilizing the situation in Ukraine, Syria, and elsewhere may draw attention to its concerns and make Russia more important for specific issues, but it also makes it a less credible negotiating partner for any future grand bargain. Not just President Obama but any US leader would be reluctant to reward what Washington sees as Russian "bad behavior," as this could encourage further Russian aggression and embolden other powers (most troublingly China) to test US resolve.

Robert Gilpin noted long ago that prestige and status (and not power, as many neorealist theorists argue) are the actual currencies of international relations.[8] If a state's status and prestige are recognized by other states, it can achieve its goals without actually having to exercise material power. The US is unwilling to open discussion on these issues of order, because this would give Russia much higher status and greater prestige than it believes is merited by its current capabilities and strength. Nor is it willing to open up discussion on issues of order that it regards to have been solved long ago with the collapse of the USSR. The US regards Russia as a declining great power, so it prefers to push any confrontation with Russia forward into the far and distant future when Russia will be even weaker relative to the US than it is now – particularly after it exhausts itself in the process of challenging the US-led international order.

Domestic Politics

If larger structural factors inhibit the US from validating Russian concerns and working out a compromise that would help avoid confrontation, domestic political factors mean that politicians from both parties agree on a hawkish position toward Russia, but vary in the extent to which they advocate support for intervening in the issues important to Russia. In the immediate term, the presidential cycle has given candidates from both parties an opportunity to demonstrate their "toughness" on security issues, with Republican candidates in particular using Russia and its assertive behavior to attack President Obama. Leading Republican candidates assert that Obama has been too soft on Russia, and particularly on Putin, from the get-go. They have criticized his administration's initial attempts to "reset" relations in Moscow after the 2008 Georgian War as tantamount to appeasement, arguing that [the reset] has only emboldened Putin to adopt more aggressive policies.[9]

Most of the Republican candidates, with the notable exception of frontrunner (but still political outsider) Donald Trump, advocate much more muscular and hawkish policies to thwart Russian "aggression," including arming Ukraine with lethal weapons, deploying missile interceptors and radars in Poland and the Czech Republic, and imposing a no-fly zone in Syria to stymie Russian air strikes in that country – even if the latter risks a direct confrontation between Russian and US warplanes. According to Florida Senator Marco Rubio (viewed by many experts as the Republican establishment's preferred nominee) "[Putin] needs to understand that there are serious costs for invading neighbors, propping up a murderous dictator like Assad, and violating the airspace of and threatening other countries."[10]

Democratic candidates have also tried to distance their foreign policy approaches from Obama's. Despite notable successes, such as the end of the Cuba embargo, the successful negotiation of a nuclear deal with Iran, and the Trans-Pacific Partnership trade deal, ongoing difficulties in the Middle East, which Obama promised to bring to an end, have left a majority of the American electorate unsatisfied. Growing authoritarianism in Russia provides a major opening for Democratic candidates to appeal to the liberalism of their constituents on issues such as democratization and LGBT rights. Like their Republican counterparts, taking a hawkish position on Russia is like pushing on an open door: Even foreign policy doves such as Vermont Senator Bernie Sanders support a policy of "standing up to Putin" and isolating the Russian leadership politically and economically.[11]

As secretary of state during the first Obama administration, Democratic frontrunner Hillary Clinton was one of the main architects of the US-Russia reset. She is now taking a tough stance on Russia to distance herself from this policy and deflect criticism from her political rivals in both parties. While defending the reset as a sound policy that garnered significant immediate achievements (the New START treaty and Russia's cooperation on Afghanistan and Iran), Clinton has tried to shift the blame for the subsequent deterioration of US-Russia relations on Russia's growing authoritarianism and Putin's need to distract attention from domestic problems by appealing to nationalism and adopting a more aggressive and anti-American foreign policy. According to Clinton, Putin's objectives are "to stymie, to confront, and to undermine American power whenever and wherever."[12]

The political climate in the US is thus unlikely to encourage rapprochement, or even a relaxation of tension between the two countries, at least until the current electoral cycle runs its course and a new administration takes office. Nevertheless, domestic political factors over time will continue to hinder the development of more cooperative relations. Russia has few friends in Washington but many enemies. Over the last few decades, a powerful anti-Russia lobby has emerged in Washington. This lobby is diverse and includes older organizations that represent ethnic groups traditionally hostile to Russia (Poles, Balts and Ukrainians); representatives of post-Soviet states that are trying to distance themselves from Moscow by integrating more closely with the West, such as Georgia and Ukraine; neo-conservative think tanks such as the Heritage Foundation and American Enterprise Institute that see Putin's Russia as a threat to US hegemony; and "liberal hawks" and democracy promotion advocates opposed to growing authoritarianism in Russia itself. According to political scientist Andrei Tsygankov, the lobby propagates a distorted view of modern-day Russia, portraying it as an imperialist and revanchist power whose worldview is fundamentally opposed to the principles and values of the West.[13]

This lobby does not unilaterally control US foreign policy toward Russia, as perhaps some Russian commentators believe, and it has been quite critical of US policy when it deems the latter insufficiently tough on Russia, as was the case with the reset. However, it has been able to shape the general political discourse in a way that is not conducive to compromise or the development of a more balanced understanding of Russia's motives and interests. Moscow has failed to develop the kind of lobbying presence in America's capital that many countries such as Israel, Japan or even Poland have, leaving it mute, without anyone pushing for its interests or articulating its viewpoint to the Washington establishment. Russia's "image problem" cannot be remedied by simply employing the most well-connected lobbyists or most effective PR strategy. The real problem is much deeper in that post-Soviet Russia does not possess the kind of attractiveness or soft power able to overcome and dispel deeply entrenched cold war-era stereotypes about Russia as an authoritarian and backward society. Russia's recent backsliding on democracy and human rights has only strengthened these prejudices.

While the US establishment tends to largely agree about the threat posed by Russia, there is more of a plurality of opinion over the issue of how best to respond to this threat. Hawks from both parties advocate a more robust response to Russia's "aggression." President Obama has so far adopted a more cautious approach and resisted calls to escalate US involvement in Ukraine or Syria, but rifts have begun to open up even within the administration itself. Evelyn Farkas, the Defense Department's top official on Russia and Ukraine, resigned in protest over the President's unwillingness to confront Russia more directly. In a subsequent op-ed in *Politico*, she warned: "Russia's challenge is so fundamental to the international system, to democracy and free market capitalism that we cannot allow the Kremlin's policy to succeed in Syria or elsewhere."[14] Any future administration will thus face strong domestic political pressure from both parties to take a tougher line on Moscow.

Differing Worldviews

Major differences in worldview also work against reaching a deeper understanding. For Russia to get what it wants, the US would have to recognize the legitimacy of Russia's desire to maintain a sphere of interest in the post-Soviet space. For most members of the American establishment, any talk about a "sphere of influence" violates the right of all nations and countries to choose their own foreign policies and alliances,[15] and reflects an anachronistic 19th-century Realpolitik understanding of international relations that is not in tune with the realities of a modern, globalized and interdependent world. To recognize Russia's or China's sphere of influence in their respective regions would be a step in the wrong direction: a return to the great power conflict and war of past centuries.[16] To be sure, prominent American Realists such as Henry Kissinger, John Mearsheimer and

Stephen Walt have urged the US to recognize Russia's right to a sphere of influence in its own backyard.[17] But their views are in the minority and have met with either staunch criticism or silence.[18]

The US elite and public have never been comfortable with Realpolitik and balance-of-power approaches to international politics. From the very early days of the republic, the founding fathers were deeply suspicious of the European balance-of-power politics and saw it as profoundly unprincipled, immoral and undemocratic.[19] Separated from the rivalries and conflicts that plagued Europe, the US emerged as a world power relatively unscathed by foreign invasion, military occupation and material devastation of war. There was no need to practice Realpolitik, and a more idealistic approach to foreign policy could emerge. According to Mearsheimer, "Realism stands opposed to Americans' views of both themselves and the wider world. In particular, realism is at odds with the deep-seated sense of optimism and moralism that pervades much of American society."[20]

To be sure, liberal idealism is only one strand of American foreign policy and it has also had to compete with isolationist and imperial strands (i.e., manifest destiny) and even moments when realism has asserted itself (most notably the Nixon-Kissinger foreign policy).[21] However, liberal idealism has dominated foreign policy thinking since the end of the cold war. America's "victory" in this struggle and its subsequent historically unparalleled dominance of the international system has validated the idealist approach and given rise to self-righteous views of American exceptionalism that often ignore the many instances of unscrupulous Realpolitik the US has frequently engaged in.[22] American elites believe that they are presiding over a unique international order that is based on universal liberal principles that serve the best interest of all humankind. Accepting Russia's demands for a "sphere of influence" would jeopardize not only American hegemony but also the future of what they believe to be a fundamentally just and fair order.[23]

The belief in liberal internationalism often goes hand in hand with the belief in liberal democracy as the most effective and just form of government. Democratic rule is not only in the best interest of domestic populations, but also of international peace and stability, as democracies enjoy conciliatory relations with one another, while autocracies are prone to aggressive and warlike behavior.[24] Trying to reach an understanding with Moscow is seen by many in Washington as a futile exercise in appeasement that will encourage even more aggression on the part of Putin's authoritarian regime, which needs to engage in aggressive and nationalistic foreign policies in order to compensate for its lack of domestic legitimacy and failing foreign policies.[25]

***

Kennan's integrative analysis of the factors shaping "Soviet conduct" allowed him to develop a nuanced and complex understanding of Soviet foreign policy. The USSR's material vulnerabilities and weaknesses, its psychological insecurities (which had deep historical roots in the repeated foreign invasions the country was forced to suffer), conspiratorial origins as a banned group, and messianic communist ideology led him to conclude that the Soviets' intentions were aggressive and constituted the gravest threat the US had ever faced to its national security. Nevertheless, Kennan also argued that the Soviets' faith in the ultimate dialectical victory of communism over capitalism would prevent them from engaging in overly risky behavior that would jeopardize this outcome. He thus concluded that the threat from Soviet communism could be contained and there was no need to roll it back directly.

We try to adopt a similar integrative approach by examining the structural, domestic-political, and ideological considerations that shape US policy toward Russia and what US leaders perceive to be Russia's challenge to the US-led global order. From a structural perspective, the US is reluctant to engage with what it sees as a declining power (Russia) either in a settlement or in direct confrontation, and prefers to delay either outcome until a future time when Russia will be much weaker. In terms of concrete policy on the ground, this means ignoring Russia's calls for a new security architecture in Europe, while at the same time taking steps to strengthen NATO and its defensive commitments in the Baltics, Poland and elsewhere in Eastern Europe to prevent Moscow from engaging in reckless behavior designed to push the US toward the bargaining table on these issues. It will also mean that the US is unlikely to take action (such as arming Ukraine with lethal weapons or enforcing a no-fly zone in Syria) that would provoke an immediate confrontation with Russia. The optimal US strategy in both Ukraine and Syria is to use these crises to hasten Russia's decline by making sure that Russia gets bogged down in the conflicts that are raging in both countries. Given the structural balance of power between the two sides, the US should bide its time and let Russia "tire itself out" by becoming embroiled in drawn-out conflicts in Ukraine, Syria and elsewhere.

Domestic politics and ideological factors make it very difficult for the US to commit itself to any kind of overarching deal with Russia, at least as long as the current regime in Moscow is in power. Given the current politically charged climate, even hinting at accepting the legitimacy of Russia's actions in Ukraine and Syria would be denounced by many as tantamount to appeasement. Even the current strategy adopted by the Obama administration of biding time and letting Russia "tire itself out" – which makes the most sense from the structural perspective (as described above) – has come under intense criticism from the Republican opposition and liberal hawks, who demand that Obama go on the offensive against Putin. So far, Obama has been able to hold his ground, and it is likely that any future president will also stick to the same prudent strategy after the campaign rhetoric dies down and they are forced to face the realities of decision-making. Nevertheless, the well-established "anti-Russia" lobby will keep the heat on any future president to show that the White House is adequately addressing the "Russian threat." Moreover, significant segments of the American elite now believe that Russia will only give up its challenge to US leadership and become integrated into the Western-led liberal order if there is democratic regime change in Russia itself. They will pressure the administration to criticize Russia for violations of democracy and human rights, and to oppose any policies of cooperation or constructive engagement that appear to strengthen or legitimize the current authorities in Moscow.

For the US, the stakes in Ukraine and Syria have been raised by Russia's great power challenge. As the current Russian government shows no sign of conceding on issues of prestige and status – with President Putin likely to be in power until 2024, if not longer – the fate of both countries will be consumed by the US-Russian struggle over the future of the international order. Russian-US relations are beginning to resemble a cold war as the US institutes containment policies in preparation for a drawn-out showdown. The issue then becomes who can hold out longer to demonstrate the necessary resolve to get the other side to back down. If this is indeed the case, history may be repeating itself, with the most detrimental consequences to be borne by the people of Ukraine and Syria.

Notes

1. "X" (George F. Kennan). "The Sources of Soviet Conduct," *Foreign Affairs*, 25(4), July 1947, pp. 566-582.

2. Weber, Yuval. "Why the U.S. Does Nothing in Ukraine," *The Washington Post*, Monkey Cage, March 18, 2015, https://www.washingtonpost.com/blogs/monkey-cage/wp/2015/03/18/why-the-u-s-does-nothing-in-ukraine/. Weber argues that this lower level of danger is partly why America's Ukraine policy has not been as vigorous toward an ostensible ally as observers would expect. A theoretical inference from Weber's article is that the Barack Obama administration downplays the structural challenge by Russia to the international order.

3. Ikenberry, John. *After Victory: Institutions, Strategic Restraint, and the Rebuilding of Order after Major Wars*. Princeton: Princeton University Press, 2001.

4. Suslov, Dmitry. "For a Good Long While," *Russia in Global Affairs*, 12(4), Dec. 18, 2014, https://eng.globalaffairs.ru/number/For-a-Good-Long-While-17211.

5. Karaganov, Sergei. "Mir nakhoditsya v predvoyennom sostoyanii" [The world is in a pre-war state], *The New Times*, Feb. 16, 2016, http://www.newtimes.ru/articles/detail/107733/.

6. Frakas, Evelyn. "Putin is Testing Our Resolve," *Politico Magazine*, Nov. 24, 2015, https://www.politico.com/magazine/story/2015/11/isil-syria-putin-nato-airspace-213393.

7. Stacey, Jeffrey. "Russia's Pyrrhic Victory in Syria," *Foreign Affairs*, March 20, 2016, https://www.foreignaffairs.com/articles/syria/2016-03-20/russia-s-pyrrhic-victory-syria.

8. Gilpin, Robert. *War and Change in World Politics*. Cambridge: Cambridge University Press, 1981, p. 31.

9. Krauthammer, Charles. "Obama's serial appeasement has backfired," *Chicago Tribune*, Jan. 7, 2016, http://www.chicagotribune.com/news/opinion/commentary/ct-iran-missile-krauthammer-putin-obama-perspec-0108-jm-20160107-story.html.

10. Rubio, Marco. "Why We Must Stand Up for Turkey and Against Russian Aggression," Dec. 1, 2015, https://medium.com/@marcorubio/why-we-must-stand-up-for-turkey-and-against-russian-aggression-ebc8094dd78c.

11. "Transcript of the Democratic Presidential Debate in Milwaukee," *The New York Times*, Feb. 11, 2016, http://www.nytimes.com/2016/02/12/us/politics/transcript-of-the-democratic-presidential-debate-in-milwaukee.html?_r=0.

12. "Clinton Calls for Tougher Response to Russia on Ukraine, Syria," *Radio Free Europe/Radio Liberty*, Sept. 9, 2015, https://www.rferl.org/a/russia-us-clinton-calls-for-tougher-response-on-ukraine-syria/27235800.html.

13. Tsygankov, Andrei. *Russophobia: Anti-Russian Lobby and American Foreign Policy*. New York: Palgrave Macmillan, 2009.

14. Frakas, Evelyn. "Putin is Testing Our Resolve," *Politico Magazine*, Nov. 24, 2015, https://www.politico.com/magazine/story/2015/11/isil-syria-putin-nato-airspace-213393.

15. Pifer, Steve. "Avoiding a New Cold War. Really?" *Brookings: Order From Chaos,* Oct. 13, 2015, http://www.brookings.edu/blogs/order-from-chaos/posts/2015/10/13-avoiding-a-new-cold-war-pifer.

16. Implicit in many of these arguments is the idea that continued US hegemony is the key to ensuring the bright liberal future for the world. See: Kagan, Robert. "The United States must resist a return to spheres of interest in the international system," *Brookings: Order From Chaos*, Feb. 19, 2015, http://www.brookings.edu/blogs/order-from-chaos/posts/2015/02/19-united-states-must-resist-return-to-spheres-of-interest-international-system-kagan.

17. Mearsheimer, John. "Why the Ukraine Crisis Is the West's Fault: The Liberal Delusions That Provoked Putin," *Foreign Affairs,* September/October 2014. See also: "Interview with Henry Kissinger: Do We Achieve World Order Through Chaos or Insight?" *Der Spiegel*, Nov. 13, 2014.

18. Recently, there has been much debate on whether Obama can be considered a realist because of his reluctance to get the US more involved in Syria and Ukraine, and his equanimity regarding ISIS, as he is said to see none of these as posing an existential threat to the US. The president himself has on occasion also referred to himself as a foreign policy realist. See: Jeffrey Goldberg, "The Obama Doctrine," *The Atlantic*, April 2016, http://www.theatlantic.com/magazine/archive/2016/04/the-obama-doctrine/471525/.

19. Bew, John. *Realpolitik: A History.* Oxford: Oxford University Press, 2016, pp. 107-122.

20. Mearshimer, John. *The Tragedy of Great Power Politics.* New York: W.W. Norton, 2001, p. 23.

21. Nau, Henry R. *At Home Abroad: Identity and Power in American Foreign Policy.* Ithaca, NY: Cornell University Press, 2002.

22. Lind, Michael. *The American Way of Strategy: U.S. Foreign Policy and the American Way of Life.* Oxford: Oxford University Press, 2006.

23. Ikenberry, G. John. "The Illusion of Geopolitics: The Enduring Power of the Liberal Order," *Foreign Affairs*, May-June 2014.

24. Russett, Bruce and Oneal, John. *Triangulating Peace: Democracy, Interdependence, and International Organizations.* New York: W.W. Norton, 2001.

25. Stoner, Kathryn and McFaul, Michael. "Who Lost Russia (This Time)? Vladimir Putin," *The Washington Quarterly*, 38(2), 2015, pp. 167-187.

PART THREE

3.3. Emerging Geopolitical Balances

BY THE WATERS OF BABYLON

Dmitry Yefremenko

The time when Russia could contemplate an exit strategy seems to have passed. It would be virtually impossible now to guarantee a negotiated settlement in Syria, or even a lasting truce, without a substantial Russian military presence in that country.

More than a century has passed since Britain, France and Russia arbitrarily divided the vast territories of the Ottoman Empire into areas of their own postwar dominance. The Sykes-Picot Agreement started the process of partitioning the Middle East into countries that cut through regions historically populated by Arabs and Turks, Kurds and Assyrians, Sunnis and Shiites, Christians and Jews, etc. The borders of those countries have subsequently changed many times, but the great powers remain consistently involved in the process. And yet, although the borders were largely artificial and the risk of conflict was quite high, the Middle Eastern order held for almost a century (assuming the 1920 Treaty of Sevres as the starting point), and some countries in the region have developed quite successfully. But the quality of governance and functionality of the

This article originally appeared in *Russia in Global Affairs* Vol. 15, No. 3, 2017.

state were never high, and the ability to resist centrifugal tendencies has often been ensured by harsh – and sometimes downright repressive – regimes. But the US intervention in Iraq to remove Saddam Hussein and the subsequent Arab Spring created such turbulence that the Middle Eastern order started to crumble, putting Iraq, Syria, Libya and Yemen on the brink of disintegration.

The paradox is that almost no one wants the existing Middle Eastern states to collapse. This is not only because of adherence to the fundamental principles of sovereignty and territorial integrity, but also because the collapse of those Middle Eastern countries would create too many threats for their neighbors and more distant countries. But risks always generate new geopolitical opportunities. Indeed, countries that have declared their commitment to the territorial integrity of Syria, Iraq, Yemen, Libya and other states in the region are keeping an eye on those opportunities. In particular, they are considering scenarios where chaos and internal confrontation gain such momentum that blocking them from the outside would be ineffective, and external players would simply prefer to wash their hands of it all. One of the scenarios currently on the negotiating table for deescalating the crisis in Syria calls for separating territorial enclaves not controlled by the Syrian government and giving them security guarantees from international mediators.

It is highly probable that a military defeat of the Islamic State (IS), a terrorist organization banned in Russia, and particularly the liberation of Mosul, Raqqa and other territories in Iraq and Syria seized by extremists, may trigger the disintegration of key states in the region. The current reconfiguration of external and internal forces, directly or indirectly involved in various conflicts in the region, may be regarded as a prelude to greater transformations.

America Returning

Over the past 18 months, the armed conflict in Syria and geopolitical processes in the Middle East in general have taken a radical turn due to the Russian military operation to support Syrian government forces. By the summer of 2016, Russia, Turkey and Iran had developed a new format of interaction aimed at coordinating their positions on a settlement of the Syrian crisis and combating IS. As US activity in Syria declined due to Donald Trump's election campaign and his unexpected victory, the Russia-Turkey-Iran triangle became a political reality that led to negotiations in Kazakhstan to complement the Geneva talks. The successful operations conducted by the Syrian Arab Army (with the support of Russia and Iran) to force armed anti-Bashar Assad opposition groups out of Aleppo and by the Free Syrian Army (with the support of Turkey) to push IS militants out of Al-Bab should be considered in the context of joint efforts undertaken by the three countries. The intensity of armed confrontation in Syria has decreased significantly, except for the efforts to crush IS.

The election of Donald Trump as the 45th president of the US stirred hopes for building a broad front led by the US and Russia to destroy IS militarily within the shortest possible time. But these hopes turned out to be premature, to say the least. A possible deal with Russia was blocked by a rabid information campaign against Trump and members of his team, who were accused of improper contacts with Moscow. However, the US took some steps to show its resolute return to the Middle East.

Trump made this return as demonstrative as possible when he ordered a missile strike against a government air base in Syria. While addressing several tactical objectives, the Trump administration nevertheless gave no clue as to how it was going to defeat IS and raised even more questions about its long-term strategy toward Syria. And yet a new system of coordinates is beginning to emerge. Full-scale support for Israel and a reversal of Barack Obama's Iran policy are key elements of this new system. The US and Iran are heading toward a new standoff. The US missile strike on the Shayrat air base in Syria reflects Washington's choice of Iran as its main opponent in the region and Syrian government forces as a target, since the new US administration views Syria as an Iranian ally and client. This sends a strong signal to Russia, whose response to the US attack was quite reserved, which not only made it possible for Russia to maintain contact with the US on the crisis settlement process in Syria, but also work out initiatives that take into account Trump's new approaches. However, these approaches may prove quite tricky for preserving statehood in Iraq and Syria.

US-Iranian Confrontation and the Future of Iraq

Paradoxically, the US operation to remove Saddam Hussein significantly strengthened Iranian positions both in Iraq and in the Persian Gulf region. As former German foreign minister Joschka Fischer rightfully pointed out, "America was powerful enough to destabilize the existing regional order, but not powerful enough to establish a new one."[1] Iran largely filled this vacuum. As a result, the US and Iran took steps to divide Iraq into spheres of influence at the end of George W. Bush's presidential term, but especially during Barack Obama's presidency. The Iranian nuclear deal signed in 2015 paved the way not only for lifting sanctions on Iran, but also for starting a dialogue with the US on the future of the Middle East, for which Zbigniew Brzezinski, Robert Gates and several other leading US foreign policy experts had repeatedly called.

Today we are witnessing a new and radical turn in US policy on Iran. Attempts to break the Iraqi sector of the Shiite arc or crescent are behind the renewed efforts to isolate Iran. But is this possible? Iran cannot be equated to the Shia majority in Iraq because the latter is not consolidated. Iran is not only an ally and protector, but also a kind of arbiter for Iraqi Shiites. The US may try to rely on one of the Shiite forces in Iraq, but this would most likely trigger an internal conflict among Shiites and prod most of them into siding with their coreligionists in the east. In other words, a new confrontation with Iran would create a situation where the Shia-dominated central government in Baghdad would become even weaker and eventually start gravitating toward Iran.

It is unlikely that the Americans will be able to find strong support among Sunnis until IS is defeated or at least forced out of Iraq. But the US may try to form a new, post-IS balance of power in Iraq that would take into account the interests of moderate Sunnis and give them a fraction of influence in the central government and control over parts of the territories currently held by IS forces. But this task is quite difficult as it is, even without anti-Iranian escapades. In fact, a delay in a new attack on Mosul was caused not so much by military-tactical or humanitarian considerations as by deep disagreements over who will take and control the city. US attempts to diminish Iran's influence and strengthen the Sunnis will most likely undermine the Haider al-Abadi government's positions.

The main opponent of the present government in Baghdad – former Iraqi prime minister Nuri al-Maliki – remains a figure who provokes disagreements between key religious and ethnic groups despite his efforts to form a new broad-based coalition.

With IS far from being fully crushed and the US seeking to set back Iran, preserving the integrity of Iraq appears to be an increasingly illusory pursuit. Kurds have become the key to the future of not only Iraq, but of the entire Greater Middle East. In fact, the Kurds in Iraq and Syria are the most valuable US ally in the fight against IS in the region. Iraqi Kurdistan has been an important US outpost since 1991. The alliance with the US made it possible for Iraqi Kurds to survive (under Saddam Hussein) and it subsequently gave them autonomy close to sovereignty along with some economic advantages. But the US kept the Kurds from pushing for full independence. However, now that US policy priorities in the region have changed, the situation has become particularly favorable for Iraqi Kurdistan to proclaim its sovereignty. Another factor conducive to this step is that the Kurds control many disputable territories, including large oil fields near Kirkuk. But the situation in Iraq may change in several months and the Kurds will run out of luck.

Iraqi Kurdistan President Masoud Barzani has called an independence referendum within the next several months. That decision apparently reflects an agreement between the region's two main parties and the Barzani and Talabani tribes that support them. The central government in Baghdad will most likely have to accept the results of the referendum due to Constitutional reasons. But the borders of an independent Kurdistan may be challenged, since the current Iraqi Constitution localizes the Kurdish autonomy within Dohuk, Erbil, Sulaymaniyah and Halabja Provinces. Control over Kirkuk remains an open question because of its valuable oil fields and mixed ethnic composition. The idea of making Kirkuk the capital of Iraqi Kurdistan is quite popular among the Kurds, but doing so may trigger a new confrontation between the Kurdistan Democratic Party (Barzani) and the Patriotic Union of Kurdistan (Talabani), which controls the city. It is highly unlikely that Baghdad would try to force the Kurds out of Kirkuk after the defeat of ISIS.

The US officially supports the territorial integrity of Iraq. But under Trump, the US will be less inclined than under Barack Obama and George W. Bush to commit large sums of money and use its influence to prevent Iraq's disintegration. The US also listens attentively to Israel, which would welcome the emergence of an independent Kurdish state. If Iraqi Kurdistan leaders choose the right time to hold their referendum and proclaim their independence, the US will most likely accept the breakup of Iraq as a fait accompli and focus on consolidating its dominant positions in a new state. If Iran's influence in Iraq continues to grow, Kurdistan will serve as the main US bridgehead in the territory that is currently part of Iraq.

Turkey is the main threat to the independence of any part of Greater Kurdistan. However, if Erbil proclaims independence, Turkey is unlikely to resort to violence to suppress the move. The Peshmerga are a serious force, and starting a full-scale war against Iraqi Kurds would inevitably destabilize Turkish Kurdistan and draw Syrian Kurds into the conflict. Both the US and Russia are using their influence to keep Turkish President Recep Tayyip Erdogan from responding too aggressively to the emergence of the first independent Kurdish state. At the same time, Turkey and Iraqi Kurdistan are bound by the oil business that may become even more profitable if it is fully legalized through interstate trade. But of course, in order to pacify Erdogan, the leaders of Iraqi Kurdistan will have to distance themselves from the Kurdistan Workers' Party and the idea of consolidating Kurdish lands. But these assurances will not make the Kurdish irredenta disappear.

The independence of Iraqi Kurdistan (which could tentatively be called South Kurdistan) would, on the one hand, mean the collapse of the regional order established by the Sykes-Picot Agreement. On the other hand, South Kurdistan may become a new regional equilibrium in the mid-term, some kind of balancer that would prevent the excessive strengthening of both Turkey and Iran. In this respect, Russia could regard the emergence of South Kurdistan as a positive development.

The situation of Sunnis in Iraq is coming to the fore as IS nears defeat. If the Kurdish-controlled territories are separated from Iraq, the share of Shiites in the remaining part of the country would increase, thus prodding Shiites into building a state system that excludes territorial division on religious or ethnic grounds. Sunnis would be offered positions in the central government (possibly by quota) regardless of which Shia political leaders head it. Agreements over the distribution of other important posts may also be amended.

For example, the post of president, currently assigned to Kurds, may become part of the "Sunni quota." But this compromise would have to pass the test from both sides. Radical Shiite groups would continue to push for the maximum advantages from Shia dominance, while many Sunnis would demand control over towns and territories where they have a majority. It is highly unlikely that the advocates of "Sunnistan" would limit their aspirations to just a political struggle. If the authorities in Iraq accept the separation of the Sunni territories, the way would be paved for the ultimate disintegration of Iraq.

External forces would undoubtedly be drawn into these processes, with the main confrontation flaring up between Iran and the Arab monarchies. The US and Turkey would also significantly contribute to the conflict. As for Russia, it should be vitally interested in strengthening political, economic and military-technical cooperation with the government in Iraq as well as with South Kurdistan, whether autonomous (for the time being) or independent. Russia does not want to get directly involved in processes that may lead to the emergence of "Sunnistan" in Iraq. At the same time, it is important to maintain contact with those Sunni forces in Iraq that are determined to look for political solutions to existing problems.

The territorial separation of the Sunnis in Iraq would not affect Russia directly, but through Syria. The emergence of "Sunnistan" would also reverberate through the region. But will today's Middle East ever look like the map drawn by Army Lt. Col. (ret.) Ralph Peters?[2] Borders can only be drawn along ethnic and sectarian lines when leading domestic and international actors are not prepared to commit enough resources to avert such a scenario. What makes the situation around Iraq distinct is that key actors are unlikely to accumulate and use sufficient resources to prevent the partial or complete disintegration of Iraq. The situation in Syria is different because the major external players have already committed significant resources to support the warring factions and achieve their geopolitical goals.

Syrian Alternatives

Just as the liberation of Mosul will determine the future of Iraq, the contours of Syria's future will start taking shape after ISIS is pushed out of Raqqa and other Syrian territories. Although ISIS structures of governance have already been relocated from Raqqa to the vicinity of Deir al-Zour, taking Raqqa would be an event of great political and symbolic significance. It seems that the US and Russia have agreed in principle that Raqqa will be stormed under American control. It is now up to the US to choose the striking force that will do the fighting on the ground. Syrian Kurds are the most likely choice, which would significantly restrict US-Turkish activities in Syria and in the region as a whole.

This choice is quite acceptable for Russia, which maintains working contact with Syrian Kurds and calls for constitutional guarantees of autonomy in the territories under their control. With the tacit consent of the US and Russia, Kurdish territories can be cobbled together. But international actors will not support the independence of Rojava or its integration with Iraqi Kurdistan in the foreseeable future. Rojava may become a very important factor of stabilization in Syria, as well as a deterrent against Turkey's neo-Ottoman aspirations.

After IS has been forced out of Raqqa, control over this city and some of the adjacent territories would most likely be handed over to one or several Sunni groups opposing Bashar Assad. By that time, it should become clear how to implement the agreements on deescalation zones. Four scenarios are possible:

- The conflict flares up again, forces regroup, and a broad coalition is formed to overthrow Assad.
- The conflict is allowed to simmer, in order to tie up the Syrian government forces, opposing Sunni groups, Iran and Hezbollah, Russia, Turkey, and Arab monarchies.
- New efforts are launched to settle the conflict on the basis of an agreement addressing key issues between Russia and the US at first, and then between other domestic and external actors.
- Key actors give their tacit consent to Syria's breakup after the possible disintegration of Iraq.

The first scenario means that the crisis would keep growing and could develop into a large regional war, because a broad anti-Assad coalition would inevitably enter into confrontation with Iran and Russia. The second scenario is less risky for both the US and Israel, even though flare-ups and regroupings are also possible. Also, it gives no guarantees against the reincarnation of IS or similar terrorist organizations.

The search for a political solution may be fruitful if Russia and the US agree on a formula for compromise not only on Syria, but the entire Middle East. Such a compromise may also include agreements concerning Russian and American interests in other parts of the world. However, an agreement between Russia and the US is a necessary, but not sufficient, condition for a breakthrough in settling the Syrian crisis. The reverse side of a multipolar world is that even an agreement between the US and Russia cannot guarantee the desired result in such regional conflicts.

In general, a political settlement in Syria may include a formula for the political system, economic influence and security that would guarantee the long-term, peaceful co-existence of various ethnic and religious groups, with broad autonomy of the territories under their control and an inclusive central government. It could also draw on the Taif National Reconciliation Accord, which put an end to the civil war in Lebanon, and the Iraqi Constitution of 2005. However, in the case of Syria, the probability that Russia, the US, Iraq, Turkey and the Arab monarchies will get involved is quite high. Thus, a Syrian settlement will require a compromise on their further presence in the country if at least Syria's formal integrity is preserved. One may assume that the presence of certain external actors in one form or another will become an element of security guarantees for various parties involved in the Syrian conflict. The creation of deescalation zones, which are not controlled by the central government, will speed up all processes. The territorial configuration will most probably change, but the Americans are likely to stay in Syrian Kurdistan, the Russians will keep their presence on the Mediterranean coast and in territories populated predominantly by Alawites, and the Turks will assert their presence in Idlib. A key question is the military presence in Syria of Iran's Islamic Revolutionary Guard Corps (IRGC) and Hezbollah groups. This is utterly unacceptable for the Trump administration, Israel, and Saudi Arabia, and quite undesirable for Turkey. However, it is these forces that provide Assad with reliable support.

If a compromise is possible at all, Russia should become the main guarantor for the Alawites and their political and security structures. Russia's exit from Syria, whether voluntary or due to some extraordinary circumstances, would create a power vacuum that the US, Turkey, and the Gulf countries, on the one hand, and Iran, on the other, would immediately try to fill. Adverse consequences for the region would not be far off. In other words, the time when Russia could contemplate an exit strategy seems to have passed. It would be virtually impossible now to guarantee a negotiated settlement in Syria or at least a lasting truce without Russia's substantial military presence in that country.

Russia's long-term military presence in Syria is more preferable for Turkey and Israel than Iran's. In fact, only Russia's presence can ensure a balance of power in Syria acceptable for Iran if the latter is forced to give up plans to deploy its troops and Hezbollah units in Syria due to external pressure or domestic problems.

The issue of Assad's future could delay negotiations indefinitely. But unless this issue is resolved in a civilized manner, there will be no chance to form an inclusive central government in Syria. Currently only Russia and Iran, acting together, can tell Assad how long he can stay in office and how he should leave. Iran can be convinced to support Russia's position if the Iranian leaders see an opportunity to ensure their interests when new forces come to power in Syria. On the whole, Iran is facing a serious dilemma in Syria. Iran would like to keep the current state of affairs, which allows it to extend its influence in some form or another to Iraq, Syria, Libya and Yemen as parts of a single "Islamic resistance front." Iran would also like to see the Shiite branch of Islam, currently stymied by the Saudi monarchy, consolidate its positions on the Arabian Peninsula. However, overstrain becomes a serious obstacle toward this goal. If Iran nonetheless decides to keep or even expand its military presence in Syria (including creating Naval bases in the Mediterranean), it may end up in dangerous isolation. An alternative could be guarantees of political influence in Damascus in exchange for the withdrawal of the IRGC and Hezbollah units from Syria. Political leaders in Damascus agreeable for Iran should keep their levers of power. Essentially, this entails preventing a politically motivated restructuring of militarily efficient units of the Syrian Arab Army (including the 5th Assault Corps currently being created), the Republican Guard and Alawite-dominated security services. This will most likely be the red line and price Syria's opponents would have to pay if they are truly committed to a political settlement and territorial integrity in Syria.

If the Syrian state collapses, the leading actors would have to understand that neither side can win in this conflict, and that no acceptable formula can be found for peaceful coexistence of the main ethnic and religious groups. But external forces would keep their presence in various parts of Syria even after its breakup.

The partial disintegration of Iraq (after the separation of Kurdistan) could provide an external impetus for the breakup of Syria. Yet the real problems would begin with the emergence of "Sunnistan" in Iraq, which more than likely would merge with Sunni-controlled regions of Syria and cover a territory almost identical to what IS controlled before the offensive on Mosul and Raqqa. But even if the international community recognizes the disintegration of Syria as a fait accompli, relative peace can be achieved only in some parts of the country. "Sunnistan" would seek to control Damascus and Aleppo, while "Alawistan" would remain under external pressure as long as Iran has a substantial military commitment there. Finally, once Syria falls apart, it would be hard to stop the chain reaction sending ripples of disintegration throughout Lebanon, Jordan and the entire Arabian Peninsula. Turkish Kurdistan and Iranian provinces with large Kurdish, Azerbaijani and Arab communities would also face the risk of destabilization.

Balance of Cooperation/Rivalry between Russia, Turkey and Iran

Let us take another look at the prospects of trilateral interaction between Russia, Iran and Turkey. The level of cooperation they achieved in the second half of 2016 and the beginning of 2017 is truly unprecedented. But the idea of such cooperation is not new. In his work *The Russian-Eastern Agreement of 1896*, Ismail Gasprinsky, a renowned Crimean Tatar intellectual and ideologue of Jadidism, suggested that the Russian Empire could pursue a positive and mutually beneficial rapprochement with both Turkey and Persia. Gasprinsky was critical of the West's goals: "Acting either against Russia or against Muslims, Europeans in both cases reap the benefits and move forward.*** If one looks at how heartlessly Europe oppresses the whole of the East economically, turning into a beast each time when it comes down to a pence, centime or pfennig, it becomes clear that the East should expect no good from the West."[3] Gasprinsky suggested reaching an agreement with the Ottoman Empire and Persia to establish Russian Naval bases on the Mediterranean Sea and in other places close to the Indian Ocean. He believed that such an agreement would have allowed Turkey and Persia to "calmly engage in internal revival, borrowing forms not from the West, but from Russia as a country that is closer to them as a civilization and in terms of people's way of life."[4]

One hundred twenty years later, Turkey and Iran have complicated relations with the West, sort of giving Gasprinsky's ideas a new lease on life. Under certain circumstances, some elements of this discourse may be reproduced in modern political rhetoric. However, it was the temporary alignment of divergent interests of each of the three countries due to internal and external factors that provided a real basis for the Russia-Turkey-Iran triangle. Ultimately, Russia, Turkey and Iran will draw together, but not along anti-Western lines, and their possible estrangement will certainly not be caused by a sudden outburst of affection for the "values of the free world."

There is no guarantee that the triangle will last in the short or long term. Even a slight change in the combination of factors or efforts that brought Russia, Iran and Turkey together could undermine their interaction and eventually upset it completely. In fact, Turkey may yield to US pressure aimed at wrecking the alliance. If this pressure coincides with internal transformations accompanying the establishment of Erdogan's personalistic regime, a revision of Turkey's positions would ruin the triangle.

At the same time, there are some important circumstances that help keep the trilateral format working, since the only alternative to the Astana peace talks would be a new outbreak of more violent confrontation in Syria. In addition, with the trilateral format gone, the sides would no longer be able to control each other's activities. The lack of mutual trust between Russia, Turkey and Iran can be made up for if each of them opts for a strategy that gives all of them a positive balance of gains/losses, while reducing related risks to an acceptable level.

The Goals of Russian Policy in the Greater Middle East

Russia needs to reevaluate its goals in the Greater Middle East. While the decision to provide direct military support to Assad was made in the fall of 2015 largely in the context of the Ukraine crisis and Western efforts to isolate Russia, in 2017, a foreign policy priority is to consolidate Russian positions as one of the centers of power in the region.

It should be a key position that allows Russia to use its influence and have a foothold in different parts of the region. This means that Russia should not be viewed solely as Assad's ally or a secret patron of the Shiite arc. It is vitally important to avoid a situation where Russia's actions will be interpreted as prejudiced against certain religious or ethnic groups in the region. Russia should maintain partner relations with Iran, Turkey, Israel, Egypt and Jordan, and raise the dialogue with Saudi Arabia, Qatar and the United Arab Emirates to the level of partnership. And, of course, Russia should achieve an acceptable level of understanding with the US and its main NATO partners on how to resolve conflicts in the region (including coordination of efforts if Iraq and Syria fall apart). By and large, this can be viewed as an attempt to transform the Russia-Turkey-Iran triangle into a multilateral format incorporating all key actors in the Greater Middle East. This task cannot be solved without Russia.

Russia's long-term presence in the region will require considerable resources. Clearly, Russia should offset those costs by gaining major economic preferences in Syria and other parts of the Greater Middle East, including participation in postwar reconstruction and development of natural resources. Political and military-strategic achievements should be converted into economic dividends.

Ultimately, our policy in the region should become part of a comprehensive strategy aimed at creating favorable conditions for the development of Russia as a country that helps, along with China, reformat the geoeconomic and geopolitical landscape in Greater Eurasia. This process will have to go hand in hand with the integration of the Eurasian Economic Union and China's Silk Road Economic Belt project, the expansion of the Shanghai Cooperation Organization, and the creation of continental transport and logistics chains, as well as latitudinal and longitudinal development corridors. The Russia-Turkey-Iran triangle could provide the basis for this process in the Greater Middle East. Interest from Middle Eastern countries in megaprojects associated with Greater Eurasia's geoeconomics may become an important factor encouraging the search for compromises and relaxation of tension. Greater Eurasia will gain integrity only when the stabilized Greater Middle East becomes its natural part. However, the latter forebodes new turbulence, since global geopolitical transformations will inevitably meet resistance from some of the national and supranational actors seeking to preserve their privileged positions in the present world order.

332 | DMITRY YEFREMENKO

Notes

1. Fischer, Joschka. "The Middle East's Lost Decade," *Project Syndicate*, March 18, 2013, https://www.project-syndicate.org/commentary/winners-and-losers-of-the-iraq-war-by-joschka-fischer?barrier=accesspaylog.

2. Peters, Ralph. "Blood Borders. How a better Middle East would look," *Armed Forces Journal*, June 1, 2006, http://armedforcesjournal.com/blood-borders/. Col. Peters suggested that a reimagining of Middle Eastern and Asian borders along ethnic, sectarian and tribal lines might ease regional tensions. The article and the accompanying map were – and continue to be – widely taken as Washington's blueprint for imperial meddling.

3. Gasprinsky, Ismail. *Russko-vostochnoye soglasheniye: Mysli, zanetki i pozhelaniya* [Russo-Eastern agreement: thoughts, notes and wishes]. Bakhchisarai, 1896.

4. *Ibid.*

RUSSIA: THE POWER BROKER IN THE MIDDLE EAST?

Andrei Kortunov

To maintain its current position as a critical power broker in Syria, as well as in a broader Middle East context, the Kremlin must figure out how to cope with three recent developments. First, the defeat of ISIS has stirred up old rivalries and animosities among the remaining forces in the region. Second, the current Israeli-Iranian and US-Iranian rifts complicate Russia's role as an "honest broker" in the region. Finally, if Damascus regains control over most of Syrian territory, its current dependence on Moscow will inevitably decrease.

Historically, the Middle East has never been a strategic priority for Russia compared to Europe, the Northeast Pacific or even Central Asia. Unlike many other major European powers, Russia had no colonial ambitions in the region; it never considered the Middle East its "sphere of influence" or a critically important geostrategic or economic transit corridor. Until very recently, Russia had no experience in direct use of its military power in the region, much less a claim to become a key external power broker in the Middle East.

This article originally appeared in *Russia in Global Affairs* Vol. 16, No. 4, 2018.

After the collapse of the Soviet Union, many in Moscow and in the West argued that the residual Russian influence in the Arab world, inherited from the heyday of global Soviet imperial outreach, was doomed to decline continuously, turning the Kremlin into an explicitly marginal player in regional politics. Indeed, Russia's interests and attention were limited mostly to three non-Arab states on the periphery of the Arab world. The first was Turkey – a highly controversial, but very important partner in the Black Sea area and the Caucasus, in terms of trade, investment, energy and in tourism. The second was Iran – another difficult ally, which played an active role in many international matters very important to Moscow – from civil wars in Tajikistan and Afghanistan to the problem of Caspian Sea partition. The third was Israel, with its large Russian and Russian-speaking diaspora and a thick fabric of political, economic, social, cultural and human relations between the two countries.

As for the Arab core of the Middle East region, the climax of Russian activism at the beginning of the 21st century was a successful effort to build a Russian-German-French coalition opposing the US-led international coalition that invaded Iraq in the spring of 2003. However, even concerted efforts by Moscow, Berlin and Paris did not prevent the Iraq War. Neither did that ad hoc trilateral collaboration grow into a multilateral strategic partnership on a broader range of Middle East issues. The US, despite all the mistakes and blunders of its Middle East policies, remained the unquestionable external hegemon of the Arab world. Russia could hope for only very modest progress in dealing with select Arab nations like Egypt, Algeria, Saudi Arabia and Syria.

The relative stability of the region started to crumble in the wake of the Arab Spring. The changing situation presented Moscow with both new challenges and new opportunities. On the one hand, the Kremlin had reason to be concerned about a spillover effect of the Arab Spring, particularly in post-Soviet Central Asia, but also in the Northern Caucasus and other Muslim-populated regions of the Russian Federation. Politicians and pundits in Moscow viewed the Arab Spring through the lens of earlier "color revolutions" in Ukraine, Georgia and Kyrgyzstan, which were regarded as direct threats to Russia's security interests and Putin's political system.

On the other hand, the Arab Spring and the apparent enthusiasm of major Western counties to embrace ongoing changes in the Arab world presented the Kremlin a chance to demonstrate that Russia was different. Moscow stood by its strategic partners in the Middle East, articulated concerns about possible negative side effects of the region's swift and uncontrolled political and social transformations, and cautioned against foreign support to antigovernment, antiregime forces that were riding the wave of the Arab Spring.

Vladimir Putin used the disappointment and frustration aroused both within and outside the Middle East by the awakening of populist movements there to offer his own narrative of contemporary world politics. The traditional Western narrative had defined the main global dividing line as democracy vs. authoritarianism. Whatever served the cause of democracy should be encouraged and supported; whatever furthered the cause of authoritarianism should be denounced and opposed. Russia's new, post-Arab Spring narrative argued that such a juxtaposition was no longer relevant in the postmodern world. The real dividing line was not democracy vs. authoritarianism, but "order" vs. "chaos." For all the shortcomings and deficiencies of authoritarian regimes, these regimes were the preferred option over an uncontrolled, chaotic drive toward democracy. Whoever supports chaos, whether willingly or unwillingly, explicitly or implicitly, ends up on the "wrong side of history"; whoever stands for order against chaos is on the "right side." This interpretation may be regarded as biased, oversimplified and self-serving, but it has clearly gained a lot of traction in the Middle East, especially among conservative political regimes concerned about a possible new wave of the Arab Spring.

Within this context, the initial stage of the Russian military operation in Syria launched in September 2015 should be regarded primarily as a "pedagogical" action. Russia's intention was not to diminish the US's position in the Middle East, much less to drive it out of the region. It was clear from the very beginning that Moscow could not hope to replace Washington in the Arab world as the prime security provider: It simply did not have the economic, political or military resources to do that. If the US decided for its own reasons to withdraw from the region, the vacuum left would be filled not by Russia, but by Islamist radicals – not a very attractive outcome for Moscow. Therefore, the goal was not to drive the US out, but to change American policy in Syria (and, hopefully, in the region at large) by demonstrating the "right" approach to managing regional crises. This goal was particularly important in view of the ongoing Ukraine conflict: The Kremlin was concerned about how that conflict would impact its relations with the West, and was willing to demonstrate that Russian involvement was not necessarily part of the problem, but could be a big part of the solution.

This stage of Russian military involvement in Syria lasted about a year, during which time Moscow persistently tried to engage Washington. Its efforts culminated in September 2016 with Russian Foreign Minister Sergei Lavrov and [then] US secretary of state John Kerry signing a ceasefire deal for Syria. The sides also agreed to a joint US-Russian air campaign against ISIS and other extremist groups, and new negotiations on the country's political future.

However, the deal turned out to be short-lived. Both sides accused each other of failing to deliver on their respective commitments. The conclusion drawn in Moscow was that instead of trying to engage with the West in Syria and beyond, Russia should focus on building a "coalition of the willing" composed of regional actors interested in reaching a ceasefire in Syria.

As it tried to forge an alliance of regional actors, Moscow counted on the major comparative advantage that distinguished Russia from other major external powers involved in Middle East crises: It enjoyed good relations with practically all local players – Sunnis and Shiites, Iran and Arab states of the Gulf, Israelis and Palestinians, Turks and Kurds, etc. Russia's regional activism was also inadvertently encouraged by the Trump administration, which could not decide how to approach either Syria or the region at large. The launch of the Astana process in the very end of 2016 turned out to be a significant political victory for Moscow. Throughout 2017, Russia consistently tried to capitalize on this initial success by broadening the range of participants in the Astana process and expanding the conversation beyond tactical deescalation and ceasefire mechanisms to a more sustainable political settlement.

The second stage of Russia's direct engagement in the region turned out more successful than the first. However, it also demonstrated a number of limitations. Iran and Turkey turned out to be unable or unwilling to control many nonstate groups fighting in Syria. Impressive military success on the ground reduced the incentive for Damascus to discuss a political settlement in Geneva, and made Bashar Assad more self-confident and arrogant. As it tried to engage Turkey, Moscow alienated Syrian Kurds, who turned to the US for support and protection. Finally, Donald Trump turned out to be a loose cannon in the region, much more inclined to use US military power against the Damascus regime than his predecessor, but without making any serious commitments to a political settlement and postconflict reconstruction in Syria. The so-called Congress of Peoples of Syria that Russia convened in Sochi in early 2018 clearly failed to produce a breakthrough in the situation on the ground; neither did it show visible progress in conceptualizing the political transformation of Syria toward of a more pluralistic, representative and decentralized state.

To maintain its current position as a critical power broker in Syria, as well as in a broader Middle East context, the Kremlin must figure out how to cope with three recent developments that call for significant adjustments in the Russian strategy.

First, the defeat of ISIS, which is definitely a positive development for everyone engaged in Syria and neighboring countries, has an important downside. Old regional rivalries, animosities, fears and conflicts that were put aside to fight the common enemy are back onstage. It might become increasingly difficult for Russia to forge even tactical alliances in the region, not to mention strategic coalitions.

Second, the current Israeli-Iranian and US-Iranian rifts immensely complicate Russia's role as an "honest broker" in the region. Neither Israel nor Iran is completely happy with the Russian policy of balancing its relations with the two states; each of the parties is trying to pull Moscow to its own side. The risks of alienating either Tehran or Jerusalem, or even both, are rising.

Lastly, if Damascus finally wins a complete military victory and regains control over most of Syrian territory, its current dependence on Moscow will inevitably decrease. Russia and its partners could arguably win the war, but they cannot win the peace in Syria – in the sense that they do not have resources needed to launch the process of postconflict reconstruction. No matter who assumes power in Damascus by the end of the war, the leadership of Syria will have to look for other partners and allies with pockets deeper than Moscow's, Tehran's or Ankara's.

WILL US PULLOUT FROM SYRIA INCREASE RISK OF CONFLICT WITH RUSSIA?

Fyodor Lukyanov

It is noteworthy that the withdrawal of US troops from Syria announced by Trump has not caused any exultation in Moscow. Putin's initial reaction was skeptical; furthermore, leaks in the US press imply that the US president has "handed over" Syria to Turkey. And the most curious aspect is that the stationing of Russian and US troops in close proximity ensured necessary and inevitable communication, at least at the military level. Given the current state of US-Russian relations, Syria has been almost the only area of relatively constructive interaction.

On Dec. 20, 2018, speaking at his annual press conference, Russian President Vladimir Putin surprisingly praised US-Russian collaboration on Syria.

"Despite all the disagreements, our specialists, our military personnel, security services and foreign ministries have established a rather constructive dialogue to address acute issues in combating terrorism in Syria. Overall, we are satisfied with our cooperation," he said.

This article originally appeared in *Russia in Global Affairs* on Dec. 29, 2018.

This may seem odd, because the two countries' stances through-out the Syrian conflict have been as different as chalk and cheese on a wide range of issues. They backed opposing warring parties and had at best different views on the desirable outcome of the confronta-tion. Hence, when President Donald Trump ordered the withdrawal of American troops from Syria, most US commentators viewed it exclusively through the lens of a zero-sum game, claiming the US had capitulated to Russia. Thus, the countries' shared objective of eliminating ISIS and their joint success in accomplishing this goal are practically disregarded, despite the threat the caliphate posed to both. In turn, geopolitical rivalry in the region is considered the real "big game."

And what about Russia? Is the Kremlin exulting over Trump's snap announcement? What aims is Russia setting for itself now, and what are some key results in 2018?

When Moscow decided to launch a military operation in Syria in 2015, several goals were established. More than three years later, virtually all of them have been achieved. Radical Islamists have been crushed. President Bashar Assad has retained and strengthened his power. Russia's regional clout has grown dramatically alongside its military and political impact on the global stage. However, one aim has not been fulfilled. Syria has failed to amplify and boost the US-Russian agenda, and the constructive, albeit reluctant, interaction between the two countries' militaries seems likely to be on the wane and may even be viewed as something no longer necessary.

Syria is a poster child of Russian success, rather unexpectedly even to most of those who launched the operation. The balanced combination of rigidity and flexibility, the use of military force, dip-lomatic astuteness and political maneuvering with a clear ultimate aim in mind – to preserve the Syrian regime – have borne fruit. Re-gardless of continuing skirmishes, the highly charged atmosphere in general and the extremely entangled relationships between numer-ous parties to the conflict, Russia continues to implement its plans.

To some extent, Russia owes its success to inconsistent poli-cies of other stakeholders, primarily those of the US. It should be noted that the policy is less incoherent under Trump than under his predecessor. Washington has ultimately failed to formulate its goals in Syria, while European nations, beset with internal problems and possessing little force-based leverage, quit as independent actors in

Syria long ago. Some of them are now back in the game thanks to Russia, which has been seeking EU financial support for restoration efforts. Negotiations among Russia, Turkey, Germany and France took place this fall.

It should be mentioned that these circumstances made life easier for Russia but did not pave the way for its success in Syria. This year, Moscow has coped with challenges that could have easily derailed the process and forced it to backslide. These include crises linked to the use of chemical weapons and their military and political repercussions, the Turkish military offensive in Afrin, the Idlib stand-off – which could have degenerated into a full-scale conflict – and the accidental downing of a Russian aircraft by Syrian air defenses caused by an Israeli air raid on Syria. This is not to mention nasty, albeit minor, skirmishes, as well as the stalled political settlement process and the confrontation between Iran and Saudi Arabia on the one hand and between Iran and Israel on the other.

All of this did not discourage Russia to the point of altering course. The preserved Astana format is a miracle in itself, since it bears witness to the cooperation of states that are largely distrustful of each other and have different interests in most regards. However, the Russia-Turkey-Iran triangle demonstrates a new type of partnership. The parties are united by the desire not to attain a common goal, but for each to achieve its own. However, each party understands that the other two make it all possible.

Russia's success in Syria has been the bridge to a shared stance on the Middle East. Without it, Russia would not have cultivated trade relations with Saudi Arabia and OPEC, which have turned Russia into a key actor in the global oil market. Even the Soviet Union failed to achieve that much in this realm. Moreover, one can see remarkable advances in Russian diplomacy in Libya, where a range of local actors have been trying to secure Moscow's backing. There are some advocates of active involvement in Libyan affairs in Russia as well. Such an undertaking, however, apparently exceeds the amount of available resources.

It is noteworthy that the withdrawal of US troops from Syria announced by Trump has not caused any exultation in Moscow.

First, as Putin put it, "A statement about a pullout and the actual departure of troops" is not always the same. Many policymakers believe that the withdrawal parameters can be adjusted along the way, with some units staying on the ground. In addition, since American military forces are deployed in Iraq, strikes can be carried out if necessary.

Second, the US withdrawal creates additional problems for Russia. The US units in the Kurdish-controlled regions stood in the way of Turkish military operations there. If the leaks in the US press about Trump's conversation with Turkish President Recep Tayyip Erdogan can be trusted, the US president actually "handed over" Syria to Turkey. Now Ankara is promising to continue the anti-Kurdish campaign. On the one hand, it implies further Turkish actions on the territory under Assad's jurisdiction, which would exacerbate the already tense situation between the two. On the other hand, the delicate Astana balance will have to pass one more endurance test.

The third and most curious aspect is that the stationing of Russian and US troops in close proximity ensured necessary and inevitable communication, at least at the military level. While this interaction can hardly be referred to as cooperation, the parties have shown that they are both taking their responsibility very seriously as both American and Russian generals want to avoid accidental clashes, which could escalate uncontrollably. In that respect, the undoubtedly dangerous incident near Deir al-Zour in February 2018 – about which more information should be revealed – is illustrative. The episode allegedly involved mercenaries from a Russian private military company. The sides have preferred to turn the page on it, at least publicly.

Given the current state of US-Russian relations, Syria has been almost the only area of relatively constructive interaction. Just as during the cold war, the military can exercise a more sober and practical approach than politicians. The higher the risk of a collision, the more cautious military leaders are. Following the end of the Syrian story, the two major powers' military forces may still interact in the Black and Baltic seas. However, in these cases the situation is more fraught with risk, given the absence of military standoff and the presence of political ardor. Naturally, one can lament that what could be termed as rule-based US-Russian hostility, which has characterized the situation in Syria until now, is almost the apex of bilateral relations. However, such is the current phase. In other spheres, nothing of the kind can be detected, with hostility being more chaotic and, therefore, particularly dangerous.

ABOUT THE CONTRIBUTORS

In order of appearance

Fyodor Lukyanov (collection editor)—Graduate of the Moscow State University School of Philology. Worked as journalist for radio station Golos Rossii (Voice of Russia) and several print publications. Founded the journal *Rossia v globalnoi politike* (*Russia in Global Affairs*) in 2002, becoming its editor in chief. Currently Chairman of the Presidium of the Council on Foreign and Defense Policy, and Research Director of the Valdai International Discussion Club.

Yevgeny Primakov (deceased)—Full Member of the Russian Academy of Sciences. Served as minister of foreign affairs of the Russian Federation (1996-1998); prime minister (1998-1999); and chairman of NIS GLONASS.

Aleksandr Dynkin—Member of the Russian Academy of Sciences. Director, Institute of World Economy and International Relations, Russian Academy of Sciences (IMEMO RAN).

Vladimir Pantin—Doctor of Sciences in Philosophy. Head of the Department of Comparative Political Studies, IMEMO RAN.

Vladimir A. Orlov—Founder, PIR Center for Nuclear Nonproliferation Studies. Currently Director of the Center for Global Trends and International Organizations, Diplomatic Academy, Russian Ministry of Foreign Affairs, and member of the UN Secretary General's Advisory Board on Disarmament Matters.

Aleksei Malashenko—Doctor of Sciences in History. Research Director, Dialogue of Civilizations Research Institute, Berlin. Board member of the International Federation for Peace and Conciliation; former chair of Carnegie Moscow Center's Religion, Society, and Security Program.

Rafael Khakimov—Doctor of Sciences in History. Politician, philosopher and historian. Vice-President and Full Member of the Tatarstan Academy of Sciences. Director, Institute of History, Tatarstan Academy of Sciences.

Vasily Kuznetsov—Doctor of Sciences in History. Director, Center for Arab and Islamic Studies, Institute of Oriental Studies, Russian Academy of Sciences.

Andrei Baklanov—Ambassador Extraordinary and Plenipotentiary, Saudi Arabia (2000-2005); head of the International Relations Department, Federation Council of the Russian Federal Assembly (2009-2012); Deputy Chairman of the Board, Association of Russian Diplomats.

Aleksandr Novak—Graduate of the Norilsk Industrial Institute. Served as deputy mayor of Norilsk and deputy finance minister of the Russian Federation. Currently Minister of Energy of the Russian Federation.

Anastasia Likhachova—Deputy Dean for Research and Deputy Director, Center for Comprehensive European and International Studies, National Research University Higher School of Economics (NRU-HSE).

Anatoly Adamishin—Graduate of Moscow State University. Served as deputy foreign minister of the USSR (1986-1990), first deputy foreign minister of the Russian Federation (1993-1994) and minister of CIS affairs (1997-1998). Currently a member of the Board of Advisers, *Russia in Global Affairs*.

Yevgeny Satanovsky—Graduate of Institute of Oriental Studies, Russian Academy of Sciences. Former member of Russian Federation Council and Russian Jewish Congress. President, Institute of the Middle East.

Anatoly Vishnevsky—Doctor of Sciences in Economics. Director, Institute of Demography, NRU-HSE.

Aleksandr Golts—Graduate of the Moscow State University School of Journalism. Independent defense analyst.

Aleksei Arbatov—Full Member of the Russian Academy of Sciences. Director, International Security Center, IMEMO RAN.

Ruslan Pukhov—Graduate of the Franco-Russian dual-degree program between the Paris Institute of Political Studies and the Moscow State Institute of International Relations (MGIMO). Director of the Centre for Analysis of Strategies and Technologies (CAST); member of the Public Council under the auspices of the Russian Defense Ministry.

Prokhor Tebin—Doctor of Sciences in Political Science. Member of the Russian International Affairs Council and the Valdai International Discussion Club. Independent military/naval expert.

Veronika Kostenko—Research Associate, Laboratory of Comparative Social Studies (LCSS), NRU-HSE.

Eduard Ponarin—Ph.D. in Sociology, University of Michigan. Tenured professor at NRU-HSE; head of the LCSS.

Pavel Kuzmichov—Academic researcher at the LCSS.

Aleksandr Aksenyonok—Doctor of Sciences in Law. Ambassador Extraordinary and Plenipotentiary of the Russian Federation; veteran diplomat and Arabist who has held assignments in many Arab countries. Served as ambassador to Algeria and Slovakia, and as special envoy to the Balkans.

Irina Zvyagelskaya—Doctor of Sciences in History. Senior Research Associate, Institute of Oriental Studies, Russian Academy of Sciences; head of the Center for Middle East Studies, IMEMO RAN.

Sergei Lavrov—Graduate of MGIMO. Former Russian representative to the UN and president of the UN Security Council. Currently Minister of Foreign Affairs of the Russian Federation.

Pyotr Stegny—Doctor of Sciences in History. Ambassador Extraordinary and Plenipotentiary of the Russian Federation; member of the Russian International Affairs Council.

Andrej Krickovic—Ph.D. in Political Science, UC Berkeley. Assistant Professor, Department of World Economy and World Politics, NRU-HSE.

Yuval Weber—Ph.D. in Government, UT Austin. Inaugural DMGS-Kennan Institute Fellow, Daniel Morgan Graduate School.

Dmitry Yefremenko—Doctor of Sciences in Political Science. Deputy Director, Institute of Scientific Information on Social Sciences, Russian Academy of Sciences.

Andrei Kortunov—Graduate of MGIMO. Director General, Russian International Affairs Council. Member of expert and supervisory committees and boards of trustees of several Russian and international organizations.

INDEX

AFGHANISTAN
Counterterrorist coalition, 134
Drug export problems, 134, 302
Extremism, 55
Forcible democratization, 285
Islamic threat, 55
Lessons drawn from wars in, 183 et seq.
Local forces, reliance on in warfare, 188
Negotiating with terrorists, 191
Russia and US warfare strategies
    compared, 174
US war strategy, 173

AIR OPERATIONS IN SYRIA
See Warfare

AL QAEDA
Arab-Israeli conflict and, 17
Black September responsibility, 184
Credit claims for terrorist activities, 134
Goals, 5
Iraqi invasion and, 260
ISIS compared, 87
Organizations operating under brand
    name, 148
Revolutions, support for, 227
Separatism, 6
Terrorism stereotyping based on, 139

AL-JAZEERA, 241

ALGERIA, 241, 262

ARAB SPRING
Generally, 224 et seq.
See also: Democracy, Revolution
    (entries below)
Arab-Israeli conflict and, 234, 289
Authoritarian regime collapses as
    stage of democratic process, 293
Destabilizing factors for international
    politics, 245
Egypt, catalysts in, 118, 125
Established regimes swept away by, 278
Ethnic antagonisms heightened by, 279
Extent prediction, 292
Future alliances, potentials for, 289
Historical background, 279
Horizontal and vertical aspects, 291
Informal alliances and conflicts, 297
Iranian support, 289
Iraqi war as cause, 320
Regimes swept away by, 278
Religious antagonisms heightened by,
    279
Social-political phenomenon, treat-
    ment as, 258
Stability impacts, generally, 334
Sunni-Shiite alliance, potentials for, 289
Syrian civil war
    Generally, 278
    See also Syria (entry below)